*Vietnamese
Foreign Policy in
Transition*

Vietnamese Foreign Policy in Transition

edited by

CARLYLE A. THAYER
RAMSES AMER

St. Martin's Press, NEW YORK

Published by
Institute of Southeast Asian Studies
30 Heng Mui Keng Terrace
Pasir Panjang
Singapore 119614
Internet e-mail: publish@iseas.edu.sg
World Wide Web: http://www.iseas.edu.sg/pub.html

First published in the United States of America in 1999 by
St. Martin's Press, Scholarly and Reference Division,
175 Fifth Avenue, New York, NY 10010

The responsibility for facts and opinions expressed in this publication rests exclusively with the authors and their interpretations do not necessarily reflect the views or the policy of the Institute.

Library of Congress Cataloguing-in-Publication Data

Vietnamese foreign policy in transition / edited by Carlyle A. Thayer and
    Ramses Amer.
      p.   cm.
    Includes bibliographical references and index.
    ISBN 0-312-22884-8 (cloth)
    1. Vietnam--Foreign relations.   I. Thayer, Carlyle A.   II. Amer,
    Ramses.
    DS556.57.V54   1999
    327.597'009'049--dc21   99-41755
                                                            CIP

ISSN 0218-608X
ISBN 981-230-025-2 (softcover, ISEAS, Singapore)
ISBN 981-230-059-7 (harcover, ISEAS, Singapore)

This hardcover edition (ISBN 0-312-22884-8) is published by St. Martin's Press, New York for distribution in North America and Europe.

Printed in Singapore by Seng Lee Press Pte Ltd.

CONTENTS

INTRODUCTION

Carlyle A. Thayer and Ramses Amer

Very little has been published in English about Vietnam's foreign policy over the last decade. This stands in marked contrast to the outpouring of books dealing with *doi moi* and Vietnam's economic reforms. The most recent book on Vietnamese foreign policy is based on conference papers originally presented in 1995 on the eve of Vietnam's membership in the Association of Southeast Asian Nations (ASEAN) and the normalization of Vietnam's relations with the United States, and subsequently updated for publication (James W. Morley and Masashi Nishihara, eds., *Vietnam Joins the World*, 1997). This volume carries the analysis further, providing a longer-term perspective on these major developments.

These and other developments prompted the co-editors to approach the organizers of the European Vietnam Studies Conference series and request that they include an international relations stream in their discussions. Dr. John Kleinen, the conference organizer, readily agreed. A general announcement was sent out to the scholarly community.

The Third European Vietnam Studies Conference (EuroViet III) was hosted by the International Institute for Asian Studies and the Centre for Asian Studies, Amsterdam, at the University of Amsterdam from 2 to 4 July 1997. Carlyle Thayer and Ramses Amer served as co-organizers for the international relations stream.

We vetted a number of proposals before deciding on the final selection. A special EuroViet e-mail group was formed. This served as the basis for circulating abstracts and completed papers prior to the conference. As co-organizers, we were especially pleased with the professionalism of the panelists who provided copies of their abstracts and papers in advance of the deadline. These were then circulated to every other participant and to Derek Tonkin, the former ambassador from the United Kingdom to Vietnam, who acted as discussant.

With one exception, all chapters in this volume were originally commissioned for delivery at EuroViet III. The international relations stream was divided into two panels. The first panel focused on the role of ideology and comprised three papers: Li Ma, "China and Vietnam Faced with the Politics of Democratization of the West: How A Common Situation Becomes A Common Interest"; Eero Palmujoki, "Ideology and Foreign Policy: Vietnam's Marxist-Leninist Doctrine and the Global Change, 1986–1996"; and Carlyle A. Thayer, "Vietnamese Foreign Policy: Multilateralism and the Threat of Peaceful Evolution".

The second panel was concerned with Vietnam's three most important relationships—ASEAN, China and the United States. It comprised four papers: Ramses Amer, "Sino-Vietnamese Relations: Past, Present and Future"; Chang Pao-min, "Vietnam and China: New Opportunities and New Challenges"; David Wurfel, "Between China and ASEAN: The Dialectics of Recent Vietnamese Foreign Policy"; and Bui Thanh Son, "Vietnam Foreign Policy in the 1990s and Vietnam-U.S. Relations". The papers provoked considerable discussion from the audience, which included the former Belgium ambassador to Vietnam and the former head of the BBC World Service's Vietnamese Section.

By prior agreement, the contributors met later at the conference for an in-house discussion where the decision was made to revise the papers and seek publication. Later, Kent Bolton was approached and asked to prepare a chapter on the normalization of U.S.-Vietnam relations to provide an American perspective on this important issue. The final chapter of this book was written by the two co-editors. The conclusion presents a summary of the findings and the main themes in the different chapters of the volume. The bibliography contains a full list of all references cited by the various authors. In addition, it contains an extensive list of works on Vietnam's foreign relations.

The contributors to this volume come, quite literally, from the four corners of the earth. They hail from academic institutions located on four separate continents: Europe (Finland, France, Sweden), America (Canada and the United States), Asia (China, Taiwan and Vietnam) and Australia. English is the second language for five out of the eight contributors. The scholarship presented in this volume represents the best of the next generation of Vietnam specialists as well as the considered views of more established and senior academics. All are political scientists and foreign policy specialists by training.

It is our expectation that the contributions to this volume will highlight the complexity of the foreign policy issues facing Vietnam, be they in the formulation of adequate policies within Vietnam itself or in its dealings with major foreign counterparts such as ASEAN, China and the United States. Because of the differences in methodological approach and source materials used (including a diversity of non-English language sources), the contributors occasionally differ in the salience that they attach to particular factors in their analysis. This should be viewed as a strength rather than a weakness because, when taken as a whole, the various contributions reveal the difficulties and complexities in assessing various events and factors shaping the foreign policy-making process in Vietnam and its external relations. In the conclusion, we have attempted to bring together the major observations and findings of the different contributors. It is our assessment that the individual contributors do indeed complement each other in a stimulating way. It also displays that, both on an individual basis and taken together, the contributions bring the analysis of Vietnam's foreign relations to a higher level and they generate an enhanced amount of knowledge and information about Vietnam's foreign relations.

As co-editors, we would like to acknowledge the early expression of interest by the Institute of Southeast Asian Studies and comments made by anonymous reviewers on this manuscript. In light of this input, individual chapters were revised and edited for publication.

The co-editors would like to thank especially Beverley Lincoln for her expert help in getting various drafts of this manuscript into shape for submission, and Sue Moss and Nguyen Hong Thach for invaluable research assistance in the preparation of the bibliography.

Carlyle A. Thayer and Ramses Amer
Canberra and Stockholm
December 1998

Will Thayer

ever write anything

that is not boring?

VIETNAMESE FOREIGN POLICY: MULTILATERALISM AND THE THREAT OF PEACEFUL EVOLUTION

*Carlyle A. Thayer**

Paradigm lost

During the mid-to-late 1980s, a major transformation took place in how Vietnam's policy élite conceptualized foreign policy. The roots of this transformation were twofold. They lay in domestic circumstances arising from the socio-economic crisis which confronted Vietnam at that time. And secondly, they also lay in external influences arising from the "new political thinking" fashionable in Gorbachev's Soviet Union.[1] Vietnam turned from a foreign policy model heavily structured by ideological considerations to a foreign policy model which placed greater emphasis on national interest and *realpolitik*. Vietnamese analysts now tended to emphasize global economic forces and the impact of the revolution in science and technology over military aspects of power when weighing the global balance.[2] The shift in foreign policy paradigms was not a smooth one as party conservatives resisted jettisoning ideology completely. According to one former party-insider, as late as the end of 1992 Vietnam still used ideological considerations in setting foreign policy priorities in confidential internal party documents.[3] The old and new foreign policy models are not mutually exclusive. Ideology and national interest are not dichotomous terms: they can and do overlap and co-exist.

The influence of ideology on Vietnam's foreign policy prior to the mid-to-late 1980s may be illustrated as follows. From the inception of the Democratic Republic of Vietnam as an established state in Southeast Asia, its élite accepted the "two camp" thesis that the world was divided between the forces of socialism and imperialism.[4] In the late 1960s Vietnam adopted a framework known as the "three revolutionary currents".[5] According to this model, global order was determined by three trends (or revolutionary currents): the strength of the socialist camp headed by the Soviet Union; the strength of the workers" movement in advanced industrial countries; and the strength of the forces of national liberation in the Third World. In practical terms, Vietnam allied itself with the Soviet Union as the "cornerstone" of its foreign policy. Hanoi's leaders also viewed Indochina as a strategic entity and sought to develop an integrated alliance system with Laos and Cambodia. Vietnam's 1978 invasion of Cambodia and 25–year treaties of friendship and co-operation with Laos and the Soviet Union were logical end products of this orientation. They resulted in a decade-long polarization of regional relations. Vietnam was left isolated and dependent on the Soviet Union and Eastern Europe for political, military and economic support.

ASEAN was in the forefront of diplomatic efforts to secure the withdrawal of Vietnamese military forces from Cambodia. This partly took the form of an embargo on trade, aid and investment. These pressures eventually played a part in convincing Hanoi's leaders to seek a negotiated end to the conflict. In December 1986, at the sixth national party congress, as is well known, Vietnam adopted the policy of *doi moi* or renovation. This policy was mainly concerned with overcoming a domestic economic crisis by the adoption of socio-economic reforms whose centre piece was the dismantling of the central planning apparatus in favour of a market-orientated economy. Vietnam also sought to open itself to foreign investment.

It was clear to Hanoi's leaders that *doi moi* could not be accomplished without a comprehensive settlement of the Cambodian conflict. In 1987, the Politburo of the Vietnam Communist Party secretly adopted Resolution no. 2, which set in motion a strategic readjustment in Vietnam's national security policy.[6] Vietnam made the decision to withdraw from Cambodia and Laos and to reduce its large standing army.

Vietnam's ideologically-derived world-view began to change in tandem with a re-thinking of Soviet foreign policy. It was not until May 1988, however, that Vietnam's new foreign policy orientation was codified. This took the form of Politburo Resolution no. 13 which stressed a "multi-directional foreign policy" orientation.[7] This resolution is now recognized as a major landmark. It is important to note that this followed, and was not contemporary with, the adoption of renovation in economic policy. The emphasis was "to maintain peace, take advantage of favourable world conditions" in order to stabilize the domestic situation and set the base for economic development over the next ten to fifteen years. Politburo

Resolutions nos. 2 and 13 *inter alia* thus set in motion changes in Vietnamese national and foreign policies which contributed to a diplomatic settlement of the Cambodian conflict in October 1991.

In late 1988 Nguyen Van Linh, then Secretary-General of the Vietnam Communist Party, told visiting Philippine Foreign Minister Raul Manglapus that Vietnam was "eager to join ASEAN".[8] At the same time, Malaysia's Prime Minister Mahathir indicated that "ASEAN could accept Vietnam as a member of the grouping in future should it subscribe to the ideas of ASEAN."[9] In early 1989 Indonesian Armed Forces Commander-in-Chief General Tri Sutrisno stated that ideology would not be an impediment to Vietnam's membership in the Association.[10] Early the following year (January 1990), Thai Prime Minister Chatchai Chunhawan publicly stated his support for the incorporation of Indochina into ASEAN but only after the Cambodian conflict had been settled.[11] In November 1990, President Soeharto of Indonesia became the first ASEAN head of state to pay an official visit to Vietnam. His trip set off intense speculation about the possibility of Vietnam becoming ASEAN's next member.[12] Finally, in March 1991, Malaysia's Prime Minister proposed the initiation of a dialogue between ASEAN and the non-member states of mainland Southeast Asia (Vietnam, Myanmar, Laos and Cambodia). This was immediately welcomed by Vietnam, which also signaled its desire to attract investment from ASEAN businessmen.[13]

An important modification of Vietnam's "multi-directional foreign policy" was adopted by the seventh national party congress in June 1991.[14] Vietnam now sought "to be friends with all countries". Vietnam's *Strategy for Socioeconomic Stabilization and Development Up to the Year 2000*, which was adopted by the seventh congress, declared that Vietnam would "diversify and multilateralise economic relations with all countries and economic organisations ..." In August, immediately following the congress, an international symposium on Interaction for Progress: Vietnam's New Course and ASEAN Experiences was co-hosted in Hanoi by the Vietnam Institute of Social Science, the Central Institute of Economic Management and the Information and Resource Center of Singapore. The seminar was addressed by Phan Van Khai, first vice chairman of the Council of Ministers, who signaled Vietnam's desire to co-operate with ASEAN members. Another Vietnamese official stated that "ASEAN can become the bridge between Vietnam and the world".[15] In September, during the course of a visit to Hanoi by Thailand's Foreign Minister, Arsa Sarasin, Vietnam expressed its willingness to accede to the 1976 ASEAN Treaty of Amity and Cooperation and then followed up by officially notifying the Philippines of its intention.[16]

The October 1991 Cambodian peace agreement and the collapse of the Soviet Union in December that year represented a major watershed in the development of an "omni-directional" approach to foreign policy. The Cambodian settlement meant that Vietnam was no longer an international pariah state subject to an aid and trade boycott. After the Cambodian settlement, Vietnam moved rapidly to normalize its relations with the countries of Southeast and East Asia. Vietnam initially gave priority to the ASEAN states and China before turning to South Korea, Western Europe, Australasia, Japan and Central Europe. Official figures released at the end of September 1991 indicated that ASEAN states had invested in thirty-four projects with a total prescribed capital of US$173 million. This represented "12.4 per cent of foreign investment projects and 7.2 per cent of total legal capital invested ..."[17] In 1994 alone, Vietnam received presidents and prime ministers from Mongolia, the Philippines, Singapore, Sweden, South Korea, Japan, India and Canada.

In late 1991–early 1992 Vietnam moved to restore relations with the individual members of the Association of South East Asian Nations and with ASEAN as a regional organization. This represented a complete reversal of a decade-long period of confrontation. Vo Van Kiet, then chairman of the Council of Ministers, led a high-level government delegation to Indonesia, Thailand and Singapore in October–November 1991.[18] The following year he visited Malaysia, the Philippines and Brunei. Kiet's trips marked a return of Vietnam into the regional fold and a turning back of the clock to 1976–77 when Vietnam-Southeast Asia relations were at an all time high.[19] Since Kiet's ground-breaking visits, Do Muoi, Secretary-General of the Vietnam Communist Party, has paid visits to Singapore, Malaysia, Thailand, New Zealand, Australia, Japan, South Korea and Myanmar.[20]

The end of the Cambodian conflict brought with it an end to ASEAN's trade and aid embargo. This led to unprecedented levels of commercial interaction. ASEAN investment increased tenfold in just three years (1991–1994), and made up 15 per cent of total direct foreign investment. ASEAN states became involved in over 147 projects with a paid-up capital of US$1.4 billion by the first half of 1994. Thirty-seven development agreements were signed between Vietnam and ASEAN businesses during this period.

On the eve of ASEAN membership, 60 per cent of Vietnam's foreign trade was with ASEAN states. In 1994, Singapore overtook Japan to become Vietnam's biggest trading partner. Four of the ASEAN countries ranked among the top fifteen foreign investors in Vietnam. Singapore and Malaysia ranked sixth and seventh, respectively, after Hong Kong, Taiwan, South Korea, Australia and France.[21] The industrializing economies of Thailand and Malaysia also made them important models for Vietnamese emulation.

Since 1992, in preparation for membership, Vietnam joined six ASEAN committees and five ASEAN projects on functional co-operation, including science and technology, environment, health services, population, tourism, culture, civil aviation and maritime transportation. In 1992 and 1993, Vietnam and Laos attended the annual ASEAN Ministerial Meetings as observers. In July 1992 both acceded to the 1976 ASEAN Treaty of Amity and Cooperation (or Bali Treaty). By so doing they renounced the use of force or the threat to use force in foreign relations. And they committed themselves to the non-violent resolution of any conflict which might arise under mechanisms spelled out in the 1976 Bali Treaty. Two years later, at the ASEAN Ministerial Meeting in Bangkok, ASEAN officially invited Vietnam to become its seventh member. Vietnam became a founding member of the ASEAN Regional Forum in mid-1994. Its application for membership in ASEAN was approved in late 1994 and Vietnam joined in July 1995.[22]

Since the seventh party congress (1991), Vietnam has succeeded in diversifying its foreign relations. The major accomplishments of this new orientation were fivefold: normalization of relations with China (November 1991), the restoration of official assistance from Japan (November 1992) and in 1995 normalization of relations with the United States, membership in ASEAN and the signing of a framework agreement with the European Union. For the first time, socialist Vietnam had established relations with all five permanent members of the UN Security Council and equally importantly, with the world's three major economic centres: Europe, North America and East Asia. Vietnam's overall diplomatic relations expanded to include diplomatic ties with 163 countries by the end of 1996. In 1989, Vietnam had diplomatic relations with only twenty-three non-communist states.

During 1995 Vietnam exchanged thirty-five major delegations with ASEAN states including the visit of President Le Duc Anh to the Philippines and the visit of the King of Malaysia to Vietnam. Figures released at the end of the year revealed that ASEAN states had invested in 234 projects with a total investment capital reaching US$3.2 billion. As of 16 May 1997, these figures had risen to 312 projects with a total capitalization of US$7.6 billion or 20 per cent of the total foreign direct investment in Vietnam. Singapore ranked first in both the number of projects (156) and capital invested (US$5.1 billion).[23]

On 15 December 1995, Vietnam signed the protocol acceding to the agreement on the Common Effective Preferential Tariff (CEPT) scheme as a first step in joining the ASEAN Free Trade Area.[24] Vietnam is now obligated to extend most-favoured nation and national treatment to ASEAN member countries. Under the terms of this protocol Vietnam is also required to provide information on its trade regime and move to meet a series of tariff reduction deadlines starting 1 January 1996. Vietnam uses 2,218 tariff lines. Vietnam nominated 857 lines in its immediate inclusion list (nearly 39 per cent of the total). Of these, 548 have zero tariffs while the remaining 309 items attract tariffs in the 1–5 per cent range. Vietnam has already met the deadline of January 2006 by which tariffs on all items in the immediate inclusion list must be lowered to between 0–5 per cent.

Vietnam has retained 1,189 tariff lines (54 per cent of the total) on its temporary exclusion list and 26 tariff lines on its sensitive list (1 per cent of the total). It must phase in tariff reductions on the temporary exclusion lines in five equal instalments beginning in January 1999 and ending by January 2003. Thus, by 2003, 92 per cent of all tariff lines used by Vietnam will fall under the CEPT scheme. Most of Vietnam's sensitive list includes unprocessed agricultural products; these must be phased in starting January 2001 and ending by January 2010.

In sum, in both political and economic relations Vietnam has achieved very favourable circumstances for its integration with the region and the global economy (Vietnam's defence relations are discussed below).[25] This chapter will now offer an assessment of how Vietnam views the advantages of multilateralism, that is, membership in ASEAN.

The benefits of multilateralism

Vietnamese officials state that three main factors accounted for Vietnam's decision to join ASEAN: the desire to have amicable relations with regional states, to attract foreign investment, and as a catalyst to its domestic reform process (unstated reasons are discussed below).[26] On the anniversary of Vietnam's first year as an ASEAN member, foreign minister Nguyen Manh Cam said that Vietnam made the right decision to join ASEAN despite the difficulties it now faced in liberalizing the economy in an effort to catch up with the other six members.[27] He also noted difficulties caused by differences in the political systems, noting in particular Vietnam's socialist government, planned economy, lack of experience with the free market, and the lack of English-speaking officials; but Vietnam would meet its obligations to open its economy under the AFTA by 2006. "We want to strengthen the trend towards regionalism and international integration. This will promote peace and stability", he said.

In 1996, at the end of its first full year of membership, Vietnam was more committed to ASEAN than previously. For example, Vietnam reorganized its bureaucracy by creating a National ASEAN Committee headed by a Deputy Prime Minister with responsibility for co-ordinating all institutions that interacted with ASEAN or ASEAN-affiliated bodies. An ASEAN Department was created within the Foreign Ministry. In 1995 Vietnam participated in the fifth ASEAN summit and the first Asia-Europe Summit Meeting. Vietnam also agreed to host an informal sixth summit meeting in Hanoi in December 1998. Vietnam also met its obligations under the Common Effective Preferential Tariff agreement by drawing up a programme for the reduction of import duties on a list of over 1,600 products. Among the Vietnamese foreign policy élite there was a general consensus that the decision to join ASEAN was correct and had been a success.[28] This assessment must be viewed within the context of the multiple economic and political objectives Vietnam sought to achieve when it first joined.

In 1994 when Vietnam made the decision to apply for membership in ASEAN it did so with the prime strategic objective of securing a more peaceful international environment in which to guarantee Vietnam's national security against external threat. According to one Vietnamese writer, "Politically, due to ASEAN's high international prestige, ASEAN membership would enhance Vietnam's diplomatic standing and integrate Vietnam's security with the security of the whole of Southeast Asia, thus creating an external environment favorable for economic development."[29]

A secondary objective was to secure the most favourable external conditions for carrying out economic renovation. Within these broad strategic objectives Vietnam specifically sought to transform its relations with ASEAN states from suspicion to trust and from competition to partnership by moving to resolve such problem areas as the repatriation of Vietnamese refugees,[30] demarcation of continental shelves, overlapping territorial claims (involving Malaysia, the Philippines and Thailand) and fishing disputes. These legacies of history were seen as irritants which could impede the development of close ASEAN-Vietnam relations. An improvement in Vietnam's relations with ASEAN would also serve to change Vietnam's image and increase its prestige in global affairs.

Vietnam also sought membership in ASEAN to enhance its

bargaining position with other states, specifically China and the United States. Vietnam is now more strategically important to Beijing and Washington as a member of ASEAN. Despite the normalization of relations with China in late 1991, there has been no resolution of overlapping territorial claims in the South China Sea. Indeed, Chinese assertiveness in the Spratly Islands in 1992 served as a catalyst for ASEAN membership. Membership in ASEAN, in Hanoi's view, transformed this particular problem from a bilateral one between Beijing and Hanoi to a multilateral one involving China and ASEAN as a group. At the same time as Vietnam conducts bilateral talks with China on territorial disputes, as it does with other ASEAN members such as the Philippines, it also stands behind ASEAN declaratory policy on the settlement of territorial conflicts. However, as Vietnamese analysts point out, "Vietnamese history shows that one-sided relations have led to political isolation and economic difficulties.... Therefore, Vietnam's ASEAN membership should be achieved in a way that would strengthen instead of harm Vietnam's relations with China."[31]

Likewise, Vietnam sought membership in ASEAN as a means of improving its relations with the United States. In 1994 when Vietnam applied for membership in ASEAN, it was still subject to a U.S.-imposed trade and aid embargo. By securing membership in ASEAN Vietnam hoped it would transform its image from a "communist trouble maker" to that of a socialist developing country striving to develop a "market-orientated economy". In Hanoi's view, its conversion into a potential "partner for peace" would be attractive to decision-makers in Washington. ASEAN membership would also provide some measure of protection for Hanoi from Washington on such issues as human rights and democratization. According to one Vietnamese political analyst, Vietnam would be "quite happy to hide behind" Malaysia and Singapore on those issues.[32]

Vietnam also set the broad objective of achieving external support for its economic development, which it saw as a concomitant of an improvement in the strategic environment. In other words, a transformation in Vietnam's political relations would also lead to a transformation in Vietnam's economic relations, which in turn would reinforce its domestic policy of renovation. As a first priority, Vietnam sought to integrate its economy with that of the Asia-Pacific region and global economy. Joining ASEAN meant participation in the ASEAN Free Trade Area and gaining familiarity with the norms and practices of international trade. This in turn facilitated membership in APEC and eventual membership in the World Trade Organization.[33] As a member of ASEAN, Vietnam could also expect to learn from the developmental experience of its individual members. This would accelerate the development of a competitive market-oriented economy.

As a member of ASEAN and a participant in AFTA, Vietnam expected to benefit from increased trade and investment from ASEAN states.[34] Intra-ASEAN trade expanded and Vietnam reoriented its exports to take advantage of this large market. This trend was evident even before Vietnam formally joined the Association. Imports from ASEAN accounted for nearly one-half of Vietnam's total imports. About 30 per cent of Vietnam's exports went to ASEAN states. The volume of trade with ASEAN countries rose markedly in dollar value terms and was expected to expand further with Vietnam's participation in ASEAN's CEPT scheme. Vietnam's membership in AFTA will not greatly affect the other ASEAN economies as trade with Vietnam comprised about 2.5 per cent of the existing intra-ASEAN total. But participation in AFTA could result in trade creation and trade diversion benefits for Vietnam. Vietnam was expected to increase its imports from ASEAN, particularly from Singapore. These imports would replace more costly, domestically-manufactured goods and may even have the indirect effect of dampening the smuggling of Chinese goods. ASEAN, Thailand in particular, was expected to divert its trade by importing more from Vietnam under AFTA arrangements. Vietnam was to import quality materials from ASEAN not only for domestic production but for export. As an ASEAN member, Vietnam enjoys Generalized System of Preferences (GSP) status in selling to Europe and North America. Vietnam's textile, garment, leather and electronic assembly industries were expected to benefit most.

Vietnam expected that membership in AFTA would result in increased foreign direct investment to the extent that the ASEAN region as a whole was seen as a stable and profitable market. Vietnam also expected to receive high technology transfers from member states which were created by foreign investment initially. As of May 1997 three ASEAN countries—Singapore, Malaysia, and Thailand—ranked among the ten largest foreign investors in Vietnam (Indonesia ranked eighteenth, the Philippines twenty-first). Singaporean investment is concentrated in the fields of hotel construction and tourism. Malaysia and Indonesia invested in Vietnam's oil sector while Thailand has concentrated on mineral exploitation and processing. ASEAN investment in Vietnam was expected to rise as investors sought to exploit Vietnam's lower labour costs in resource and labour intensive industries.

These were Vietnam's expectations up until the onset of the Asian financial and economic crisis of 1997–98. In mid-1997, coinciding with the devaluation of the Thai baht, Vietnam began to experience a decline in the rate of GDP growth and a fall-off in direct foreign investment. Vietnam's economic picture worsened in 1998 because the countries which were worst hit by the regional economic crisis (Japan, South Korea, Thailand) were also among Vietnam's largest trading and investment partners. Vietnam responded by turning inwards and by putting a premium on the maintenance of domestic political stability.

Eighth party congress

Vietnam's paradigm shift in foreign policy from a model stressing ideology to one with an emphasis on national interest has provoked internal party debate.[35] Vietnam's diversification of foreign relations, including developing ties with the United States, has not been without its critics as well. This became particularly evident immediately following the normalization of U.S.-Vietnam relations and Vietnam's admission into ASEAN. These events took place during the process of preparing the first draft of the party's *Political Report* to the eighth national party congress.

In August 1995, Politburo member (and prime minister) Vo Van Kiet prepared a twenty-one page classified memorandum for consideration by the Politburo.[36] Kiet touched on a number of internal party issues and warned that if Vietnam did not step up the process of renovation the leadership risked being removed from power. In his discussion of foreign relations Kiet argued that confrontation between socialism and imperialism had given way to multipolarity as the dominant feature of the global system. According to Kiet, "Unlike the past, national interests, regional interests, and other global interests (peace, environment, development, globalisation of manufacturing) play an ever more important role in creating conflicts and forming new alliances..." In his view the four remaining socialist countries (China, Vietnam, North Korea and Cuba[37]) "cannot act and have no international value as a united economic force" as each was still searching for a suitable path of development. Kiet also mentioned "hot spots" which could flare up, a pointed reference to Chinese actions in the South China Sea.

According to Kiet, changes in the international system resulted in greater acceptance of Vietnam's one-party state by the international community. He listed normalization of diplomatic relations with the United States and membership in ASEAN as two major achievements of his government. In so doing he downplayed the threat posed by the United States to Vietnam. Indeed, he argued for a strengthening of relations with Washington: "Vietnam will benefit more if we go down that path". In sum, according to the Vietnamese prime minister, Vietnam now faced the most favourable international environment since 1945 and it should take determined steps to take advantage of this situation.

Vietnam's ideological conservatives, in contrast, still stressed the importance of conflict and competition between socialism and imperialism. In their view socialism was temporarily on the decline and capitalism inevitably would be replaced.[38] Party conservatives are particularly concerned by the threat to one-party rule posed by the process of "opening up" and "integration into the world economy". These critics argue that Vietnam's "socialist orientation" would be undermined by the development of a market economy at home and by political and cultural influences from abroad.[39] In its starkest form, Vietnam was seen as the victim of a campaign of "peaceful evolution" orchestrated by "foreign reactionaries and imperialists" (overseas Vietnamese and the United States). One conservative has argued that ideology—Marxism-Leninism and the Thoughts of Ho Chi Minh—must be defended equally along with the country's air space and land and sea territory.[40]

Kiet's memorandum was circulated at a time when preparations were just getting under way to prepare the draft strategic policy documents to be presented to the eighth party congress scheduled for 1996. They triggered strong reactions from conservative Politburo members Dao Duy Tung and Nguyen Ha Phan. Tung had carriage of ideological matters, while Phan was responsible for economic affairs. Tung was being privately tipped as the person who would replace Do Muoi as party Secretary-General.[41] Phan addressed a number of closed meetings of party cadres where he branded Kiet's views a "deviation from socialism" but refrained from attacking Kiet by name. Vietnam's ideologues also played on deep anxieties about the newly developing relationship with Vietnam's former arch enemy, the United States, by highlighting the social evils which accompanied the open door policy and by warning of the threat of peaceful evolution.

The conservatives also drafted a ten-page document entitled, "American Strategies to Transform Socialist Vietnam After the Normalization of United States-Vietnam Relations" (*Chien Luoc Chuyen Hoa Viet Nam*), which they circulated among high-ranking officials to counter Kiet's memorandum. The document was dated 23 October and was classified secret. It argued that membership in ASEAN and normalization of relations with the United States, far from being diplomatic victories, were part of a clever new U.S. strategy of "selective economic development" to undermine VCP rule by encouraging the development of democratic forces. The conservative memo argued, "America will push not only for economic freedom but also political freedom. America will urge Vietnam to discard communism... [which] will be replaced by foreign investors and capitalist businesses". The document also warned that U.S. investment was designed to dominate the Vietnamese market and the United States would seek out and support reformist elements in the party.

At least two major drafts of the *Political Report* were drawn up before the final version was presented to the eighth congress.[42] When all three versions are compared it is notable that the foreign policy section was the most heavily edited and amended. Most remarkably, the foreign policy sections of the first two drafts failed to mention ASEAN (Vietnam's membership in ASEAN was noted in passing in the first section which dealt with successes achieved after ten years of renovation). A reference was finally inserted as the second point in a five point list of Vietnam's foreign policy objectives. Point two read, "To do our utmost to increase our relations with neighbouring countries and other ASEAN members, constantly consolidate relations with traditional friendly countries, attach importance to relations with developed countries and economic-political centers of the world, at the same time upholding all the time the spirit of fraternal solidarity with developing countries in Asia, Africa, Latin America, and the Non-Aligned Movement".[43] The inclusion of a reference to ASEAN was made as a result of the strenuous objections by ASEAN ambassadors stationed in Hanoi after they saw the public draft released in April. They were reportedly furious that such an important event as Vietnam's membership in ASEAN had been given such scant attention.

A political report to a national party congress is, by its nature, a consensus document. Each section of the political report is drafted by a specialist committee and is circulated internally before being released for wider discussion. Draft copies of the political report are routinely discussed at provincial party congresses held prior to the national congress and by specially convened meetings involving relevant specialists. It is not surprising then to find that the section of the 1996 *Political Report* which dealt with "the characteristics of the international system", reflected the views of ideological conservatives as well as the more pragmatic orientation of policy practitioners.[44] The *Political Report*, for example, noted that "[t]he collapse of the socialist regimes in the Soviet Union and Eastern European countries has driven socialism into temporary regression.

However, that has not changed the nature of the times; mankind is still in the era of transition from capitalism to socialism..." The *Political Report* goes on to note that "[t]he revolution in science and technology continues to develop at an increasingly higher level, rapidly increasing productive forces while accelerating the process of shifting the world economic structures and the internationalization of the economy and social life". The *Political Report* also juxtaposes the potential for conflict arising from competition in the areas of economics, science and technology with the potential for co-operation arising from global peace and stability. Or, to round out this point, the *Political Report* notes the role of "socialist countries, the communist and workers' parties, and the revolutionary and progressive forces"[45] alongside peaceful coexistence and co-operation by "countries with different socio-political systems".

The threat to peaceful evolution

National defence, internal security and foreign relations are seen as mutually reinforcing. According to the 1996 *Political Report*, Vietnam's first foreign policy priority is "consolidating the peaceful environment and creating further favourable international conditions to step up socio-economic development and national industrialization and modernization in [the] service of national construction and defence...".[46] Vietnam's once highly secretive military establishment has sought to expand international relations with its ASEAN counterparts as well as other countries.[47] During 1996, for example, defence contacts were made with at least fifteen non-ASEAN countries. The list includes: Australia, Bulgaria, Burma, Cambodia, Canada, China, Cuba, France, India, Italy, Japan, Laos, South Korea, United Kingdom and the United States.[48] Since 1992 Vietnam has also hosted visits by naval warships from France, Canada, Italy and the United Kingdom.

Beginning in 1994 Vietnam's defence minister visited all ASEAN states except Brunei. Since joining ASEAN, Vietnam has hosted visits by Thailand's Defence Minister, Chief of Staff, Army Commander-in-Chief and a delegation from the National Defence Institute; the chiefs of staff from Indonesia's Armed Forces and Air Force; the Philippine's National Defence Secretary and Commander of the Infantry Force; a delegation from Malaysia's Armed Forces Staff College; and Singapore's Defence Minister and a military delegation led by the Chief of the Army. Going in the opposite direction were the Vietnamese Defence Minister and the head of the army's General Department of Technology who both visited Singapore.

The Vietnamese military are also making their first appearances at region-wide security meetings. In 1996 Vietnamese representatives attended the ASEAN Regional Forum inter-sessional meetings on confidence building held in Tokyo in January and Jakarta in April, and the Asia-Pacific Security Dialogue hosted by Thailand in March. Vietnam also sent representatives to the Forum for Defence Authorities in the Asia-Pacific Region, the first regional meeting of defence planners, held in Japan in October. In another first, Vietnam publicly released a Defence White Paper to the ASEAN Regional Forum meeting in Manila in mid-1998.[49]

Vietnam's remarkable opening to the outside world—politically, economically and militarily—has provoked expressions of deep-seated anxiety if not fear that the very process of opening could also undermine Vietnam's one-party system. Ideological conservatives, located in the Vietnam Communist Party, the Vietnam People's Army, the ministries of interior and national defence and elsewhere in the party-state apparatus, have formed a loose coalition to put a break on this process. The same 1996 *Political Report* (section 8, foreign policy) which called for a foreign policy of "openness, diversification and multilateralisation of foreign relations, in the spirit that Vietnam wishes to be a friend of all nations…" also carried this warning (section 7, national defence and security): "to prevent and foil all designs and activities attempting social-political destabilisation, encroachment on independence, sovereignty and territorial integrity, and detriment to our national construction and development".[50]

"Peaceful evolution" is a term first used by China in the late 1970s, which was borrowed by Vietnam to describe the strategy used by imperialism to undermine socialism in Eastern Europe and the Soviet Union.[51] In 1989, Vietnam was shaken by the disintegration of communist rule in Eastern Europe. The VCP Central Committee rejected political pluralism at its sixth plenum (20–29 March), and condemned imperialism for undermining the socialist bloc at its seventh plenum (15–24 August). The army strongly endorsed the resolutions of both plenums.[52] The then Defence Minister General Le Duc Anh, for example, argued that "the army could not remain isolated from the country's political problems at a time when Vietnamese socialism was under attack."[53] Or in the words on an editorial appearing in the army newspaper:

> The imperialists forces' present scheme—which they hope will work—lies in their attempts to carry out a "peaceful evolution" aimed at restoring imperialism in those parts of the world where the socialist system has already been established …

Western countries are using pluralism and the multiparty system—an attribute of bourgeois democracy—as a deadly political weapon to discredit the communist party and then eliminate the latter's leading role, and to eventually deliver power into the hands of anti-socialist forces ...

Thus, through "political pluralism" the imperialist forces have tried by all means to gradually change the political nature of the socialist system. They regard this political maneuver as the most important spearhead, because in their belief, if they can change a political system then they can change everything ...

The imperialists have therefore chosen the tactic of "silk worms eating mulberry leaves" to begin by degenerating one Eastern European socialist country into a moderate capitalist country and then advancing toward degenerating other Eastern European countries.[54]

In June 1991, as noted above, the seventh party congress endorsed a foreign policy of "diversification and multilateralization" of relations and "making friends with all countries". Later that year the Soviet Union collapsed. This led to an accentuation of anxieties that Vietnam's internal weaknesses might be manipulated by hostile forces outside the country and that Vietnam "was next". Maj. Gen. Nguyen Van Phiet argued, for example:

Today, the factors threatening our socialist regime's existence and our fatherland's independence stem not only from certain counter-revolutionary armed violence in the country, or from the deterrent, aggressive military strength of imperialism from the outside; they are also shaped and influenced by our country's weaknesses and deficiencies in the economic, social, political, ideological, cultural, educational, and artistic fields as well as and in our life-style. These are weaknesses and deficiencies caused by the socio-economic crisis. Pursuing their scheme of abolishing socialism, hostile forces inside the country and imperialism are deepening our weaknesses and carrying out many policies and tricks of sabotage, confrontation, and aggression against our people in all domains of social life. In conjunction with applying military deterrence, they are implementing the "peaceful evolution" strategy, launching attacks and sabotage activities in the economic, political, ideological, educational, and cultural fields and in daily life, while colluding with reactionary forces inside the country for the purpose of overthrowing the present political regime. They are concentrating on undermining the unity among the party, state, people, and armed forces, and on inciting enmity among nationalities... [sic] These are the factors threatening the security of our regime and endangering the independence and sovereignty of the Vietnamese fatherland. This could even be called an undeclared, non-shooting "war of aggression".[55]

General Doan Khue argued that Vietnam was already in the sights of hostile external forces:

> Following the failure of socialism in Eastern Europe and the Soviet Union, hostile forces, on the one hand, have been expanding the results of their victory in those countries, and, on the other, stepping up their offensive against the remaining socialist countries, which include Vietnam.
>
> Their plots and actions are aimed at accelerating the combined use of unarmed and armed measures against us to undermine in a total manner our politics, ideology, psychology, way of living, and so on, and encircling, isolating, and destroying us in the economic field, with the hope that they could achieve so-called "peaceful evolution" and make the revolution in our country deviate from its course. They have been trying to seek, build, and develop reactionary forces of all kinds within our country; at the same time to nurture and bring back groups of armed reactionaries within our country; and to combine armed activities with political activities, hoping to transform the socio-economic crisis in our country into a political crisis and to incite rioting and overthrowing when opportunities arise. They may also look for excuses to effect an intervention, to carry out partial armed aggression, or to wage aggressive wars on various scales.
>
> Our people thus have the task of dealing with and being ready to deal with any circumstances caused by hostile forces; peaceful evolution, riot and overthrow, encirclement, blockade, surprise attacks by armed forces, aggressive wars on various scales. The politico-ideological front is a hot one to fight back "peaceful development" and to defend the fatherland.[56]

The theme that Vietnam is threatened by "peaceful evolution" has been a constant refrain by Vietnam's ideological conservatives from the collapse of the Soviet Union to the present. For example, an editorial published in the party's newspaper at the start of 1997 argued:[57]

> Apart from opportunities, the new situation has posed many dangers for our party and people. Because these dangers are interrelated and equally grave, we should not belittle any of them. Together with other dangers, hostile forces are implementing their "peaceful evolution" strategy against our country in a bid to do away with Marxism-Leninism and Ho Chi Minh's ideology, undermine the ideological single-mindedness within our party and among our people, negate our party's leadership role and get rid of the socialist regime in our country. "Human rights" and "free market-orientated economy" are the two key prongs of the so-called "pro-democracy movement" designed to privatise the overall economic system, transform our party and state,

instigate the people, sow disunity among our internal ranks and cause our socio-economic system to be side-tracked from the socialist orbit. The struggle against "peaceful evolution" is, therefore, difficult and complicated by nature.

Vietnamese leaders have warned that "hostile forces"—including tourists and backpackers—are busy trying to steal state secrets, and employees sent abroad for training are being recruited as spies. Internally, the rhetoric of Vietnam's conservatives has been supplanted by sporadic action, such as during the anti-social evils campaign of early 1996, efforts to form party cells in joint ventures involving foreign partners, and action to control the use of the Internet.

Disadvantages of multilateralism

Vietnam joined ASEAN primarily for the political and strategic benefits it calculated it would gain *vis-à-vis* China and the United States. Perhaps the major political disadvantage for Vietnam, long accustomed to asserting its sovereignty and independence,[58] has been the need to meld Vietnam's position to fit in with the ASEAN consensus. As noted by one Vietnamese writer, "despite announcing its commitment to the Treaty of Amity and Cooperation signed in Bali in 1976, Hanoi is not so certain whether it accepts the rules of the game, that is, accepts all the written and unwritten norms of the relationship among ASEAN countries without any exceptions."[59]

Vietnam faces several possible economic disadvantages as a result of ASEAN membership. Vietnam and the other ASEAN economies are essentially competitive not complementary, particularly in the areas of foreign investment and development assistance. Vietnam's developing industry faces potentially stiff challenges from its ASEAN counterparts.[60] In August 1996, ASEAN Secretary-General Ajit Singh told Vietnam it would need to end its quota system (which favours state enterprises), eliminate other non-tariff barriers, and enhance the transparency of its trade regime. These steps may aggravate Vietnam's trade imbalance with ASEAN and increase an already growing trade deficit. More than half of Vietnam's trade deficit of US$3.5 billion (1996 figures) is with other ASEAN countries. There is also the possibility that Vietnam's tax base could be undermined by the in-flow of goods from ASEAN states as part of the AFTA regime. At present Vietnam earns a portion of its domestic revenue from tariffs on imported goods. When these tariffs are lowered or eliminated the flow of revenue from this source to the central government will decline. Vietnamese policy-makers are now considering off-setting taxes, such as consumption and turnover taxes, to counter-balance these expected losses. This is a highly complex economic issue with the finer technical points being debated by Vietnamese economists and party officials.

The major disadvantage of ASEAN membership in the eyes of some ideological conservatives lay in the potential for economic success to contribute to political instability if not speed up the erosion of one-party rule in Vietnam. Ideological conservatives therefore engaged in a rearguard action to bolster the state-owned sector of the economy while placing constraints on the private sector. They also sought to control and limit foreign investment.

In 1998, party conservatives became alarmed by two developments affecting ASEAN. The first concerned the impact of the regional economic crisis on Vietnam's domestic stability. ASEAN's disarray in dealing with this issue also served to reinforce those voices in Vietnam which urged a go-slow approach to economic integration. The second issue concerned a move by Thailand, supported by the Philippines, to modify ASEAN's long-cherished principle on non-interference in the internal affairs of another member state. Thailand's proposal was aimed at Myanmar whose domestic policies, it was argued, spilled over and threatened regional stability. Vietnam supported the status quo. These two developments caused Vietnam to lower its expectations about the benefits and advantages of ASEAN membership.

Conclusions

Reformers and foreign policy pragmatists argue that sometime between the seventh and eighth national party congresses Vietnam has "lost direction" and suffered from a "loss of orientation". In sum, not only has a "paradigm been lost" but Vietnam is still suffering from a crisis of faith in its foreign relations. Vietnam's foreign minister Nguyen Manh Cam has called for a "deepening of relations" with foreign countries. What does this mean in practical terms? On the surface it means going beyond the simple framework of "diversifying relations" and "making friends with all countries" to develop multi-faceted relations. But Vietnam has hardly succeeded in going beyond the economic dimension. After foreign direct investment, aid, and trade, where does the relationship go? For example, the sudden burst in developing new military relations appears impressive; on closer examination little has been accomplished. Vietnamese are mainly concerned to work out the details of how they might acquire needed spare parts and other equipment. They are extremely wary of developing any relationship in depth. Vietnamese military officials restrict bilateral discussions to generalities. Hanoi-based defence attaches are near unanimous in expressing frustration at the low level and superficial nature of their access to Vietnam's armed forces. Foreign diplomats who have sought to engage the Vietnamese in discussions on regional security issues and draw them further into the process of regional security dialogue have become frustrated by Vietnam's unwillingness to engage in depth. Vietnam's bland and vaguely worded 1998 Defence White Paper was particularly disappointing in this respect.

Vietnam emphasizes its own independence, stability, socialist orientation and integration with the world. This had led to a shallow-ness or flatness in relations, especially on the political, security and defence planes. Bilateral and multilateral ties are advancing at a glacial pace in these areas. Note the anodyne flavour of the following report:[61]

> The party leader [Do Muoi] said that the visit of the Singapore defence minister would make an important contribution to the promotion of mutual understanding and to the consolidation of bilateral friendship and co-operation between the two countries.
>
> He expressed his pleasure at the fruitful development of relations between Vietnam and Singapore as well as between Vietnam and other members of the Association of Southeast Asian Nations (ASEAN), thus creating favorable conditions for Vietnam's socio-economic development. He further said that Vietnam wished, together with other ASEAN countries, to build Southeast Asia into a region of peace, stability, co-operation, development and prosperity.
>
> Prime Minister Vo Van Kiet highly appreciated the friendship and co-operation between the two countries. He briefed his guest on the socio-economic situation of Vietnam.

Vietnam's "loss of orientation" has led to a certain formalism in the conduct of its foreign policy. It would appear that deep-seated insecurities within the party structure account for this. There is a fear about developing close political ties with non-socialist states and the impact this might have on domestic affairs. This results in super-ficial professions of friendship and co-operation across a spectrum of activities while substantial relations fail to develop further. Relations are established but not consummated. The fear of "the threat of peaceful evolution" on the part of conservative ideologues will affect the pace of Vietnam's integration into ASEAN and the development of fully rounded bilateral relations with regional states. More par-ticularly, Vietnam's fear of "the threat of peaceful evolution", will remain a domestic political issue as Vietnam develops its relations with the United States and participates in multilateral organizations in which the U.S. is a dominant player.

Notes

* The author would like to thank Nguyen Hong Thach for research assistance in the preparation of this chapter.
1. Ramesh Thakur and Carlyle A. Thayer, *Soviet Relations with India and Vietnam* (London: Macmillan, 1992), pp. 53–61 and 69–70; and Thayer, "The Soviet Union and Indochina", in Roger E. Kanet, Deborah Nutter Miner and Tamara J. Resler, eds, *Soviet Foreign Policy in Transition* (Cambridge: Cambridge University Press, 1992), pp. 236–55.
2. Vu Khoan, "Mot so van de quoc te cua dai hoi VII" and Nguyen Manh Cam, "Gia tri lau ben va dinh huong nhat quan" in Bo Ngoai Giao, *Hoi nhap quoc te va giu vung ban sac* (Hanoi: Nha xuat ban chinh tri quoc te, 1995), pp. 71–76 and 223–30, respectively.
3. See Bui Tin, *Following Ho Chi Minh: The Memoires of a North Vietnamese Colonel* (London: Hurst & Company, 1995), p. 191. For a general overview of the changing role of ideology in Vietnamese foreign policy, consult Eero Palmujoki, *Vietnam and the World: Marxist-Leninist Doctrine and the Changes in International Relations, 1975–93* (London: Macmillan Press Ltd, 1997).
4. Gareth Porter, "Vietnam and the Socialist Camp: Center or Periphery?", in William S. Turley, ed., *Vietnamese Communism in Comparative Perspective* (Boulder: Westview Press, 1980), pp. 225–64.
5. Carlyle A. Thayer, "Vietnamese Perspectives on International Security: Three Revolutionary Currents", in Donald H. McMillen, ed., *Asian Perspectives on International Security* (London: Macmillan Press, 1984), pp. 57–76.
6. Carlyle A. Thayer, "Vietnam's Strategic Readjustment", in Stuart Harris and Gary Klintworth, eds, *China as a Great Power: Myths, Realities and Challenges in the Asia-Pacific Region* (Melbourne: Longman Australia Pty Ltd, 1995), pp. 185–201; and Thayer, *The Vietnam People's Army Under Doi Moi*, Pacific Strategic Paper no. 7 (Singapore: Institute of Southeast Asian Studies, 1994), pp. 14–17.
7. Nguyen Dy Nien, "Tiep tuc doi moi va mo cua vi su nghiep cong nghiep hoa, hien dai hoa dat nuoc", *Tap Chi Cong San*, no. 12, June 1996, p. 47.
8. *Indonesian Newsletter* (Information Section, Embassy of the Republic of Indonesia in Canberra), no. 1, January 1989, 1.
9. *Bernama* in English, 0503 GMT, 16 December 1988.
10. *Antara* in English, 0204 GMT, 13 January 1989.
11. Christopher Goscha, "Could Indochina Join ASEAN?" *Bangkok Post*, 24 November 1990.
12. Kawi Chongkitthawon, "Vietnam's Backdoor to ASEAN", *The Nation*, 24 November 1990. During Soeharto's visit Vietnam made clear it would rather join ASEAN than a new regional body designed to incorporate the Indochina states.
13. Hanoi International Service in English, 1000 GMT, 15 March 1991;

and Radio Malaysia (English), News Bulletin, 1830 hours, 21 March 1991, item 8. Vietnam has also supported the expansion of ASEAN membership to include the C-L-M (Cambodia, Laos and Myanmar) states. For an upbeat assessment of the implications of ASEAN's expansion, see Hoang Anh Tuan, "Nhung Tac Dong Cua Viec Mo Rong Tu ASEAN-7 Len ASEAN-10", *Nghien Cuu Quoc Te* 1, no. 16 (February 1997): 40–45.

14. Vu Khoan, "Mot so van de quoc te cua dai hoi VII", op. cit., p. 75.

15. Remarks by Pham Van Tiem, chairman of the State Price Committee quoted by Andrew Sherry, Agence France Presse (AFP), Hanoi, 25 August 1991.

16. Kavi Chongkittavorn, "Vietnam now casting its eyes towards Asean", *The Nation*, 24 September 1991. It was also reported that ASEAN members considered it premature to admit Vietnam as a full member.

17. *Vietnam Weekly* (Hanoi), 21 October 1991, p. 13. Figures for indi- vidual countries: Indonesia 4 projects, US$13.8 million; Malaysia 4 projects, US$66.5 million; Philippines 4 projects, US$40. million; Singapore 8 projects, US$18 million and Thailand 14 projects, US$34.2 million.

18. Murray Hiebert and Michael Vatikiotis, "Asean's embrace", *Far East- ern Economic Review*, 14 November 1991, p. 19.

19. Carlyle A. Thayer, "ASEAN and Indochina: The Dialogue", in Alison Broinowski, ed., *ASEAN Into the 1990s* (London: Macmillan Publish- ers, 1990), pp. 138–61. Kiet, then first vice chairman of the Council of Ministers, first visited Malaysia in early 1991 to attend a World Bank seminar.

20. Do Muoi held an informal summit with Thai Prime Minister Chatchai in Chiang Mai in January 1991.

21. Data on foreign investment provided by the State Committee for Co- operation and Investment as of 11 August 1994.

22. For Vietnamese views on the ARF, consult Vu Tung, "Dien dan khu vuc ASEAN (ARF) va an ninh chau A - Thai Binh Duong", *Nghien Cuu Quoc Te* 3, no. 5 (September 1994): 28–33; and Nguyen Phuong Binh, "Vai tro cua ASEAN trong viec xay dung co che an ninh khu vuc", *Nghien Cuu Quoc Te* 4, no. 6 (December 1994): 30–34.

23. Le Quoc Phuong, "FDI of ASEAN Countries in Vietnam to Increase", *Saigon Times Daily*, 21 May 1997. Figures for the other ASEAN states: Malaysia 56 projects, US$1.1 billion; Thailand 72 projects, US$949 million; Indonesia 13 projects, US$333 million; and the Philippines 15 projects, US$191.5 million. Brunei's investment figures are negligible.

24. This discussion is based on "Vietnam in ASEAN", in Suthad Setboonsarng, ed., *AFTA Reader*, vol. 4, *The Fifth ASEAN Summit* (Jakarta: ASEAN Secretariat, September 1996), pp. 36–38.

25. For a current assessment, see William S. Turley, "Vietnamese Secu- rity in Domestic and Regional Focus: The Political-Economic Nexus", in Richard J. Ellings and Sheldon W. Simon, eds, *Southeast Asian Security in the New Millennium* (Armonk: M.E. Sharpe, 1996), pp. 175– 220.

26. Doan Manh Giao, "Why Vietnam Joins ASEAN", paper presented to

international seminar on Vietnam and ASEAN: Business Prospects and Policy Directions, Kuala Lumpur, 19 December 1995.

27. Lee Kim Chew, Hanoi, "Vietnam 'Has No Regrets About Joining ASEAN' ", *The Straits Times*, 10 September 1996.

28. Nguyen Manh Hung, "Nhin lai mot nam Viet Nam gia nhap ASEAN", *Nghien Cuu Quoc Te*, no. 13 (1996): 3-5.

29. Hoang Anh Tuan, "Why Hasn"t Vietnam Gained ASEAN Membership", *Contemporary Southeast Asia* 15, no. 3 (December 1993): 283.

30. Kawi Chongkittawon, *The Nation*, 29 January 1992.

31. Ibid., pp. 288-89.

32. Quoted by Adam Schwarz, "Joining The Fold", *Far Eastern Economic Review*, 16 March 1995. An article written prior to Vietnam's membership in ASEAN also noted the similarity in policy on human rights between Vietnam and ASEAN; see: Nguyen Phuong Binh, "Ve viec Viet Nam gia nhap ASEAN", *Nghien Cuu Quoc Te* 3, no. 5 (September 1994): 26.

33. Vietnam was admitted into APEC in November 1998 following a decision to do so at the APEC Summit in Manila in 1996. Vietnam has applied for membership in the WTO.

34. This section relies on Bala Ramasamy, "The Second Enlargement of ASEAN: The Inclusion of Vietnam", *ASEAN Economies* 25, no. 2 (June 1996): 29-47. Updated figures are from Le Quoc Phuong, "FDI of ASEAN Countries in Vietnam to Increase", op. cit.

35. Carlyle A. Thayer, "Sino-Vietnamese Relations: The Interplay of Ideology and National Interest", *Asian Survey* 34, no. 6 (June 1994): 513-28; Adam Schwarz, "Joining The Fold", op. cit., noted, "At home, conservatives in Vietnam's leadership once feared Asean membership would strain ties with China." For a discourse on the broad themes of Vietnamese foreign policy, consult Tran Quang Co, "Tuong lai cua cac quan he giua Viet Nam va cac nuoc chau A - Thai binh Duong: tac dong den phat trien kinh te cua Viet Nam" and Nguyen Manh Cam, "Gia tri lau ben va dinh huong nhat quan" in *Hoi nhap quoc te va giu vung ban sac*, op. cit., 103-114 and 223-30, respectively; and Phan Doan Nam, "Ve mot so mau thuan noi len tren the gioi hien nay", *Nghien Cuu Quoc Te*, no. 13 (1996): 7-18.

36. "Thu Vo Van Kiet goi Bo Chinh Tri", *Viet Luan* [Paris], no. 1053 (5 January 1996): 30-31 and 58-60.

37. Laos was omitted from Vo Van Kiet's list.

38. Le Kha Phieu, "Can Bo, Chien Si Luc Luong Vu Trang Kien Dinh Muc Tieu Doc Lap Dan Toc va Chu Nghia Xa Hoi, Duong Loi Ket Hop Hai Nhiem Vu Chien Luoc", *Nhan Dan*, 25 March 1996, pp. 1-2. Phieu replaced Do Muoi as party Secretary General in December 1997.

39. Bui Phan Ky, "May van de ve xay dung va bao ve To quoc xa hoi chu nghia trong boi canh the gioi ngay nay", *Tap Chi Cong San*, no. 16 (August 1996): 18-20.

40. Le Xuan Luu, "Ve moi quan he giua xay dung va bao ve To quoc trong giai doan cach mang moi", *Tap Chi Cong San*, no. 10 (May 1996): 7-10 and 14.

41. *Far Eastern Economic Review*, 16 February 1995, p. 12; Harish Mehta, *Business Times* [Singapore], 9 August 1995.

42. Dang Cong San Viet Nam, *Du Thao Cac Van Kien Trinh Dai Hoi VIII cua Dang (Tai Lieu Dung Tai Dai Hoi Dang Cap Co So)*, Mat (Secret), Luu Hanh Noi Bo (Internal Circulation), December 1995; "Du Thao Bao Cao Chinh Tri cua Ban Chap Hanh Trung Uong Dang Khoa VII Trinh Dai Hoi Lan Thu VIII cua Dang", *Nhan Dan*, 10 April 1996 supplement; and "Bao Cao Chinh Tri", *Quan Doi Nhan Dan*, 30 June 1996. For a general overview of the eighth congress and foreign policy, see Vu Khoan, "Dai hoi VIII va cong tac doi ngoai", *Tuan bao Quoc Te*, no. 26, 26 June–2 July 1996, 1 and 10.

43. Communist Party of Vietnam, *VIIIth National Congress Documents* (Hanoi: The Gioi Publishers, 1996), p, 78.

44. The following quotations are taken from part two of the Political Report, Communist Party of Vietnam (1996), op. cit., pp. 33–35.

45. The eighth congress was attended by 35 foreign delegations including non-communist ruling parties from neighbouring states such as the People's Action Party (PAP) from Singapore and United Malays National Organization (UMNO) from Malaysia. Indonesia's GOLKAR declined to attend. The communist parties from all socialist states in power (China, Laos, North Korea and Cuba) as well as communist and socialist parties and national liberation movements not in power (for example France, Russia, Japan, Belarus, Ukraine, Bulgaria, USA, Germany, Italy, Portugal, Argentina, India [CPI (M) and CPI], Lebanon, Brazil, Greece, Chile) attended.

46. Communist Party of Vietnam (1996), op. cit., p. 77.

47. Carlyle A. Thayer, "Force Modernisation in Vietnam", *Contemporary Southeast Asia* 19, no. 1 (June 1997): 1–28, which discusses Vietnam's defence contacts with individual ASEAN states. For a positive Vietnamese assessment of ASEAN defence co-operation, including an endorsement of joint military exercises, see Minh Duc, "Hop Tac Quan Su, Quoc Phong cua cac nuoc ASEAN", *Tap Chi Quoc Phong Toan Dan*, February 1997, pp. 69–71 and 13.

48. In the period from 1991 to the end of 1995, Vietnam also revived or established defence contacts with the Czech Republic, Israel, Kazakhstan, North Korea, Russia, Slovak Republic, and the Ukraine. These are discussed in Thayer, "Force Modernisation in Vietnam", op. cit.

49. Socialist Republic of Vietnam, *Vietnam: Consolidating National Defence, Safeguarding the Homeland* (Hanoi: Ministry of [National] Defence, 1998).

50. Communist Party of Vietnam (1996), op. cit., pp. 75–76. A BBC translation, prepared from the text of the Political Report published in *Quan Doi Nhan Dan*, read, "we must effectively prevent and crush all plots and activities of peaceful evolution and subversive violence and be ready to deal with any other complicated situations that could arise."

51. Palmujoki, *Vietnam and the World*, op. cit., pp. 202–3 and 206.

52. General Le Duc Anh writing in *Tap Chi Quoc Phong Toan Dan* (December 1989).

53. Report of interview by *Quan Doi Nhan Dan* carried by AFP, Hanoi, 23 December 1990.

54. *Quan Doi Nhan Dan*, 13 September 1989.

55. Maj. Gen. Nguyen Van Phiet, "Applying Results of Study on Democracy-Discipline Measures in Air Defence Service", *Quan Doi Nhan Dan*, 17 March 1992.

56. General Doan Khue, "Understanding the Resolution of the Third Plenum of the VCP Central Committee: Some Basic Issues Regarding the Party's Military Line in the New Stage", *Tap Chi Quoc Phong Toan Dan*, August 1992, pp. 3–15 and 45.

57. "Tang Cuong Hon Nua Cong Tac Bao Ve Chinh Tri Noi Bo", *Nhan Dan*, 3 January 1997, 1 and 7.

58. See Truong Giang Long, "Mot So Van De Trong Qua Trinh Ho Nhap Viet Nam-ASEAN", *Tap Chi Cong San*, no. 3, February 1997, pp. 57–59, which stresses the need for Vietnam to maintain its independence and sovereignty as a member of ASEAN.

59. Pham Cao Phong, "How Asean's newest member is coping", *Business Times Weekend Edition, Trends*, 29–30 June 1996.

60. Achara Ashayagachat and Tran Van Minh, "VN Businesses Uneasy Over New Tariff Cuts", *Bangkok Post*, 30 December 1995.

61. Vietnam News Agency, Hanoi, in English 1447 GMT, 27 November 1996.

2

IDEOLOGY AND FOREIGN POLICY: VIETNAM'S MARXIST-LENINIST DOCTRINE AND GLOBAL CHANGE, 1986–96

Eero Palmujoki

Introduction

During the Cold War period both political doctrines as well as political ideologies were assumed to be very stable in spite of changes in the political context. Similarly, they played an important role particularly in explaining the politics in Marxist state systems. It was assumed that the doctrines at the "core", or the "central" beliefs of decision makers remained unaltered despite changing circumstances. Undoubtedly the rigid Cold War constellation supported this approach in the field of international studies. The credibility of the Marxist-Leninist doctrine as a fundamental theory of social and international relations and as a basic explanation of the Communist decision-makers' behaviour was seriously challenged when the socialist systems collapsed in Eastern Europe and the Soviet Union. The European Communist parties made remarkable changes to their ideology and political programmes in order to adapt better to the new political situation. Marxism-Leninism in various cultural forms has survived as state ideology in the People's Republic of China (PRC), Vietnam, North Korea and Cuba, and dominates political rhetoric in these countries.

This chapter deals with the development of the Marxist-Leninist doctrine and Vietnam's foreign policy during the decade of great upheavals in international relations and between three congresses of the Vietnam Communist Party, 1986–96. It poses the following questions: "What is the role of Marxism-Leninism in politics and international relations when many of its basic assumptions have lost their significance in the post-Cold War situation?", and "How are doctrinal changes explained?" The approach to political doctrine used in this chapter refers to the manner in which political arguments are constructed. It does not deal with political behaviour or the cognitive structure of the decision-makers but with political communication. This approach is thus called a rhetorical approach to the study of political doctrine.

The point of departure is that rapid overall change of the political doctrine and ideology is unlikely. It is obvious that the doctrine is composed of different politico-cultural strata. In order to shed light on these questions, this chapter examines two traditions in Vietnamese Marxism-Leninism before exploring the present connection between foreign policy and the current application of the Marxist doctrine. A third approach seems to be emerging, including elements of earlier approaches along with new ideas concerning economic growth and political power which emphasize Vietnam's position in the Asia-Pacific system.

Rhetoric and Vietnamese Marxist-Leninist doctrine

The dominant paradigm in doctrinal studies has been the cognitive approach which assumes that the cognitive elements of the decision makers, including political doctrine and political culture, form a general orientation to action, which supposes that the actors act in a certain way in sets of situations. This is based on an assumption that the actor is constantly motivated to maintain a coherent interpretation of political reality.[1] Nathan Leites, in his pioneering work, *A Study of Bolshevism*,[2] introduced the concept of an operational code in order to reveal those doctrinal and cultural elements which form the political strategy of Soviet leaders. In analysing the Bolshevik leaders' operational code, Leites managed to formulate some main characteristics of Soviet Marxism-Leninism which could be generalized as permanent components of Marxist-Leninist doctrine. They include politics as a struggle between two opposite poles, a vision of future and past as a concomitant to this struggle, and justification of the means employed in relation to the ends, together with a number of minor epithets of Marxism-Leninism.[3] The concept of the operational code was established in Communist studies,[4] studies on political culture,[5] and some general foreign policy studies[6] in order to refer to those cognitive elements which give meaning to (decode) political experience. Similarly, it gives the prediction for the most probable orientations of the decision makers in future situations.

In summary, cognitive doctrinal studies define doctrine as a set of beliefs that try to explain reality and set the goals for political action.

Doctrine is thus a particular form of a broader ideology operating at the decision-making level.[7] An attempt is made to analytically construct the links between the cognitive intentions of the individual decision maker to the process of preparing official statements and vice versa. The analytical scheme of these doctrinal studies was divided into world-view, policy goals, and instruments used. It is widely employed by the decision makers and policy planners themselves when they describe their decision-making process.[8]

However, these doctrinal studies have been unable to solve the problem of how to show that the textual material refers to the essential cognitive elements of the decision makers and how these elements really influence political behaviour. The operationalization of the cognitive approach has been more successful in the projects where individual cognitive models have been tested by specific interviews.[9] However, in a situation where the textual material originates only from the actual policy-making process, the operationalization of political doctrine cannot be achieved due to the singular character of policy decisions.

In the present work, I want to focus within doctrinal studies on the analysis of political communication and language. This is not to deny its cognitive basis, but the problems that have been unresolved in previous doctrinal studies are avoided. Although the cognitive approach seems to be theoretically more ambiguous than the analyses of political language, one may also ask whether cognitive studies failed to see the corruption and biases of the Marxist-Leninist language on the eve of the collapse of the socialist world system when they really believed that this language reflected not only the cognitive structure of the decision makers but also that of the larger strata of the population living in socialist countries. In this respect, I believe that this illusion will continue, if these aspects are not taken into consideration when analysing the political doctrines of the remaining socialist countries. In this approach communication and argumentation are the main focus. More particularly, the main questions are: how are political arguments constructed with special reference to political doctrine? And what happens in the case of political change?

As the main weight of rhetoric is on the active side of language, semiotics is concerned more with permanent characteristics of language, with different communicational modes and the structures of expressions. However, when dealing with the constant modalities in the expression of thought, rhetoric comes close to semiotics. These constant modalities are formal structural rules embedded in every linguistic system. In political language these rules (code) used to be more restrictive than in many other fields of communication. This is the special realm of the doctrinal approach.

Accordingly, in a rhetorical approach, the doctrine involves two obvious components: the vocabulary and the code. Political vocabularies have an important task in the parlance of Marxist-Leninist governments. Socialist countries indicated which audience they were addressing, and the place of this audience in the socialist world, by varying the stress which was given to a variety of ideological concepts. The vocabulary which was used connected the arguments of the Marxist-Leninist doctrine, and to the code.

In order to emphasize the role of the code in Marxist-Leninist parlance, I propose the term "doctrinal code". The concept of code has been utilized in various studies on social semiotics and social linguistics. The role of code in these studies is that codes "transmit the culture and so constrain behaviour".[10] In these studies code is a system where the speaker and the hearer have a variety of choices to interpret what is said.[11] However, contrary to this "systemic" approach to code, I am inclined to emphasize the view that natural language may include several codes among which some might be much more restrictive than others. It depends on the nature of the language analysed. When Marxist-Leninist language is analysed, it is assumed that the Marxist-Leninist doctrine provides the particular rules of argumentation. These rules may amount to such a restrictive code, the doctrinal code.

Several elements which stand out in relief from the Vietnamese Marxist-Leninist doctrinal code were already formulated by Leites when studying the Soviet operational code. The tendency to examine political reality according to two opposite poles, and to examine the future and the past according to these poles are obvious characteristics in Vietnamese Marxist-Leninist argumentation. The third element is the ritualistic pattern of argumentation established in Marxism-Leninism particularly by Stalin.[12] That the texts do not focus on new information but on repetitions of words and phrases and other textual organizations that are unnecessary for a general communicational pattern, is also clearly seen in Vietnamese Marxist-Leninist language.

This "mantra content" which does not aim at normal communication but at "autocommunication", as Yuri Lotman calls it, is an important part of the Marxist-Leninist doctrinal code. The meaning of this kind of communication is accessible only to those who already know the premises of communication.[13] For example, the widely-used phrase in Vietnam's foreign policy during the 1970s, "the offensive posture of world revolutionary forces" (*the tien cong cua luc luong cach mang)* did not refer to any concrete state of affairs; but it did strengthen autocommunication and the doctrine, as Vietnam was viewed as an important part of these revolutionary forces. It also referred to the doctrinal system, whose fundamental aim was to justify the leadership role of the Vietnam Communist Party.

The Vietnamese varieties of setting opposite poles

Obviously there were characteristics in Vietnamese cultural codes which facilitated the adoption of Marxist-Leninist parlance in Vietnam. In his thorough study, Trinh Van Thao[14] traced the interesting lineage of the political rhetoric between the Vietnamese Communist leadership and the intellectuals of the anti-colonial literati class of the late nineteenth and early twentieth centuries. In his broad sociological study, he examined the intellectual history of 222 Vietnamese intellectuals and political leaders across three generations in order to follow the continuity and change of politico-philosophical thinking during the last hundred years. Apart from showing how the leading Vietnamese Communists came from families of the literati class, who were attached to Confucian education, he points out how certain rhetorical expressions and semiotic modes prevailed in the political language during the period covered by his examination.

The most obvious was the pragmatic approach that the Communists adopted in the 1940s when the anti-colonial campaign broke out. This approach, which emphasized the present realities and ponders possible action in response to it, was very important according to the Confucian scholar gentry's rhetoric when the methods of opposing French colonialism were contemplated at the turn of the century. This pragmatism was very evident in the policy of the National United Front. The phrase *"biet dich, biet ta"* (knowing the enemy, knowing us) was widely used in the Communist Party leadership when they mobilized national forces against the French. It includes the idea of distinguishing friend from foe. By this phrase and with different variations of it, the Party leadership not only managed to concentrate national forces but also used it as an analytical tool in concrete situations when political methods were under consideration.[15] It contains the idea of two opposite poles, and this illustrates how communication should be understood in the parlance of the Vietnamese revolutionaries. However, it was not only a ritualistic phrase which was routinely used in a way as happened to many concepts in the subsequent development of Vietnamese Marxism-Leninism. The idea of distinguishing friend from foe, or even distinguishing between "ourselves, our friends and our enemies" (*phan biet ta, ban, thu*) was not totally abandoned, when Soviet origin and more formalist vocabulary took a dominant position in Vietnamese parlance.[16]

The concept which partially replaced the distinction between friend and enemy was also based on the idea of two opposite poles. It was not, however, based on pragmatic contemplation in actual politics, but was a crucial part of the Stalinist doctrine on the development from a semi-feudal country to a socialist and Communist society. The question "who will win over whom" (*ai thang ai*) was an abbreviation from a longer sentence "who will win over whom between the two roads" (*ai thang ai giua hai con duong*). It turned out to be a fundamental concept from which most of the discussions in Party circles could be deduced, whether the issue concerned economy, culture or foreign policy.[17]

The struggle waged between two roads was a Stalinist modification of the concept of the class struggle developed for the purposes of revolution in an agrarian society with weak capitalist and working classes. The other key concept here was the "transitional period to socialism" (*thoi ky qua do len chu nghia xa hoi*) or simply "transitional period" (*thoi ky qua do*). Accordingly, the *"ai thang ai"* struggle is waged when society is advancing to socialism and bypassing the stage of capitalist development. This struggle with its various forms is characteristic of the transitional period.[18]

The struggle waged between two roads means that it is a broader form of class struggle in contrast to the thinking of Marx and Engels. Thus, those who travel the socialist road include not only the working class but also the peasants and the members of the progressive intelligentsia, taken collectively, while the travellers on the capitalist road are not only the bourgeoisie but also other reactionary elements and agents of the imperialist clique, together with the forces of "spontaneous capitalism" (*tu phat tu ban chu nghia*). Revolutionaries cannot resolve this struggle for their advance without proletarian dictatorship, i.e. without the absolute power of the Communist Party. Therefore the reference to *ai thang ai* always points to the necessity for Communist Party power.[19]

There are clear similarities between *ai thang ai* and the concept of distinguishing friend from foe. With a certain reservation, *ai thang ai* could be regarded as a special form of the friend/foe conception. Like the friend/foe conception, *ai thang ai* works in mobilizing the masses in the struggle to achieve a common goal with the idea of two opposite poles. In this sense, the postulate of the culturalist approach that culture provides continuity even in cases of political change seems to be reasonable in the Vietnamese case.[20] However, owing to its crucial role in the Marxist-Leninist doctrine *ai thang ai* was much more rigid than distinguishing friend from foe. It was bound to the concept of the struggle between two roads, and was not bound to any actual situation like the friend/enemy concept. As one purpose of the friend/enemy concept was to divide and neutralize all other potential opponents, the *ai thang ai* concept is in this respect more dogmatic. It recognizes only friend or enemy; namely the followers of the socialist or capitalist roads.

Despite different political and social domains and different concepts, the particular concept systems derive from the question of "who will win over whom?" The purpose of it, at this mature stage of Marxism-Leninism, is to show the difference between two roads in all social discourse. Therefore the *ai thang ai* concept made every message predictable because the audience knew the premises of communication.

Doi moi, international relations and doctrinal change

The doctrinal change in Vietnamese Marxism started after Mikhail Gorbachev proclaimed his *perestroika* campaign in the Soviet Union. The signs of doctrinal change occurred as early as in the spring of 1986 when the broad reform movement, later known as the *doi moi* (renovation) campaign, was launched. Officially it was launched to revitalize the socialist economy, the Marxist-Leninist political system and the Communist Party organization in the framework of the Marxist-Leninist doctrine, but it resulted in changes to the doctrine itself.

The emergence of new vocabulary indicated for the first time doctrinal changes. Hence the most important area where the new vocabulary occurred was international relations. In spite of the fact that the discussion on foreign relations cannot be separated from the general reform movement, Vietnam's international situation, and the deadlock on the Kampuchean question particularly, promoted this reorientation in foreign policy. These changes mean the removal of some old concepts, such as *ai thang ai* and three revolutionary currents and adoption of some new, largely Gorbachevian terms to foreign-policy vocabulary. The new keywords were the world's scientific-technological revolution (*cach mang khoa hoc—ky thuat the gioi*), dependency (*su thuy thuoc*) or interdependence (*su le thuoc lan nhau*), the internationalization trend (*xu the quoc te hoa*) and an international order (*mot trat tu quoc te*), which followed all of these.

This did not, however, mean that all orthodox Marxist-Leninist concepts and international class struggle as a basic assumption disappeared from Vietnamese Marxist-Leninist thinking. In fact the Vietnamese defined *doi moi* as an organic part of Marxism-Leninism. When the Gorbachevian campaign in the Soviet Union started to threaten Communist Party power, the Vietnamese carefully distinguished their *doi moi* from the Soviet *perestroika*. This took place at a fairly early stage. Although the Russian word *perestroika* may include the idea of "renovation" in its broad sense, it stands for "restructuring", and in the new Soviet vocabulary it referred particularly to "the restructuring of society". The Vietnamese were fully aware of this. They had a term equivalent to *perestroika* in a sense of "reorganizing", *cai to*, and sometimes "restructuring", *cau truc lai*.[21]

The fact that *cai to* applied to the Soviet Union, and perhaps to the other socialist countries, and *doi moi* to Vietnam, was made clear. Thus *cai to* did not refer to the Vietnamese reform campaign. However, both *doi moi* and *cai to* did belong, together with all the reforms carried out in the socialist countries, according to a Vietnamese analysis, to the same historical trend and developed from "the dialectics of history".[22] The political significance of this differentiation was later confirmed by the Foreign Minister, Nguyen Co Thach, in the situation where the Soviet *perestroika* and Vietnam's *doi moi* had already established their own course. Thach argued for Soviet-Vietnamese co-operation as follows: "With the great undertakings of restructuring (*cong cuoc cai to*) in the Soviet Union and the renovation (*cong cuoc doi moi*) in Vietnam, we have grounds to be optimistic about the relations of Vietnam's future co-operation with the Soviet Union and other socialist countries".[23]

Obviously, the interpretation that *doi moi* should contain the Marxist-Leninist doctrinal code, and all destructive elements that might thwart the idea of totalitarian mobilization and control, were discarded so far as possible. Nevertheless, in the new conceptualization of international relations there were elements which were difficult to fit into the old code. A concept like interdependence which followed from the scientific-technological revolution and the internationalization trend can be fitted into Marxist economic theories but it obscures the idea of two opposing poles. This, of course, weakens the doctrinal code. This development was not, however, uniform. As noted above there were serious attempts to fit old premises to new vocabulary.

The weight which was given in this situation to the concept of a transitional period (to socialism) illustrates this attempt. The Vietnamese were now ready to admit that this period would be longer than they had supposed, and that the situation was more complex than the simplistic versions of the two roads of the development. In two articles published in the philosophical quarterly *Tap Chi Triet Hoc*,[24] the materialistic basis for new thinking about foreign affairs was outlined. In this, the concept of transitional period was particularly emphasized. Interestingly enough, mainly Gorbachevian arguments parallel some main themes of western studies of international political economy. Accordingly, the world's scientific technological revolution advanced with unexpected speed, with different impacts on both the capitalist and the socialist countries. This has created new production forces leading to the internationalized economy and changing the political relations all over the world. Second, the focus of the struggle between capitalism and socialism turned to the Third World, where both the capitalist and the socialist countries try to exploit the governments of the Third World countries to attract them to their side in order to secure the global position of these systems. Hence the interests of the underdeveloped countries and the socialist countries do not always coincide and the real danger is that the Third World countries will be left at the very nucleus of this conflict. The third element which was pointed to was a group of global issues, familiar already from Gorbachev's foreign policy themes. This group included the issues that both affected the capitalist and the socialist countries equally: environmental problems, population growth, famine, illiteracy, etc., which impede progress and increase the risk of war.[25]

The foreign policy line which should be adopted in this stage of the transitional period should be, according to these articles, peaceful coexistence. This is not to acknowledge that the former policy of revolutionary struggle was wrong, but that the materialistic base of this policy had changed. The concept of three revolutionary currents represented all the relations of production, and because the scientific-technological revolution had created new kinds of production and production branches, the materialistic basis of the currents had changed. In fact, when analysing the factors that had changed the world structure during recent decades, the articles seem to imply that the concept refers rather to the past than to the present. This is particularly the case with the development of the Asian newly industrialized countries (the NICs), where the main emphasis has been on the scientific-technological revolution.[26]

The policy of peaceful coexistence suggested by these articles is clearly based on the Marxist-Leninist doctrine of the two roads and not on the new preconditions offered by the scientific-technological revolution.[27] Nevertheless, there emerged more radical suggestions for the theoretical basis of the foreign policy discussion. Phan Doan Nam, writing in the theoretical journal of the Vietnam Communist

Party, touched on the very heart of Vietnam's Marxism-Leninism. The writer, reportedly a close subordinate of Nguyen Co Thach[28] and later editor-in-chief of the *Vietnam Courier*, proposed rejecting the idea of distinguishing friends and enemies and particularly the connection of this idea to peaceful coexistence. He argued that "we would not avoid making mistakes if we distinguish friend from foe in international relations only on the basis of the national angle without considering the interests of other nations in the struggle for the common goal of the era".[29] He criticized the commonly accepted Marxist-Leninist interpretation of peaceful coexistence and pointed out that

> two states cannot be in peaceful coexistence if they still consider each other as enemies. Peaceful coexistence... is an international order in which countries of different socio-political systems can live as friendly neighbours and cooperate in all areas, economic, scientific technological and so forth.[30]

Similarly, the Western concept of international relations, which saw global order arising from a balance of power between states and not as a struggle between two camps, went against basic Marxist-Leninist premises. As one Vietnamese analyst has pointed out, this new interpretation of international relations is more properly termed global "disorder" (rather than global "order"); this suggests the wider acceptance of pragmatic argumentation.[31]

Accordingly, in a new situation of international relations, where any fair estimation of the world's political, military, and economic changes, even in the middle range, is problematic, particular attention should be paid to regional affairs and regional co-operation. This called for a definition of independence and sovereignty with special attention to regional conflicts as well as to regional possibilities.[32]

After the Tiananmen Square incident in Beijing in June 1989 the Vietnamese party leadership firmly assailed new political ideas, particularly in international relations theory, and reasserted the primacy of orthodox Marxist-Leninist doctrine.[33] Nevertheless it was clear that the new pragmatic approach had already gained a strong hold among some cadres and officials in the Vietnam Communist Party itself. However, the Communist Party had emphasized during its Seventh Party Congress in 1991 its commitment to Marxist-Leninist rule and proletarian dictatorship. Similarly, the pragmatic and influential Foreign Minister, Nguyen Co Thach, was replaced after this congress by a career diplomat, Nguyen Manh Cam, who, although he is pragmatically oriented, has had less room to move than his predecessor. Party sources reported that Thach's candidate, Deputy Foreign Minister Tran Quang Co, rejected the position because the foreign ministry lost its representation on the Politburo and the Secretariat.[34]

Foreign policy and domestic rule: towards an Asian model?

Six months after the Seventh Party Congress, the Soviet Union disintegrated and foreign moral support for orthodox Marxism-Leninism evaporated. Thus the Vietnamese orientation towards Southeast Asian countries and the Association of Southeast Asian Nations (ASEAN), which had started already in the late 1980s, gained strength. The deadlock between Vietnam and ASEAN caused by the Kampuchean question was broken when the Vietnamese withdrew from Cambodia and the country was placed under the United Nations Transitional Authority in Cambodia. In this new situation, where one tendency, the striving to maintain the old political rule, draws from orthodox Marxist-Leninist vocabulary, and the other, the attempt to integrate into the Southeast Asian regional system, calls for a pragmatic approach, the political language becomes more and more heterogeneous and the doctrinal code disintegrates. While political parlance dealing with domestic rule retained its auto-communicative function, foreign policy language was directed more to normal communication.

After the disintegration of the Soviet Union, the relationship between internal rule and foreign relations widened further. The Vietnamese increasingly moved towards a common Asian model in which economic growth, international economic relations and foreign policy were interconnected but sovereignty and the domestic political system were protected. This politico-economic model, first introduced by the Asian newly industrialized countries, emphasized economic growth based on an export intensive economy as a primary factor in the development of society. This calls for a strong government which is committed both to economic growth and political stability as primary objectives and which has control over the labour force, education and exchange rate. Nevertheless this model has been strongly challenged after the Asian economic crises of 1997–98, from the point of view of political power and ideology. It is certain that Hanoi prefers this model instead of flexible currency rates and economic transparency strongly advocated by the International Monetary Fund.

Although the Asian politico-economic model was never clearly articulated by the Vietnam Communist Party, political and economic discussions after the Sixth Party Congress and the statements in the

Eighth Party Congress documents indicate this new approach. Both new political vocabulary together with concrete measures for harmonizing the Vietnamese economy with the ASEAN countries emerged. Nevertheless, the model also includes new elements justifying the power of the Communist Party. Interestingly enough, it came as an integral part of a broader discussion on human rights and democratic freedoms in Asia. In the new situation, where the Asian economies were in a constant state of economic growth, the Vietnamese welcomed the general ideas of authoritarian political rule and economic development in the Asia-Pacific area. There were attempts to fit this new foreign policy approach into the old doctrine when the Soviet Union collapsed and Hanoi was faced with dealing with the capitalist world system on its own. The critical question which Marxist-Leninist theoreticians posed was: why did socialism collapse in the Soviet Union, the "motherland of the world's socialist revolution?"

The answer reached by the conservative theoreticians can be condensed as follows: The question of *ai thang ai* during the transitional period is a crucial law that determines whether society is developing towards socialism or capitalism. The socialist road of development can be maintained only if the proletarian class holds political power. The threat to this power is posed by the imperialists, who are eager to use reactionary circles inside their country. The conclusion was that imperialism took advantage of the reform process for "peaceful evolution" (*dien bien hoa binh*) to break up the Communist Party in the Soviet Union. Therefore the collapse was due to subjective failures of the Party leadership in their evaluations of class struggle during the transitional period. The lesson for Vietnam is that the Vietnamese should stick firmly to the basic premises of Marxism-Leninism to prevent imperialism from defeating Vietnam peacefully.[35]

Although the concept of peaceful evolution was loudly echoed by the conservatives in the Communist Party and by persons connected with security and defence matters, pragmatically orientated foreign ministry officials also repeated it routinely. As mentioned above, this discussion became an integral part of a broader discussion on negative foreign values in Asian societies. Besides the fact that the term linked Vietnamese vocabulary to the rhetoric of Beijing, it also came close to the principles that some Southeast Asian leaders had advocated in order to resist liberal western ideas of democracy as totally alien phenomena to Asian societies.[36] In practice ASEAN member states have adopted the principle of non-interference in the internal affairs of another member state. Thus it can be seen that the political rhetoric of these two different code systems share a common vocabulary when authoritarian political power comes under challenge from adverse external influence.

When Vietnam became a full member of ASEAN in July 1995, the Vietnamese seemed to adopt common ASEAN vocabulary including such key concepts as "regionalism", "regional resilience" and "unity in diversity".[37] Membership was preceded by closer interaction with the ASEAN countries and negotiations with ASEAN as a regional body in its own right. Typically, the ASEAN countries made no particular demands on Vietnam's political system, but the main concern was how seriously Vietnam was pursuing a policy where "economics have clear priority over politics" and mutual co-operation and interdependence are accepted as the basics of regional co-operation.[38] Thus ASEAN members lobbied Vietnam to accept, at least partly, the NIC model of development in order to participate in ASEAN co-operation.

The fact that the *doi moi* discussion laid particular emphasis on international economic matters and interdependence evidently helped the Vietnamese to adopt ASEAN's new political vocabulary. Although traditional Marxist-Leninist rhetoric has survived, the major shift from class struggle to economic growth as a major driving force of the society was written into policy documents adopted by the Eighth Congress. The general axiom of the NICs, which made economics a top priority, was included in the Central Committee's Political Report by means of traditional rhetoric: "To closely combine economic renewal with political renewal from the start, with economic renewal as the focus while step by step conducting political renewal".[39] This meant that the Party had to be ready to counter "extremist and fanatic democratism" and thwart all attempts to abuse issues of "democracy" and "human rights" destabilizing the internal developments of the country.[40] ASEAN member states also shared this sentiment, and thus provided Vietnam with international support.

In spite of the fact that "two strategic tasks of building socialism and defending the homeland" remained in the official party programme, emphasis was put on "the multi-sector commodity economy", which called for more open international relations. This meant that despite some references to class struggle, the distinction between friend and foe as well as mention of the struggle between two roads were deleted from the party's eighth congress documents. Now the emphasis was placed on Vietnam's integration into the regional and world economies, which included, first, the preparations for participating in the ASEAN Free Trade Area (AFTA), and then the Asia Pacific Economic Cooperation (APEC) forum and the World Trade Organization (WTO).[41] The focus on foreign relations was shown by the Party Congress on international economic relations and not on ideologically motivated alliances.

Vietnam's integration into ASEAN was, of course, also dictated by security concerns. However, negotiations for Vietnam's membership clearly indicated the salience of economic matters and Vietnam's ability to participate in AFTA. As part of the internationalization of Vietnam's foreign relations, Vietnam was deeply involved with the same problems as other ASEAN members. These economic and political issues raised the question of globalization (*toan cau hoa*) and its affects on Vietnam, including the role of new information technology, global financial networks and the necessity of nation states to integrate into regional systems.[42] Vietnam's ASEAN membership has increased the importance of these questions as through ASEAN Vietnam takes part in forums where the concrete issues of political globalization are dealt with. APEC draws Vietnam into Asia-Pacific co-operation, and in the Asia Europe Summit Meeting (ASEM) Vietnam together with other East and Southeast Asian countries engage in political and economic dialogue with the countries of the European Union. In addition, the ASEAN Regional Forum (ARF) includes both Asia-Pacific powers and the European Union to discuss Asian security matters. In order to take advantage of these forums Vietnam identifies more closely with the general ASEAN approach to internationalization and globalization.[43]

Conclusion

As discussion within the Vietnam Communist Party on international relations has shown, the change in the Marxist-Leninist doctrine involved several elements. The present political development indicates that some political concepts have been rather temporary and changeable, although they had a prominent role in the doctrinal system. However, the most stable concepts have also been under consideration whereas the doctrinal code has been rather rigid for decades. This rigidity is a symptom of the political rule and the function of political language in the Marxist-Leninist system, but obviously also reflects the continuity which the political culture provides for the political system. Despite this rigidity, which culture offers to the political doctrine, it may also accelerate new kinds of political orientations. As the Vietnamese literati class' revolutionary rhetoric supported the adoption of Marxism-Leninism into Vietnam, so a similar pragmatic approach can be seen in the cadres' discussion on the orientation towards the regional system and in their arguments for integrating into the world's economic system. In this discussion, the role of the doctrinal code has been very weak, disappearing almost completely when the arguments are drawn from the present realities and not from Marxism-Leninism. This pragmatism approaches the economically motivated arguments by which many Southeast Asian governments have grounded the authoritarian political systems in their countries.

It is suggested, therefore, that the cultural aspect of politics should be looked upon as dynamic. As far as political language and political rhetoric are concerned, they may contain several different vocabularies. In the case of the present study, attention was paid to the two most obvious vocabularies; that of pragmatic rhetoric with its obvious origins in the Vietnamese literati class' argumentation and its deep attachment to Asian pragmatism; and that of formal Marxism-Leninism, which was adopted by Vietnam in a rather orthodox form, owing to the close contacts between the Vietnamese Communists and the Soviet Communist Party. New political vocabularies are again becoming established, but this does not mean that the old ones are being totally neglected. They are rather building on top of each other. For example, in the present situation, the Vietnamese discussion on international relations might include relics of Marxist-Leninist formalism, together with pragmatic contemplation originating from older rhetoric, combined with the concepts of Gorbachevian "new thinking" and the general concepts of political economy. A brand new foreign policy vocabulary is also emerging. ASEAN's concepts of regionalism and resilience, for example, are reflected in Vietnam's new approach. The adoption of ASEAN's old slogan of "unity in diversity" also reflects this approach, but it also shows how distant is the old concept of socialist unity, which was previously enthusiastically advocated by the Vietnamese, and in which diversity was not accepted even nominally. This shows how much present Vietnamese ideas on international relations have distanced themselves from Marxist-Leninist ideology.

The changes in the international system may alter doctrine. As in general, so also in the case of Vietnam, these changes do not depend solely on Vietnamese political choices, but on general developments in the Asia-Pacific region. Hence, the question of how the Vietnamese succeed in taking advantage of the Asia-Pacific region's growing importance on a global scale will also indicate their ability to adapt the new political vocabulary to their own political traditions. Similarly, the current Asian economic crises may also create a new situation. One solution may be the emphasis of the indigenous character of Vietnamese political thinking as the new emphasis on Ho Chi Minh's ideas. The Vietnamese solution to this question may develop by adopting general ASEAN thinking on the state and international relations combined with Vietnamese tradition.

Notes

1. See S.W. Rosenberg, and G. Wolsfeld, "International Conflict and the Problem of Attribution", *Journal of Conflict Resolution* 21, no. 1 (March, 1977): 75–103.
2. Nathan Leites, *A Study of Bolshevism* (Glencoe, Illinois: The Free Press Publishers, 1953).
3. Ibid., pp. 15–25.
4. Alexander L. George, "The 'Operational Code': A Neglected Approach to the Study of Political Leaders and Decision-Making", in Erik P. Hoffman and Frederic J. Fleron Jr., eds, *The Conduct of Soviet Foreign Policy* (New York: Aldine Publishing Company, 1980), pp. 165–90; Douglas E. Pike, "Operational Code of the North Vietnamese Politburo", *Asia Quarterly* 1 (1971): 91–102.
5. Lucian W. Pye, "Introduction: Political Culture and Political Development", in Lucian W. Pye and Sidney Verba, eds, *Political Culture and Political Development* (Princeton: Princeton University Press, 1965); Harry Eckstein, "A Culturalist Theory of Political Change", *American Political Science Review* 82, no. 3 (September 1988): 789–804.
6. Katarina Brodin, *Studiet av Utrikespolitiska Doktriner: Teori och tva empiriska tillampningar*, Stockholm: Departementens offsetcentral, 1977; and D. Heradsveit, and O. Narvesen, "Psychological Constraints on Decision-making: A Discussion of Cognitive Approaches: Operational Code and Cognitive Map", *Cooperation and Conflict* 13 (1978): 77–92.
7. K.J. Holsti, *International Politics: A Framework for Analysis* (Englewood Cliffs: Prentice-Hall, 1977), pp. 373–74; J.F. Triska and D.D. Finley, *Soviet Foreign Policy* (Toronto: Macmillan, 1968), pp. 112–13 and 115; and R. Judson Mitchell, *Ideology of a Superpower: Contemporary Soviet Doctrine on International Relations* (Stanford: Hoover Institution Press, 1982).
8. Peter Berry, *Sovjetunionens Officielle Utrikespolitiska Doktrin* (Stockholm: Utrikespolitiska institutet, forskningsrapport, 1972); Katarina Brodin, *Studiet av Utrikespolitiska Doktriner* op. cit., and Hans Mouritsen, "Prediction on the Basis of Official Doctrines", *Cooperation and Conflict* 16 (1981): 25–38.
9. See Rosenberg and Wolsfeld, "International Conflict and the Problem of Attribution", op. cit., pp. 75–103.
10. Basil Bernstein, *Class, Codes and Control: Theoretical Studies towards a Sociology of Language*, vol. 1 (London: Routledge and Kegan Paul, 1971), p. 122.
11. M.A.K. Halliday, *Language as a Social Semiotic: The Social Interpretation of Language and Meaning* (London: Edward Arnold Publishers, 1978), pp. 5–6; and M.A.K. Halliday, "Language as Code and Language as Behaviour: A Systemic-Functional Interpretation of the

Nature and Ontogenesis of Dialogue", in Robin P. Fawcett et al., eds., *Semiotics of Culture and Language: Language as Social Semiotic*, vol. 1 (London: Frances Pinter Publishers, 1984), pp. 24–27.

12. See Ilmari Susiluoto, "Deritualization of Political Language: The Case of the Soviet Union", in Sakari Hanninen and Kari Palonen, eds, *Texts, Contexts, Concepts: Studies on Politics and Power in Language* (Jyvaskyla: The Finnish Political Science Association, 1990), pp. 69–75.

13. Yuri M. Lotman, *Universe of the Mind: A Semiotic Theory of Culture* (London: I.B. Tauris and Co. Ltd Publishers, 1990); H. Broms and H. Gahmberg, "Communication to Self in Organizations and Cultures", *Administrative Science Quarterly* 28 (September 1983): 482–95.

14. Trinh Van Thao, *Vietnam: Du confucianisme au communisme* (Paris: Edition's L'Harmattan, 1990).

15. See Vo Nguyen Giap, *People's War, People's Army* (Hanoi: Foreign Language Publishing House, 1961); To nghien cuu lich su chien tranh, Hoc vien quan su, "Tai thao luoc kiet xuat cua ong cha ta", *Hoc Tap* 11 (1972): 25–26; Truong Chinh, *Selected Writings* (Hanoi: Foreign Language Publishing House, 1977, 619–21); Hoc vien Nguyen Ai Quoc, Khoa lich su Dang, *Lich su Dang cong san Viet Nam*, tap I, *1920–1954*. Chuong trinh cao cap. (Hanoi: Nha xuat ban tuyen huan 1988), pp. 224–25.

16. See Nguyen Duy Trinh, "30 nam dau tranh ngoai giao vi doc lap, tu do cua to quoc va xay dung chu nghia xa hoi", *Hoc Tap* 10 (1975): 12.

17. Tran Con, "Nhan thuc ve van de dau tranh giai cap, dau tranh giua hai con duong o nuoc ta hien nay", *Tap Chi Triet Hoc*, 1 (40), 3 (1983): 43–65; Pham Nhu Cuong, "Phan dau nang cao chat luong cua cong tac giang day nghien cuu ly luan Mac - Le-nin theo tinh than cua nghi quyet dai hoi Dang lan thu V"; Ho Van Thong, "May van de chung trong nhan thuc tu tuong ve thoi ky qua do hien nay o nuoc ta"; and Tran Con, "Suy nghi ve cuoc dau tranh giai cap, dau tranh giua hai con duong hien nay", in Truong Dang Cao Cap Nguyen Ai Quoc, Khoa triet hoc, *Quan triet nghi quyet dai hoi lan thu V cua Dang* (Hanoi: Nha xuat ban sach giao khoa Mac - Le-nin, 1984), pp. 44–75, 101–122 and 123–34, respectively.

18. Hoang Tung, *May van de ve cong tac chinh tri va tu tuong trong chang duong hien nay cua cach mang xa hoi chu nghia* (Hanoi: Nha xuat ban Su that, 1983), p. 86.

19. Tran Con, "Nhan thuc ve van de dau tranh giai cap, dau tranh giua hai con duong o nuoc ta hien nay", op. cit., pp. 43–65; see also Hoang Tung, *May van de ve cong tac chinh tri va tu tuong trong chang duong hien nay cua cach mang xa hoi chu nghia* op. cit; Tran Con, "Suy nghi ve cuoc dau tranh giai cap, dau tranh giua hai con duong hien nay", op. cit., pp. 45–47; Ho Van Thong, "May van de chung trong nhan thuc tu tuong ve thoi ky qua do hien nay o nuoc ta", op. cit., pp. 101–102; and Pham Nhu Cuong, "Phan dau nang cao chat luong cua cong tac giang day nghien cuu ly luan Mac - Le-nin theo tinh than cua nghi quyet dai hoi Dang lan thu V", op. cit., pp. 44–75.

20. See Eckstein, "A Culturalist Theory of Political Change", op. cit., pp. 792–93.

21. For example, Hoang Nguyen, "Doi moi tu duy trong cong tac doi ngoai", *Tap Chi Triet Hoc*, 2 (57), 6 (1987): 71; Le Thi, "Tu duy moi ve

cuoc dau tranh tu tuong, dau tranh bao ve hoa binh, chong chien tranh hat nhan hien nay", *Tap Chi Triet Hoc*, 4 (59) (1987): 23; Van Tao, "Van de hoa binh trong su chuyen hoa cua cac mau thuan co ban cua thoi dai", *Tap Chi Cong San* 1 (1988): 74; Nguyen Co Thach, "Tat ca hoa binh, doc lap dan toc va phat trien", *Tap Chi Cong San* 8 (1989): 7; and Quoc Tuy, "Doi moi tu duy doi ngoai va nhung nguyen tac co ban cua Le-nin ve chinh sach doi ngoai", *Tap Chi Cong San* 12 (1989): 13.

22. Van Tao, "Van de hoa binh trong su chuyen hoa cua cac mau thuan co ban cua thoi dai", op. cit., p. 74.

23. Nguyen Co Thach, "Tat ca hoa binh, doc lap dan toc va phat trien", op. cit., p. 7.

24. Hoang Nguyen, "Doi moi tu duy trong cong tac doi ngoai", op. cit., pp. 66–78 and Le Thi, "Tu duy moi ve cuoc dau tranh tu tuong, dau tranh bao ve hoa binh, chong chien tranh hat nhan hien nay", op. cit., pp. 21–31.

25. Le Thi, "Tu duy moi ve cuoc dau tranh tu tuong, dau tranh bao ve hoa binh, chong chien tranh hat nhan hien nay", op. cit., pp. 21–25.

26. Hoang Nguyen, "Doi moi tu duy trong cong tac doi ngoai", op. cit., pp. 67–72.

27. Le Thi, "Tu duy moi ve cuoc dau tranh tu tuong, dau tranh bao ve hoa binh, chong chien tranh hat nhan hien nay", op. cit., pp. 28–30 and Hoang Nguyen, "Doi moi tu duy trong cong tac doi ngoai", op. cit., pp. 73–76; see also Quoc Tuy, "Doi moi tu duy doi ngoai va nhung nguyen tac co ban cua Le-nin ve chinh sach doi ngoai", op. cit., p. 16.

28. See Gareth Porter, "The Transformation of Vietnam's World-view: From Two Camps to Interdependence", *Contemporary Southeast Asia* 12, no. 1 (June 1990): 9.

29. Phan Doan Nam, "Mot vai suy nghi ve doi moi tu duy doi ngoai", *Tap Chi Cong San* 2 (1988): 54, 79.

30. Ibid., p. 79.

31. Tran Trong Thin, "Can can quan su dang thay doi chien luoc gi cho ngay mai?" *Tap Chi Cong San* 4 (1991): 57 and 59.

32. Ibid., p. 57; and Phan Doan Nam, "Van de phoi hop giua an ninh, quoc phong va ngoai giao trong giai doan cach mang moi", *Tap Chi Cong San* 3 (1991): 31; and Nguyen Trong Thu, "Ve trat tu quoc te moi", *Tap Chi Cong San* 5 (1991): 60.

33. Nguyen Van Linh, "Phat bieu cua dong chi tong bi thu Nguyen Van Linh. Be mac hoi nghi 7 cua BCHTUD", *Tap Chi Cong San* 9 (1989): 5–12; see also Do Minh, "Co nen lay chu nghia Mac-Le-nin lam nen tang tu tuong hay khong", *Tap Chi Cong San* 5 (1991): 56–57, and Nguyen Van Duc, "Mot trat tu the gioi moi hay la mot hinh thai dau tranh moi?" *Tap Chi Quoc Phong Toan Dan* 1 (1992): 57–61.

34 . Murray Hiebert, "More of the same", *Far Eastern Economic Review*, 11 July 1991, p. 10 and "Cutting red tape" *Far Eastern Economic Review*, 22 August 1991, p. 11.

35. See the discussion in *Tap Chi Cong San*: Doan Chuong, "Bai hoc thoi dai", *Tap Chi Cong San* 2 (1992): 5–9; Song Tung, "Vi sao chu nghia xa hoi hien thuc o Dong Au va Lien xo sup do?" *Tap Chi Cong San* 2 (1992): 10–13, and 17; Le Xuan Luu, "Ban chat cach mang va khoa

hoc cua chu nghia Mac - Le-nin", *Tap Chi Cong San* 3 (1992): 3-7; Tran Ba Khoa, "Canh giac voi am muu dien bien hoa binh cua cac the luc thu dich", *Tap Chi Cong San* 1 (1993): 18-20; and Bui Phan Ky, "May suy nghi ve chien luoc quoc phong trong boi canh quoc te moi", *Tap Chi Cong San* 5 (1993): 58-62.

36. Le Tinh, "The gioi nam 1992 co gi moi?" *Tap Chi Cong San* 1 (1993): 57-60; Nguyen Manh Cam, "Tren duong trien khai chinh sach doi ngoai theo dinh huong moi", *Tap Chi Cong San* 4 (1993): 11-15; and Nguyen Ngoc Truong, "Vietnam's New Home", *Far Eastern Economic Review*, 29 July 1995; see also Carlyle A. Thayer, "Comrade Plus Brother: The New SinoVietnamese Relations", *The Pacific Review* 5, no. 4 (1992): 402-06.

37. See Nguyen Ngoc Truong, "Vietnam's New Home", op. cit., p. 33.

38. Report of an International Symposium on Interaction and Progress, Vietnam's New Course and ASEAN Experiences, Hanoi, 20-23 August 1991, *Vietnam Commentary*, no. 24 (November-December 1991): 35-38.

39. Communist Party of Vietnam, *VIIIth National Congress Documents* (Hanoi: The Gioi Publishers, 1996), p. 27.

40. Ibid., p. 28.

41. Ibid., pp. 198-199.

42. Phan Doan Nam, "Mot vai suy nghi ve van de 'toan cau hoa' ", *Tap Chi Cong San* 8 (1996): 52-55.

43. Tran Ba Khoa, "Doi thoai va hop tac an ninh o chau A -Thai Binh Duong hien nay", *Tap Chi Quoc Phong Toan Dan* 7 (1996): 120-22.

3

CHINA AND VIETNAM: COPING WITH THE THREAT OF PEACEFUL EVOLUTION

Li Ma*

Introduction

The international order which emerged after the Second World War was disrupted by the events which took place between 1989 to 1991. China (already isolated after the Tiananmen Square incident) and Vietnam, as with the rest of the communist world, were shaken by the collapse of communism in Eastern Europe and the USSR. The main objective of these countries was the survival of their regimes, which needed to break the isolation that the West tried to impose on them,[1] while continuing their economic opening. The Chinese and Vietnamese regimes achieved success through economic reforms, going down a new path, which they called the "socialist market economy". They did so while maintaining politically rigid authoritarian regimes. In the West there was a general consensus that an economic opening would result in economic development and eventually, after a long process, lead to a political opening in the form of democratization. This preordained evolution—the so-called "peaceful evolution" towards democracy—was of course rejected by Chinese and Vietnamese leaders.

Parallel to this rather theoretical position, Western leaders, following Presidents George Bush and William Clinton, announced a general policy favouring democracies in the world: the politics of democratization.[2] Applying this to Asian states, this political stance seemed to indicate that the peaceful evolution was too slow, and that it was necessary to bring it about by fostering its accomplishment. The success of American policies would result in the end of Asian communist regimes. This explains why Chinese and Vietnamese leaders constantly denounce "the threat of peaceful evolution", which they perceive to be a new form of aggression that could lead to a "new Cold War".

The first section of this chapter analyses the common situation of China and Vietnam and their decision to embark on economic opening up, which brings to them performance legitimacy. Next, the chapter considers the foundations of peaceful evolution and its applicability to China and Vietnam. The chapter then discusses the hypothesis and deficiencies of Western democratization policies as applied to these countries. In the second section, the chapter considers the common interests and the consequences of Western policies for Sino-Vietnamese relations: frequent contact, the necessity for regional stability and the common destiny of these two countries which chose the path of the socialist market economy. Finally, the chapter concludes with a discussion of the motivations of the United States for opposing the development path pursued with relative success by China and Vietnam.

The common situation of China and Vietnam faced with the West

When the Cold War ended, the world was quick to claim the end of communism. Nevertheless, Cuba was not the only communist state left, and there existed in Asia an important group of communist regimes. In 1991, these regimes seemed to be remainders, anachronisms which would collapse in short order. Several years later, China and Vietnam, having chosen to open up (contrary to North Korea, for example) achieved impressive economic growth.[3] Their regimes do not seem to be endangered. Those who predicted a rapid collapse were wrong; they now replaced "rapid" with "unavoidable collapse".

The end of the Cold War and the decline of ideology in international relations may explain why the West does not explicitly refer to the communist nature of these regimes in its denunciations. Instead, these nations are now treated like classical authoritarian states and condemned for denying their citizens liberty and for abusing human rights. This may come from the fact that, unlike the USSR in the 1950s, these regimes did not seek to export communism outside of their borders. Instead, they tried to survive and to develop.

Vietnam and China: the opening to the world

To survive and develop as communist regimes, each of the Asian regimes wanted to pursue their proper diplomatic and economic paths. Two different forms, however, can be observed. North Korea chose to close its borders (although it briefly tried to open in 1992), withdraw into itself and pursue autarchy. North Korea now seems to be in a stalemate.

In contrast, China and Vietnam, the other remaining communist states, made the decision to pursue economic opening well before 1991. China embarked on its course in 1978 under Deng Xiaoping. Vietnam followed in 1986 with the launching of reforms partially inspired by Gorbachev's *perestroika*. China not only undertook economic reforms, but also opened diplomatically in order to break out of the isolation which resulted after the events of Tiananmen Square in 1989. The isolation ended after China collaborated with the West during the 1991 Gulf War. Vietnam chose another path to end its isolation. In September 1989 it withdrew its military forces from Cambodia and then pursued political reconciliation with China. In November 1991, after the Seventh Congress of the Vietnam Communist Party, Vietnam finally normalized its relations with China. It also decided to break with Russian-style reforms in favour of emulating the Chinese example. For example, during the period of normalization, a Vietnamese delegation visited Guangzhou, Shenzhen, and Nanning to observe Chinese reforms closely.[4] The Vietnamese regime ended its diplomatic isolation in 1995, when it joined ASEAN and normalized its relations with the United States.[5] It is clear that these policies of economic and diplomatic opening (including adherence to international organizations, a neo-functionalism in favour of the state[6]) was born of necessity in order to avoid economic stagnation.

Performance legitimacy and common problems

The economic success and the dynamics that came with Chinese and Vietnamese societies transformed the nature of the legitimacy of these regimes. Now they possess "performance legitimacy";[7] they are forced to continue economic growth. If this growth slows down, they will have to face internal discontent. Indeed market openings give rise to several inequalities between regions or in the social distribution of new wealth. A dynamics of growth is necessary to wipe out the resentment provoked by these heterogeneities, and to give hope of a better future. A recession would certainly give rise to a lot of social agitation, and a calling into question of the politics of the regime. On the other hand, China and Vietnam practise an "economic diplomacy", using diplomacy to sustain their strategy of economic development. Recently China even used the attraction of its huge internal market to impose some economic choices on other nations.[8] This strong diplomatic position would be lost in the case of a clear slowdown of the growth, or a recession.

Vietnam also began to experience the same disorders and problems linked with opening up and economic growth that China had already faced for several years. These problems include inequalities of income between regions (North and South for Vietnam, or coastal and interior regions for China), corruption, the problem of autonomy of provinces, and the flow of the unemployed moving from city to city in search of jobs.[9] Since Vietnam is much smaller, some of these problems are less acute than in China, but they have the same qualitative nature, and Vietnam carefully studies their evolution and the way Chinese authorities deal with theirs. For example, because they think that Tiananmen was fostered by inflation, Vietnamese leaders want to keep the level of inflation within reasonable limits.[10] One of the important elements enabling a successful practice of reforms is the direct association of army executives in business. Since the army directly benefits from economic reforms, it is not nostalgic for the past and has offered no opposition to reforms. This artful utilization of the army (which also has some drawbacks, when corruption is so important) is a practice China initiated, which Vietnam has followed.[11] This represents a guarantee of social stability, given the fact that the army will be willing to protect current reforms.

The decision to open to the outside world and the success that resulted does not permit the regimes of China and Vietnam to go backwards. They are thus in the same defensive position in front of a very common point of view, according to which this first step is the beginning of an irreversible movement towards "market democracy". The section below examines this mechanism and its supposed theoretical basis.

Peaceful evolution and the cases of China and Vietnam: some empirical arguments but a theoretical vacuum

In the field of international relations, most of the literature dealing with the future evolution of Chinese and Vietnamese regimes assumes that a political opening is inevitable. The opening of the economy is only the first step. It is followed by a political opening which in turn leads to democratization, and later, to a regime closely resembling liberal democracy. This is the process of so-called peaceful evolution. The general scheme is as follows:[12] economic reforms benefit part of the population, which transforms itself progressively into a middle class; this middle class then organizes itself into a "civil society", i.e. several social organizations (trade unions, associations, professional groups) independent from the state;[13] under the pressure of civil society, the regime democratizes itself, following an evolution which can last one generation.[14] The former authoritarian regimes of the Asian "tigers"—which became the Newly Developed Countries (for example South Korea, Singapore, Taiwan)—are often cited as examples of this evolution. It is admitted that when an income threshold was reached these countries adopted democratic regimes under the pressure of their civil societies.

It is easy to understand how people are seduced by this argument: it seems unavoidable, progressive, causal, and unstoppable. It is tempting to apply it to the cases of China and Vietnam. However, when we examine it, several important defects appear. First, each step of the evolution should be carefully proved, but this is not yet the case. And the link proposed between economy and politics is still criticized by a number of scholars.[15] Second, the arguments which are used are empirical rather than theoretical. Finally, the authoritarian communist regimes of China and Vietnam differ from the former authoritarian capitalist regimes of the Asian "tigers": even if the theory applies to capitalist regimes, does it also work for the socialist market economy that is put into practice by these two countries? We examine below several steps which have still to be proved before saying that the peaceful evolution of the Chinese and Vietnamese regimes is inevitable.

A link between development and democracy?

The first link which can be studied is the one between the development (more precisely the global wealth which goes with it) of a country and its political regime: the advantage of this approach is that the degree of development can be quantified (for example with a Gross National Product or the Gross Domestic Product by inhabitant), independently of all hypotheses on the economic structure of the country producing this wealth. Using several simple criteria (linked, for example, to executive recruitment or to the constraints existing on the chief executives) which of course can always be criticized, it is then also possible to define an "index" of democracy, and to study the correlations between this index and the wealth of the country. This approach was first proposed by Martin Lipset in 1959,[16] and then developed in a number of studies,[17] to show—empirically—that there exists in effect a correlation between the socio-economic development and democracy index of the regime.

Donald Emmerson[18] even proposed to call the following proposal "Lipset's law": "The more well-to-do a nation, the greater the chances that it will sustain democracy." Contrary to what is claimed too optimistically by several authors,[19] correlation does not mean causality; in other words, if one goes with the other, this does not mean that one necessarily implies the other. This point, made originally by Lipset, is underscored by Emmerson:

> This does not justify the optimistic liberal's hope that an increase in wealth, in the size of the middle class, in education, and other factors will necessarily mean the spread of democracy.[20]

To prove this causality, a theory should be proposed, rather than using only empirical arguments.

On the other hand, if one only considers the empirical arguments concerning this correlation between level of development and democratization, one may note that there exists important exceptions to this rule. India is a democratic country which has a rather modest level of development, whereas most of the oil exporting countries are very rich while remaining authoritarian kingdoms. This "law" thus possesses several flaws: it is only empirical, and there exist counter-examples. There are few reasons why it should apply to China and Vietnam. Finally, even if this empirical law was universal (it is not the case), this would not imply an immediate democratization of China and Vietnam, because their GNP per capita is still quite low.

Does capitalism bring democracy?

A link between capitalism and democracy is also a frequently-held point of view. Let us first point out that this is not the same hypothesis as the previous one: one should examine the link between an economic system and democracy: this system does not necessarily produce a rich country (there are capitalist states in bankruptcy).

The link between democracy and capitalism is implicitly present in the argument of Francis Fukuyama, celebrating the "end of history" and the triumph of liberal democracies.[21] Nevertheless, he points out elsewhere almost reluctantly, "The relationship between capitalism and democracy is an indirect one. That is, capitalism in itself does not generate direct pressure for democracy."[22] As before between development and democracy, the causal and necessary link that could exist between capitalism and democracy has not yet been obtained. This link may never be proved, because in fact a number of historical or contemporary counter-examples show that capitalist regimes can very well stay authoritarian (and absolutely non-democratic) during several decades, without any form of evolution towards democracy. Hence Ralf Dahrendorf showed that the industrialization of Germany under the Second Reich (1870–1918) did not lead to democratization.[23] We can thus say, with Kyong-won Kim, that "clearly, we cannot argue that a capitalist economy always leads to a democratic polity".[24]

This brief overview of studies showing that there is a missing theoretical link between capitalism and democracy should not lead us to forget that, in the cases of China and Vietnam, what is being attempted there is the introduction of a market economy with strong state control, in other words, a socialist market economy. The section below discusses this economic system and its possible links with democracy.

A link between market socialism and democracy?

According to the official positions of the governments of China and Vietnam,[25] the economic system of these countries is "socialist market economy", i.e. a market economy controlled by the state and collectivities, with several public and collective companies being in competition through the market.[26] The viability of this "third way" is questioned by several western scholars. Allan Goodman argues that "economies undergoing the transition to a free market usually become too complex to be controlled by a state bureaucracy";[27] and Peter Berger[28] argues that this system—which he thinks was already experimented on without success by Yugoslavia and Hungary—does not work, mainly because the managers have no motivation. On the other hand, Pranab Bardhan and John Roemer propose a new type of market socialism that is supposed to be viable and efficient.[29] Nevertheless, we may note that if this system works[30]—we may have an empirical answer—the question of its necessary evolution towards democracy is open. To our knowledge, this point has not yet been treated by scholars in political science.[31]

Finally, even if market socialism is an impossible economic structure in practice, the transition towards a market economy, which is presently being attempted by China and Vietnam, raises the possibility of a link between development and democracy. As was shown in the discussion above, this link has not been convincingly demonstrated.

It is then clear that the inevitable "peaceful evolution" of China and Vietnam towards a democratic regime is not a foregone conclusion. These two countries have chosen a path of development through fostering a socialist market economy, and we saw that the general link between development and democratization was incoherent, while a possible evolution of a socialist market economy towards democratization was an unexplored field of research.

As several scholars have argued,[32] modernization in a centralized (socialist) authoritarian system does not necessarily result in the growth of a civil society independent from the state. Rather, a bureaucratic élite may emerge which is apolitical and does not support democracy. The economic opening of a communist regime does not necessarily lead to a political opening. As Robert Scalapino has argued, it is likely to result in the birth of what he calls "authoritarian-pluralism".[33] This is a system in which a relatively independent civil society exists and in which the degree of liberty is small, but still greater than that in former communist regimes. This type of regime is not a liberal democracy. It does not correspond to peaceful evolution, either in economic or political domains.

The democratization politics of the West

The end of the Cold War has not been perceived and analysed by everyone in the same manner. According to the common point of view, the dream of George Bush of a "New World Order", or the "End of History" of Francis Fukuyama had some credibility at its best until the Gulf War. Since then no general scheme seems to have emerged, which could make global sense out of the new international system. This is not the point of view of G. John Ikenberry,[34] who sees in the present world a liberal democratic order dominated by the West, under the leadership of the United States. According to him, before launching containment politics against communism in 1947, President Truman presented his model of the liberal democratic order[35] in a speech at Baylor University. This model was supposed to give to the world an "economic peace" through international institutions such as the International Monetary Fund. According to Ikenberry, this approach of international relations had been frozen by the Cold War, and could continue its full expansion when the latter ended. This liberal democratic order is not yet reality for the world is not presently an ensemble of liberal democracies, but it seems clear that the Western leaders, following the United States, seek to impose it, through a general policy of democratization. After giving several examples of American leaders announcing these politics, we will expose some of its inconsistencies, dangers, and maybe get rid of its evangelism.

A new politics of "enlargement" of market democracies

In 1990, Secretary of State James Baker indicated that "beyond containment lies democracy".[36] Later, he stated that:

> ... shared democratic values can ensure an enduring and stable peace in a way that the balance of terror never could. Real democracies do not go to war with each other.[37]

This official position in favour of democracy, put into acts by the Bush Administration, was resumed by Clinton's Administration. Hence the National Security Adviser Anthony Lake indicated in 1993 that "the successor to a doctrine of containment must be a strategy of enlargement, the enlargement of the world's free community of market democracies".[38] This politics, called "idealpolitik" by the Deputy Secretary of State Strobe Talbott, relies on the idea that:

> Countries whose citizens choose their leaders are more likely than those with other forms of government to be reliable partners in trade and diplomacy, and less likely to threaten the peace.[39]

According to Talbott, the priority of American diplomacy is to sustain democracy everywhere in the world. He indicates also that the United States, "in collaboration with its democratic allies, must work hard helping nascent democracies through their phase of greatest fragility".[40] President Clinton himself indicated in which states the United States would have to give priority for the democratization process:

> in states that affect [U.S.] strategic interests, such as those with large economies, critical locations, nuclear weapons, or the potential to generate refugee flows into [the United States] or into [its] friends and allies.[41]

China and Vietnam perfectly fit into this description. When Vietnam and the United States normalized their relations, President Clinton made a noteworthy speech in which he said that normalization:

> ... will advance the cause of freedom in Vietnam, just as it did in Eastern Europe and the former Soviet Union. I strongly believe that engaging the Vietnamese on the broad front of economic reform and the broad front of democratic reform will help honor the sacrifice of those who fought for freedom's sake in Vietnam.[42]

As far as China is concerned, violation of human rights, the Chinese presence in Tibet and arms sales to so-called sensitive countries were the causes of recurrent tensions with the West (in particular the United States). In recent years, until 1995, the U.S. renewal of the most favoured nation clause for China provided the opportunity for delivering criticism of China's lack of democracy and human rights abuses. The return of Hong Kong to China provided the Western press opportunities to regularly criticize the democracy situation in China. This policy seems, at the same time, too pure and too simple to be free from any problem and suspicion concerning its real motives. This point is discussed below.

A blameworthy politics

Let us first note that this doctrine does not seem to be consistent with the idea that peaceful evolution should be inevitable in communist regimes which undertake economic opening. If peaceful evolution is supposed to happen by itself, according to a law of nature governing societies, why interfere with this process? Beyond this call for coherence, some more fundamental critiques, which we develop below, can be formulated against this enlargement politics.

Democracy and stability

One of the arguments which is used is the stability of democratic regimes, which would result in a safer world if all regimes were democratic. This reasoning goes back to Kant, who wrote that democracies are less likely to go to war, because a democratic leader must persuade his citizens of the necessity to fight.[43] This is quite an idealistic vision, which has not yet been proved; it is in fact used by American leaders as an axiom. In his critical review of the question, Mohamed Hassan indicates that there are democracies creating instabilities (one can consider as an example for this the U.S. actions in Vietnam from 1965 to 1975), and he recalls also that the Southeast Asian area contains several non-democratic states, whereas regional stability there is quite high. He asserts, with reason, that "the linkages between democracy and stability are by no means straightforward, and neither have they been satisfactorily established with regard to many points".[44] Furthermore, it has been argued that (true) democracies never go to war with each other.[45] Instead it is clear that democracies can go to war with non-democratic regimes; it seems that in a case of disagreement a democratic regime is less patient and is less reluctant to go to war with a non-democratic regime.[46] In two wars involving the United States since the last world war—the Vietnam war and the Gulf war—the democratic regime sought to limit its own human losses, without being concerned by the enemy's. In these two wars the human losses of Vietnam and Iraq were enormous compared to the Americans. This does not favour the notion of democratic stability.

Democratization and war

The democratization process of an authoritarian regime can be long and dangerous. It is not enough to organize free elections, one must also change the behaviour of "subjects" and transform them into "citizens"; one must also put in place efficient democratic institutions. During this evolution, a regime in transition and the central government are fragile (see, for example, the present situation of Cambodia). For reasons of internal stability, it can be prone to populism and an aggressive nationalism in the foreign realm. Edward Mansfield and Jack Snyder have conducted a data analysis which quantitatively confirms this general scheme. According to them, a state which evolves rapidly from an autocracy to a democracy has twice the probability to fight in a war within the ten years following democratization, than states which remain autocratic.[47] These authors did not conclude that one should not try to push authoritarian regimes in the direction of a democratic evolution, but instead that this peaceful evolution must be escorted, and done softly, instead of being roughly brought about.

The resistance against democratization by a large number of non-western cultures

After having defended world-wide democratization since 1974, through what he called "the third wave of democratization",[48] Samuel Huntington recently adopted a more mitigated position, and developed a widely read thesis of "clash of civilizations" to explain the reluctance of numerous cultures to westernization and democratization.[49] He remarked that several cultures (or civilizations) want modernization, but not necessarily westernization, democracy or human rights.[50] By popularizing the idea of a clash between civilizations, it could become a self-fulfilling prophesy. Furthermore, Samuel Huntington explicitly suggests that westerners should look to themselves and face together the menace that the emergence of Islamic or Sinic civilizations represent for their leadership in world affairs. This position has been strongly criticized.[51] If western leaders follow Huntington's recommendations, this won't improve the relations between the West and communist (and non-communist) Asian countries (and other "civilizations"). G. John Ikenberry considers that this would be a "declaration of a new Cold War".[52]

Is the United States looking for hegemony?

The "idealpolitik" of Clinton's Administration is certainly not so generous as its supporters would like to persuade us. Maybe it is not liberty and the welfare of other people, with the supposed international stability that this would provide for the world and for the West, which is sought, but better commercial and strategic interests. Asian leaders recall that the democratization of Russia accompanied its economic collapse, and that this eliminated the great challenger of the United States. They consider that Western pressures in favour of democratization in Eastern and Northern Asia are motivated by the wish to destabilize the regimes of an area with great economic growth, as was indicated scathingly by Malaysian Prime Minister Mahathir:

> [Their] sanctimonious pronouncements on humanitarian, democratic and environmental issues are likely to be motivated by a selfish desire to put as many obstacles as possible in the way of anyone attempting to catch up and compete with the West.[53]

Some western scholars have the same point of view: see for example Samir Amin, who argues that:

> ce projet de démantèlement de la Chine est à l'ordre du jour: c'est l'agenda de la politique des Etats-Unis et du Japon, pour lesquels la Chine grande puissance (fut-elle capitaliste) constitue une perspective inacceptable.[54]

China and Vietnam denounce a return of ideology

Whatever the real reasons motivating Western pressures in favour of democratization, it is clear that the Communist regimes of China and Vietnam cannot accept them, if they don't want to disappear. Chinese and Vietnamese leaders regularly denounce the "new Cold War" or the "return of ideology" in international relations. Hence the official New China News Agency on 23 August 1995 accused Washington of having an "anti-Chinese", "anachronistic and a hegemonic mentality", and wanting "China permanently [to stay] poor and backward, [while submitting] to the exploitation of western great powers". It also condemned the American media which presented China as a *"new empire of Evil"* having aggressive behaviour.[55] In parallel, the seventh and eighth congresses of the Vietnam Communist Party in 1991 and 1996, respectively, were the occasions to repeat the rejection of pluralism and peaceful evolution.[56] To publicly defend peaceful evolution can be a crime punishable by a jail sentence in Vietnam.

Hence several sore points between the United States, Vietnam and China can be interpreted as coming from an "informal ideology" in the relations between these states.[57] Yet this ideology is not uniquely

. informal, since one can also find some anti-communist aspects in American laws which seem to be remnants of the Cold War.[58]

The United States seeks explicitly to use the economic opening and developments in China and Vietnam to help the "cause of liberty", according to its definition of liberty which includes economic and political standards. This "double liberty" is supposed to exist fully only in the liberal democratic system presently practised by Western countries. This type of evolution would represent the end of the communist regimes of China and Vietnam, the end of the "socialist market economy" as they are trying to build it. We examine here the different elements which put these regimes in a common situation faced with Western pressures.

Common interests and consequences for China and Vietnam

The "natural" peaceful evolution of China and Vietnam towards becoming liberal democracies is thus not at all certain. Other paths are possible in the future. These two countries, in fact, have short-term goals which are very close. These are for them common interests which represent problems to solve and questions to settle. These different points are presented below.

The parallel situations mentioned here must not obscure the fact that bilateral relations were in bad shape before 1991.[59] The deterioration of the relations began to be serious in January 1974 when China forcibly took control of the Paracels archipelago, which was also claimed by Vietnam. These borderline problems later gave rise to several confrontations between the two armies, but it was the Vietnamese invasion of Cambodia that provoked the much more serious Sino-Vietnamese clash of February–March 1979. Gradually a status quo emerged in which the situation along the border was marked by minor clashes. In March 1988, the Spratly's archipelago was the scene of naval clashes between the two armies. The Vietnamese withdrawal from Cambodia later permitted the revival of contacts between the two countries, and bilateral relations were finally re-established in November 1991. Despite this, some problems are still to be settled between the two countries, essentially dealing with borderline questions (a disagreement on several milestones along the terrestrial borderline of 1,130 km)[60] and with Spratly and Paracels archipelagos, which are still claimed by each of the two countries (among others).

Present common interests of China and Vietnam

Regional stability

After normalization, despite regular discussions on the question of demarcating the land and maritime borders the two countries have yet to settle these issues. However, this does not prevent the establishment of good relations. The two countries, in fact, realized that their common situation brought with it common interests, i.e. some identical problems and short-term objectives. Among those was the necessity for sustainable economic growth, foreign investments, and regional stability.[61] For this reason, China and Vietnam decided to find solutions to settle peacefully their border disputes gradually. This willingness is certainly very important because a regional conflict would frighten away foreign investors, slow down economic growth, and endanger the pursuit of economic reforms and consequently the internal stability of each country. It is impossible to avoid disagreement on these issues but each country has some self-interest in keeping tensions to a minimum.

Trade relations

Border trade is also a common interest between the two countries.[62] A large number of Chinese companies invest in Vietnam. The Chinese provinces of Yunnan and Guangxi largely benefit from this new market and also the proximity of the Vietnamese port of Haiphong (120 km to the southeast of Hanoi), which allows them to dispose of their goods more readily than by going through Canton. On the other hand, the north of Vietnam, poorer than the south, takes advantage of the proximity of China to make up for lost time. In 1996, cross-border trade represented US$1 billion, three times more than in 1995 and fifteen times more than in 1991 (smuggling excluded).[63] The trade exchanges were not symmetrical; Vietnam was inundated by cheaper Chinese products than it could produce locally. A rail connection between China's Yunnan province and Vietnam's Lao Cai province was re-opened in February 1996 to better facilitate and control the trade exchanges.[64]

The success of the socialist market economy

The main common interest between the two countries lies in the existence and success of the socialist market economy and economic reforms. This comes from the fact that Vietnam followed the Chinese experiment. Hence a Vietnamese diplomat indicated:

> At the beginning, we didn't take China as a model for development.
> We based (development) on the Vietnamese reality. But in reality,

there are similarities between our situation and that of China. The Chinese are ahead of us, which is why we can draw on their experiences. Vietnam wants to observe China's situation and study it as an example of a socialist market economy.[65]

The next section considers the consequences for Sino-Vietnamese relations.

Outcome for Sino-Vietnamese relations

Very frequent contacts

The similar situations confronting China and Vietnam and their common interests have brought several outcomes for Sino-Vietnamese relations. First, they have enforced contacts between the two countries. Since normalization in November 1991, high-level visits have been carried out on a mutual basis by each side. In 1991, Vietnamese Prime Minister Vo Van Kiet and General Secretary of the Vietnam Communist Party, Do Muoi, went to China. In 1992, Chinese Prime Minister Li Peng went to Hanoi. In November 1993, Vietnamese President Le Duc Anh went to China. In November 1994, Chinese President Jiang Zemin went to Vietnam. In November 1995 Do Muoi revisited China. In June 1996, Li Peng was the guest of honour at the eighth congress of the Vietnam Communist Party. Most recently, in October 1998, Prime Minister Phan Van Khai travelled to Beijing. These regular contacts resulted in several joint communiqués, which repeated the will of the two countries to pursue economic co-operation, and not to use force to settle border problems.[66] Since December 1992, while discussions on land and sea borders were taking place,[67] several military delegations were regularly exchanged.[68]

No alliance but a common destiny

The similarity of the situations and regimes, and the perception of a common threat from the West at one point reportedly led to a consideration of reviving the alliance relationship between China and Vietnam. According to Carlyle Thayer, this question was suggested by China during 1991, with the intention of creating an alliance including the USSR, China, Vietnam, North Korea and Mongolia. Vietnam responded positively to this proposal. With the demise of USSR, China abandoned the idea.[69] Presently, an alliance between China and Vietnam is not on the agenda. Such an explicit return to ideology in their relations would not be well received by their neighbours. It certainly would be considered incompatible with Vietnam's membership in ASEAN by the other members of the association. In fact, before Vietnam's membership in ASEAN, this question was considered a potential danger by the states of the region. In particular, regional states feared the possibility of a Sino-Vietnamese agreement on the question of the Spratlys.[70] Now this possibility seems remote indeed.

China and Vietnam thus cannot at the same time pursue their politics of modernization and opening and, at the same time, form an alliance. Vietnamese leaders understand this. According to Zachary Abuza, since 1992 in the security area they have adopted the "comprehensive security approach". This approach includes the three following components: good bilateral relations with all countries; no formal alliance relations; and the maintenance of a peaceful foreign environment, in order to allow economic development.[71] On the other hand, the common situation that China and Vietnam are in strongly favours the establishment of informal agreements imposed by circumstances for the Chinese economic model which is being exported to Vietnam, as was noted above.

The similarity of their situations can also have undesirable effects. Both regimes possess "performance legitimacy" that need to maintain high growth rates. They both share a common interest in undertaking economic and political reforms in parallel. Any abrupt unilateral change would result in a spill over into the domestic affairs of the other. In order to prevent this from happening the two regimes are forced to undertake reforms together.

Is the search for peaceful resolution of borderline disputes linked to the success of economic reforms in the two countries?

As long as the reforms in each country operate well, the border disputes will continue to be frozen, waiting for peaceful resolution. In the case of an internal crisis, or in case the reforms run into difficulties, in one or the other country, this would certainly bring internal problems. The result could be an aggressive nationalism in order to divert the attention of the population away from domestic problems. The emergence of nationalism could well result in belligerent acts in the South China Sea. On the other hand, the use of force to settle land and sea disputes, or in the case of China the use of force to respond to "provocations" by Taiwan, would certainly lead to a flight of investors and a rapid decline of economic activity in the area. This would bring big problems for the continuation of the economic reforms in the two countries. In sum, their reforms require stability.

Looking for the motivations of the western politics of democratization in China and Vietnam

It is then legitimate to say that the peaceful settlement of border problems is without doubt linked to the pursuit of economic but not political reforms. A too pronounced Western pressure for a change of regime could endanger not only the internal order of China or Vietnam, but also the stability of the whole region.

What is the real goal of American leaders when they state the application of a politics in favour of democratization in the world? Do they really want to have a safer world, composed of liberal democracies? This is clearly an idealist position and the American leaders should know well that in practice a political system does not evolve so easily. Do they want, in the short term, to enable nationals of authoritarian countries to live better, under a freer system? It is difficult to believe that American leaders are so altruistic and preoccupied by the fate of nationals of other countries. The real motivation could belong to larger scale fields, such as diplomacy and strategy.[72] In this framework, the short-term result of democratization in China and Vietnam would certainly be the slowing down of economic growth, and the eruption of internal troubles and tensions in the region. China and Vietnam are presently experimenting with their own economic reforms. It would be premature and dangerous to force them to undertake political change. Is it the intention of the West to force these countries down the path taken by the former Soviet Union? The risks of such a policy are well understood by Chinese and Vietnamese leaders. The present sorry state of the Russian Federation symbolizes for them one of the possible outcomes of the democratization process. Besides, this point of view seems to be in part confirmed by Pentagon documents which state that one of the main goals of U.S. security strategy in the post-Cold War is "deterring potential competitors from even aspiring to a larger regional role".[73] It is then tempting to think that the democratization politics of the United States and the will of the West to see China and Vietnam evolve towards more liberty in the political and economic spheres, have for main and real motivation the prevention—through destabilization—of the emergence of a new socio-economic model (socialist market economy), and at the same time of a potentially great challenger for the United States. This point of view may be seen as exaggerated,[74] but it is not more ridiculous than "idealpolitik": the missionaries of democracy try certainly to hide their real motivations.

The West quickly and nearly unanimously hailed *glasnost* (political reforms) and *perestroika* (economic reforms) in Gorbachev's Soviet

Union. The result was a disaster for the political unity of the country and the living conditions of the inhabitants. Furthermore, concerning the so-called human rights question, one can agree with Peter Nolan that democratization does not necessarily lead to an improvement in the human rights situation as is gratuitously thought by its advocates:

> The provision of the right to vote periodically in elections may appear as less and less adequate a compensation for the loss of other human rights consequent upon economic failure.[75]

To be convinced, it is sufficient to examine the present situation of Russia. The question asked several years ago by Jagdish Bhagwati—"Who was right, Gorbachev or Deng Xiaoping?"[76]—now has an obvious empirical answer.

Conclusion

This chapter has examined the usual arguments developed by the West, according to which economic development and opening necessarily leads to a political opening. The argument presented here is that these views are in fact dogma. Those who argue that there is a casual relation between economic development and opening and democracy have not convincingly demonstrated their case. They have relied on empirical analysis which suggests that there is a correlation, but the causal link has not been proved in theory or practice. If there were a casual and automatic link, why in the post-Cold War era has the United States dropped its policy of containment in favour of the enlargement of democracy?

If "democratic enlargement" were applied to the Asian communist regimes, it would be interpreted by their leaders as the rest of an ideological coloration within international relations. China and Vietnam are doubly concerned by this possibility because they initiated a general policy of opening up their economies (and societies) to the West. The decision by China and Vietnam to pursue an economic opening while maintaining closed political systems puts them in a common situation. This has resulted in the emergence of common interests, of which the most important are the maintenance of regional stability and success in developing a socialist market economy.

Which should China and Vietnam pursue first: economic opening or political opening? A comparison of the situation in China and Vietnam with that of the former Soviet Union shows that their choice is empirically the better one. Russia is a superficial democracy; the fact that its citizens have the right to vote should not obscure this. Human rights are in a poor state and the economy is a disaster. This leads one to ask what is the real intention of the West? Is it to foster the personal liberty of the Chinese and Vietnamese people, or is the West's real objective to prevent the successful development of a viable socialist market economy? If China and Vietnam achieve success in their unique path of development, they would emerge over time as dangerous competitors. According to the OECD and the World Bank, if China continues its present rate of economic growth it will emerge as a major power around the year 2010.[77] In this case, the enlargement politics of Clinton's Administration would have the same mercantile and ideological coloration as the containment policies it replaced.

Notes

* The author would like to thank Carl Thayer for his assistance in editing this chapter.

1. François Joyaux, *La politique extérieure de la Chine*, Que sais-je? (Paris: PUF, 1993), pp. 106-7; see also Jean-Claude Pomonti and Hugues Tertrais, *Vietnam, communistes et dragons* (Paris: Le Monde-Editions, 1994).

2. These policies are most visibly promoted by American leaders, but democracy is a fundamental value in all Western countries, and promoting democracy is a general objective of most Western leaders. Therefore, in this chapter, policies which advocate the spread of democracy are termed Western rather than U.S.

3. In 1994-95, China achieved a GDP growth rate of 11 per cent while Vietnam achieved a figure of 7.9 per cent. During the period 1978-95, China achieved a yearly average growth rate of 9.4 per cent while Vietnam's economy grew on average at 7.1 per cent. See *World Development Record* (Washington: World Bank, 1996).

4. Karen Sutter, "China's Vietnam Policy: The Road to Normalization and Prospects for the Sino-Vietnamese Relationship", *Journal of Northeast Asian Studies* (Summer 1993): 21-46; see also United States Foreign Broadcast Information Service (USFBIS), *Daily Report—China*, no. 91-215, 6 November 1991.

5. The American ambassador finally arrived in Hanoi on 9 May 1997.

6. Gerald Chan, "China and International Organizations", *China Review* (1995): 115-35.

7. See Steve Chan, "Regime Transition in the Asia/Pacific Region: Democratization as a Double-Edged Sword", *The Journal of Strategic Studies* 18, no. 3 (1995): 52-67.

8. For example, when diplomatic relations were established with South Africa (before South Africa had chosen the Taiwan camp), or when a proposal by the United Nations Human Rights Commission to condemn China for violating human rights was motivated by trade reasons. France did not support the proposal, breaking the unity of the European Commission on the question; Agence France-Presse, 16 April 1997.

9. Lang Son, "Vietnam beats China at its own game", *The Economist*, 5 November 1994; Adam Schwarz, "Enemy No. 1: Economic opening has unleashed corruption scourge", *Far Eastern Economic Review*, 11 July 1996.
10. Lang Son, "Vietnam beats China at its own game", op. cit.
11. See "Vietnam", *L'Asie Nouvelle* (Paris), no. 1407, 31 May 1996.
12. This presentation is, of course, simplistic; the discussion will be more precise below. For more detailed studies, see James W. Morley, ed., *Driven by Growth: Political Change in the Asia-Pacific Region*, revised edition (Armonk and London: M.E. Sharpe, 1999).
13. On civil society, see Ernest Gellner, *Conditions of Liberty: Civil Society and Its Rivals* (London: Penguin, 1994).
14. See Clifford J. Shultz II and Khai Lee, "Vietnam's Inconsistencies Between Political Structure and Socio-economic Practice: Implications for the Nation's Future", *Contemporary Southeast Asia* 15, no. 2 (1993): 179–94; Larry Diamond and Marc Plattner eds, *Capitalism, Socialism, and Democracy Revisited* (Baltimore: John Hopkins University Press, 1993), pp. 1–10; Minxin Pei, "The Puzzle of East Asian Exceptionalism", *Journal of Democracy* 5, no. 4 (1994): 90–103; and Allan E. Goodman, "The Political Consequences of Normalization of US-Vietnam Relations", *Contemporary Southeast Asia* 17, no. 4 (1996): 420–29.
15. One of the first books on this question is Joseph A. Schumpeter, *Capitalism, Socialism, and Democracy* (New York: Harper and Row, 1950); this book is discussed in Diamond and Plattner, eds., *Capitalism, Socialism and Democracy Revisited*, op. cit., pp. 1–132; see also the special issue of the *Journal of Democracy*, on the theme "Economic Reform and Democracy", October 1994, pp. 3–175.
16. Seymour M. Lipset, "Some Social Requisites of Democracy: Economic Development and Political Legitimacy", *American Political Science Review* 53 (1959): 69–105.
17. For more recent works, see for example Larry Diamond, "Economic Development and Democracy Reconsidered", *American Behavioral Scientist* 25, no. 4 (1992): 450–99, and John B. Londregan and Keith T. Poole, "Does High Income Promote Democracy?", *World Politics* 49 (1996): 1–30.
18. Donald K. Emmerson, "Region and Recalcitrance: Rethinking Democracy Through Southeast Asia", *The Pacific Review* 8, no. 2 (1995): 232.
19. Diamond, "Economic Development and Democracy Reconsidered", op. cit.; and Londregan and Poole, "Does High Income Promote Democracy?", op. cit.
20. Lipset, "Some Social Requisites of Democracy: Economic Development and Political Legitimacy", op. cit., p. 103.
21. Francis Fukuyama, "The end of History", *The National Interest* 16, no. 4 (Summer 1989): 18.
22. Francis Fukuyama, "Capitalism & Democracy: the Missing Link", in Diamond and Plattner, eds., *Capitalism, Socialism and Democracy Revisited*, op. cit., p. 102.
23. Ralf Dahrendorf, *Society and Democracy in Germany* (New York: Doubleday, 1969).
24. Kyung-won Kim, "Marx, Schumpeter, and the East Asian Experience", in Diamond and Plattner, eds, *Capitalism, Socialism, and Democracy Revisited*, op. cit., p. 19.

25. For the Chinese position see Yang Jianwen, "China's socialist market economy", *Studia Diplomatica* 49, nos. 4–5 (1996): 19–46; and for the Vietnamese position see Do Muoi, "Speech at the Closing Session of the Ninth Plenum", 14 November 1995.

26. See also Yves Chevrier, "Un pays en voie de banalisation? Les paradoxes politiques de la réforme chinoise", *Relations Internationales*, no. 81 (printemps 1995): 39–58.

27. Goodman, "The Political Consequences of Normalization of US-Vietnam Relations", op. cit., p. 425.

28. Peter Berger, "The Uncertain Triumph of Democratic Capitalism", in Diamond and Plattner eds, *Capitalism, Socialism, and Democracy Revisited*, op. cit., pp. 1–10.

29. Pranab Bardhan and John E. Roemer, "Market Socialism: A Case for Rejuvenation", *Journal of Economic Perspectives* 6, no. 3 (1992): 101–16.

30. It must be stressed that criticism of the socialist economic system by classical liberal scholars like Friedrich von Hayek do not apply to market socialism. See his *Knowledge Evolution and Society* (London: Butler and Tanner, 1983).

31. It should be recalled that one of Schumpeter's conclusions was that socialism is compatible with democracy, but democratic socialism is certainly not democratic *capitalism*, the final stage of the process of peaceful evolution. Schumpeter was one of the first scholars to have studied this domain. See Schumpeter, *Capitalism, Socialism, and Democracy*, op. cit. For a more recent point of view, consult Alex Callinicos, "Liberalism, Marxism, and Democracy: A Response to David Held", *Theory and Society* 22, no. 2 (1993): 283–86.

32. See, for example, Nicholas Lardy, "Is China Different?", in David Chirot, ed., *The Crisis of Leninism and the Decline of the Left* (Seattle: The University of Washington Press, 1991); and Kyung-won Kim, "Marx, Schumpeter, and the East Asian Experience", op. cit.

33. Robert Scalapino, *The Politics of Development: Perspectives on Twentieth-Century Asia* (Cambridge: Harvard University Press, 1989), pp. 20–43; and Scalapino, "Northeast Asia—Prospects for Cooperation", *The Pacific Review* 5, no. 2 (1992): 101–11.

34. G. John Ikenberry, "The Myth of Post-Cold War Chaos", *Foreign Affairs* 75, no. 3 (1996): 79–91.

35. This approach is not new; *it was already proposed* by Immanuel Kant in 1795. See *Perpetual Peace* (New York: McMillan, 1957).

36. See Gregory A. Raymond, "Democracies, Disputes, and Third-Party Intermediaries", *Journal of Conflict Resolution*, no. 38 (1994): 25.

37. See Bruce Russet, *Grasping the Democratic Peace: Principles for a Post-Cold War World* (Princeton: Princeton University Press, 1993), p. 129.

38. Cited in Richard Haas, "Paradigm Lost", *Foreign Affairs* 74, no. 1 (1995): 44.

39. See Strobe Talbott, "Democracy and the National Interest", *Foreign Affairs* 75, no. 6 (1996): 47. See also Douglas Brinkley, "Democratic Enlargement: the Clinton Doctrine", *Foreign Policy*, no. 106 (1997): 111–27.

40. Ibid., p. 58.

41. William J. Clinton, *A National Security Strategy of Engagement and Enlargement* (Washington D.C.: The White House, July 1994), p. 19.

42. Office of the Press Secretary, The White House, "Remarks by the President", in "Announcement on Normalization of Diplomatic Relations with Vietnam", Washington D.C., 11 July 1995, p. 3.

43. Kant, *Perpetual Peace*, op. cit.

44. Mohamed J. Hassan, "The Nexus Between Democracy and Stability: The Case of Southeast Asia", *Contemporary Southeast Asia* 18, no. 2 (1996): 165; see also a discussion of the question in Steve Chan, "Regime Transition in the Asia/Pacific Region: Democratization as a Double-Edged Sword", op. cit.

45. Among many recent publications on this subject, see David Lake, "Powerful Pacifists: Democratic States and War", *American Political Science Review* 86, no. 1 (1992): 24–37. For an historical assessment, see James Lee Ray, "The Democratic Path to Peace", *Journal of Democracy* 8, no. 2 (1997): 49–64 and James Lee Ray, *Democracy and International Conflicts: An Evaluation of the Democratic Peace Proposition* (Columbia: University of South Carolina Press, 1995).

46. Christopher Layne, "Kant or Cant: The Myth of Democratic Peace", *International Security*, no. 19 (1994): 5–49; and David Spiro, "The Insignificance of the Liberal Peace", *International Security*, no. 19 (1994): 50–86.

47. Edward D. Mansfield and Jack Snyder, "Democratization and War", *Foreign Affairs* 74, no. 3 (1995): 79–97. These authors use a classification of regimes and wars from 1811 to 1980.

48. Samuel P. Huntington, *The Third Wave: Democratization in the Late Twentieth Century* (Norman: University of Oklahoma Press, 1991).

49. Samuel P. Huntington, "The Clash of Civilizations?", *Foreign Affairs* 72, no. 3 (1993); these positions have then been developed in his book, *The Clash of Civilizations and the Remaking of World Order* (New York: Simon and Schuster, 1996).

50. The failure of democratic transition to occur in Southeast Asia has been also discussed recently by Emmerson, "Region and Recalcitrance: Rethinking Democracy Through Southeast Asia", op. cit.

51. See the responses to Samuel Huntington, *Foreign Affairs* 72, no. 4 (1993): 2–26; see also *Commentaires* 66 (1993) and *Foreign Affairs* 76, no. 2 (1997): 162–69.

52. G. John Ikenberry, "Just like the Rest", *Foreign Affairs* 76, no. 2 (1997), 163.

53. Mohamad Mahathir, "East Asia will find its own roads to democracy", *The International Herald Tribune*, 17 May 1994, p. 3.

54. Samir Amin, "Y a-t-il un projet chinois?", *Alternatives Sud* 3, no. 3 (1996): 106.

55. See Patrick Sabatier, "Pékin accuse Washington de vouloir mener une nouvelle guerre froide", *Libération*, 24 août 1995, p. 7.

56. Frederick Brown, "Vietnam's tentative transformation", *Journal of Democracy* 7, no. 4 (1996): 78–81; see also Carlyle Thayer, "Vietnam: Coping with China", *Southeast Asian Affairs* (1994): 351–67.

57. See also AFP, "Le Vietnam exprime son mécontentement devant une campagne de presse du FBI", 9 March 1996; Jialin Zhang, "US-China relations in the post-cold war period: a chinese perspective", *Journal of Northeast Asian Studies* 14, no. 2 (1995): 47–61; Steven Levine, "Perception and Ideology in Chinese Foreign Policy", in Thomas

Robinson and David Shambaugh, eds, *Chinese Foreign Policy, Theory and Practice* (Oxford: Clarendon Press, 1994), pp. 30–46.

58. For example, the U.S. Government will not provide financial aid to U.S. companies which want to invest in a developing country if this country is "Marxist-Leninist"; see Office of the Press Secretary, The White House, "Fact Sheet: Background Paper on Economic Relationships", 11 July 1995, 2, cited by Goodman, "The Political Consequences of Normalization of US-Vietnam Relations", op. cit. See also Jeremy Grant, "US-Vietnam frustrations mount", *Financial Times*, 15 July 1996.

59. For a study of Sino-Vietnamese relations, see Ramses Amer, "Sino-Vietnamese Relations and Southeast Asian Security", *Contemporary Southeast Asia* 14, no. 4 (1993): 314–31; and chapter four in this volume.

60. See AFP, "Vietnam-Chine: quatrième round de pourparlers sino-vietnamiens sur les frontières terrestres et maritimes", 21 September 1996.

61. See Thayer, "Vietnam, Coping with China", op. cit.; and Clifford J. Shultz II and William J. Ardrey, IV, "The Future Prospects of Sino-Vietnamese Relations: Are Trade and Commerce the Critical Factors for Sustainable Peace?", *Contemporary Southeast Asia* 17, no. 2 (1995): 126–46.

62. Shultz and Ardrey, "The Future Prospects of Sino-Vietnamese Relations", op. cit.

63. "Marché frontalier sino-vietnamien; les échanges bilatéraux ont le vent en poupe", *Le courrier du Vietnam*, 2 February 1997.

64. AFP, "Vietnam-Chine: les liaisons ferroviaires entre le Vietnam et la Chine rétablies le 12 février", 30 January 1996.

65. Cited by *Asahi Evening News*, "Vietnam searches for role model", 8 November 1993.

66. See "Communiqué commun sino-vietnamien, 22 novembre 1994", *Beijing Informations*, 5 December 1994; and also Thayer, "Vietnam, Coping with China", op. cit.

67. Nine rounds of discussions on border problems were organized between 1993 and 1996; see AFP, "Vietnam-Chine: quatrième round de pourparlers sino-vietnamiens sur les frontières terrestres et maritimes", 21 September 1996.

68. AFP, "Vietnam-Chine: visite du chef d'état-major de l'armée chinoise au Vietnam", 17 April 1995.

69. Carlyle Thayer, "Comrade Plus Brother: The New Sino-Vietnamese Relations", *Pacific Review* 5, no. 4 (1992): 402–6; see also *Bulletin de sinologie*, no. 80 (juin 1991): 13.

70. Amer, "Sino-Vietnamese Relations and Southeast Asian Security", op. cit.

71. Zachary Abuza, "International Relations Theory and Vietnam", *Contemporary Southeast Asia* 17, no. 4 (1996): 409.

72. Noam Chomsky argues (*World Orders, Old and New*, London: Pluto Press, 1994) that there is a discrepancy between what U.S. leaders say in public speeches and the actions they take. According to this view, U.S. leaders do not really try to bring about democracy in non-democratic states but are content to maintain a profitable trade relationship. In this context, a public speech advocating democracy is

mainly designed for internal American consumption. A contrary view holds that American actions are congruent with their public speeches. For example, the United States votes in favour of UN resolutions condemning China for human rights violations. Or, the U.S. opposed Chinese membership in GATT and now opposes Chinese membership in the WTO for essentially political reasons.

73. Excerpts from "Pentagon's Plan: Prevent the Reemergence of a New Rival", *New York Times*, 8 March 1992; see also Paul Tyler, "US Strategy Plan Calls for Insuring No Rivals Develop", *New York Times*, 8 March 1992.

74. For example, see the views of William J. Murphy who argues that American foreign policy is not very consistent over the years, due in part to in-fighting. Murphy, "Power Transition in Northeast Asia: US-China Security Perceptions and the Challenges of Systemic Adjustment and Stability", *Journal of Northeast Asia Studies* (Winter 1994): 61–84.

75. Peter Nolan, "Democratization, Human Rights and Economic Reform: The Case of China and Russia", *Democratization* 1, no. 1 (1994): 97.

76. Jagdish Bhagwati, "Democracy and Development", in L. Diamond and M. Plattner, eds., *Capitalism, Socialism and Democracy Revisited*, op. cit., p. 35.

77. See "La Chine devrait figurer au premier rang des puissances économiques mondiales dans une quinzaine d'années", *Les Echos*, 11 January 1996.

4

SINO-VIETNAMESE RELATIONS: PAST, PRESENT AND FUTURE*

Ramses Amer

Purpose and structure

The purpose of this chapter is to analyse how disputed issues influence the relationship between China and Vietnam, with a focus on developments since the full normalization of political relations in November 1991. However, the period 1975–91 will also be subject to attention given its importance as a background to developments in the 1990s. The chapter is divided into two main parts. The first is an empirical overview of how the Sino-Vietnamese relationship had evolved within two broad periods of time, 1975–91 and 1992–98. In the second part an analysis is made of the relative importance of different issues in explaining the changing pattern of interaction. As the main purpose of the chapter is to study the post 1991 period, that period is given more detailed attention in the empirical part of the study and the contentious issues in bilateral relations during that period—primarily the impact of the territorial disputes—is given extensive attention. In the concluding section, the overall pattern of interaction between China and Vietnam is assessed. The failures and successes in managing disputed issues and the possible future management of such issues and their impact on Sino-Vietnamese relations are discussed.

Background[1]

Relations between China and Vietnam were very close in the 1950s, and for two decades China provided the Democratic Republic of Vietnam (DRV) with extensive economic and military assistance. China also sent thousands of advisers to assist the Vietnamese in various fields. However, irritants developed during the 1960s and into the first half of the 1970s due to different perceptions of the Union of Soviet Socialist Republics (USSR) and divergent views on relations and negotiations with the United States of America (USA). After the Paris agreement in 1973, the Vietnamese claimed that Chinese leaders had advised them to diminish the level of the fighting in the South for a couple of years, advice perceived as aiming to keep Vietnam divided. China rejected this claim.

Sino-Vietnamese relations, 1975–91[2]

Relations between China and Vietnam went through dramatic changes from seemingly good and normal relations in 1975 to war in 1979, and from continued tension during most of the 1980s to full normalization of relations in late 1991. The major events of the relationship will be presented in a chronological fashion with a focus on the shifts in the pattern of interaction and the issues and events that characterized this period.

Officially normal relations but conflicting issues in evidence: April 1975 to March 1978

Following the end of the Vietnam War in late April 1975, relations between China and Vietnam began to deteriorate over a number of issues. One was differences in opinion concerning the USSR and China's uneasiness about Vietnam's relations with the USSR. This became apparent during a visit by the Secretary-General of the Vietnam Communist Party (VCP),[3] Le Duan, to China in September. During this visit, and for the first time in discussions between the two sides, Le Duan officially raised the issue of sovereignty over the Paracel and Spratly archipelagos in the South China Sea. The visit ended without the usual joint communiqué.[4]

Both China and Vietnam carried out actions to emphasize their territorial claims in the South China Sea prior to the September 1975 meeting. In January 1974, China had seized control over the whole Paracel archipelago from the Republic of Vietnam (RVN); previously China had taken control over parts of the archipelago in 1956. The DRV seized six islands in the Spratly archipelago from the RVN in April 1975. Each of these actions was interpreted as aggressive by the other party. The land border between China and Vietnam became a disputed issue because of shifts in the position of border demarcations that had been made since 1955. These divergences led to border skirmishes and clashes from 1974 onwards.[5]

The question of China's economic assistance to Vietnam was also a source of friction. The first major cut in Chinese assistance came in February 1977 when China announced that it could not provide new loans. Two reasons were given; first, China needed the money for domestic purposes, and, second, large amounts of funds allocated earlier had yet to be disbursed.[6] This was entirely at variance with Vietnam's requests for increased economic assistance for reconstruction work.[7]

Cambodia came to play an important role in Sino-Vietnamese relations. Relations between China and Cambodia were good from 1975, whereas relations between Cambodia and Vietnam were less harmonious but seemed to have been manageable, at least officially, until the end of 1977, when in fact a military conflict had been going on for about a year. The roots of the conflict were both ideological and nationalistic.[8] China sought to mediate between the two countries from 1975 to 1977.[9] Initial Chinese reporting on the conflict in early 1978 was fairly neutral but China's pro-Cambodian stand gradually became more apparent.[10] It appears the Chinese decision to support Cambodia was taken after a visit by Le Duan to China in November 1977 but it was not implemented until 1978.[11]

Although China raised the issue of Vietnam's treatment of the Chinese minority at Chinese Vice Prime Minister[12] Li Xiannian's talks with Vietnamese Prime Minister Pham Van Dong in June 1977, the ethnic Chinese in Vietnam did not become a major issue of controversy until 1978.[13] In late 1977 China began a re-appraisal of its policy towards the Overseas Chinese. Institutions and organizations dealing with the Overseas Chinese, which had been disbanded or neglected during the Cultural Revolution, were re-established. China also started to look to the Overseas Chinese to support its economic reconstruction. The re-activated policy implied that China was prepared to take greater interest in the situation of the ethnic Chinese in Vietnam.[14]

From public dispute to war: April 1978 to March 1979[15]

Despite the many disputed issues which plagued the relationship between China and Vietnam up to the beginning of 1978, it was the exodus of the ethnic Chinese from Vietnam to China in the spring of 1978 that triggered the public deterioration of relations. Prior to the exodus, the misunderstandings had been kept out of the public arena. The first public indication that ethnic Chinese were leaving Vietnam and arriving in China came on 30 April 1978 when the Head of the Overseas Chinese Affairs Office of the State Council in Beijing broke the news that a large number of "Chinese residents" had suddenly returned from Vietnam. He stated that since early April 1978 Vietnam had stepped up the "expulsion" of "Chinese residents" and the number of expelled persons had reached 40,000. Then on 24 May a spokesman of the Overseas Chinese Affairs Office of the State Council accused Vietnam of "unwarrantedly ostracizing and persecuting Chinese residents" and "expelling" many of them back to China.

On the bilateral level, China moved to cancel its funding for some 70 projects in Vietnam during the month of May. The funds were to be used to take care of the expelled "Chinese residents". China stepped up its reaction to the exodus by unilaterally deciding to send ships to repatriate persecuted "Chinese residents". On 27 May, Vietnam rejected the allegations that it was maltreating its ethnic Chinese and proposed talks to settle the differences. Despite the initial Chinese refusal to negotiate, talks on repatriation of ethnic Chinese from Vietnam started on 13 June and went on to 19 July when China proposed to refer the matter to negotiations at the level of vice foreign ministers, which Vietnam accepted. In the wake of this "breakdown" of the repatriation talks, two Chinese ships that had been lying off the Vietnamese coast since mid June were called back to China. Talks at the level of vice foreign ministers started on 8 August and lasted until 26 September. No agreement was reached because neither side was willing to compromise.

Meanwhile, on 12 July, China sealed its border with Vietnam and decided that "Chinese Nationals" residing in Vietnam who wanted to return to China had to apply for official repatriation certificates to be issued by the Chinese embassy in Hanoi. They also needed exit visas from the Vietnamese authorities and they had to cross the border at certain fixed locations. China's move has to be understood in the context of the influx of ethnic Chinese. By mid July over 160,000 people had entered China.[16]

The rift in Sino-Vietnamese relations over the issue of the ethnic Chinese in Vietnam was further fuelled by divergences of opinion with regard to Cambodia as well as to Vietnam's relations with the USSR. Any earlier reluctance to publicly attack each other over disputed issues were removed once the dispute over the ethnic Chinese became public.[17]

Events in foreign relations were to cause Sino-Vietnamese relations to deteriorate further. One such event was the admission of Vietnam to the Soviet-led economic grouping, the Council for Mutual Economic Assistance (CMEA), on 28 June 1978. Vietnam's earlier reluctance to join the CMEA, in order not to provoke China, was removed by the earlier cut-offs of Chinese assistance.[18] China reacted by terminating all remaining economic and technical aid to Vietnam and by withdrawing all experts.[19]

Vietnam's relationship to the USSR was further strengthened on 3 November 1978, when Vietnam accepted a long-standing proposal and signed a Treaty of Friendship and Cooperation between the two states.[20] Vietnam's decision to enter into an alliance with the USSR came about after efforts to normalize relations with the United States in 1978 had failed despite Vietnam dropping all its preconditions. The United States had instead opted for full normalization of relations with China, a process which was completed on 1 January 1979. Thus, two strategic alliances had been created, a Soviet-Vietnamese and a Sino-American.[21]

During 1978 the armed conflict between Cambodia and Vietnam continued unabated leading up to the Vietnamese military intervention in Cambodia, launched on 25 December. The intervention resulted in the overthrow of the Cambodian Government and a new administration was installed—the People's Republic of Kampuchea (PRK).[22] The Vietnamese intervention was a major blow to China, since a friendly government had been overthrown and China had not been in a position to prevent it. Earlier restraints on the publicity given to "the need to teach Vietnam a lesson" completely disappeared and following several weeks of a mounting war of words, China launched a co-ordinated attack along the land border with Vietnam on 17 February 1979. China claimed to have captured the provincial capitals of Cao Bang, Lang Son and Lao Cai, as well as 17 other cities and counties before announcing the pull-out on 5 March.[23]

From continued deep differences and military tension to early contacts: April 1979 to mid-1988

The Chinese withdrawal was followed by attempts at negotiations between China and Vietnam from April 1979 to March 1980, but the positions were too disparate to enable the two parties to reach an understanding.[24] The bilateral relations remained tense during these talks and for the major part of the 1980s. The tension was most visible along the common border with mutual accusations about military incursions. Increased Chinese military activities along the border seem to have been linked to Vietnamese offensives in Cambodia, and in the period up to August 1987 six major flare-ups were registered.[25] Beginning in early 1988 tension began to mount in the Spratly archipelago, leading to clashes and resulting in China seizing some of the islands in March.[26] On a more positive note, tension along the common land border steadily decreased during the second half of 1988 and by the end of the year border trade had been resumed.[27]

On the diplomatic front a slight warming of Sino-Vietnamese relations could be noticed as early as in late 1985, exemplified by a message of congratulations from China's President to his Vietnamese counterpart on the occasion of Vietnam's Fortieth National Day celebrations. Low level contacts and greetings on special events continued, while the level of tension fluctuated along the common border.[28] The bilateral contacts between 1985 to 1988 coincided with the changes in Soviet foreign policy implemented by Mikhail Gorbachev.[29]

The normalization process: early 1989 to November 1991

From early 1989 higher level Sino-Vietnamese contacts were reported. In January 1989, one of Vietnam's Deputy Foreign Ministers visited Beijing and held talks with his Chinese counterpart and with China's Foreign Minister.[30] Another meeting took place in August 1989 when Vietnam's Foreign Minister met with China's Vice Foreign Minister in connection with the Paris Conference on Cambodia.[31] Although these contacts did not bring about any significant improvement of bilateral relations, they were important signs of an interest in improving relations, a process which was facilitated by the full normalization of relations between China and the USSR in May 1989. However, relations were impeded by the continued differences over Cambodia as well as bilateral issues such as territorial disputes.[32]

This situation prevailed up to early September 1990 when a then secret Vietnamese high-level visit to China took place. Vietnam was represented by the Secretary-General of the VCP, Nguyen Van Linh and the Prime Minister, Do Muoi, but not the Foreign Minister, Nguyen Co Thach.[33] The absence of Nguyen Co Thach from the September summit was a clear indication that China objected to him.[34] The international diplomacy of the Cambodian conflict following the summit suggested that China and Vietnam had reached an understanding on some of the issues relating to the conflict but not on all.[35] Despite these positive signs the Cambodian conflict was not resolved in 1990 and the normalization process between China and Vietnam lacked momentum on the political front.

This state of affairs with increased economic interaction but a stalled normalization process prevailed up to mid-1991 when it gained momentum, an evolution which paralleled the process of resolving the Cambodian conflict leading up to the Paris Agreements in

October 1991. Resolving the Cambodian conflict certainly facilitated the contacts between China and Vietnam, and improved Sino-Vietnamese relations had positive repercussions on developments relating to Cambodia.[36]

A change in the Vietnamese leadership also helped to move the normalization process forward. At the Seventh Congress of the VCP, Nguyen Co Thach was dropped from the Politburo and the Central Committee, and following the congress he lost his government posts. China's response was to invite General Le Duc Anh to visit China.[37] He paid a then undisclosed visit to China in late July. In September, Vietnam's newly appointed Foreign Minister, Nguyen Manh Cam, visited China and this cleared the way for a high-level summit from 5–10 November 1991, during which the bilateral relations were officially fully normalized.[38]

Sino-Vietnamese relations 1992–98[39]

Since the November 1991 summit, relations between China and Vietnam have been characterized by two contradictory trends, one positive with expanding contacts and co-operation in many fields, and the other negative with continued differences relating primarily to the territorial disputes. The positive trend has been prevalent throughout the period but has at times been slowed down by the fluctuating levels of tension relating to the border disputes, in particular those in the South China Sea area.

A good start turns into tension: January to mid-September 1992

The year 1992 began with overall good relations. In February China's Foreign Minister Qian Qichen visited Vietnam, and a memorandum of understanding and agreements in principle were reached relating to communication, transportation, and economic co-operation. There was also an agreement to establish working groups to discuss the territorial disputes.[40] In March, during a visit to China by Vietnam's Minister of Transport and Post, agreements concerning post, telephone, telecommunication, and transport were signed. At the same time a Vietnamese defence delegation and a delegation from the VCP visited China.[41]

However, during 1992 China made several moves which brought about renewed tension. In February, China passed a new law on territorial waters which stipulated that the Paracel and Spratly archipelagos and most of the South China Sea waters were to be regarded as part of its national territory.[42] In May, China signed an agreement with the Crestone Energy Corporation, a U.S. company, on oil and gas exploration in a 10,000 square mile area in the South China Sea. Vietnam reacted negatively and claimed that the area was located on its continental shelf.[43] In July, Vietnam accused China of having landed troops on "Da Lac coral reef" in the Spratly archipelago.[44] In September, China began drilling for oil in a disputed area of the Gulf of Tonkin, which prompted Vietnam to protest.[45] It can also be noted that Vietnam claimed in September, that since June 1992 nearly 20 Vietnamese ships transporting goods from Hong Kong had been seized by China. Following official Vietnamese requests China had released some of the ships but not all.[46]

Continued differences of opinion relating to the demarcation of the land border prevented the resumption of rail traffic between the border provinces of Lang Son and Guangxi. Vietnam accused China of occupying a stretch of some 300 meters of the railway, including Vietnam's pre-1979 end station.[47] However, border crossings were opened in early 1992.[48]

Talks on the border issues dominate bilateral relations: mid-September 1992 to March 1994

The border problems were discussed during a visit by one of China's Vice Foreign Ministers to Hanoi in September but no agreement was reached. However, the two sides agreed to hold talks on the land border and other territorial disputes in Beijing in October.[49] The October talks were the first to be held between experts from the two countries and they agreed that the next round of talks would concentrate on the land border.[50]

The visit by China's Prime Minister Li Peng to Vietnam in late November and early December provided the opportunity to ease tension and to address the border issues at the highest political level. In terms of co-operation between the two countries, agreements were signed on economic, scientific and cultural co-operation. China decided to grant Vietnam interest-free credit worth about US$14 million. The two sides agreed to step up co-ordinated efforts aimed at curbing smuggling along the common border. However, no significant progress was reported with respect to the conflicting claims in the South China Sea; but both parties emphasized that the differences would be settled through negotiations.[51]

Following Li Peng's visit, discussions on the territorial issues continued during the Vietnamese Defence Minister's visit to China later in December. In February 1993 experts from the two countries held their second round of border talks; in May China's Defence Minister visited Vietnam and border issues were discussed, and in August a Vietnamese Government delegation visited Beijing and the two sides reached a "general understanding and consensus" on "fundamental principles" for solving the territorial issues.[52]

More importantly, a Chinese Government delegation visited Vietnam in October, and on 19 October an agreement was signed which included basic principles for settling the territorial disputes relating to the land border and to the "dividing" of the Gulf of Tonkin. Furthermore, the two countries were to concentrate their efforts on resolving those two disputes while at the same time continuing talks on other maritime issues, i.e. in the South China Sea. They also agreed to set up joint working groups at the expert-level to deal with the land border and Gulf of Tonkin issues.[53]

Despite the differences regarding the territorial disputes, good bilateral relations were generally maintained. This was exemplified by the conclusion of an agreement on scientific and technological co-operation in April 1993.[54] A significant indication of the good relationship was the visit by Vietnam's President, Le Duc Anh, to China in November when the territorial disputes were discussed and both sides "contended" with the recent agreement on principles for resolving the "border issues". They also "asserted" the necessity to settle the "remaining issues", relating to land and sea borders, through negotiations in order to find a solution which would meet the "aspiration and interests" of both sides. The need to strengthen economic relations was stressed and the problem of smuggling along the border was discussed.[55]

In fact the large amount of smuggled goods from China was a major preoccupation for Vietnam as it had a detrimental repercussion on economic development, particularly in the north of the country. This issue was addressed at the high-level talks in November 1993. Vietnam made some unilateral moves such as imposing a tariff on various imported goods in August 1993 and taking measures to curb smuggling along the border later in 1993.[56]

During 1994 the joint working groups at the expert-level on the land border and the Gulf of Tonkin were set up and began to hold talks. The first meeting of the joint working group on the land border met in February and in March the joint working group on the Gulf of Tonkin held its first meeting.[57]

Renewed deep differences relating to the South China Sea: April–June 1994

The activities of the Crestone Energy Corporation in the South China

Sea continued to be a source of tension, and in April 1994 Vietnam launched official protests against seismological surveys carried out by Crestone in the "Tu Chinh coral reef" area.[58] On 5 May, a spokesman for Vietnam's Foreign Ministry emphasized that the Tu Chinh area "lies fully" within Vietnam's Exclusive Economic Zone (EEZ) and continental shelf, and that no area was disputed there.[59]

The tension in the area was further increased when on 10 May a spokesman for China's Foreign Ministry was reported as saying that "the Blue Dragon sea area belongs to the adjacent waters of the Nansha islands", i.e. the Spratlys. He also stated that an exploration contract signed between Vietnam and American Mobil Oil Company in the Blue Dragon oil field was "illegal".[60] The following day Vietnam's Foreign Ministry reiterated that the areas of "Tu Chinh" and "Thanh Long" were located within its EEZ and continental shelf and that Vietnam "has the sovereign right to explore and exploit natural resources in these areas". It was also emphasized that the two areas "are in no way related" to the Spratly archipelago or its adjacent waters.[61]

On 12 May, the Chinese Foreign Ministry stated that any contract signed by Vietnam with oil companies for prospecting and exploiting oil deposits in waters around the Spratly islands would infringe on China's "rights and interests". It was also stated that the "Lanlong Sea" was located within the waters of the Spratly archipelago.[62]

In an interview with *The Strait Times* (Singapore), published on 19 May, Vietnam's Prime Minister, Vo Van Kiet, was quoted as reiterating Vietnam's position and refuting China's sovereignty claims to the "Blue Dragon oilfield". Nevertheless, he said that Vietnam would try to resolve the issue by "peaceful means". He also addressed the issue of overlapping Chinese and Vietnamese sovereignty claims to the Paracel archipelago by stating that it was a separate issue from the Spratly dispute and that it was a bilateral issue. He also said that he favoured a negotiated settlement of the Paracel dispute. Finally, in response to reports about a Chinese build up of its strike capability in the area by deploying warplanes to the Paracels, the Prime Minister said that it was "unlikely" that force would be used as it would not benefit China and Vietnam "to go to war".[63]

After these Chinese and Vietnamese claims, counter-claims and rebuttals of the standpoint of the other side during the first half of May, there followed a period of about one month of relative calm during which the two sides refrained from openly publicizing their differences. This relative calm was temporarily interrupted, on 16 June, when a spokesman of the Chinese Foreign Ministry made a statement demanding "once again" that Vietnam put an end to its "acts of infringement" on China's sovereignty. He said that since mid-May Vietnam had sent exploratory vessels to "Wan'an Reef" (Vanguard bank) located in the "area" of China's "Nansha"; i.e. Spratly, sea area. He reiterated that China had "indisputable" sovereignty over the Spratly islands and their adjacent waters. He also complained that Vietnam had "repeatedly harassed" the scientific surveys and fishing activities of Chinese vessels in the area, thus "seriously" violating Chinese sovereignty and putting in "serious jeopardy" the contract between China National Offshore Oil Corporation and Crestone Energy Corporation.[64]

Vietnam's response came the next day through a statement by a spokesman of the Vietnamese Foreign Ministry. He rejected the Chinese claim that the Tu Chinh area—called "Wan'an Reef" by China—was part of the Spratly archipelago. He also said the Chinese contract with Crestone Energy Corporation in the area was in defiance of the "principles" of international law and practice. He reiterated the "undeniable fact" that Tu Chinh area was located "entirely" within Vietnam's EEZ and continental shelf.[65]

Gradually bringing the border disputes under control: late June to November 1994

In late June and early July 1994, the interaction between the countries shifted away from the deep differences relating to the South China Sea, to talks. The second round of talks of the joint working group on the land border was held, a Vietnamese army delegation visited China, and the second round of talks between the joint working group on the delineation of the Gulf of Tonkin was held.[66] Interestingly enough the talks on the Gulf of Tonkin do not seem to have been affected by the protest by the Chinese Foreign Ministry against Vietnam's seizure of Chinese fishing boats in the Gulf of Tonkin on 2 July. China requested the immediate release of the Chinese fishermen and boats and demanded that no such incidents should occur in the future.[67] In response a spokesperson of the Vietnamese Foreign Ministry stated that Chinese boats had been seized in two separate incidents and he "affirmed" that the Chinese boats had violated Vietnam's territorial waters and that the seizure of the boats was in accordance with Vietnamese and international laws. He went on to state that the Vietnamese side was still carrying out its investigation and that the boats would be dealt with in conformity with the above laws and in "line" with relations between Vietnam and China.[68]

Talks between the two countries on the territorial issues also took place in connection with international meetings such as the ASEAN Ministerial Meeting (AMM) and the inaugural meeting of the ASEAN Regional Forum (ARF) in Bangkok. The Foreign Ministers of China and Vietnam met and discussed those issues during the ARF meeting. According to a report by the Thai newspaper *The Nation*, quoting China's foreign affairs spokesman Shen Guofang, the two sides had agreed to hold talks at the level of Vice Foreign Minister to discuss joint development in areas with overlapping claims in the South China Sea. The talks also resulted in agreement on the basic principles concerning the territorial disputes. Shen was quoted as saying that "positive progress" had been made in negotiations between the two "governments" and that this had laid a solid foundation for a "proper settlement of border and territorial questions through peaceful negotiations". The Thai newspaper also quoted the Vietnamese Foreign Minister as saying that both countries had agreed to "exercise self-restraint and not do anything to make the situation deteriorate".[69]

In the series of bilateral talks on the territorial issues, the second round of government-level talks were held in August. According to *Xinhua News Agency*, the two sides reviewed the work of the joint working groups on the land border and the Gulf of Tonkin. They agreed that the territorial issues, including the Spratly issue, should be settled through negotiations and that both sides would refrain from the use or threat of force. Furthermore, the territorial disputes would not be allowed to affect the "normal" development of bilateral relations.[70]

Of interest in this context are the statements made by Deputy Foreign Minister Vu Koan in an interview published by the Japanese newspaper *Sankei Shimbun* on 22 August. He elaborated on Vietnam's standpoint over China's proposal to engage in joint development in areas of the South China Sea and said that the problem was in which area this would take place. He reiterated that the Chinese contract with an "American company", i.e. Crestone, was within Vietnam's EEZ and continental shelf and was not linked to the conflict over the Spratlys. He concluded that China's "intention" in proposing joint development was to justify a Chinese presence within Vietnamese waters under the "name" of joint development.[71]

The border talks in August were followed by a period marked by two conflicting patterns of interaction. The first pattern displayed good bilateral relations, and was marked by a visit to China by Vietnam's Deputy Prime Minister Phan Van Khai during the second half of September; by celebrations of the forty-fifth anniversary of the establishment of the People's Republic of China in late September;

the third round of talks of the joint working group on the land border in Hanoi on 22–27 October; and the visit by Jiang Zemin, Secretary-General of the Central Committee of the Chinese Communist Party (CCP) and Chinese President to Vietnam in November.[72] The second pattern displayed tension relating to the territorial disputes, and included China reiterating its "indisputable" sovereignty over the Spratly archipelago on 8 September and Vietnam responding the following day by reaffirming its sovereignty claim to the archipelago.[73] In addition, on 14 October, China protested against Vietnamese attempts at inviting foreign investors to submit tenders to develop the Gulf of Tonkin. It was stated that the Chinese Government had "declared" that foreign companies were not allowed to engage in activities "violating China's rights and interests" in the Gulf of Tonkin. Vietnam did not respond to the Chinese protest as such, but issued a statement, on 17 October, demanding that China "inform its own people to stop their chronic violations" of Vietnam's territorial waters and EEZ. It is notable that both sides also elaborated on the bilateral efforts aimed at achieving a "delimitation" of the area through negotiations.[74] Finally, on the same day, a spokesman for the Chinese Ministry of Foreign Affairs stated that China was "gravely concerned" that Vietnam was prospecting for oil together with oil companies from other countries in the "Wanan reef area of China's Nansha (Spratly) sea waters".[75] The following day, Vietnam's Foreign Ministry responded by stating that the area referred to by China was in fact the "Tu Chinh area" and was located within Vietnam's continental shelf, and thereby refuted China's claim to it. Vietnam also stated that it was carrying out "normal" activities in the area by itself and in collaboration with foreign partners.[76]

Jiang Zemin visited Vietnam from 19–22 November.[77] In the joint communiqué issued on 21 November, the achievements in strengthening bilateral relations were reviewed and the two sides pledged to "accelerate" the development of relations on a "deeper and broader scale". Emphasis was put on the importance of "stepping up" cooperation in such fields as economy and trade. In order to promote such co-operation, three agreements were signed: the first established a "Sino-Vietnamese Committee on Economic and Trade Cooperation", the second was an agreement on "Automobile Transport" and the third an agreement on "Cooperation in Guaranteeing the Quality of Import and Export Commodities and in Mutual Certification". The communiqué also addressed the bilateral border disputes and the two sides "reaffirmed" that they would "persist" in peaceful negotiations as the avenue to solve their "boundary and territorial issues". They also agreed to "strive" for an "early" settlement of the disputes relating to the land border and the Gulf of Tonkin in accordance with the agreement on basic principles reached in October 1993, while at the same time pursuing negotiations and setting up an expert group to deal with the "issue involving the seas". Furthermore, the two sides agreed that pending a settlement of the territorial disputes they would refrain from "taking actions" which would "complicate or enlarge the disputes", and would also refrain from using or threatening to use force.[78]

Stability in bilateral relations and continued talks on border issues including the South China Sea: December 1994 to March 1996

Following these high-level talks, the territorial disputes were primarily handled through peaceful negotiations for the remainder of 1994 and into 1995. This was exemplified by the third round of talks of the joint working group on the Gulf of Tonkin in December 1994. The joint working group on the land border held its fourth round of talks in January 1995.[79] Seemingly the talks on the land border were not affected by a statement from the Chinese Foreign Ministry which urged Vietnam to cease its geological surveys in the Spratly archipelago because such activities encroached on China's territorial sovereignty.[80] Vietnam responded by reiterating its own sovereignty claim to the archipelago.[81] Overall relations also do not seem to have been affected by this episode, as exemplified by the publicized clearing of the remaining land mines in Guangxi province along the border with Vietnam during the months of February and March, the fourth round of talks of the joint working group on the Gulf of Tonkin in late March, and the visit to Vietnam by a Chinese military delegation in April.[82]

In mid-May, Vietnam's Foreign Minister visited Beijing to hold talks with his Chinese counterpart and they discussed the territorial disputes as well as the overall bilateral relations. Both sides concurred on the need to settle the territorial disputes through peaceful negotiations. They also discussed ways to further strengthen bilateral relations, in particular in the field of economic co-operation, and in this spirit an agreement on taxation was signed.[83]

This visit was followed by continued talks on the territorial issues at the expert- and government-levels. In late May, the joint working group on the land border held its fifth round of talks[84] and in June the joint working group on the Gulf of Tonkin held its fifth round of talks.[85] In July, the third round of talks on the border issues at government level was held. Apart from reviewing the progress made at the expert level relating to the land border and the Gulf of Tonkin, the two sides decided to form a "joint working group on sea border" to work on the territorial issues in the South China Sea.[86] In October the expert-level talks on the land border continued with the sixth meeting of the joint working group. According to a statement of the spokeswoman of Vietnam's Foreign Ministry on 19 October, the two sides agreed on a "number of technical measures leading to the signing of a border agreement".[87]

In mid-November two important bilateral meetings took place in Hanoi; the "Sino-Vietnamese expert group on maritime issues" held its first round of talks and the "Sino-Vietnamese Commission for Economic and Commercial Cooperation" also held its first meeting. The talks within the "Commission" resulted in both sides agreeing to take measures to ensure that all bilateral agreements be observed and "realized" and that "effective" measures be taken to "intensify" the control of cross-border trade in order to "attain" a "healthy and orderly development".[88] According to the report by *Xinhua News Agency*, from the talks on the "maritime issues" the two sides exchanged views on "substantive" matters and reached consensus on "work procedures" for the settlement of the Spratly dispute through bilateral negotiations in the "future". According to this report the Chinese delegation had reiterated China's "indisputable" sovereignty over the Spratly islands and the surrounding waters, China favoured a settlement of the Spratly dispute by peaceful means in accordance with "legal principles" and international law, including the 1982 UN Convention on Law of the Sea (UNCLOS), and that China held the opinion that if the dispute could not be settled for the time being the two sides could, as a temporary measure, "put it aside" and "seek" joint development or co-operation.[89]

It was in this atmosphere of ongoing dialogue on the border issues and of deepening economic co-operation that the Secretary-General of the VCP, Do Muoi, arrived in China for a summit meeting on 26 November. In Beijing, Do Muoi held talks with his Chinese counterpart Jiang Zemin and other Chinese leaders. The talks reviewed the achievements in expanding bilateral relations since normalization of relations, and discussed ways to further strengthen relations.[90] In the joint communiqué issued on 2 December, the two sides expressed satisfaction at the development of friendly relations between the two "parties" and the two countries and agreed to "properly" resolve the "issue of territory along the borders" on the basis of international law, international "practices", and through peaceful negotiations. They also expressed "happiness" about the "obvious" progress in expanding trade and developing economic co-operation during 1995 and agreed to give "full play to the potential" of economic interaction. In this context the communiqué announced that an agreement "in principle" on railway "transportation" had been reached.[91]

In an interview with the *Voice of Vietnam* following the visit to China, Vietnam's Foreign Minister elaborated on the discussions on the border disputes and on the railway agreement. He stated that on the "basis" of the progress made in "recent" expert-level talks on the land border, China and Vietnam had agreed on "various principles to open the border rail route". He confirmed that expert-level talks would continue on the land border, Gulf of Tonkin and South China Sea. With respect to the land border he said that the two parties had agreed that in order to create favourable conditions to resolve the issue and "achieve" the "signing" of a treaty "as soon as possible", all conflicts in "border areas" should be resolved "quickly" and on the "spot".[92]

During the months of January and February 1996, bilateral relations focused on the preparations for the resumption of railway traffic. Discussions between the Chinese Ministry of Railways and the Vietnamese Ministry of Communication and Transport were held and custom procedures were announced on 31 January. Furthermore, work on the repair and upgrading of the two railway links was carried out enabling the resumption of traffic on 14 February.[93] On that occasion the Vice Foreign Ministers met in Lang Son to review the implementation of earlier bilateral agreements and to "speed" up negotiations on the territorial disputes.[94] A visit to Vietnam in January by a military delegation from the Chinese province of Guangzhou provided the opportunity to discuss such issues as the maintenance of "order" in border areas and ways of strengthening "border defence" co-operation through "dialogue".[95] These events and meetings overshadowed the seventh round of talks of the joint expert group on the land border in late January.[96]

It was in this atmosphere of good bilateral relations and ongoing dialogue on the border issues that the two Prime Ministers met in connection with the first Asia-Europe Meeting (ASEM) in Bangkok in early March. Li Peng stated that the two countries had reached "consensus" on the border issues. With reference to specific disputes, he said that negotiations on the land border had "entered the substantial stage" and that talks on "demarcating" the Gulf of Tonkin were about to be resumed. Vo Van Kiet reportedly "agreed and welcomed Li's views".[97]

Renewed tension relating to the South China Sea in April and May 1996

The dialogue over the border issues was brought to an abrupt, albeit temporary, halt during the months of April and May. In April, controversy erupted following the signing of a "business" contract between Petrovietnam and Conoco Vietnam Exploration and Production B.G., a U.S. company, for the exploration and exploitation of "oil plots 133 and 134" in the South China Sea. Vietnam insisted that the plots were located within its continental shelf and that the area was "completely" under Vietnam's sovereignty and jurisdiction.[98] China viewed the contract as an encroachment on its sovereignty and its "marine rights and interests", and also took the opportunity to reiterate its "indisputable" sovereignty over the Spratly islands. In fact the spokesman for the Chinese Foreign Ministry claimed that the "entire" area encompassed by the contract was located within the area of the "Wan'antan Bei–21 contract" between the China National Offshore Oil Corporation and Crestone Energy Corporation.[99] Despite this controversy, co-operation continued in other fields such as an agreement on bilateral co-operation in the field of meteorology signed on 18 April, and an agreement on co-operation in the field of public health, signed in connection with a week-long visit by Vietnam's Public Health Minister to China beginning on 15 April.[100]

The other source of tension relating to the territorial disputes emerged on 15 May when China issued a statement defining the baselines of its territorial sea adjacent to the Chinese mainland and to the Paracel islands. China stated that this was done in accordance with its 1992 law on the territorial sea and contiguous zone.[101] Vietnam responded through a Foreign Ministry statement which reiterated Vietnam's stand that the Chinese law of 1992, stipulating that the Paracel and Spratly archipelagos are Chinese territory, violates Vietnamese sovereignty. Furthermore, it was stated that "China's delineation of the baseline" around the Paracel archipelago was a "severe violation" of Vietnam's territorial sovereignty.[102]

Stability returns followed by expanding relations: June 1996 to February 1997

In June the two sides moved to decisively mend fences. The Eighth National Congress of the VCP held in late June gave the Chinese and Vietnamese leaderships the opportunity to display the good and close bilateral relationship between the two countries and the two ruling parties. The Chinese delegation was headed by Prime Minister Li Peng. He met with the Secretary-General of the VCP and with

Vietnam's Prime and Foreign Ministers. At the VCP Congress, he also delivered a speech that reviewed the achievements made by the VCP in developing Vietnam as well as the achievements in strengthening Sino-Vietnamese relations. Alluding to the territorial disputes, he stated that the two sides would continue their efforts aimed at reaching "solutions" to "some unresolved problems" in the spirit of "friendly consultation and seeking common ground while reserving differences".[103]

The visit by the Chinese Prime Minister and the party delegation to Vietnam was followed by the second round of talks of the joint expert group on the "sea issues" in July. Reportedly the talks were held in an atmosphere of "friendship and frankness". The Vietnamese version of the talks is that the two sides compared notes on the "sea issues" "relating" to both countries including the question of sovereignty over the Paracel and Spratly archipelagos. They agreed to continue to seek "long term and basic resolutions" on the basis of international law including the 1982 UNCLOS.[104]

Another positive move was the announcement on 20 August that the Tra Vinh-Lung Ping border gate between the Vietnamese province of Cao Bang and the Chinese province of Guangxi had been opened. The opening followed an agreement at the government-level aimed at facilitating commercial and cultural exchanges between people in the border areas. A further indication of the good relations was the visit to Vietnam in late August by the Chief of the General Staff of the Chinese People's Liberation Army during which the need to enhance and strengthen bilateral relations and co-operation between the two countries, parties and armies was stressed. Also in late August came an agreement on co-operation in broadcasting between the Voice of Vietnam and the Central People's Broadcasting Station of China.[105]

This positive development in bilateral relations continued throughout the rest of 1996 and into early 1997. With regard to the border disputes, the fourth round of talks at the government-level took place in September. The two sides reviewed the expert-level talks that had taken place relating to the territorial disputes. They also discussed how to speed up the negotiation process on the border issues and agreed on guidelines for the coming talks of the joint working groups.[106] The ninth round of talks of the joint working group on the land border was held in October.[107]

Frequent visits by government, party and military delegations took place, displaying the expanding bilateral links during that period. Among the visits, it can be noted that during the first half of November the Vietnamese Deputy Minister of Trade visited China to hold talks with his Chinese counterpart and the Minister for Foreign Trade and Economic Cooperation. The Chinese Minister said that since normalization of relations the frequent high-level visits had considerably accelerated the development of bilateral ties, in particular economic and trade relations. She also elaborated on the issue of trade imbalance and said that China "stands to strike a balance" between trade partners through development, instead of by resorting to "any negative means" and that China was willing to settle the issue together with Vietnam through consultation on an "equal basis". According to the Vietnamese Deputy Minister both sides agreed that economic and trade ties had witnessed a "smooth" improvement and they would continue to strive for improved economic and trade relations.[108] Also in November, Qiao Shi, Chairman of the Standing Committee of the National People's Congress, visited Vietnam and met with senior Vietnamese leaders. He repeatedly stressed that China was conducting a foreign policy aimed at developing friendly relations with its neighbours and that China's development would not pose a threat to other countries in the region. He also stressed that China would not become a superpower.[109] In early December, the Chinese Minister of Public Security visited Vietnam for talks with the Vietnamese Minister of the Interior, and both sides expressed their satisfaction with the development of the "multi-faceted" co-operation.[110] Another sign of the expanding bilateral relations was the re-opening of the cargo railway between the two countries on 13 December, with the first train leaving Shanghai for Da Nang port.[111]

Despite these overall positive developments, the controversy relating to oil exploration in the South China Sea re-surfaced as an issue of contention during a press conference at the Ministry of Foreign Affairs in Hanoi on 5 December. In reply to a question about Vietnam's response to the transfer of the contract originally signed by Crestone Energy Corporation to the "Bank and Oil and Gas Group", the spokesperson replied that Vietnam had repeatedly "confirmed" that "Tu Chinh" area in the South China Sea was "conclusively" within Vietnam's continental shelf. He stated that the "move" was a violation of Vietnam's sovereignty and that Vietnam "regards" the contract as invalid "no matter to whom it was transferred".[112]

On 19 December at another press conference, the spokesperson of Vietnam's Foreign Ministry elaborated on the development of relations between China and Vietnam by highlighting the visits to Vietnam by the Chinese Prime Minister and the Chairman of the National People's Congress during 1996. He also said that bilateral trade in 1996 was estimated at US$1 billion. With regard to the territorial disputes, he said that bilateral talks had "gained positive results". No reference was made to the earlier controversy over the transfer of the Crestone contract.[113]

The month of January 1997 displayed similarities to the pattern of interaction in bilateral relations in December 1996, with mutual visits and an agreement on "cross-border banking" signed between the "Vietnam agriculture bank" and its Chinese counterpart.[114] The controversy relating to oil exploration in the South China Sea was brought up again at a press conference of Vietnam's Ministry of Foreign Affairs on 23 January. In response to a report that the "Baken Oscar company" had acquired all the shares of the Crestone Energy Corporation in December 1996, the spokesperson reiterated Vietnam's stand on the "Tu Chinh" area and said that Vietnam "considers" the agreement between Crestone and the Chinese Offshore Oil Corporation "completely illegal and void", no matter who the contract was transferred to.[115]

From late January to early March, bilateral relations remained good with the eighth round of talks of the joint working group on the Gulf of Tonkin held in late January. In late February and early March, a military delegation visited Vietnam and held talks with, among others, Vietnam's Defence Minister, and in March a VCP delegation visited China at the invitation of the Central Committee of the CCP.[116]

Chinese oil-drilling causes renewed tension in the South China Sea: March to mid-April 1997

Apart from the brief controversies in December 1996 and January 1997 relating to the transfer of the contract of Crestone Energy Corporation, all seemed to be evolving well in bilateral relations. Therefore, it came as a surprise when *Voice of Vietnam* announced on 15 March that China had sent an oil rig (Kanta[n]–03) together with two "pilot ships Nos 206 and 208" to carry out exploratory oil drilling in areas lying within Vietnam's continental shelf between the co-ordinates 17° 13'45'N north latitude and 108° 39'30'E longitude. The report outlined Vietnam's response to the Chinese action and highlighted Vietnamese demands that China "immediately" halt its activities and withdraw the oil platform and "prohibit" similar activities in the future, but thus far it had not "brought" about any response from China.[117]

The first official Chinese reaction came on 18 March when a spokesman of the Ministry of Foreign Affairs said that China's "normal operation" within its EEZ and continental shelf was "indisputable". He stated that oil exploration was carried out in the northern part of the South China sea "within" the EEZ and continental shelf zone "claimed" by China.[118]

On 20 March, the Deputy Head of the Information and Press Commission at Vietnam's Foreign Ministry replied to questions by foreign journalists on the controversy relating to Chinese oil exploration in the South China Sea. He said that the area in which the Chinese oil rig was operating was "totally" within Vietnam's EEZ and "territorial shelf". He continued by stating that Vietnam had conducted seismic surveys in the area since 1983 and that at the appropriate time, it would engage in oil exploration of its own or set up joint ventures with foreign partners. He stated that Vietnam was protecting its sovereignty and sovereign rights while at the same time pursuing a consistent policy of resolving "all" disputes "through" diplomatic channels, and that this approach had been applied in the current situation.[119]

On 27 March a spokesman for China's Foreign Ministry elaborated on the controversy relating to the oil exploration at a "regular" news conference. He stated that China "holds the rights" over the EEZ and continental shelf zones, in which its "drilling ship" operated, in accordance with international "laws" including the 1982 UNCLOS. He then said that it was "beyond reproach" that the ship carried out "normal" exploration in the zones "claimed" by China. Finally, he shifted his attention to the handling of the controversy by saying that China "cherishes" its "friendship" and co-operation with Vietnam and "is ready to hold friendly consultations" in order to "properly solve certain problems" in bilateral relations.[120]

Eventually talks were held in Beijing on 9 and 10 April. According to a report by the *Vietnam News Agency*, official Vietnamese sources reported that the talks did not result in any "bilateral solution" of the dispute over the operation of the Chinese oil rig within Vietnam's continental shelf. The report claimed that the expert-level talks were held at Vietnam's "request".[121] Interestingly enough, on 9 April, a Vietnamese expert was quoted, in a report by the *Voice of Vietnam*, as saying that since 1 April the Chinese oil rig and its "tugboats" had been withdrawn from Vietnam's EEZ and continental shelf. Thus, the Chinese action causing the dispute had ceased and Vietnam's demand for a withdrawal had been satisfied.[122]

Despite the controversy over Chinese oil drilling activities, mutual visits by delegations from the two countries continued throughout the month of March and into April. For example, the Chinese State Councillor visited Vietnam on 17–21 March, and met with Vietnam's Prime and Foreign Ministers. In early April, Vietnam's Interior

Minister led a VCP delegation on a visit to China and met with Jiang Zemin. Also during the first half of April a Vietnamese military delegation visited China for talks with, among others, China's Defence Minister. According to official reports the dispute relating to the oil drilling was not discussed during these visits; instead references were made to the good and expanding relations.[123]

Stable bilateral relations: mid-April 1997 to mid-January 1998

In mid-April, China and Vietnam reverted to handling the territorial issues through negotiations. The third round of political consultations between senior officials from the Association of Southeast Asian Nations (ASEAN) and China, held in Anhui Province, China, on 17 and 18 April, gave the Deputy Foreign Ministers of Vietnam and China the opportunity to discuss bilateral relations and more specifically the territorial disputes. According to *Vietnam News Agency*, both sides agreed to "promote" talks in order to "solve" the land border issue, to "demarcate" the Gulf of Tonkin and to pursue the talks on "issues of territorial water".[124]

The talks at the expert level on the territorial disputes continued with the third meeting of the joint working group on the "sea issues" held in Hanoi on 22–25 April. The talks focused on the "scope and content" of negotiations and on the "preliminary opinions" relating to the possibility for co-operation in "certain" areas.[125] From 7–12 May, the tenth round of expert-level talks on the land border was held.[126]

From mid-April overall co-operation was expanded and visits reported. On 19 April the *Voice of Vietnam* announced that Vietnamese officials had discussed joint border control with their Chinese counterparts.[127] In another report by the *Voice of Vietnam* on 12 May, it was announced that the Chinese Ministry of Foreign Affairs had ratified the opening for traffic of the sea route extending from Beihai in China to Hon Gai and Haiphong in Vietnam.[128] In mid-May a delegation of the Vietnam Fatherland Front (VFF) visited China, and in early June the General-Director of the Vietnam News Agency also visited China and met with China's President Jiang Zemin and the President of Xinhua News Agency.[129] Also in early June, a delegation from the Chinese Ministry of Communication led by Vice Minister Hong Shanxiang visited Vietnam. During the visit, a protocol on the implementation of an agreement on road transport between the two countries was signed on 3 June. The protocol stipulates "concrete" provisions on passenger and luggage transportation through the border gates along the land border.[130] The links between the armed forces of the two countries were further reinforced through two visits to China by Vietnamese army delegations on 10–17 June and on 21–28 October.[131]

The most important event in bilateral relations in 1997 was the high-level summit held in mid-July. The Secretary-General of the VCP, Do Muoi, led a delegation to China on 14–18 July. During the visit Do Muoi held talks with his Chinese Counterpart Jiang Zemin, with Prime Minister Li Peng and with other Chinese leaders.[132] The talks reviewed the progress made in terms of overall co-operation between the two countries. Jiang Zemin noted that bilateral economic relations had developed and that the "sphere" of bilateral co-operation continued to expand. He also noted that the friendly and co-operative relations provided "favourable" conditions for solving "certain remaining historical matters".[133] Do Muoi stressed that Vietnam paid great attention to its relations with China and that developing these relations was an important part of Vietnam's foreign policy. He expressed hope that the leaders of the two countries would accelerate the co-operation in various fields. He also expressed the view that the "negotiation process" should be accelerated to resolve "remaining issues" in bilateral relations.[134] It was also reported that the two Secretary-Generals had agreed on the need to speed up the negotiations on territorial disputes and to make efforts to settle the land border and Tonkin Gulf disputes before the turn of the century and to promote negotiations on disputes relating to "territorial water and islands".[135] The territorial disputes between the countries were given particular attention during discussions between the foreign ministers of the two countries in connection with the summit. Both ministers stressed the readiness of their respective country to speed up negotiations and consultations on the land border and Tonkin Gulf issues in order to resolve them at an early date.[136]

Discussions between Do Muoi and Prime Minister Li Peng focused on co-operation between the two governments and particular attention was devoted to economic co-operation. Both sides concurred on the need to expand and upgrade bilateral economic co-operation and relations. In this context, Li Peng stated that China would continue to offer Vietnam a limited amount of "free aid".[137] Discussion on steps to further economic and trade ties were also held between Vice Prime Ministers Wu Bangguo and Phan Van Khai in connection with the summit.[138]

Following the high-level summit, Vietnam's Foreign Minister Nguyen Manh Cam elaborated on the agreements reached in an interview with the daily *Nhan Dan*. In terms of economic co-operation he stated that two-way trade was valued at US$1 billion in 1996, thus making China Vietnam's sixth largest trading partner. Furthermore, China had invested more than US$70 million in forty-one projects.[139] During the summit, a long-term co-operation plan was discussed. This included upgrading and expanding Chinese-built factories in Vietnam, in particular the Thai Nguyen Iron and Steel Complex and the Bac Giang Nitrogenous Fertilizer Plant. In terms of commerce the two sides would strive to further strengthen official trade through the control of cross-border trade and by co-ordinating efforts aimed at curbing the smuggling of goods and combating drug trafficking.[140]

The Vietnamese Foreign minister provided detailed information on the border disputes. First, in order to create favourable conditions for talks on the land border, Tonkin Gulf and "sea borders" issues, both sides were in agreement, since 1991, to maintain stability, to exercise self-restraint by not taking actions that might cause the situation to deteriorate, and not to use or threaten to use force. Second, both agreed to settle the "issues relating to boundaries" in the South China Sea and the Tonkin Gulf on the basis of inter-national law, in particular the 1982 UNCLOS. Third, during the high-level summit the two Secretary-Generals agreed to speed up negotiations on the land border and Tonkin Gulf issues in order to reach agreements on the land and sea boundaries by the turn of century and to promote further negotiations on the disputes relating to "territorial water and islands" in the spirit of "mutual respect and concession" with the aim of reaching a "fundamental and lasting solution acceptable to all relevant sides".[141]

Parallel to the high-level summit in Beijing, the joint working group on the Tonkin Gulf met in Hanoi on 16–18 July for its ninth session of talks. The two sides reportedly reached a consensus that discussion had entered into "real stage". They discussed "at length" the application of international law in "consideration" of the natural conditions of the Tonkin Gulf in order to reach a fair and mutually acceptable solution.[142]

On 13–15 August, the fifth round of government-level negotiations on the territorial disputes was held in Beijing. The two sides reviewed the expert-level talks on the land border, Tonkin Gulf and the "sea issues" since September 1996. They discussed "concrete" measures to speed up the negotiation process in order to implement the "consensus" reached by the leaders to sign agreements on the land border and Tonkin Gulf issue by the year 2000. The two sides also agreed to continue with negotiations on the "East Sea issues", i.e. the South China Sea issues, and they were "unanimous" on a number of "measures" to maintain stability during negotiations.[143]

Economic co-operation remained a high-priority issue in Sino-Vietnamese relations as exemplified by the visit to Vietnam of the Chinese Vice Prime Minister in charge of economic affairs, Wu Bangguo, on 23–26 October. During his visit he held talks with his Vietnamese counterpart, with the Secretary-General of the VCP Do Muoi, with Vietnam's President Tran Duc Luong and with Prime Minister Phan Van Khai. During the talks between Wu and his Vietnamese counterpart, both sides expressed satisfaction with the expanding commercial links and they discussed ways in which to make such links more balanced. Two loan agreements were signed. The first related to a Chinese loan to Vietnam of US$23.75 million to upgrade several industrial plants, and the second related to a Chinese loan of US$170 million to refurbish the Thai Nguyen Iron and Steel Complex. Furthermore, China undertook to provide Vietnam with non-refundable aid totalling US$10 million to help meet the interest payment for the second loan.[144] Agreements were also reached on expanded co-operation in terms of transfer of technology in the fields of agriculture and of civil aviation. Furthermore, co-operation at the provincial level would be expanded between the Chinese provinces of Guangxi and Yunnan and Vietnamese border provinces. Finally, it was agreed to initiate negotiations aimed at reaching an agreement on the regulation of cross-border economic activities.[145] In a subsequent statement by the Chinese Ambassador to Vietnam, some of the problems that would need to be addressed and resolved within the framework of such an agreement were identified, namely the dubious quality of goods, smuggling, and drug trafficking. He also predicted that an agreement would be reached during the first half of 1998.[146]

In the context of the situation along the land border, it can be noted that beginning in late October 1997, reports have publicized the preparation and launching of a new campaign to remove land mines along the common border. According to a report from Hong Kong in late October, China is to finance the mine clearing operation. According to a Chinese report, the operation was launched on the Chinese side on 28 November 1997.[147]

In December, Li Ruihuan, a member of the Standing Committee member of the Political Bureau of the CCP Central Committee, paid a well-publicized visit to Vietnam. He met with President Tran Duc Luong, Prime Minister Phan Van Kai, and with VCP Secretary-General Do Muoi. Discussions touched upon the multifaceted aspects of bilateral relations including the territorial disputes and economic relations. The two sides also reviewed the developments in the two countries during 1997. In his capacity as Chairman of the

National Committee of the Chinese People's Political Consultative Conference (CPPCC) Li met with the President of the VFF, Le Quang Dao. On this occasion, Li stated that the CPPCC would further promote ties and exchanges with the VFF.[148]

Further positive signals in bilateral relations can be noted from late December and during the first half of January 1998. First, on 29 December President Jiang Zemin congratulated Le Kha Pieu on his election as Secretary-General of the VCP and on 14 January Le Kha Pieu met the Chinese Ambassador to Vietnam and expressed his satisfaction with the developments in the relations between the two countries.[149]

Interplay between bilateral co-operation and the sporadic emergence of tension relating to the border issues: late January to October 1998

In the midst of all these signs of good bilateral relations, serious tension over an area along the land border was suddenly reported in an interview by the *Vietnam News Agency* with Ngo Dinh Tho, Deputy-Chairman of the People's Committee of Quang Ninh Province, aired in a broadcast by the *Voice of Vietnam* on 22 January. According to the Vietnamese official, China had in May 1997 built a one-kilometre long stone wall in a river which is shared by Dong Mo in the district of Binh Lieu in Quang Ninh Province on the Vietnamese side, and the district of Fangcheng in Guangxi Province on the Chinese side. This stone wall extended some 6 to 8 metres from the bank at the Dongzhong border post. According to the Vietnamese, the construction was a "severe violation" of the "provisional agreement concerning border affairs" from November 1991. Despite Vietnamese attempts through contacts at district-, provincial- and government-levels to stop the construction of the wall and then to bring about the removal of the wall, the Chinese side had not yielded to the demands. The wall caused detrimental effects during the rainy season: the irrigation system on the Vietnamese side was destroyed, flash flooding occurred causing damage, and serious land erosion was noted. In response, Vietnam built a stone wall in late September to prevent further erosion and in order to rebuild the irrigation system. In so doing the Vietnamese "strictly" observed the 1991 agreement by informing the Chinese beforehand about their purpose and action. Despite this, on 11 December 1997 the Chinese began to fill up the border river and by 22 January the following year, nearly two hectares had been filled, thus encroaching upon Vietnamese territory. Interestingly enough, the Vietnamese claimed that the border is clearly defined in the area so these events did not take place in a disputed area.[150]

The Chinese response came on 24 January when Zhu Bangzao, spokesman for the Ministry of Foreign Affairs, commented on the Vietnamese version of the events. He stated that the "truth of the matter" was that since August 1997, the Vietnamese had been building an embankment and increased the height and consolidated a check dam in the area and by so doing artificially changed the alignment of the boundary river. These actions had "seriously" damaged the "interests" of the Chinese side. This had compelled the Chinese to build a bank to protect farmland and to avoid land erosion. When the bank was built, the "interests" of the Vietnamese side were taken into "full" consideration.[151]

The controversy was discussed during the eleventh round of talks of the joint working group on the land border, held in Hanoi from 12–22 January. It was not reported if any agreement was reached on the matter but, reportedly, the two sides "frankly exchanged views" on the matter. The two sides also "reviewed" the aerial surveys over the border for mapping purposes, they exchanged views on the draft agreement on the land border, and "discussed various conflicts" in the border region.[152]

Following this public display of the dispute in the border area, both China and Vietnam reverted to reporting on more positive aspects and activities such as mine clearance activities, increasing economic interaction along the land border, upgrading of roads, and the establishment of a coach service between the provinces of Lao Cai and Yunnan.[153]

Expert-level talks on the Tonkin Gulf continued with the tenth meeting of the Joint Working Group held in Beijing on 24–30 March. Reportedly the meeting took place in an atmosphere of "friendship and frankness". The two sides "appraised" the progress made during the previous year and exchanged views on issues related to border demarcation in the Tonkin Gulf. Both sides concurred on the need to accelerate the talks with the goal of reaching an agreement on how to resolve the demarcation of the Tonkin Gulf by the year 2000.[154] Expert-level talks have also continued on the land border issue with the twelfth round of talks of the Joint Working Group held in Beijing on 26 May to 5 June. The two sides reportedly agreed to speed up the negotiation process and to shorten the intervals between the talks with the aim of meeting the goal of signing an agreement on the land border by the year 2000.[155] From 8–10 July, the fourth round of talks between "maritime experts" from the two countries was held in Beijing. The two sides reportedly discussed the scope and agenda of the talks and the possibilities for bilateral co-operation on maritime issues.[156]

Good bilateral relations continued to prevail as exemplified by the talks between Vietnam's Prime Minister Phan Van Khai and his Chinese counterpart Zhu Rongji and between Vietnam's Foreign Minister Nguyen Manh Cam and his Chinese counterpart Tang Jiaxuan in connection with the second ASEM in London in early April 1998.[157] Another sign of the good bilateral relations was the week-long visit by the Vietnamese Defence Minister to China in early June. He met not only with his Chinese counterpart but also with the Chinese President and with the Chief of Staff of the People's Liberation Army.[158]

However, in April, Vietnam officially complained on three occasions about Chinese plans to use the Paracel islands for tourism and reiterated Vietnam's sovereignty claims to both the Paracel and the Spratly archipelagos.[159] In early May Vietnam publicized its release of 53 crewmen from four Chinese fishing vessels which had been seized by Vietnamese naval forces off the coast of Quang Binh Province in late March 1998.[160] Finally, on 20 May a spokesperson from the Vietnamese Ministry of Foreign Affairs stated that the Chinese ship *Discovery 08* was operating in the Spratly archipelago and even "deeply" into Vietnam's continental shelf, and that this was a violation of Vietnam's territorial sovereignty. The spokesperson also said that Vietnam had made no attempt to seize the Chinese ship but that Vietnam had asked the Chinese to withdraw *Discovery 08* from Vietnam's "waters".[161] The Chinese response came on 21 May when Zhu Bangzao, spokesman for the Ministry of Foreign Affairs, in reply to a question, stated that China had "indisputable" sovereignty over the Spratly islands and their surrounding waters. He went on to say that the presence of Chinese ships in these waters "for normal" activities was within China's sovereign rights.[162] Interestingly enough, on the following day the spokesperson from the Vietnamese Foreign Ministry, in response to a question relating to the activities of "China's exploration ship No 8", said that the ship and two armed fishing vessels had withdrawn from Vietnam's "sea area". The Vietnamese approach to the problem was said to have been in line with the "persistent" policy of settling disputes through diplomatic negotiations. In this spirit Vietnam had "patiently" maintained contact with China on the operation of the Chinese ships in Vietnam's "sea territory".[163] Furthermore, on 17 July the Vietnamese Foreign Ministry stated that Vietnam was very concerned about the new Chinese law on "privileged economic zones and continental shelf".[164]

There were signs of more tension over the border disputes in

September. First, on 4 September the spokesperson of Vietnam's Foreign Ministry stated that Vietnam has "irrefutable" sovereignty over the Paracel and Spratly archipelagos. This was in response to newspapers reports that China was conducting scientific surveys in the Spratly archipelago and "its adjacent zone", which according to the Vietnamese lay "deep in Vietnam's continental shelf in the "Tu Chinh area". The spokesperson reiterated the Vietnamese stand on some issues. First, that "Tu Chinh area" is within Vietnam's EEZ and continental shelf and that the area "has no connection" with the Spratly archipelago. Second, that Vietnam had "repeatedly declared" that it considers the contact signed by the Chinese with the "Crestone company of the US" illegal and demands its annulment. Finally, the activities of China and the "US company" to prospect oil in the "Tu Chinh area" were said to "clearly violate" Vietnam's sovereignty.[165] China's response came on 8 September when Zhu Bangzao, spokesman of China's Foreign Ministry, stated that China had made "serious representations" to Vietnam "strongly demanding" that it withdraw from two submerged reefs that it had "unlawfully occupied". The two submerged reefs were referred to as "Aonan" and "Jindun", located to the southeast of "Nanhuitan" in the Spratly archipelago. China also demanded that Vietnam dismantle all "facilities" which had been "illegally" erected and that the Vietnamese side "guarantee" that no such "acts of occupation" would occur again. The spokesman also reiterated that China had "indisputable" sovereignty over the Spratly archipelago and its adjacent waters.[166] On the next day the Vietnamese responded to the Chinese accusation by reiterating Vietnam's sovereignty claim over the Paracel and Spratly archipelagos. It was also stated that the two "economic-scientific-technological service stations for the Vietnamese fishery" were civilian facilities and that they were located on the "Ba Ke submerged reef area" within Vietnam's continental shelf. Furthermore, it was clarified that the submerged reef "does not belong" to the Spratly archipelago. Finally, the Vietnamese stated that the operations carried out were "normal civil" within the country's sovereignty and in accordance with international laws, in particular the 1982 UNCLOS.[167]

Following this public display of tension relating to activities in the South China Sea the two sides reverted back to more co-operative interaction. First, during 17–22 September, a delegation from the CCP led by Wei Jianxing, member of the Political Bureau of the Standing Committee of the CCP Central Committee, made a well-publicized visit to Vietnam. The delegation was received by VCP Secretary-General Le Kha Pieu, the Vietnamese Prime Minister, and the former VCP Secretary-General Do Muoi. In these meetings Wei told his Vietnamese hosts that China wanted to work with Vietnam towards a higher level of co-operation in the fields of economics and trade. He also said that the "constant" exchange of visits by party and state leaders of the two countries played an "irreplaceable" role in friendly bilateral co-operation. The Vietnamese leaders stressed that to develop relations and co-operation with China is of great importance to Vietnam.[168] Second, on 25 and 26 September the sixth round of talks at the government-level was held in Hanoi. A report by *Xinhua News Agency* provided little information about the talks themselves and instead focused on statements made following a meeting, held after the talks, between a Vietnamese Deputy Prime Minister and the head of the Chinese delegation. The Vietnamese Deputy Minister expressed his country's satisfaction with the progress of border negotiations with China. Furthermore, Vietnam "appreciated" the co-operative attitudes by both sides during the government-level talks. The head of the Chinese delegation said that China wanted to co-operate further with Vietnam to accelerate the negotiation process in order to achieve the target set by the leaders of the two countries to "conclude" border agreements before the year 2000.[169]

This was followed by a high-level visit to China by Vietnam's Prime Minister Phan Van Khai during 19–23 October 1998.[170] In the talks between the Vietnamese Prime Minister and his Chinese counterpart Zhu Rongji, both sides spoke "highly" of bilateral economic co-operation and of trade relations, and they discussed ways to further promote such interaction. In the talks Zhu noted the "positive progress" in the negotiations on border "issues". He also noted the 1997 agreement between the two Secretaries-General that the two countries "should settle boundary issues and demarcation of the Beibu [Tonkin] Gulf by year 2000". Reportedly the Vietnamese Prime Minister "echoed" his counterpart's remark. The two ministers agreed to "speed up" negotiations to settle the land border and Tonkin Gulf disputes within the "set" period of time. Following the talks the two Prime Ministers attended a signing ceremony for three documents: a treaty of mutual judicial assistance, an agreement on border trade, and a "consular treaty".[171] In talks between China's President and Secretary-General of the CCP Jiang Zemin and the Vietnamese Premier, both sides noted the progress made in bilateral relations during the 1990s. Jiang elaborated on the border issues and expressed his "delight over the important progress" made in the government-level negotiations during the "last year and more". He also stressed the importance of resolving the border issues at an "early date". Also Li Peng, Chairman of the Standing Committee of the Chinese National People's Congress, met with Prime Minister Khai. During the meeting Li expressed his hope that China and Vietnam make "a greater effort" to reach agreements on the "demarcation of borders" this century. During both these meetings the Vietnamese Prime Minister also stressed the need and importance of resolving the border issues.[172]

Issues of contention in Sino-Vietnamese relations

Issues of contention in the late 1970s[173]

Three major issues contributed to the deterioration of relations between China and Vietnam from 1975 to the Chinese attack on Vietnam in February–March 1979: different perceptions of the USSR, relations with and influence in Cambodia, and the status of ethnic Chinese in Vietnam. Each of these three issues will now be examined in more detail, and will be followed by a discussion about the relative importance of the territorial disputes, ideology and internal change.

The Soviet factor
The *"Soviet factor"* was a source of controversy prior to 1975 and it was predictable that it would feature prominently in Sino-Vietnamese relations in the post 1975 period as well. Earlier research has shown the importance of the Soviet factor in explaining China's policy towards Vietnam during that period.[174] China's ambition seems to have been to curtail the influence of the USSR in Vietnam. In pursuit of this goal it was logical for China to encourage Vietnamese tendencies to distance itself from the USSR and to diversify its foreign relations or, in the contrary case, to show displeasure at indications of Vietnam strengthening its links with the USSR. However, Vietnam did not intend to sever its relations with the USSR, or to conduct a foreign policy leading to a one-sided dependence upon the USSR, as illustrated by Vietnam's attempts at diversifying its foreign economic relations in 1976 and 1977 by courting countries in western Europe. Other indications that Vietnam was trying to avoid a one-sided dependence on the USSR was that Vietnam did not join the CMEA until after China had terminated most of its economic assistance, and did not sign the Treaty of Friendship and Cooperation with the USSR until hopes of normalization with the United States were dashed.[175]

Did China encourage Vietnam's attempts at diversifying its foreign relations? China did express support for such attempts in 1976 and 1977 but did not try to counter-balance the Soviet influence in

Vietnam, for instance by offering increased economic assistance between 1975 and 1977, although Vietnam requested such help from China. On the contrary, China decreased its economic assistance,[176] possibly convinced that Vietnam would not, in any case, embark upon an anti-Soviet foreign policy. China might have been more willing to increase its economic assistance if Vietnam had shown some inclination to clearly distance itself from the USSR, but this is by no means certain. In this context it is worth recalling that one of the reasons given for not providing Vietnam with new loans in February 1977 was that China needed the money for internal use. This could be seen as an indication that China was facing financial difficulties that prevented it from giving Vietnam more assistance.[177] However, it can also be interpreted as Chinese displeasure with Vietnam.[178] Given the outcome, China's policy towards Vietnam could even be perceived as contributing towards pushing Vietnam into a closer relationship with the USSR. This was totally at variance with China's overall goal to curtail the Soviet influence. However, the Soviet factor was not the only issue of contention in Sino-Vietnamese relations. Thus, other factors may have contributed to the seemingly counter-productive Chinese policy towards Vietnam.

The Cambodia factor
The differences concerning relations with Cambodia and Laos could be seen as an attempt by both China and Vietnam to counter the influence of the other party in these two countries. In other words, Sino-Vietnamese competition for influence was the cause of the deterioration of their relations. In earlier research on the dynamics of the Sino-Vietnamese relationship, it was argued that the competition for influence, primarily over Cambodia, was the major reason behind the deterioration of bilateral relations in the post 1975 period.[179] This line of explanation is based on the assumption that whatever the state of relations between China and Vietnam, each country would resent a strong influence by the other party in Cambodia and Laos. From a geo-strategic perspective these two countries are of paramount importance to Vietnam's security, while they are of less importance to China. However, it is highly unlikely that China and Vietnam would have perceived the other party's influence in Cambodia and Laos so negatively if their bilateral relations had not already been tense over other issues.

Relations between Vietnam and Laos were very good in the post 1975 period and evolved into a formal alliance through the signing of a Treaty of Friendship and Cooperation in July 1977,[180] whereas relations between Vietnam and Cambodia were manageable at the diplomatic level up to the end of 1977 but deteriorated sharply during 1978, leading to Vietnam's military intervention in late December 1978. China might not have been pleased with Vietnam's influence in Laos but the situation seems to have been acceptable as long as China's relations with Vietnam were still manageable. The relations between Cambodia and Vietnam caused problems for China as early as May and June 1975 when military clashes occurred between Cambodia and Vietnam. At this time China's interest was to promote good neighbourly relations and therefore China tried to mediate. This mediation produced fairly good results since a relative calm prevailed along the Cambodia-Vietnam border from mid-1975 to the end of 1976.[181]

The second period of problems began in 1977 when military clashes between Cambodia and Vietnam gradually escalated and led to the break in diplomatic relations at the end of 1977 and continued warfare in 1978. China's initial response was to renew its mediation efforts but during 1978 China gradually shifted to a policy of supporting Cambodia.[182] How can this change in Chinese policy be explained? One reason was that China's relations with Cambodia were better than its relations with Vietnam. China could be seen as supporting a friendly country, or could be siding with Cambodia because of its own deteriorating relations with Vietnam. Thus, it can be argued that China would not have backed Cambodia if Sino-Vietnamese relations had been friendly. In other words, Vietnam's policy towards Cambodia was tolerable to China only as long as Sino-Vietnamese relations were good. The Soviet factor may also have come into play, as noted above, since China's shift in policy towards the Cambodian-Vietnamese conflict could have been influenced by a perception that co-operation was expanding between the USSR and Vietnam, and Vietnam's policy towards Cambodia was perceived as facilitating and expanding Soviet influence in the region. Thus, China had to side with Cambodia to curtail the expansion of Soviet influence.[183]

Vietnam's policy towards Cambodia in the post 1975 period was initially characterized by efforts aimed at establishing close bilateral relations, ideally as close as the relations between Vietnam and Laos. Another phase began once Cambodia had broken off the diplomatic relations and the military conflict had been publicly disclosed. In response, Vietnam changed its policy and severely criticized the foreign and domestic policies of the Cambodian Government and gave support to opposition groups. Vietnam gradually came to view Cambodia's policy as encouraged, and later orchestrated, by China. From a security viewpoint Vietnam perceived that it was facing a two-front struggle against a Chinese-led threat, with one front in the north bordering China and the other in the south-west bordering Cambodia. Eventually, Vietnam launched a military intervention and overthrew the Cambodian Government.[184]

It may be debated to what extent the relations between Cambodia and Vietnam *per se* led to the deterioration of Sino-Vietnamese relations during the first half of 1978. It is more evident that, as relations between China and Vietnam had already deteriorated by the time of Vietnam's military intervention in Cambodia in late December 1978, this intervention can be directly linked to China's military attack on Vietnam in February–March 1979. Although strategic alliances had been formed between the USSR and Vietnam and between China and the United States, respectively, in 1978 this evolution had not brought about a large-scale Chinese military action against Vietnam. Vietnam's intervention in Cambodia can be seen as providing China with the pretext to take military action against Vietnam or it can be seen as compelling China to take action. However, China officially stated that the action was a self-defence measure in response to Vietnam's military provocations.[185]

The ethnic Chinese factor
The third issue in Sino-Vietnamese relations to be discussed in this context is the dispute over the ethnic Chinese in Vietnam. The ethnic Chinese factor was the factor which brought the conflict out in the open and decisively led to the breakdown in bilateral relations. However, it can be argued that the conflict over the ethnic Chinese was aggravated by the differences related to other issues.

If attention is first focused on the ethnic Chinese factor as such, i.e. the situation in which the ethnic Chinese were living in Vietnam, and second, on China's and Vietnam's perceptions of the other party's behaviour, the following observations can be made. The situation in which the ethnic Chinese in Vietnam were living underwent dramatic changes in 1978 with sweeping economic reforms involving the abolition of private trade and a currency reform. These economic measures affected the Chinese to a large extent since they were predominant in the economic life of the former RVN and this led to an increase in the number of Chinese people leaving Vietnam. In northern Vietnam, many ethnic Chinese were living in the regions bordering China and most of them left for China in the spring and summer of 1978 amidst rising tension and rumours about an imminent war. Other factors such as the question of citizenship and the economic reforms affecting the relatively small private sector of northern Vietnam contributed to increase the number of departures but did not trigger the exodus.[186]

From China's viewpoint, the failure to get the Vietnamese to accommodate its demands in general and to get any Vietnamese concessions in the two rounds of negotiations on the issue of the ethnic Chinese must have been perceived as Vietnamese intransigence. The return of the empty Chinese ships that were sent to repatriate "persecuted Chinese residents" in late July 1978 was tantamount to a loss of face for the Chinese authorities. To add to China's frustration it had to endure the burden of taking care of the 260,000 people (of whom 230,000 were ethnic Chinese) who fled to China during 1978 and 1979. In short, the unfolding of events relating to the ethnic Chinese factor shows that China was not in a position to make Vietnam comply with any of its demands on the issue, a state of affairs which was unacceptable to China.[187]

From Vietnam's viewpoint the measures undertaken in the economic field in 1978 were necessary for the transformation of the country to a socialist society and these measures were not directed at any specific ethnic group. Any attempt by China to raise the issue of Vietnam's treatment of the ethnic Chinese was regarded as unwarranted interference in Vietnam's internal affairs. There was also Vietnamese suspicion regarding China's intentions *vis-à-vis* the ethnic Chinese. The deterioration of Sino-Vietnamese relations over the ethnic Chinese also prompted Vietnam to gradually apply more discriminatory policies towards the remaining ethnic Chinese, particularly so in the wake of China's attack on Vietnam in early 1979.[188]

There can be no doubt that Vietnam's tactics during the dispute over the ethnic Chinese were caused by suspicions about China's intentions. Likewise, China's course of action was motivated by Vietnam's behaviour but this was not necessarily the only factor determining China's policy. The re-activation of China's policy towards the Overseas Chinese, beginning in late 1977, meant that China was ready to take a greater interest in the treatment of Chinese minorities in other countries. Research on China's response to the treatment of Chinese communities in the Southeast Asian region indicates that China has a tendency to react strongly to the treatment of the ethnic Chinese in a country when there is an overall deterioration of bilateral relations. On the other hand, when bilateral relations are good, China is not likely to jeopardize these relations by reacting to the treatment of the ethnic Chinese.[189] Yet another factor could have been China's perception of the role played by the USSR. China might have perceived Vietnam's treatment of the ethnic

Chinese and its refusal to accommodate China's demands as evidence of Soviet influence. From China's perspective, the USSR encouraged Vietnam's "persecution" of the ethnic Chinese and its refusal to bow to China's demands.[190]

Thus, China's behaviour in the dispute over the ethnic Chinese could have been influenced by a perceived Soviet instigation of Vietnam. However, there is no evidence to support the view that Vietnam would have been more amenable to China's demands if Soviet-Vietnamese relations had been bad. Vietnam's behaviour was determined by its perception of China as a growing threat. Only in a situation with good Sino-Vietnamese relations would it have been possible to contain the conflict over the ethnic Chinese.

It should be noted that in the context of the large-scale outward migration from Vietnam in the late 1970s, what became known as the "boat people" crisis, the ethnic Chinese made up an estimated 60 per cent to 70 per cent of the refugees up to mid-1979.

The territorial disputes
The territorial disputes in the South China Sea between China and Vietnam were purely bilateral issues and were bound to erupt in the post 1975 period with a unified Vietnam asserting its national interests in that area. China may not have expected Vietnam to claim sovereignty over the Paracel and Spratly archipelagos since, in the pre 1975 period, only the RVN had upheld Vietnamese claims. After 1975, attempts were made at negotiating the delimitation of the territorial waters in the Tonkin Gulf but no agreement was reached.[191] The disputes in the South China Sea and in the Tonkin Gulf contributed to the deterioration of bilateral relations by adding yet another issue to the growing rift between the two sides; however it is difficult to discern its specific impact. The land border conflict was more an indication of the divergences with regard to other issues and of the overall deterioration of relations in the post 1975 period rather than an important disputed issue in itself. All the territorial conflicts became increasingly publicized in 1979 following China's attack on Vietnam.[192]

Ideology and domestic changes
To assess the relative importance of a factor such as ideology is problematic since domestic and foreign policies are influenced by ideology as well as nationalistic and strategic considerations.[193] Such policies can be altered by changes in the top leadership of a country although the official ideology will remain the same. In the context of this study the question is whether differences in ideological

perceptions and domestic changes in the two countries could have had an impact on bilateral relations.

Since both China and Vietnam were ruled by communist parties, there could be no divergences regarding the leading role of the party. With regard to the situation in the world there were major differences since China viewed the USSR as an enemy whereas Vietnam perceived the USSR as a friendly socialist country and eventually as an ally. The sharp differences in the perceptions of the USSR can be seen as differences in strategic outlook rather than as an ideological issue.

On the domestic front China went through dramatic changes between 1975 and 1979. There was a shift from the Cultural Revolution to the modernization and open-door policies launched in 1978. Two of China's most important leaders, Zhou Enlai and Mao Zedong, both died in 1976. After a brief spell in power Mao's widow and her close associates; i.e. the "Gang of Four" were ousted from power. Hoa Guofeng emerged as leader only to subsequently lose out in a power struggle with Deng Xiaoping.[194] In Vietnam, the top leadership did not go through such dramatic changes during this period but in terms of domestic policies the socialist transformation went from gradual to total by 1978. Thus, the two countries went through two opposite experiences.

The effects on Sino-Vietnamese relations of some of the domestic changes have already been noted. One was the re-activation of China's policy towards the Overseas Chinese. Another was the exodus of ethnic Chinese from Vietnam. One of the factors that caused the exodus was the intensification of the policies of socialist transformation. China criticized Vietnam for carrying out the policies in a way which China saw as discriminatory.[195] A relevant question is whether the political changes in China influenced China's policy towards Vietnam. The political turmoil might have made China less responsive to Vietnam's attempts at diversifying its foreign economic relations. However, taken as a whole, the period 1975 to early 1979 does not show that the changes in the Chinese leadership improved relations with Vietnam; on the contrary, the trend was towards worsening relations. Maybe relations between leading personalities on both sides contributed to the failure in maintaining normal relations and in handling the emerging differences. Le Duan's visits to China in September 1975 and November 1977 cannot be assessed as anything but failures.

Issues of contention in Sino-Vietnamese relations during the 1980s and in the normalization process[196]

If attention is shifted to the Sino-Vietnamese confrontation during the 1980s, i.e. following the Chinese attack on Vietnam in February–March 1979, the first observation is that the divergences regarding the three major issues of contention remained, as exemplified by the failure of the negotiations from April 1979 to March 1980.

The Soviet factor

The Soviet factor continued to be a point of disagreement during the 1980s. However, the state of affairs was more of a standstill than during the period 1975 to 1978 with the alliance between the USSR and Vietnam and with Sino-Vietnamese contacts virtually non-existent for about half a decade. Eventually, the importance of the Soviet factor diminished following the gradual improvement of relations between China and the USSR, which began in 1982 and gained momentum during the second half of the 1980s leading to full normalization of relations in May 1989. With the Chinese perception of a reduced Soviet threat to its security, the alliance between the USSR and Vietnam became less of a concern to China.[197]

The Cambodia factor

The Cambodia factor came to be the focal point of the Sino-Vietnamese conflict during the 1980s. China was in a position to actively work against Vietnam's presence and interests in Cambodia and effectively pursued a two-track policy against Vietnam. First, China gave financial and logistic support to the three Cambodian parties[198] that were waging a military struggle against the PRK and the Vietnamese in Cambodia.[199] Second, on the diplomatic front, China in co-operation with the United States worked towards the goal of isolating Vietnam internationally and of denying international recognition to the PRK. This policy of isolation and non-recognition was applied both at the regional level in co-operation with ASEAN and at the global level through decisions at the United Nations.[200] To add pressure on Vietnam, China maintained a strong military presence along the border and forced Vietnam to permanently station large numbers of troops in the area. China increased its military activities as a response to Vietnamese offensives in Cambodia, but did not launch any new large scale attack. As it seems, China perceived continued pressure as a more efficient method than a new attack.

China's aim was to force Vietnam to withdraw from Cambodia, to bring about the disintegration of the PRK and to bring the Coalition

Government of Democratic Kampuchea (CGDK) to power. Such an evolution would also have removed the Soviet influence in Cambodia. However, this aim was not achieved since Vietnam's withdrawal from Cambodia was eventually carried out at a pace decided upon by Vietnam, thus enabling the PRK to gain enough strength to resist the CGDK forces after the final withdrawal of Vietnamese troops in September 1989. Vietnam carried out troop withdrawals on a yearly basis from 1982, and, beginning in 1985, Vietnam pledged to withdraw all troops from Cambodia by the end of 1990, at the latest. Thus, the process started before Soviet pressure could have been applied to Vietnam. Vietnam's economic difficulties may have made Vietnam more willing to speed up its withdrawal, but the way in which it was carried out indicates that it was primarily linked to the gradual strengthening of the PRK's defence capability.[201]

The Vietnamese withdrawal from Cambodia was not sufficient to fulfil China's demands and it did not take place under international supervision, which China had repeatedly demanded. However, China gradually softened its demand for the dismantling of the PRK and began supporting a quadripartite power-sharing solution with equal representation for all parties. As it turned out, the power-sharing formula agreed upon by the Cambodian parties was a Supreme National Council (SNC), created in September 1989, with twelve members—six from the State of Cambodia (SOC)[202] and two each from Front uni national pour un Cambodge indépendant, neutre, pacifique et coopératif (FUNCINPEC), the Khmer People's National Liberation Front (KPNLF), and the Party of Democratic Kampuchea (PDK).[203]

The creation of the SNC followed the presentation of a plan, on 28 August 1990 by the five permanent members of the UN Security Council, that aimed to facilitate and contribute to a comprehensive political settlement of the Cambodian conflict.[204] Thus, the August plan was supported by China. The first official Vietnamese reaction, on 31 August, was a statement "appreciating" the efforts of the permanent members of the Security Council.[205] The subsequent evolution showed that Vietnam had fully accepted it. Earlier research suggests that Vietnam's acceptance of the August plan was brought about through an agreement with China at a secret high-level meeting in Chengdu in early September.[206] It seems probable that compromises were reached on certain aspects of the Cambodian issue. One could be seen in the acceptance of the composition of SNC, which fell short of China's demand for equal representation and of Vietnam's demand for non-inclusion of the PDK. Another aspect was Vietnam's acceptance of the August plan with its proposed extensive role for the United Nations in Cambodia, while China accepted the Vietnamese withdrawal as completed.[207] However, there are indications that differences continued to persist with regard to Cambodia until the breakthrough in inter-Cambodian negotiations in 1991. It appears the normalization process between Vietnam and China and the willingness of the Cambodian parties to make decisive compromises were mutually reinforcing during the period from late June to September 1991. The agreements between the Cambodian parties and the subsequent signing of the Paris Agreements gradually removed the Cambodian issue from the agenda and made possible the full normalization of relations between China and Vietnam.[208]

Other issues
Other issues include the territorial disputes; i.e. overlapping claims to the Paracel and Spratly archipelagos, to maritime and continental shelf areas in the South China Sea and in the Gulf of Tonkin, and to areas along the land border. The border disputes were not resolved during the normalization process and have continued to cause tension in the 1990s.

A major issue in the late 1970s was the Chinese minority in Vietnam. This was not an issue that was brought to the forefront of the conflict during the 1980s and does not seem to have been a major issue in the normalization process. Attention had by then shifted away from the ethnic Chinese who remained in Vietnam to those who fled from Vietnam to China in 1978 and 1979. China held the standpoint that they should be repatriated to Vietnam but Vietnam was reluctant to accept them back.[209] In all, this group was estimated at about 270,000 people at the time of normalization.

Issues such as ideology and domestic evolution gradually changed from the situation in the late 1970s. At that time, different economic policies were being carried out in the two countries whereas in the late 1980s and early 1990s both countries were implementing policies of economic liberalization. The CCP and VCP were also brought closer together by the demise of the communist parties in Eastern Europe and the USSR. Another factor which contributed to closer relations between China and Vietnam, as well as between the ruling parties, could have been a feeling of being under siege from non-communist countries repeatedly raising human rights issues, a pressure which has increased with fewer communist-ruled countries in the world.[210] The fear of peaceful evolution was also beginning to emerge as a concern which brought the two ruling parties closer together.

If the political leadership in both countries failed to contain the deteriorating relations in the late 1970s, the leaders of the late 1980s and early 1990s successfully brought about the full normalization of bilateral relations. The Vietnamese top leadership was completely revamped by the late 1980s compared with the late 1970s, and this may have facilitated contacts with the Chinese leaders. However, the exclusion of the then Foreign Minister Nguyen Co Thach from the September 1990 visit to China and the breakthrough in the normalization process following his removal from his government posts and from the Politburo and the Central Committee of the VCP at the Seventh Party Congress in late June 1991, indicate that he was in bad odour with the Chinese. This certainly contributed to weaken his position, but other factors also came into play, such as his failure to obtain normalization of relations with the United States following the withdrawal from Cambodia and discontent with the way he was running the Foreign Ministry.[211]

Issues of contention since normalization of relations in late 1991

Since normalization of bilateral relations, the territorial issues have been the major source of controversy and therefore the major part of the discussion and analysis will be devoted to the border disputes. The only other issue officially recognized as a problem has been the smuggling of Chinese goods into Vietnam and its negative impact on the Vietnamese economy. However, the issue of the ethnic Chinese still lingers on.

Territorial disputes
The territorial disputes between China and Vietnam have been the most serious source of tension in bilateral relations since 1992. Among the territorial disputes, the land border and the Tonkin Gulf issues seem to be recognized by the two sides as more likely to be re-solved in the foreseeable future. In fact the goal is to resolve the land border issue before the year 2000. It is noteworthy that more progress seems to have been achieved in negotiations on the land border compared with talks on other territorial disputes. Progress relating to the Tonkin Gulf issue is more difficult to assess. Little progress, if any, has been achieved with regard to the territorial dis-putes in the South China Sea proper, i.e. the competing sovereignty claims to the Paracel and Spratly archipelagos as well as the overlap-ping claims to waters and continental shelf areas to the East of the Vietnamese coast. Talks have been initiated on the disputes in the South China Sea but the parties have yet to agree on which disputes to include on the agenda, with Vietnam pushing for the inclusion of

the Paracels as an issue alongside that of the Spratlys, whereas China only wants to discuss the latter issue. To further complicate matters, China views the disputes over water and continental shelf areas as part of the Spratly conflict whereas Vietnam views them as separate from that conflict.

The territorial disputes caused serious tension in bilateral relations from May to November 1992, and the differences relating to oil exploration in the South China Sea and the signing of contracts with foreign companies for oil exploration were particularly deep from April to June 1994, in April and May 1996 and in March and April 1997. During 1998 there were no extended periods of tension relating to the border disputes but brief periods of tension were noted such as in January due to a localized conflict along the land border. There were brief controversies arising from developments in the South China Sea during the months of April, May, July, and September. However, it should be noted that despite these differences the overall trend seems to be that bilateral relations are improving and co-operation expanding.

The system of talks and discussions relating to the territorial disputes is both highly structured and extensive; from bottom to top it looks as follows: expert-level talks (on a regular basis); government-level talks, i.e. deputy/vice Minister (meets once yearly); foreign ministerial-level talks (on a regular basis), and, high-level talks, i.e. secretaries-general of the CCP and VCP, presidents and prime ministers (at yearly high-level summits).

The talks at the expert and government levels deserve further attention in order to ascertain the progress made thus far. Talks at the expert level date back to October 1992, and up to late 1995 the talks focused mainly on the land border demarcation and the delineation of the Gulf of Tonkin. The talks at the government level began in August 1993 and the sixth round of talks was held in September 1998. The major achievement thus far has been the signing of an agreement on 19 October 1993 on the principles for handling the land border and Gulf of Tonkin disputes.[212] It was further agreed to set up joint working groups at the expert level to deal with the two issues. The working group on the land border met on twelve occasions during the period February 1994–June 1998 and the working group on the Gulf of Tonkin met ten times during the period March 1994–March 1998. Talks at the expert level on the territorial disputes in the South China Sea proper, the so-called "sea issues", were initiated in November 1995 with the second round of talks in July 1996, the third round in May 1997, and the fourth in July 1998.

The bilateral talks have been positive and constructive and have shown that the two countries wish to handle the disputes by negotiations and peaceful means and that they wish to refrain from the use of force. The 1993 agreement is the most formal indication of their commitment, and this commitment has been reiterated in the discussions and in the joint communiqués of the yearly high-level visits since normalization in 1991. In this context it should also be noted that an agreement was reached during the high-level summit in July 1997 to resolve the land border dispute before the year 2000 and Tonkin Gulf dispute by the year 2000.

The re-opening of the railway in February 1996 stands out as the most significant achievement in managing bilateral relations and increasing co-operation without formally resolving the territorial disputes. The major reason for not resuming the railway traffic earlier during the 1990s was the disputed border area of 300 metres between the provinces of Guangxi and Lang Son. This issue has still not been settled despite the fact that the railway linking Pingxing and Dong Dang goes through the disputed area. Since the area is under Chinese control, the part of the railway passing through it has been restored and is operated by China. Thus, Vietnam has agreed to allow China to control and manage the railway in the area but Vietnam has not renounced its claim to it. The rationale behind Vietnam's concession is not publicly known, but one reason could be that Vietnam was looking for expanded economic interaction with China and resumed rail transport would facilitate official trade. It could also be that Vietnam obtained Chinese concessions on other matters in exchange. However, since Vietnam has not renounced its sovereignty claim to the area, it is unlikely that China made any concessions on the territorial issues, nor that China can be expected to be more amenable to Vietnamese claims to other disputed areas along the land border or in relation to the other territorial disputes.

Despite the positive evolution described above, with bilateral talks at different levels and the resumption of railway traffic, the border disputes have not been formally resolved and so far the parties have been unable to prevent the territorial disputes from causing serious tension. The question is which party acts in such a way as to cause increased tension from time to time? A closer look at the developments shows that a majority of the crisis situations have been caused by Chinese activities. Thus, the track record over recent years suggests that China needs to alter its behaviour by refraining from actions which cause tension. Although Vietnam has shown a higher degree of restraint, some of its actions relating to contracts with foreign companies have also caused tension in bilateral relations.

The most recent controversy relating to the situation in the South China Sea was caused by the construction of facilities by Vietnam on two submerged reefs. China claimed that these submerged reefs form part of the Spratly archipelago, and hence were part of China's territory. Therefore, China perceived Vietnam's action as a violation of China's territory. Vietnam argued that the submerged reefs do not form a part of the Spratly archipelago and that they are located within Vietnam's EEZ and continental shelf.

In view of this situation, the two parties need to strive for the establishment of a "code of conduct" which would prevent the reoccurring periods of tension. To establish a code of conduct is not a novel idea as exemplified by the agreement in August 1995 between China and the Philippines on a code of conduct to be followed by the two countries in order to avoid an increase in the level of tension relating to their dispute over most of the Spratly archipelago. They also agreed on the need to resolve their differences by peaceful means through negotiations.[213] Another example of a similar agreement is that reached in November 1995 between the Philippines and Vietnam on a code of conduct to be followed in order to maintain stability in the area disputed by them, i.e. most of the Spratly archipelago. This code of conduct included a commitment to resolve the Spratly dispute peacefully through negotiations.[214] These two agreements and the experiences gained from their implementation could serve as the bases for establishing an agreement on a code of conduct between China and Vietnam.

In view of the situation of the last few years, the basic rule of a possible code of conduct would be respect for the status quo, and that both parties refrain from actions which could alter the status quo and thus cause tension in relations. The problem is to determine what should be the status quo in some of the areas of overlapping claims, particularly in parts of the South China Sea where Vietnam does not recognize China's extensive claims to EEZ and continental shelf areas. These areas were formerly termed "historical waters" by China but, as was shown in an earlier section of this chapter, China has through its legislation and statements gradually turned them into the EEZ and continental shelf of the Paracel and Spratly archipelagos. Consequently, Vietnam regards the Chinese moves to sign contracts with foreign oil companies and to engage in oil exploration in areas off the Vietnamese coast as violations of Vietnam's sovereign rights and as attempts to turn areas to which Vietnam's claim was previously uncontested into contested ones. Whatever the merits of the claims of the two parties and their interpretations of the

1982 UNCLOS to support their claims, the issue of foremost importance is to achieve a situation in which both parties refrain from actions which would alter the status quo.

It is necessary to point out that respect for the status quo should not be seen as passing a judgement on the question of sovereignty over the disputed Paracel and Spratly archipelagos, nor about the merits of the claims to EEZ and continental shelf areas in the South China Sea, or for that matter in the Gulf of Tonkin. Respecting the status quo is necessary to avoid the risk of tension escalating into confrontation, thus threatening the positive achievements in strengthening bilateral relations and expanding co-operation which have taken place since normalization of relations.

What then are the prospects for a Sino-Vietnamese agreement on the establishment of a code of conduct? They do not seem to be particularly good since thus far only Vietnam seems to be amenable to the idea. In fact, according to information obtained in Hanoi, Vietnam had proposed that a code of conduct be agreed between China and Vietnam but this proposal has not been accepted by China.[215]

Although it is risky to draw a conclusion stemming from one incident, it is noteworthy that the dispute in May 1998 relating to the activities of a Chinese exploration ship in areas of the South China Sea claimed by Vietnam was settled without leading to the deep tension that characterized the incident in March and April 1997. Since there were fewer public statements in connection with the May 1998 incident, it is difficult to fully assess how the more successful management of the incident was brought about. Obviously, downplaying public rhetoric and more restraint by the two parties were contributing factors. Judging from the Vietnamese statement, the approach by "diplomatic negotiations" and patience in dealing with China did bear fruit in this latest incident.

An additional observation that can be drawn from the developments in 1998 is that both China and Vietnam have been more reluctant to engage in longer periods of accusations and counter-accusations in connection with incidents in the South China Sea that have caused tension in bilateral relations. However, this does not imply that either side refrains from publicizing their discontent or from protesting against actions carried out by the other party. The difference in 1998 compared to earlier years is that the official complaint or accusation is stated on a limited number of occasions and then no further public statement on the incident in question is made. This prevents an escalation in accusations and counter-accusations from taking place and thus tension does not appear to be as deep as for example in March and April 1997 during the controversy over Chinese oil-drilling in an area of the South China Sea claimed by Vietnam. If this new pattern of reaction to actions by the other party prevails in the future then some damage control mechanisms have been developed between the two countries to contain tension relating to the border disputes. Such damage control mechanisms do not, however, prevent the two sides from publicly protesting about actions committed by the other side.

Smuggling
Although the territorial disputes have been the major source of tension in bilateral relations since full normalization in late 1991, the issue of smuggling of Chinese goods and its negative impact on Vietnam's economy have also been sources of controversy. As it seems, the smuggling and the flooding of the Vietnamese market with Chinese goods was most controversial during the earlier part of the 1990s. Judging by the publicity given to the problem by the Vietnamese side, the situation was most serious in 1993, and drew renewed attention during 1997.

A closer look at the actions taken to curb the smuggling shows that Vietnam took some unilateral measures in 1993 by introducing tariffs on certain imported goods, and more importantly by tightening control in the border areas. Bilateral moves to address the issue have included discussions at high-level meetings during the Chinese Prime Minister's visit to Vietnam in late 1992 and during the Vietnamese President's visit to China in late 1993 as well as through such measures as the opening of more border crossings and resuming direct railway traffic between the two countries.

It seems that smuggling became less of a problem during 1994, at least judging from official statements and contacts. Instead, attention shifted to ways of increasing and expanding economic co-operation, as exemplified by the three agreements signed in November 1994 in connection with the Chinese President's visit to Vietnam. These agreements aimed at increasing trade and economic co-operation, facilitating road transport and guaranteeing the quality of imported and exported goods. Since late 1994, the two sides have continued their efforts to expand economic relations and to enforce control over cross-border trade. In recent years, they have expressed their satisfaction at the expansion of economic co-operation. In 1996 bilateral trade was estimated to have totalled US$1 billion. The developments during 1997 indicate that economic co-operation and interaction is being further expanded with increased two-way trade and Chinese loans and assistance to upgrade Chinese-built factories in northern Vietnam.

Although economic co-operation between China and Vietnam is expanding, smuggling has once again emerged as a major issue of concern during 1997. This was revealed in connection with the high-level summit in July 1997 and in connection with the visit by the Chinese Vice-Premier in charge of economic affairs to Vietnam in October 1997. The renewed concern about smuggling along the Sino-Vietnamese border can be linked to enhanced efforts on the part of the Vietnamese Government to curb smuggling during 1997 and the priority given to the current campaign by the top leadership.[216] Although both China and Vietnam have taken measures to curb smuggling in the border areas, the measures thus far have not proven to be very effective.[217] The October 1997 agreement to initiate negotiations aimed at reaching an agreement on the regulation of cross-border economic activities is a clear indication that both parties are eager to co-operate in order to bring the smuggling along the common border under control. The October 1998 agreement on border trade can be seen as the first tangible result of these negotiations.

Ethnic Chinese
The issue of the ethnic Chinese has continued to be a source of controversy in bilateral relations. As during the process of normalization, the problem does not seem to be related to the ethnic Chinese in Vietnam but to the fate of those who left for China in the late 1970s. China persists in bringing up its demand for their repatriation to Vietnam, whereas the Vietnamese continue to oppose such a repatriation. The Vietnamese stand on the matter is based on economic considerations, i.e. Vietnam could not absorb such a large number of people, now estimated at about 280,000. Vietnam also argues that the ethnic Chinese have settled in China and integrated into Chinese society and therefore their lives should not be disrupted by a repatriation process.[218] Undoubtedly Vietnam also has security concerns in mind when opposing repatriation, given that the large number of ethnic Chinese have been living under the political control and influence of the Chinese authorities since the late 1970s. Thus, the issue of the ethnic Chinese from Vietnam living in China remains a potential source of tension.

Conclusion

The relations between China and Vietnam have considerably improved during the 1990s compared with the situation that prevailed in the late 1970s. However, this improvement has not resolved all major contending issues in bilateral relations. The evolution of relations since full normalization in late 1991 has been characterized by, on the one hand, expanding and strengthening economic and political co-operation, and on the other, by a fluctuating level of tension relating to the territorial disputes.

Two of the major issues of controversy in the late 1970s and during the 1980s were removed from the agenda in the course of the normalization process in the late 1980s and early 1990s. These were (1) the divergent views concerning the role of the USSR in the world and Vietnam's close relations with the USSR; and (2) removal of the Sino-Vietnamese differences over Cambodia through the Vietnamese military withdrawal and the conflict resolution process leading up to the Paris Agreements on Cambodia of October 1991.

Among the unsettled issues the most serious ones are the territorial disputes in the South China Sea, in the Gulf of Tonkin and along the land border. Despite the ongoing talks and discussions relating to the territorial disputes at the expert, government, foreign ministerial, and top-leadership levels these issues remain unresolved and are likely to remain potential threats to good relations until they are settled in a way that is acceptable to both parties.

Another problem left over from the late 1970s is the Chinese minority in Vietnam. At that time the dispute concerned the treatment of ethnic Chinese in Vietnam whereas at present the problem seems to be linked to those who left for China in the late 1970s. China wants to repatriate them, but Vietnam is, to say the least, reluctant to accept them back.

One major preoccupation for Vietnam in the earlier part of the 1990s was the large amount of smuggled Chinese goods which flooded the Vietnamese market and forced several Vietnamese enterprises to close down. This issue was addressed at high-level talks and seems to have been brought under some sort of control. Since late 1994 attention has been focused on how to expand economic interaction and co-operation. Although economic co-operation between China and Vietnam is expanding, smuggling once again emerged as a major issue of concern during 1997. This renewed concern can be linked to enhanced efforts on the part of the Vietnamese Government to curb smuggling during 1997. Both sides have taken measures to curb smuggling in the border areas but thus far they have not proven effective. Co-operation on the matter is in the process of being reinforced.

As noted earlier, the domestic evolution in the two countries has displayed some clear differences since the late 1980s compared with the situation in the late 1970s, with both countries currently implementing policies of economic liberalization. Changes in the international political environment, i.e. the developments in Eastern Europe and the feeling of being under pressure from non-communist countries repeatedly raising human rights issues, and the fear of peaceful evolution have certainly contributed to the efforts by China and Vietnam to forge closer bilateral relations. Nevertheless, the persistence of disputed bilateral issues, primarily the territorial disputes and Chinese actions in the South China Sea, tend to hamper this process and raise Vietnamese security concerns about China's intentions and ambitions.

The political leadership in both countries failed to contain the deterioration of relations in the late 1970s but the leaders of the late 1980s and the 1990s have been more successful since they have achieved full normalization of relations. There can be no doubt that the Chinese and Vietnamese leaderships perceive the bilateral relationship as an important aspect of their foreign policy. Given the asymmetry in size, population and economic strength, China is a greater foreign policy concern to Vietnam than Vietnam is to China. The importance given by both countries to the bilateral relations can be judged from the yearly high-level summits since normalization in late 1991.

The future development of the Sino-Vietnamese relationship will be determined by how successfully the two sides handle disputed issues. Co-operation in different fields and expanding economic interaction has brought about a stable bilateral relationship but re-occurring periods of tension relating to the territorial disputes prevent the co-operation from reaching its full potential and cause uncertainty about the long-term stability of the Sino-Vietnamese relationship. Ongoing talks and discussions on the territorial disputes indicate that the two sides are striving for a peaceful settlement of the border disputes. However, they have yet to agree on how to prevent the re-occurrence of increase in tension. Unless an agreement is reached on a code of conduct to be observed by the two parties, in order to maintain the status quo there is a potential risk that tension can escalate into confrontation, thus threatening the positive achievements in expanding bilateral co-operation in recent years.

Notes

*   The author wishes to acknowledge the economic support provided by the Sasakawa Young Leaders Fellowship Fund while researching and writing this study, which forms part of a larger research project on the conflict situation around the South China Sea and possibilities of durable solutions.

1. Some studies regarding the Sino-Vietnamese relationship from the mid-1950s to 1975 are Eugene K. Lawson, *The Sino-Vietnamese Conflict* (New York: Praeger Publishers, 1984); W.R. Smyser, *The Independent Vietnamese: Vietnamese Communism Between Russia and China 1956–1969*, Papers in International Studies, Southeast Asia No. 55 (Athens: Centre for International Studies, Ohio University, 1980); and Victor C. Funnell, "Vietnam and the Sino-Soviet Conflict 1965–1976", *Studies in Comparative Communism* 11, nos. 1/2 (1978): 42–169.

2. This section is derived from Ramses Amer, "Sino-Vietnamese Normalization in the Light of the Crisis of the Late 1970s", *Pacific Affairs* 67, no. 3 (Fall 1994): 358–66.

3. The Vietnam Communist Party (VCP) changed its name from Vietnam Workers' Party (VWP) at its Fourth National Congress in December 1976.

4. Lo Chi-kin, *China's Policy Towards Territorial Disputes: The Case of the South China Sea Islands* (London and New York: Routledge, 1989), pp. 92–93 and 95–97; and Gareth Porter, "Vietnamese Policy and the Indochina Crisis", in David W. Elliot, ed., *The Third Indochina Conflict* (Boulder: Westview Press, 1982), p. 77.

5. Ibid., pp. 16–78 and 80–84; Chang Pao-min, *The Sino-Vietnamese Territorial Dispute*. The Washington Papers no. 118 (New York: The Center for Strategic and International Studies, Georgetown University and Praeger Publishers, 1986), pp. 25–35; William J. Duiker, *China and Vietnam: The Roots of Conflict*, Indochina Research Monograph no. 1 (Berkeley: Institute of East Asian Studies, University of California, 1986), pp. 72–73; and Lo, *China's Policy Towards Territorial Dispute*, op. cit., pp. 53–108.

6. "Memorandum on Vice-Premier Li Xiannian's Talks with Premier Pham Van Dong (10 June 1997)", in *Beijing Review*, no. 13, 30 March 1979, p. 22.

7. *The Truth About Viet Nam-China Relations Over the Last 30 Years* (Hanoi: Ministry of Foreign Affairs, Socialist Republic of Vietnam, 1979), p. 70.

8. For a background to the border dispute and an analysis of the conflict between Cambodia and Vietnam, see Stephen R. Heder, "The Kampuchean-Vietnamese Conflict", in Elliot, *The Third Indochina Conflict*, op. cit., pp. 22–67. For a detailed analysis of the claims of the two countries during the border conflict, see Ramses Amer, *The United Nations and Foreign Military Interventions: A Comparative Study of the Application of the Charter. Second Edition*. Report no. 33 (Uppsala: Department of Peace and Conflict Research, Uppsala University, 1994), pp. 195–201.

9. Duiker, *China and Vietnam,* op. cit., pp. 66–69; and Robert S. Ross, *The Indochina Tangle: China's Vietnam Policy 1975–1979* (New York: The East Asian Institute, Columbia University, Columbia University Press, 1988), pp. 154–67.

10. Amer, *The Ethnic Chinese and Sino-Vietnamese Relations,* op. cit., pp. 45–46.

11. Geng Biao delivered this report on 16 January 1979; see "Keng Piao's Report on the Situation of the Indochinese Peninsula", *Issues and Studies* 17, no. 1 (January 1981): 78 and 85.

12. The terms "Vice" and "Deputy" Minister will be used interchange-
    ably in the study since China uses the term "Vice Ministers" and
    Vietnam uses the term "Deputy Minister".
13. Memorandum on Vice-Premier Li Xiannian's Talks with Premier
    Pham Van Dong", op. cit., pp. 21–22; and Porter, "Vietnamese Policy
    and the Indochina Crisis", p. 83.
14. C.Y. Chang, "Overseas Chinese in China's Policy", *The China Quar-
    terly*, 82 (June 1980): 282–84. See also U.S. Foreign Broadcast
    Information Service, *Daily Report China,* E 4–10, 3 January 1978,
    pp. 78–71; and E 11–21, 4 January 1978, pp. 78–72.
15. This overview is based on Amer, *The Ethnic Chinese and Sino-Viet-
    namese Relations*, op. cit. pp. 46–77. Other studies on the issue
    include Chang Pao-min, *Beijing, Hanoi and the Overseas Chinese*,
    China Research Monograph no. 24 (Berkeley: Institute of East Asian
    Studies, University of California, 1982); Michael Godley, "A Summer
    Cruise to Nowhere: China and the Vietnamese Chinese in Perspec-
    tive", *The Australian Journal of Chinese Affairs* 4 (July 1980): 35–59;
    and Lewis M. Stern, "The Vietnamese Expulsion of the Overseas
    Chinese", *Issues and Studies* 23, no. 7 (July 1987): 102–35.
16. From 1 May 1975 to 30 September 1979 an estimated 200,000 to
    236,000 ethnic Chinese left Vietnam by boat for Hong Kong and
    Southeast Asian countries, and an estimated 230,000 others left for
    China, for a total number of 430,000 to 466,000 ethnic Chinese who
    left Vietnam by the end of September 1979; see Amer, *The Ethnic
    Chinese and Sino-Vietnamese Relations*, op. cit., pp. 105–7; and Ramses
    Amer, "The Chinese Minority in Vietnam Since 1975: Impact of
    Economic and Political Changes", *Ilmu Masyarakat* (Kuala Lumpur)
    22, July–December 1992, pp. 24–25.
17. Amer, *The Ethnic Chinese and Sino-Vietnamese Relations*, op. cit.,
    pp. 65–77 and 75; and Godley, "A Summer Cruise to Nowhere", op.
    cit., p. 43.
18. Amer, *The Ethnic Chinese and Sino-Vietnamese Relations*, op. cit.,
    pp. 93–94; and Ross, *The Indochina Tangle*, op. cit., pp. 86–97 and 189.
19. "Note of the Chinese Government to the Government of the Socialist
    Republic of Vietnam (3 July 1978)", in *Documents Related to the
    Question of Hoa People in Vietnam* (Hanoi: Ministry of Foreign Affairs,
    Socialist Republic of Vietnam, July 1978), p. 78.
20. King C. Chen, *China's War with Vietnam, 1979: Issues, Decisions, and
    Implication* (Stanford: Stanford University, Hoover Institution Press,
    1987), pp. 83 and 85; Anne Gilks, *The Breakdown of the Sino-
    Vietnamese Alliance, 1970–1979*, China Research Monograph no. 39
    (Berkeley: Institute of East Asian Studies, University of California,
    1982), pp. 216–19; and Ross, *The Indochina Tangle*, op. cit., pp. 208–9.
21. Nayan Chanda, *Brother Enemy: The War after the War: A History of
    Indochina since the Fall of Saigon* (San Diego: Harcourt Brace
    Jovanovich Publishers, 1986), pp. 263–82, 284–90 and 329–33; Grant
    Evans and Kelvin Rowley, *Red Brotherhood at War: Indochina Since the
    Fall of Saigon* (London: Verso Editions, 1984), pp. 58–60; and Gareth
    Porter, "The 'China Card' and US Indochina Policy", *Indochina Issues*
    11 (November, 1980): 1–2.
22. Heder, "The Kampuchean-Vietnamese Conflict", op. cit., pp. 22–67;

and Amer, *The United Nations and Foreign Military Intervention*, op. cit., pp. 195–201.

23. For an analysis of the decision-making process in China as well as the conduct of the war, see Chen, *China's War with Vietnam*, op. cit., pp. 69–117; Gilks, *The Breakdown of the Sino-Vietnamese Alliance*, op. cit., pp. 224–33; and Ross, *The Indochina Tangle*, op. cit., pp. 223–33.

24. Chen, *China's War with Vietnam*, op. cit., p. 118.

25. Carlyle A. Thayer, "Security Issues in Southeast Asia: The Third Indochina War (revised 17 August 1987)". Paper presented to the Conference on Security and Arms Control in the North Pacific, sponsored by the Research School of Pacific Studies, Peace Research Center, Strategic and Defence Studies Centre and Department of International Relations, The Australian National University, Canberra, 12–14 August 1987. A copy of this paper may be found at ftp:// coombs.anu.edu.au/coombspapers/otherarchives/asian-studies-archives/seasia-archives/.

26. Ramses Amer, "Vietnam and Its Neighbours: The Border Dispute Dimension", *Contemporary Southeast Asia* 17, no. 3 (December 1995), p. 302.

27. Author's discussions with officials and researchers in Hanoi from December 1988 to February 1989.

28. Thayer, "Security Issues in Southeast Asia", op. cit., p. 16 and interviews with Carl Erhard Lindahl, Swedish Ambassador to Vietnam, in December 1987, January and December 1988.

29. Ramesh Thakur and Carlyle A. Thayer, *Soviet Relations with India and Vietnam 1945–1992* (Delhi: Oxford University Press, 1993), pp. 78–79 and 130–31; and John W. Garver, "The 'New Type' of Sino-Soviet Relations", *Asian Survey* 29, no. 12 (December 1989): 1138–40.

30. Author's discussions with officials and researchers in Hanoi from December 1988 to February 1989.

31. British Broadcasting Corporation, *Summary of World Broadcasts, Part Three, Far East*, 0531/C1/10–11, 10 August 1991. Hereafter BBC/SWB/ FE.

32. Garver, "The 'New Type' of Sino-Soviet Relations", op. cit., p. 1136; and Carlyle A. Thayer, "Comrade Plus Brother: The New Sino-Vietnamese Relations", *The Pacific Review* 5, no. 4 (1992): 404.

33. *Le Monde*, 18 September 1990, p. 8; and 21 September 1990, pp. 1 and 7.

34. Thayer, "Comrade Plus Brother", op. cit., pp. 405–6.

35. The existence of continued differences was confirmed in author's discussions with officials and researchers in Hanoi in February and March 1992.

36. For a more detailed analysis of the conflict resolution process in Cambodia from late June to early October 1991, see Ramses Amer, "The United Nations" Peace Plan for Cambodia: From Confrontation to Consensus", *Interdisciplinary Peace Research* 3, no. 2 (October/November 1991): 20–26.

37. Thayer, "Comrade Plus Brother", op. cit., p. 405.

38. BBC/SWB/FE/1222/A3/1, 6 November 1991; 1223/A3/1–3, 7 November 1991; 1224/A3/1–2, 8 November 1991; and 1227/A3/1–2, 12

November 1991. Among other things a "provisional agreement concerning border affairs" was signed in connection with the summit.

39. The information relating to the territorial disputes is partly derived from Ramses Amer, "The Territorial Disputes Between China and Vietnam and Regional Stability", *Contemporary Southeast Asia* 19, no. 1 (June 1997): 89–104 and 109–113.

40. BBC/SWB/FE/1305/A3/1-3, 15 February 1992; 1306/A3/1, 17 February 1992; and 1307/A3/1, 18 February 1992.

41. Ibid., 1324/A3/2-3, 9 March 1992; and 1326/A3/1-2, 11 March 1992.

42. For the full text of "The Law of the People's Republic of China on its Territorial Waters and Their Contiguous Areas" adopted by the Standing Committee of the National People's Congress on 25 February 1992 see ibid., 1316/C1/1-2, 28 February 1992.

43. Ibid., 1385/A1/2-3, 20 May 1992; 1388/i, 23 May 1992; 1417/A2/3-4, 26 June 1992; and 1430/A1/1, 11 July 1992. See also Michael Vatikiotis, "China stirs the pot", *Far Eastern Economic Review*, 9 July 1992, pp. 14–15. Hereafter FEER.

44. BBC/SWB/FE/1428/A2/1, 9 July 1992; and 1430/A1/1.

45. Ibid., 1479/i and A2/1, 7 September 1992; and 1487/A2/6-7, 16 September 1992.

46. Ibid., 1486/A2/3, 15 September 1992.

47. Based on author's discussions with officials and researchers in Hanoi and visit to the Vietnamese border province of Lang Son in December 1994.

48. BBC/SWB/FE/1299/A3/3, 8 February 1992. See also "Hanoi, Peking reopen border crossing", *FEER*, 16 April 1992, p. 14.

49. BBC/SWB/FE/1492/A2/1, 22 September 1992.

50. Ibid., 1519/A1/2-3, 23 October 1992.

51. Ibid., 1552/A2/1, 1 December 1992; 1553/A1/1-4, 2 December 1992; 1554/A1/4-5, 3 December 1992; 1555/A1/7-11, 4 December 1992; and 1556/A1/1-3, 5 December 1992.

52. Ibid., 1560/A1/9, 10 December 1992; 1561/A2/4-5, 11 December 1992; 1565/A2/6, 15 December 1992; 1566/A2/1, 17 December 1992; 1620/A2/2, 23 February 1993; 1689/A2/4-5, 15 May 1993; 1691/A2/2-3, 18 May 1993; 1777/A1/3, 26 August 1993; 1783/G/1-2, 2 September 1993; and 1786/G/4, 6 September 1993.

53. Ibid., 1825/B/2-3, 21 October 1993.

54. Ibid., 1658/A2/3, 8 April 1993; and 1693/A2/4, 20 May 1993.

55. Ibid., 1843/G/1-3, 11 November 1993; 1845/G/5-6, 13 November 1993; 1846/G/1-2, 15 November 1993; and 1848/B/3-4 and G/4, 17 November 1993. The detailed information pertaining to the border disputes is derived from an interview with Vietnam's Foreign Minister by the *Voice of Vietnam*, ibid., 1848/B/3-4.

56. For the tariffs and the Chinese reaction, see ibid., 1834/G/1, 1 November 1993; and "China-Vietnam border trade cools off as Hanoi slaps new curbs", *Business Times* (Singapore), 27 October 1993. Information concerning the tightening of controls along the border was also obtained through author's discussions with officials and researchers in Hanoi in November 1993.

57. BBC/SWB/FE/1935/B/3, 2 March 1994; 1936/G/2-3, 3 March 1994; and 1957/B/7, 28 March 1994.

58. Ibid., 1978/B/3, 22 April 1994; 1979/B/9, 23 April 1994; 1980/B/6, 25 April 1994; and U.S. Foreign Broadcast Information Service, *Daily Report East Asia*, 94–077, 21 April 1994, p. 55; 94–078, 22 April 1994, pp. 48–49. Hereafter FBIS EAS.
59. Ibid., 94–090, 10 May 1994, p. 45; and BBC/SWB/FE/1991/B/10, 7 May 1994.
60. The report was carried by *Agence France Presse*, Hong Kong and quoted in ibid., 1996/B/5, 13 May 1994.
61. Ibid., 1996/B/5; and FBIS EAS, 94–093, 13 May 1994, p. 70.
62. BBC/SWB/FE/1997/G/4–5, 14 May 1994.
63. The interview in *The Strait Times*, 19 May 1994, p. 17 was reproduced in FBIS EAS, 94–097, 9 May 1994, 68–9.
64. BBC/SWB/FE/2024/G/1, 17 June 1994.
65. Ibid., 2027/B/3–4, 21 June 1994; and FBIS EAS, 94–118, 20 June 1994, p. 67.
66. Ibid., 94–128, 5 July 1994, pp. 69–70; 94–129, 6 July 1994, p. 66; 94–133, 12 July 1994, p. 68; and BBC/SWB/FE/2028/G/4, 4 July 1994; 2046/G/2, 13 July 1994.
67. Ibid., 2040/G/5, 6 July 1994.
68. Ibid., 2041/B/7–8, 7 July 1994; and FBIS EAS, pp. 94–129, p. 66; 94–156, 12 August 1994, p. 67.
69. BBC/SWB/FE/2057/B/4, 26 July 1994. According to a report by *Xinhua News Agency* the Chinese Foreign Minister said that the two countries had reached agreement on basic principles concerning the border disputes and "positive progress" had been made during negotiations, thus laying a "solid foundation" for the settlement of disputes ibid., 2058/G/2, 27 July 1994.
70. Ibid., 2078/B/,6 19 August 1994. The Vietnamese reports from border talks concurred with the Chinese versions on most points with the notable difference that Vietnam referred to "issues related to the East Sea", i.e. the South China Sea, instead of the Spratly issue only, as China did FBIS EAS, 94–159, 17 August 1994, p. 79; 94–161, 19 August 1994, pp. 62–3; and 94–162, 22 August 1994, p. 80.
71. Experts of the interview in *Sankei Shimbun* were translated and reproduced in BBC/SWB/FE/2085/B/1, 27 August 1994.
72. Ibid., 2109/G/1–2, 25 September 1994; 2111/G/3–5, 27 September 1994; 2117/G/1–2, 4 October 1994; 2140/B/6, 31 October 1994; and 2158/B/1, 21 November 1994.
73. For the Chinese statement, see ibid., 2096/G/3, 9 September 1994 and for the Vietnamese statement, see ibid., 2098/B/4, 12 September 1994.
74. For the Chinese statement, see ibid., 2128/G/2, 17 October 1994; and for the Vietnamese response, see ibid., 2130/B/3–4, 19 October 1994; and FBIS EAS, 94–203, 20 October 1994, p. 84.
75. BBC/SWB/FE/2130/G/2–3, 19 October 1994.
76. Ibid., 2132/B/5, 21 October 1994.
77. Ibid., 2158/B/1, 21 November 1994.
78. For the full text of the "Sino-Vietnamese Joint Communiqué" see ibid., 2160/B/1–2, 23 November 1994.
79. Ibid., 2187/B/5, 28 December 1994; and 2210/B/4, 25 January 1995.
80. Ibid., 2208/G/15, 23 January 1995.

81. Ibid. 2210/B/4.
82. Ibid., 2241/G/4, 2 March 1995; 2256/B/5, 20 March 1995; 2273/G/1–2, 8 April 1995, 2280/B/4, 18 April 1995; 2281/B/1, 19 April 1995; and 2282/B/1, 20 April 1995.
83. Ibid., 2307/G/1, 19 May 1995; and 2309/G/1–2, 22 May 1995.
84. Ibid., 2315/B/1, 29 May 1995.
85. Ibid., 2340/B/1–2, 27 June 1995.
86. Ibid., 2356/G/6–7, 15 July 1995. According to the Chinese official version, the experts would work on the "territorial waters issues... and negotiate on the Nansha issue", i.e. on the Spratly issue but not on the Paracel issue; ibid., 2356/G/6–7. In a subsequent interview with Hoang Nhu Ly, Head of the China Department of the Ministry of Foreign Affairs, published in the Vietnamese publication *Tuan Bao Quoc Te* on 2 August 1995, Hoang Nhu Ly was quoted as saying that as the Vietnamese side understood it "the sea issues that the team will discuss include those having to do with the Paracel Islands and Spratly Islands"; for a translation of the interview see FBIS EAS, 95–187, 27 September 1995, p. 97.
87. Ibid., 95–199, 16 October 1995, p. 71; and BBC/SWB/FE/2441, 23 October 1995.
88. Ibid., 2461/B/2, 15 November 1995; and 2467/G/2, 22 November 1995. For other reports of the talks on economic co-operation, see ibid., 2463/B/1, 17 November 1995; and 2468/B/4, 24 November 1995.
89. Ibid., 2463/B/1.
90. Ibid., 2474/G/2–6, 30 November 1995.
91. For the full text of the "Sino-Vietnamese Joint Communiqué", see ibid., 2477/G/1–2, 4 December 1995. The agreement on opening the railway links between the two countries relates to two links linking Dong Dang and Lao Cai on the Vietnamese side with Pingxing and Shanyao, respectively, on the Chinese side, thus connecting the provinces of Lang Son and Guangxi, and the provinces of Lao Cai and Yunnan, respectively. See ibid., 2477/B/3, 4 December 1995; 2494/B/5, 23 December 1995; and 2524/B/1, 1 February 1996.
92. Ibid., 2479/B/3–4, 6 December 1995.
93. Ibid., 2518/B/4, 25 January 1996; 2524/B/1, 1 February 1996; 2525/B/4, 2 February 1996; 2536/B/4, 15 February 1996; and 2539/G/3, 19 February 1996.
94. Ibid., 2538/B/5–6, 17 February 1996.
95. Ibid., 2515/B/3, 22 January 1996; and 2517/B/1, 24 January 1996.
96. Ibid., 2522/B/2, 30 January 1996.
97. Ibid., 2550/G/4, 2 March 1996. Also, in early March the joint working group on the Gulf of Tonkin held is sixth round of talks; ibid., 2562/B/5, 16 March 1996.
98. Ibid., 2586/B/6, 15 April 1996; and 2595/B/7, 25 April 1996.
99. Ibid., 2589/G/2, 18 April 1996; and 2590/G/2, 19 April 1996.
100. Ibid., 2591/B/6 20 April 1996; and 2595/B/7.
101. Ibid., 2614/G/10–12, 17 May 1996.
102. Ibid., 2615/B/6, 18 May 1996. The eighth round of talks of the joint working group on the land border was held in May; ibid., 2618/G/3, 22 May 1996.
103. Ibid., 2651/B/11 and G/2–3, 29 June 1996. For other reports on the

visit by the Chinese Premier, see ibid., 2647/G/2, 25 June 1996; 2650/ G/3-4, 28 June 1996; 2651/B/5-7, 10 and 12; 2652/B/4 and 6-7, 1 July 1996; 2653/B/3-4, 2 July 1996; and 2654/B/6-7, 3 July 1996.

104. Ibid., 2662/B/6, 12 July 1996; and 2665/B/3, 16 July 1996. The seventh meeting of the joint working group on the delineation of the Gulf of Tonkin was held in early August; ibid., 2688/B/4, 12 August 1996.

105. Ibid., 2701/G/1, 27 August 1996; 2704/B/5-6, 30 August 1996; and 2705/B/4, 31 August 1996. See also British Broadcasting Corporation, *Summary of World Broadcasts Weekly Economic Report. Part Three Asia-Pacific*, 0450/WB/2, 28 August 1996. Hereafter BBC/SWB/FEW.

106. BBC/SWB/FE/2724/B/4-5, 23 September 1996.

107. Ibid., 2748/B/6, 21 October 1996.

108. Ibid., 2770/G/3, 15 November 1996.

109. Ibid., 2773/B/6-7, 19 November 1996; 2774/B/4, 20 November 1996; and 2775/B/4-5, 21 November 1996. All these reports were carried by Chinese sources.

110. Ibid., 2791/B/5, 10 December 1996 and 2801/B/4, 21 December 1996.

111. BBC/FEW/0466/WB/3, 18 December 1996.

112. BBC/SWB/FE/2789/B/3, 7 December 1996.

113. Ibid., 2802/B/4-5, 23 December 1996.

114. Ibid., 2819/B/5, 17 January 1997; 2821/B/5, 20 January 1997; and BBC/SWB/FEW/0470/WB/2, 22 January 1997.

115. BBC/SWB/FE/2226/B/3, 25 January 1997.

116. Ibid., 2849/G/20, 21 February 1997; 2855/G/1, 28 February 1997; 2858/B/3, 4 March 1997; 2862/B/4, 8 March 1997; and 2869/G/2-3, 17 March 1997.

117. Ibid., 2870/B/4, 18 March 1997; and 2871/B/4, 19 March 1997.

118. Ibid., 2872/G/1, 20 March 1997.

119. Ibid., 2874/B/3, 22 March 1997.

120. Ibid., 2880/G/15, 31 March 1997.

121. Ibid., 2892/B/3, 14 April 1997.

122. Ibid., 2889/B/3, 10 April 1997.

123. Ibid., 2872/B/5; 2874/B/4; 2886/G/5, 7 April 1997; 2890/G/4, 11 April 1997; and 2892/G/3.

124. Ibid., 2900/G/5, 23 April 1997.

125. Ibid., 2906/B/5, 30 April 1997.

126. Author's discussions with officials and researchers in Hanoi in September 1997.

127. Ibid., 2899/B/3, 22 April 1997.

128. Ibid., 2919/B/2, 15 May 1997.

129. Ibid., 2922/B/4, 19 May 1997; and 2937/B/3-4, 5 June 1997.

130. Ibid., 2937/B/4; and 2938/B/3, 6 June 1997.

131. Ibid., 2945/G/3, 14 June 1997; and 2951/G/1, 21 June 1997; "Une haute délégation militaire en Chine", *Le Courrier du Vietnam*, 3 Novembre 1997, p. 2; and "Viêt Nam military delegation visits China", Viet *Nam News* 3 November 1997, p. 3.

132. BBC/SWB/FE/2971/G/1, 15 July 1997; 2972/B/7; and G/1-2, 16 July 1997; and 2973/G/1-5, 17 July 1997.

133. Ibid., 2973/G/1.

134. Ibid., 2973/G/4. According to a report carried by *Xinhua News Agency*,

Do Muoi stated that Vietnam was "willing to speed up the settlement of matters between the two countries that still remain through peaceful consultations"; ibid., 2972/G/1.

135. Ibid., 2973/G/2-5 and 2977/B/6, 22 July 1997. Author's discussions with officials and researchers in Hanoi in September 1997.

136. Ibid., 2973/G/2-3.

137. Ibid., 2973/G/1-2.

138. Ibid., 2973/G/2.

139. In an interview with the Chinese Ambassador to Vietnam, Li Jiazhong, published on 1 October 1997 by *Viet Nam News*, the Ambassador gave more updated statistics relating to economic interaction between the two countries. First, two-way trade in 1996 amounted to US$1.15 billion and during the first half of 1997 it was estimated at US$700 million, an increase of 40 per cent compared with the corresponding period in 1996. Second, there were 43 Chinese projects in Vietnam with US$76 million licensed investments. "China pays special attention to ties with Viet Nam", *Viet Nam News*, 1 October 1997, p. 5. The figures provided by the *Vietnam Investment Review* put the number of Chinese projects at 47 projects with US$87.5 million in investment. Since Hong Kong has now been re-unified with China, it can be noted that the same source puts the number of projects financed by Hong Kong investors at 196 with US$3.704 billion in investment. *Vietnam Investment Review*, 318, 17-23 November 1997, 26.

140. BBC/FE 2978/B/5-6, 23 July 1997.

141. Ibid., 2978/B/5-6.

142. Ibid., 2977/B/5, 22 July 1997. Information carried by the *Vietnam News Agency*.

143. Ibid., 3002/B/3, 20 August 1997. Information carried by the *Vietnam News Agency*. The Chinese version carried by *Xinhua News Agency* did not get into any details pertaining to the discussions, but it stated that the two sides achieved "wide-raging" consensus in their exchange of views on how to accelerate the process of border talks. Ibid., 3000/G/4, 18 August 1997.

144. It is noteworthy that in an article in *Viet Nam News* previewing the visit by the Chinese Vice Premier, it was reported that the two countries were expected to sign three "finance" agreements. Two were indeed signed but not the third one which would have been a US$110 million "credit" for the expansion of the Bac Giang Urea Factory, in "Chinese Deputy PM due to visit this week", *Viet Nam News*, 21 October 1997, p. 1. No reason for not signing the third agreement was given in foreign language Vietnamese press in connection with the visit.

145. "Vietnam-Chine: Vers l'intensification des échanges commerciaux", *Le Courrier du Vietnam*, 24 Octobre 1997, p. 1; "A l"issue de la visite de Wu Bangguo. Signature des documents de coopération Vietnam-Chine". ibid., 2 Novembre 1997, p. 2; and "Chinese Deputy Prime Minister arrives to promote bilateral trade", *Viet Nam News*, 24 Octobre 1997, pp. 1 and 4; "China agrees to major loans", ibid., 25 Octobre 1997, pp. 1 and 5; "PM says Viet Nam-China trade will increase", ibid., 27 Octobre 1997, pp. 1 and 5. See also BBC/SWB/FE/3059/B/6 and G/2, 25 October 1997; and 3061/B/4, 28 October 1997.

146. Thanh Nga, "L'ambassadeur chinois au Vietnam. Un éventuel accord de commerce frontalier début 1998", *Le Courrier du Vietnam*, 1 Novembre 1997, p. 3.
147. BBC/SWB/FE/3071/G/7, 8 November 1997; and 3091/G/1-2, 2 December 1997.
148. Ibid., 3099/B/3-6, 11 December 1997. For other reports about the visit, see "VN, China look for greater ties", *Viet Nam News*, 8 December 1997, p. 1; "VN wants better Sino-Vietnamese ties", Ibid., 9 December 1997, p. 1; "Vietnam-China. Souhait réciproque de promouvoir les relations d'amitié et de coopération", *Le Courrier du Vietnam*, 9 Décembre 1997, pp. 1–2; and "Li Ruihuan à Hô Chi Minh-Ville", ibid., 10 Décembre 1997, p. 1.
149. Ibid., 3113/B/5, 31 December 1997 and 3127/B/9-10, 17 January 1998.
150. Ibid., 3133/B/8-9, 24 January 1998. The information given in the interview highlights some interesting aspects of the "provisional agreement concerning border affairs" which is referred to as "the temporary agreement signed on 7th November 1991 to settle disputes along the Sino-Vietnamese border". In clause one, article 1, it is stipulated that both parties are to maintain the status quo along the border and that neither side is permitted to carry out "man made action" which would alter the status quo. Furthermore, in clause one, article 2, relating to construction projects along the river banks, it is stipulated that construction which can affect the river currents can only be carried out by mutual agreement. It is also stated that both sides are required to negotiate according to the principles of equality and mutual benefit when dealing with activities relating to river currents in the border area. Ibid., B/8.
151. Ibid., 3134/G/1, 26 January 1998 report carried by *Xinhua* in its domestic service in Chinese.
152. Ibid., 3133/B/9-10. Report carried by the *Voice of Vietnam*.
153. Ibid., 3135/G/1, 27 January 1998; 3145/G/2-3, 7 February 1998; and 3190/G/2-3, 1 April 1998. See also BBC/FEW/0526/WB/4, 25 February 1998; 0528/WB/4, 11 March 1998; and 0533/WG/8, 15 April 1998.
154. BBC/SWB/FE/3190/B/5-6.
155. Ibid., 3249/B/6-7, 10 June 1998.
156. 3280/B/5, 16 July 1998. This was presumably the fourth round of talks on the so-called South China Sea issues.
157. Ibid., 3195/S2/8, 7 April 1998.
158. Ibid., 3250/G/3, 11 June 1998; 3251/G/2-3, 12 June 1998; and 3252/G/4, 13 June 1998.
159. Ibid., 3199/B/8, 13 April 1998; 3202/B/4, 16 April 1998; and 3205/B/6, 20 April 1998.
160. Ibid., 3222/B/6, 9 May 1988.
161. Ibid., 3233/B/11, 22 May 1998.
162. Ibid., 3235/G/1, 25 May 1998.
163. Ibid. 3236/B/12, 26 May 1998.
164. Ibid., 3283/B/6, 20 July 1998. "The Law of the People's Republic of China on the Exclusive Economic Zone and the Continental Shelf" was adopted by the National People's Congress on 26 June 1998. For a reproduction of the Chinese language version as well as an unofficial English language translation of the law, see Zou Keyuan, *Maritime Jurisdiction Over the Vessel-Source Pollution in the Exclusive Economic*

Zone: The Chinese Experience, EAI Working Paper no. 6 (Singapore: East Asian Institute, National University of Singapore, 8 July 1998), pp. 29–36.

165. BBC/SWB/FE/3326/B9, 8 September 1998.
166. Ibid., 3328/G/1, 10 September 1998.
167. Ibid., 3329/B/10, 11 September 1998.
168. Ibid., 3335/G/2, 18 September 1998; 3337/B/7, 21 September 1998; and 3339/B/7-8, 23 September 1998.
169. Ibid., 3345/B/5, 30 September 1998.
170. Ibid., 3360/G/2, 17 October 1998; and 3362/G/1, 20 October 1998.
171. Ibid., 3663/G/1, 21 October 1998. This report was carried by *Xinhua News Agency*. *Vietnam News Agency* reported that the two Prime Ministers had "stressed determinations" to accelerate negotiations to reach the target of signing an agreement on the land boundary "before" the year 2000 and an agreement on the delineation of the Tonkin Gulf "in 2000 at the latest"; ibid., 3364/G/1, 22 October 1998.
172. Ibid., 3364/G/1-3. Reports carried by *Xinhua News Agency*.
173. This section is derived from Amer, "Sino-Vietnamese Normalization in the Light of the Crisis of the Late 1970s", op. cit., pp. 368–76.
174. See the concluding chapter in Ross, *The Indochina Tangle,* op. cit., pp. 239–66.
175. Carlyle A. Thayer, "United States Policy Towards Revolutionary Regimes: Vietnam (1975–1983)", in Dick Clark, ed., *U.S. Foreign Policy: Adjusting to Change in the Third World.* no. 85-W441 (Wye Plantation, Queenstown, MD: Aspen Institute for Humanistic Studies), pp. 121–28.
176. Ibid., pp. 86–104.
177. The "interference and sabotage" of the "gang of four" and natural calamities were the factors behind China's economic problems according the official Chinese explanation Memorandum on Vice-Premier Li Xiannian's Talks with Premier Pham Van Dong", op. cit., p. 22.
178. One reason could have been the reported removal of the pro-China faction from the politburo of the VCP at the Fourth Party Congress held in December 1976; Porter, Vietnamese Policy and the Indochina Crisis", op. cit., p. 82.
179. See Steven J. Hood, *Dragons Entangled: Indochina and the China-Vietnam War* (Armonk and London: An East Gate Book, M. E. Sharpe Inc., 1992), pp. xvi and 56–57.
180. Carlyle A. Thayer, "Laos and Vietnam: The Anatomy of a 'Special Relationship' ", in Martin Stuart-Fox, ed., *Contemporary Laos: Studies in the Politics and Society of the Lao People's Democratic Republic* (New York: St. Martin's Press, 1982), pp. 245–73. See also Gilks, *The Breakdown of the Sino-Vietnamese Alliance,* op. cit., p. 179 and Ross, *The Indochina Tangle,* op. cit., pp. 123–24.
181. Ibid., pp. 40–48 and 104–110.
182. See notes 8, 9 and 10.
183. For a more detailed argument along this line, see Ross, *The Indochina Tangle,* op. cit., pp. 189–194.
184. Based on author's discussions with officials and researchers in Hanoi in December 1987–January 1988, December 1988–February 1989, and February 1990.

185. Chen, *China's War with Vietnam*, op. cit., pp. 90–105; Gilks, *The Breakdown of the Sino-Vietnamese Alliance*, op. cit., pp. 226–31; and Ross, *The Indochina Tangle*, op. cit., pp. 224–26.

186. For a more detailed discussion along this line, see Amer, *The Ethnic Chinese and Sino-Vietnamese Relations*, op. cit., pp. 46–56; Amer, "Les politiques du Viet Nam à l'égard des Chinois d'origine depuis 1975— Continuité et changement", *Réalités Vietnamiennes*, no. 6, Cahier d'études du Centre d'Observation de l'Actualité Vietnamienne CODAVI (Aix-en-Provence: Institut de Recherche sur le Sud-Est Asiatique IRSEA, Avril-Juin 1996), pp. 26–28; and Amer, "Vietnam's Policies and the Ethnic Chinese since 1975", *SOJOURN: Journal of Social Issues in Southeast Asia*, 11, no. 1 (April 1996): 84–85.

187. For a more thorough analysis of the diplomatic wrangles between China and Vietnam over the ethnic Chinese in Vietnam, see Amer, *The Ethnic Chinese and Sino-Vietnamese Relations*, op. cit., pp. 57–77.

188. Ibid., pp. 77–89.

189. For a more detailed analysis of this issue, see C.Y. Chang, "Overseas Chinese in China's Policy", op. cit., pp. 281–303.

190. Ross, *The Indochina Tangle*, op. cit., pp. 175–89.

191. Ibid., 151–53; and Chen, *China's War with Vietnam*, op. cit., pp. 48–50.

192. This can be exemplified by the fact that both parties began publicizing their claims in more detail in the post 1979 war period as part of an effort to underscore their claims on the international stage; see for example "China's Undisputable Sovereignty over the Xisha and Nansha Islands", *Beijing Review*, 18 February 1980, pp. 15–24; and *La souveraineté du Viet Nam sur les archipels Hoang Sa et Truong Sa* (Hanoi: Département de la presse et de l'information. Ministère des affaires étrangères, République Socialiste du Viet Nam, 1979).

193. For a general discussion, consult Eero Palmujoki, *Vietnam and the World: Marxist-Leninist Doctrine and the Changes in International Relations, 1975–93* (London: Macmillan Press Ltd., 1997).

194. Chen, *China's War with Vietnam*, op. cit., pp. 70–77; and Ross, *The Indochina Tangle*, op. cit., pp. 97–104. For a discussion on the domestic sources of China's Vietnam policy during this period see ibid., pp. 255–65.

195. For a detailed analysis of China's reactions to the fate of the ethnic Chinese in Vietnam in the post 1975 period, see Amer, *The Ethnic Chinese and Sino-Vietnamese Relations*, op. cit., pp. 35–77.

196. This section is derived from Amer, "Sino-Vietnamese Normalization in the Light of the Crisis of the Late 1970s", op. cit., pp. 376–82.

197. For more details concerning the Sino-Soviet normalization process, see Chi Su, "The Strategic Triangle and China's Soviet Policy", in Robert S. Ross, ed., *China, the United States, and the Soviet Union: Tripolarity and Policy Making in the Cold War*, Studies on Contemporary China (Armonk and London: An East Gate Book, M.E. Sharpe, Inc., 1993), pp. 48–57; Robert Legvold, "Sino-Soviet Relations: The American Factor", in ibid., pp. 80–88; and Herbert J. Ellison, "Soviet-Chinese Relations: The Experience of Two Decades", in ibid., pp. 99–117. See also Garver, "The 'New Type' of Sino-Soviet Relations", op. cit., pp. 1137–43.

198. The three parties were the Front uni national pour un Cambodge

indépendant, neutre, pacifique et coopératif (FUNCINPEC), the Khmer People's National Liberation Front (KPNLF), and the Party of Democratic Kampuchea (PDK). In June 1982 they established the Coalition Government of Democratic Kampuchea (CGDK).

199. Chen, *China's War with Vietnam*, op. cit., pp. 123 and 129–132; and Gary Klintworth, "The Outlook for Cambodia: The China Factor", in Gary Klintworth, ed., *Vietnam's Withdrawal from Cambodia: Regional Issues and Realignment*, Canberra Papers on Strategy and Defence, no. 64 (Canberra: Strategic and Defence Studies Centre, Research School of Pacific Studies, The Australian National University, 1990).

200. For details on the United Nations decisions, see Amer, "The United Nations and Foreign Ministry Intervention", op. cit., pp. 89–108 and 124–45.

201. This line of explanation is derived from Amer, "The United Nations' Peace Plan for Cambodia", op. cit., p. 15; and Amer, "Indochinese Perspectives of the Cambodian Conflict", in Ramses Amer, Johan Saravanamuttu, and Peter Wallensteen, *The Cambodian Conflict 1979–1991: From Intervention to Resolution* (Penang: Research and Education for Peace, School of Social Sciences, Universiti Sains Malaysia and Department of Peace and Conflict Research, Uppsala University, 1996), pp. 112–13. For explanations along other lines see Leszek Buszynski, "The Soviet Union and Vietnamese Withdrawal from Cambodia", in Klintworth, *Vietnam's Withdrawal from Cambodia*, op. cit., pp. 32–47; Michael Leifer, "Cambodia in Regional and Global Politics", in ibid., pp. 7–10; and Frank Frost, "The Cambodian Conflict: The Path towards Peace", *Contemporary Southeast Asia* 13, no. 2 (September 1991): 135–36.

202. On 30 April 1989 the PRK officially changed its name to the State of Cambodia (SOC).

203. See *Joint statement of the Informal Meeting on Cambodia*, Jakarta, 10 September 1990.

204. The full text of the August plan is contained in United Nations document *A/45/472–S/21689*, 31 August 1990.

205. BBC/SWB/FE/0858/A3/1, 1 September 1990.

206. See Thayer, "Comrade Plus Brother", op. cit., p. 404.

207. Some of the Sino-Vietnamese compromises appear in the first resolution adopted by consensus by the General Assembly on the situation in Cambodia in October 1990; see Amer; "The United Nations and Foreign Military Intervention", op. cit., pp. 127–40.

208. Author's discussions with officials and researchers in Hanoi in February–March 1992.

209. Ibid. The issue of the ethnic Chinese who left for China in 1978–79 was included in the joint communiqué of the November 1991 summit BBC/SWB/FE/1227/A3/1, 12 November 1991; and Vietnam *Courier*, no. 26 (December 1991): 1 and 3.

210. For detailed discussion concerning the possible of the emergence of an Asian socialist community (ASC) during the normalization process, see Thayer, "Comrade Plus Brother", op. cit., pp. 402–3 and 405–6.

211. Ibid., pp. 405–6. Author's discussions with officials and researchers in Hanoi in February–March 1992 and in November 1993.

212. The August 1993 and October 1993 meetings seem to be regarded as

parts of the first round of talks at the government-level by the two sides.

213. For details relating to the negotiations and agreement see BBC/SWB/ FE/2378/B/4–5, 10 August 1995; 2379/B/3, 11 August 1995; 2380/B/2– 3, 12 August 1995; and; FBIS EAS, 95–155, 11 August 1995, p. 50; 95–157, 15 August 1995, pp. 76–77; 95–158, 16 August 1995, pp. 46– 47.

214. For details relating to the negotiations and agreement see BBC/SWB/ FE/2456/B/4, 9 November 1995; and 2459/B/2, 13 November 1995.

215. Author's discussions with Vietnamese officials in Hanoi in October and November 1997.

216. For recent reports on the priority given to the fight against smuggling see "PM Khai orders an all-out war against smugglers", *Viet Nam News,* 18 October 1997, p. 1; "Smuggling, fraud still rampant in 1997", ibid., p. 3; and "Ministry to intensify smuggling fight", ibid., 13 November 1997, p. 2.

217. Author's discussions with officials and researchers in Hanoi in September 1997.

218. Author's discussions with officials and researchers in Hanoi and Ho Chi Minh City in February–March 1992, November 1993, December, 1994, December 1995, and November–December 1996.

5

SINO-VIETNAMESE RELATIONS: PROSPECTS FOR THE TWENTY-FIRST CENTURY

Chang Pao-min

Alternation of alliance and conflict

It is perhaps already a truism to say that the relations between China and Vietnam have for centuries been characterized by periodic shifts between, or rather alternations of, two extremes, namely close alliance and bitter conflict. And ironically enough, the bases of both alliance and conflict between China and Vietnam are the same: geographical, cultural, and historical. Being contiguous with a common land border of over 1,100 kilometres, the two countries have shared similar experiences throughout a history of ten centuries. As one of the two most "sinicized" Asian countries (the other being Korea), Vietnam not only shares with China many cultural traits but also understands China better than any other Southeast Asian nation does. Indeed, the two countries could even communicate in a common language. The fact that same ideologies, first nationalism and then communism, have permeated China and Vietnam for nearly the same length of time has further bound the two countries to a common destiny in the twentieth century. Even today Vietnam and China remain two of the four functioning Communist states in the entire world, and both have also adopted virtually the same model and strategy of developing their economies.[1]

As a result of all these affinities, Vietnam has historically sought China's assistance whenever it was confronted with internal turmoil or external threat, and China has also been nearly always prepared to lend a hand to Vietnam as a brother country. Indeed, at such times, the relationship between China and Vietnam has been frequently characterized by both countries as "brotherly", "intimate", and "like lips and teeth".[2] It is perhaps necessary to emphasize that during the past century or so, China had fought for Vietnam at least three times, first against the French colonialist intrusion in 1874–75, then during the first Indochina War (1948–54), and most recently, against the Americans during the second Indochina War (1958–75). The fact that three completely different political regimes in China had been equally ready to come to Vietnam's help in spite of their own apparent weakness and irrespective of the identity and nature of the enemy is in itself sufficient proof of the strong historical ties between the two countries. As a matter of fact, China was the source of both inspiration and concrete assistance for Vietnam's nationalist movement throughout the first half of the twentieth century.[3] The first two Indochina Wars merely represent the most recent experiences that both exemplified and consolidated the close relationship between China and Vietnam which can be approximated perhaps only by China's relationship with Korea until the end of the Korean War.

However, precisely because of the age-old, pervasive cultural links, the geographical proximity between China and Vietnam, and the frequent Chinese intervention—though almost invariably at the Vietnamese initiative before the 1970s—plus the contrast in size and power between the two nations, Vietnam has always been wary of excessive Chinese influence in Vietnam, let alone outright Chinese domination, whether military or political in nature. This is particularly the case when Vietnam enjoys internal tranquillity and encounters no external threat. With the emergence and growth of Vietnamese nationalism in the twentieth century, cultural affinities with China inevitably became increasingly a political liability and actually came to be seen by most Vietnamese leaders as detrimental to the cultivation and development of a distinct new Vietnamese identity. Ironically again, the second and third Indochina Wars, which witnessed the closest ever military and political alliance between Vietnam and China and on an unprecedented scale, also coincided with the full blossoming of Vietnamese nationalism which dictated that Hanoi distance itself from Beijing when the war was over. Indeed, both internal political dynamics and external exigencies required Vietnam to adopt a strong anti-China and anti-Chinese stance in the late 1970s.[4]

What is perhaps equally significant during recent decades, however, was the historically unprecedented entanglement in Indochina of the two superpowers, the United States and the Soviet Union, both traditionally alien to Southeast Asia, which nevertheless offered Vietnam for the first time in its history an opportunity to play a balancing game against China by enlisting an outside and much stronger power to check China's traditional, entrenched influence, and to counter China's possible expansionist designs. Hence the swift turn in, and radicalization of, Vietnam's posture on and policy towards China and the ethnic Chinese almost immediately following the military reunification of Vietnam in 1975, which triggered off a new round of bitter conflict between the two countries that lasted for nearly fifteen years. And for a period of time, Vietnam clearly relied on the Soviet Union in the pursuit of both its national objectives and its imperialist ambitions, both conveniently at the expense of its friendship with China.[5]

Unfortunately for Hanoi, and to some extent also beyond its expectations, such a policy turned out economically too costly and politically counterproductive. Not only did it result in a serious drain on Vietnam's already strained resources and the severance of all economic links to the non-Soviet world, it also quickly antagonized all its immediate ASEAN neighbours, as well as the United States. What was worse, Beijing's irreconcilable stance on Vietnam and on the issue of Cambodia was accompanied by Moscow's about face during the massive Chinese attack in 1979, only to be followed by intensive diplomacy between China and the Soviet Union throughout the early 1980s, culminating in the two giants' rapprochement by the mid-1980s that rendered Vietnam's aggressive Indochina policy even more undesirable and untenable. And it was out of an acute sense of exhaustion and insecurity that Hanoi decided to give up occupying Cambodia in 1985 and to withdraw all its troops from the country, a *sine qua non* of normalizing relations with both China and all the ASEAN nations, and a move that was finally completed by September 1989. Parallel to such a turnabout in foreign policy was Vietnam's overtures to the United States and its ASEAN neighbours in the early 1990s in order to cultivate a more friendly regional environment conducive to Vietnam's security and development. The sudden, quick demise of the Cold War in the mid-1980s and the subsequent rapid disintegration of Eastern Europe and the Soviet Union in 1989–90, certainly confirmed the wisdom of Hanoi's new policy and added new impetus to Vietnam's reorientation of its policy priorities, with increasingly greater emphasis upon reconciliation and co-operation with all its immediate neighbours, China included.

The very fact that Vietnam had not treasured enough its cultural ties and traditional links with China and had not even hesitated to turn against China in Vietnam's better times caused great dismay and anger in China. Indeed, precisely because of its anticipation of Vietnamese loyalty, China could not tolerate, and would react strongly to, a hostile Vietnam. This love-and-hate complex was in fact the underlying cause—though perhaps not easily comprehensible to Western observers—of China's military attacks in 1979. It also explained the accompanying and subsequent outpouring of all the emotion-charged accusations against Vietnam.[6] China under the Communist regime, like any previous Chinese regime, had not been so concerned about a Vietnam seeking and defending its political independence from China, as turning itself into an anti-China outpost of actually or potentially hostile powers. Vietnam's open alliance with China's arch-enemy in the Cold War atmosphere—the Soviet Union—was unmistakably viewed as a real threat to China's national security. Forming such an alliance in the wake of its military victory over the United States and after thirty years of Chinese unswerving support and sacrifice was to China a brutal violation of all decent rules of conduct and morality. Hence Beijing's unusually hard-lined stand on the question of Soviet support for Vietnam and Vietnam's occupation of Cambodia. China's unswerving containment of Vietnam throughout the 1980s also came as no wonder.[7]

Nevertheless, from the Chinese perspective, Vietnam was never a brother permanently lost. In the back of the Chinese mind, precisely because Vietnam had never posed a threat to China by itself, nor will it ever be capable of doing so, Vietnam should still remain, and could also easily be won over, as China's lasting friend if only for cultural and historical reasons. Sharing a common land border with China and with a long coastal line overlooking the main sea lanes in the South China Sea, Vietnam was certainly merited as a vitally important gateway to China from maritime Southeast Asia and West Asia, which Beijing cannot afford to disregard or forsake. Beijing's determination to go out of its way to strain its relations with Hanoi during 1975–90, and for that matter, China's wholehearted support for Vietnam throughout the first two Indochina Wars, did not so much serve the purpose of seeking China's domination of Vietnam, which Beijing knows it could no longer achieve, as ensuring the long-term goal of dislodging both superpowers from their footholds in China's backyard. And somehow China was confident that Vietnam's marriage of convenience with any outside power, particularly Western in character and hostile to China, could not possibly negate or replace its century-old and multifaceted linkages with China.[8] This is why China's pressure on Vietnam did not escalate as a result of the Soviet Union's withdrawal from Indochina and its subsequent political disintegration. On the contrary, no sooner had Vietnam fulfilled its promise of evacuating from Cambodia than China opened its door to Vietnam for negotiation on normalizing relations. Indeed, from the Chinese standpoint, the threat from both the United States and the Soviet Union was no more by the early 1990s.

New opportunities in the 1990s

It was in the light of the above changes that renewal of friendship between Vietnam and China proceeded smoothly and swiftly from August 1990 when Beijing openly dropped its support for the Khmer Rouge. In the same year, Vietnam's Party Secretary-General Nguyen Van Linh was invited to a secret summit meeting with Chinese leaders in China to pave the way to normalization of relations, which culminated in Vietnamese leader Do Muoi's visit to China in November 1991 and Chinese Premier Li Peng's official visit to Vietnam in late November-early December 1992. In December 1994 Chinese Party leader Ziang Zemin again paid a visit to Vietnam in his four-country tour to Southeast Asia. In December 1995, Vietnam's Party Secretary General Do Muoi paid a second visit to China. In July 1997, Do Muoi took the trouble of paying China a third visit before his retirement. Each time such high-level exchanges took place, either a communiqué was signed pledging mutual friendship or some co-operative agreements were concluded. In mid-February 1996, the cross-border rail service between Hanoi and Nanning that had been suspended for seventeen long years was resumed with much fanfare and publicity, signaling the beginning of a new era. In fact, Chinese land borders were unofficially open to trade with Vietnam in the early 1990s even before the resumption of the rail service. This was soon followed by a massive programme undertaken by the Chinese to clear the China-Vietnam border of thousands of landmines, a move that signalled Beijing's confidence in a lasting peace to come. By the mid-1990s, the two former foes had mended their broken ties and were already on good terms. Bilateral trade also grew from virtually zero in 1985 to US$227 million in 1991, and again to US$873 million in 1996.[9]

The rapid improvement of Sino-Vietnamese relations were accompanied by new diplomatic progress made by both Vietnam and China in Southeast Asia. In the case of Vietnam, trade relations with ASEAN members developed as early as the mid-1980s and have been growing since then. What is more significant, a breakthrough was made in political ties as early as 1991, when Vietnam's prime minister made a tour of ASEAN capitals, pledging his country's goodwill and expressing Vietnam's intention to establish better ties with ASEAN. Not only was this trip well received, but it was reciprocated by Asian leaders in the ensuing years. It was also followed by a continuous stream of delegations exchanged between Hanoi and its Southeast Asian neighbours. In fact, almost immediately following the complete Vietnamese withdrawal from Cambodia, Malaysia and Indonesia were enthusiastic to strike a dialogue with Hanoi. In 1992 Vietnam became an observer at the annual ASEAN Ministerial Meeting. On 28 July 1995, Vietnam became a full-fledged member of ASEAN, exceeding even its own expectation.

Similarly, China's relations with the ASEAN countries have also improved. Indeed China has made a deliberate effort to court ASEAN in the 1990s. In 1990, Beijing scored a major breakthrough by establishing formal diplomatic relations first with Indonesia, and then with Singapore. In the following year, China asked to be, and was accepted as a consultative partner of ASEAN for dialogue purposes. In 1994 a joint committee on economic, trade, scientific, and technological co-operation was set up between China and ASEAN. In the same year, Chinese state president and party leader Ziang Zemin visited Singapore, Malaysia, Indonesia, as well as Vietnam, and in 1996 Ziang visited the Philippines. In March 1996 China asked to become a full dialogue member of ASEAN, and in June Beijing's request was accepted. In March 1997 China even dispatched a small navy fleet on a goodwill visit to Thailand, Malaysia, and Singapore.

At the international level, both Vietnam and China have also made new friends. Vietnam's progress has been particularly remarkable. Not only did Vietnam normalize its relations with almost all Western countries by 1991, but talks also began to be held between Hanoi and Washington in 1991—after nearly twenty years of no contact—on a variety of issues of common interest. In 1993, the United States dropped its objection to international lending to Vietnam by the World Bank and the Asian Development Bank, thereby turning on the green light for international aid to Vietnam. By 1994, the United States had already lifted the trade embargo against Vietnam that had been imposed for nearly three decades. And on 11 July 1995, the two countries finally established formal diplomatic relations and quickly exchanged ambassadors. If Vietnam has made a new friend in Washington, China has also scored rapid progress and unprecedented new gains in its relations with Moscow. In fact, since 1992, China's bilateral ties with Russia have developed quickly on almost all fronts, including the military. A series of agreements were signed in 1994 and 1995 not only to delineate the land border, but also to reduce the armed presence along it, to inform each other on military activities, and to co-operate on advancement of military technology. On the other hand, China's relations with the United States have remained stable, in spite of the stalling question of Taiwan. In fact, China's cultural and economic ties with the United States have continued to grow by leaps and bounds in the 1990s.

Although China-Vietnam relations in the 1990s must still be understood and analysed in the context of the historical patterns outlined in the foregoing passages, it cannot be overemphasized that both the world as a whole and the Asia-Pacific region in particular in the 1990s has undergone fundamental structural changes. The disintegration and de-communization of the Soviet bloc and the end of the Cold War has definitely removed the danger of nuclear holocaust and ushered in a new era of peace for the entire world. The complete withdrawal of the United States from the Philippines in 1992 and the corresponding drastic reduction of Soviet naval presence in the Asia-Pacific region as a whole had the further effect of reducing external threat to all Asian countries. For the first time in half a century, peace prevailed in the entire Asia-Pacific region, and there is no tense confrontation between any two nations nor civil turmoil within any one. Even for Vietnam and China, two of the three major issues that once constituted bases of bitter conflict, i.e. Cambodia and the ethnic Chinese, have become moot. And neither party feels an immediate threat from any source or from each other.

Therefore, one witnesses in the mid-1990s opportunities for both Vietnam and China not only to develop themselves rapidly, but also to co-operate with each other. On the Vietnamese side, for the first time after half a century of continuous war, the country enjoys a real breathing spell and is on friendly terms with all the neighbouring countries. After abandoning its territorial ambitions in Cambodia, Hanoi was able for the first time to concentrate its energy on reconstruction of the war-devastated country and on economic development. In fact, given the protracted and prolonged nature of war, particularly in view of the extent and depth of ecological and social damages wrought to Vietnam and their lasting after-effects, Hanoi cannot afford any new adventures beyond its borders. Indeed, since 1986, Vietnam has embarked upon the most ambitious and liberal programme of economic reform and open-door policy it has ever known. And all signs indicate that Vietnam is at the moment completely absorbed in its domestic developmental programmes. Being still one of the poorest nations in the world, Vietnam does have a lot to catch up with its prospering neighbours. It certainly needs a peaceful international environment more than any other Southeast Asian country does and for a longer period of time too, in order to make up for the lost time. For this reason alone, Vietnam is not likely to sour its newly-mended ties with either China or any other ASEAN neighbour for the immediate future.

If the unprecedented peaceful and friendly environment of the mid-1990s provides Vietnam a golden opportunity to reconstruct and develop its war-torn country, it also allows China to streamline and upgrade its growing but trouble-ridden economy. Indeed, for decades China was contained or confronted by at least one superpower, and more recently by both the Soviet Union and the United States simultaneously. That kind of predicament no longer exists in the 1990s. Although the United States still maintains a substantial naval force plus 100,000 troops in the East Asian region, both compelling military considerations and growing bilateral ties have essentially transformed the China-U.S. relations, rendering it non-antagonistic in nature.[10] Moreover, new breakthroughs have been scored in China's relations with Taiwan since the late 1980s, and the flow of goods and people between the two sides of the Taiwan Strait have been growing steadily in the 1990s in spite of lack of political progress. Even the dispute on the South China Sea islands has reached a stage of being accepted by all parties as demanding no urgent resolution. At least China does not see an American or Russian hand in the dispute. And it is no exaggeration to say that since 1949 China has never enjoyed a stronger sense of security than today.

Indeed, for a number of reasons, China will be preoccupied with domestic issues and therefore unlikely to create new problems with its southern neighbour in the foreseeable future. Foremost among such issues is clearly the party leadership's paramount concern with political stability in the post-Deng era. With the death of Deng Xiaoping in February 1997, China entered a new era, led for the first time by civilians. Although Jiang Zeming's leadership position was consolidated after the fifteenth party congress, the Asian economic crisis that has swept across the region since July 1997 presents a new threat to China's economic well-being and political stability that cannot be easily removed. The disastrous summer flooding of 1998 that occurred only "once in a hundred years" affected twenty-nine of China's thirty provinces, and the massive rehabilitation work in its wake added a new challenge to Jiang's position and leadership skills. In any case, to withstand either the external or the internal pressure alone already constitutes a crucial test of the new leadership's mandate that will last well into the twenty-first century.

The second urgent item on China's political agenda has been maintaining the stability and prosperity in Hong Kong and preparing for the resumption of sovereignty over Macau on 20 December 1999. Both are vitally important tasks that demand much of Beijing's attention and efforts. In spite of the relatively smooth transfer of power in Hong Kong, the new special administrative region of China has already gone through a whole succession of events and problems that have clearly undermined both the morale of the Special

Administrative Region (SAR) government and the confidence of the Hong Kong residents. The determination of Hong Kong to pull through the Asian economic crisis by maintaining its currency value has already devastated the local property market and increased the unemployment rate to a new fifteen-year high.[11] After all, the sheer magnitude of managing a capitalist economy and administering a free society more or less independent of diverse and multiple pressures from China poses an enormous challenge to Beijing, as well as to the new SAR government. In this connection, Beijing's new woes have certainly been compounded by the increasingly chaotic social conditions in Macau as a result of large-scale and recurrent street shootouts between the local police and criminal gangs since mid-1998.[12] Even if everything goes well for both Hong Kong and Macau from now on, it will still take Beijing at least five to ten years to accumulate both experience and confidence in running two former colonies, a phenomena unprecedented in China's history. And any problems developing in either one in the coming ten years or so would definitely draw worldwide attention and criticisms of China, thereby damaging its international prestige.

Even if the Hong Kong and Macau question were settled to the satisfaction of all parties concerned, there is still the increasingly urgent and thorny problem of reunification with Taiwan. And the fact that Taiwan has been deliberately stalling any new or serious negotiations since the missile crisis clearly renders the entire problem all the more difficult to solve. By the year 2000, Taiwan will unquestionably become the single most important issue on China's political agenda. Indeed, it is perhaps no exaggeration to say that barring unforeseeable new threats from either Russia or the United States, if China will be preoccupied with any political issue in the twenty-first century, it will be Taiwan. Clearly, however, the resolution of the Taiwan problem demands a combination of diplomatic skills and political manoeuvring of a completely different order than in the case of Hong Kong and Macau. It would certainly require a time much longer than the resolution of the Hong Kong and Macau issues. This means that the task of reunification will consume much of China's attention and energy in the twenty-first century, so much so that all other international issues are likely to occupy secondary places. This is already based on the assumption that the transfer of Hong Kong and Macau turns out to be all smooth sailing. In light of all the above, China will remain very much inward-looking both economically and politically at least for the coming decade, if not longer.

For all the reasons outlined above, Vietnam and China have got every reason to maintain and even improve their bilateral relations.

Indeed, as a technologically more advanced country beginning to accumulate huge sums of foreign exchange reserves, China is in a position to extend a variety of technical and economic assistance to Vietnam. By the same token, Vietnam also constitutes a new, substantial market for China's vastly expanding consumer industry. In other words, for the immediate future, the two economies can be made to complement each other to the benefit of both parties. What is perhaps even more important, precisely because Vietnam shares a common culture with China and understands China more thoroughly than any other ASEAN country, it could play a sort of bridging role between China and maritime Southeast Asia, by conveying the latter's anxieties to China more accurately on the one hand, and by reducing their excessive fears of China as an emerging power on the other. And any progress made in this respect would surely enhance mutual understanding and mutual trust between all the parties concerned and therefore promote the stability of the entire Southeast Asian region.

New challenges in the twenty-first century

To be sure, the new opportunities offered by a Pax Asiana by no means automatically remove all sources of tension or areas of potential conflict between China and Vietnam. Nor have the emerging realities in the Asia-Pacific region completely overshadowed the traditional pattern of relations between the two countries. In fact, on the geopolitical level, the rapid diplomatic progress achieved by Vietnam in the international community since 1991 has not been exclusively the result of Hanoi's own efforts. It also reflects the changing priorities of the major powers in the West and of the ASEAN countries in Southeast Asia. Indeed, after the end of the Cold War and particularly with the rapid disintegration of the Soviet bloc, Western countries led by the United States tended to view the economically prospering China as potentially the most dangerous source of threat to regional security, and therefore sought to counter the emerging power of China, if not also to harness its growth, by all means, however discreet they might be.[13] Indeed, the return of Hong Kong and Macau to China by the year 2000 only augments further Beijing's capability to project its military power seaward and southward. The United States certainly will lose its decades-long privilege of access to one of the best and also strategically located harbours in Asia. In view of the combined weakness of all Southeast Asian countries, the recent conflict between China and Vietnam, and the latter's strong nationalist orientation, Washington apparently calculated that lending a hand to Vietnam served both its own national interest and the purpose of regional security. And such reassessment of the Asian situation was clearly shared by other members of the Western community. Hence Washington's swift response to Vietnam's peace initiatives in the early 1990s after nearly twenty years of stalling. Hence also the quick acceptance of Vietnam by the international community as a whole.[14]

Similarly if not even more strongly, the ASEAN countries, which have for decades seen China as the source of threat to the security and stability of Southeast Asia, also saw a power vacuum in Southeast Asia after both the Soviet Union and the United States had departed from the Southeast Asian scene, and therefore developed a new sense of urgency on the issue of restraining an emerging China. Although Beijing has embraced capitalism in many ways since 1979, distrust of China in Southeast Asia has deep historical, cultural, as well as ideological roots that cannot be easily removed, particularly for Malaysia and Indonesia.[15] Indeed, the very thought of China becoming an economic giant is dreadful enough, to say nothing about the political and military strength that economic power can easily generate. Although for nearly fifteen years ASEAN was closely aligned with China in a united opposition to Vietnam's occupation of Cambodia, the main objective of confining Vietnamese power within its original boundaries had already been achieved with the peace settlement of the Cambodia issue. Guided by the new priority of restraining China's power and harnessing its possible expansionist designs in Southeast Asia, ASEAN member countries after 1990 naturally saw Vietnam as a new ally in their common fear of China and a reliable outpost against Chinese influence in Southeast Asia. After all, the threat posed by a Vietnam distanced, if not also alienated, from China is manageable at the worst. By pulling Vietnam on to its side, ASEAN's bargaining power *vis-à-vis* China on a variety of political and economic issues, including the unresolved territorial dispute in the South China Sea, can be further strengthened. Hence the enthusiasm of ASEAN to court Vietnam and to admit it into the regional organization even when the memory of past enmities are still fresh.

All these strategic considerations apparently also match perfectly Vietnamese thinking in the new era. The demise of Russia as a military superpower has left the United States as the only alternative source of counterweight that could check possible southward expansion of China. It is no wonder that as early as 1985, Vietnam considered normalizing relations with Washington as the number one priority task of its foreign policy.[16] But the departure of the

United States from the Philippines, the drastic reduction of American military presence in Southeast Asia, and decades of mutual enmity between Hanoi and Washington, rendered any real and firm U.S. backing for Vietnam unreliable at the best, thereby leaving Vietnam's ASEAN neighbours as the only potential allies in any new round of conflict with China. And precisely because there are outstanding territorial issues unresolved between Vietnam and China, and also because all the other ASEAN countries wish to keep China out of the region, Hanoi could find ready support from its Southeast Asian neighbours on a variety of issues of common concern. Hence Vietnam's eagerness to befriend ASEAN and to join the organization in spite of its apparent lack of preparation and its wide differences from other ASEAN nations in ideology, politics, and culture.

The new power vacuum emerging in Southeast Asia since the early 1990s, the confluence of strategic interests of Vietnam, ASEAN, and the United States, and the resulting new realignment of forces, therefore, contain seeds of conflict between Vietnam and China. Although it is the common desire of all parties concerned to maintain peace and stability in the Asia-Pacific region, there are after all still unresolved bilateral issues between China and Vietnam which could easily generate new tension and conflict. The coming into effect of the 1982 UN Convention on the Law of the Sea in November 1995 and the almost immediately ensuing scramble for Exclusive Economic Zones in Northeast Asia certainly could not but have further alerted both China and Vietnam to the implications for the South China Sea.[17] It cannot be overemphasized that both China and Vietnam are energy-short countries, and economic development in both countries is bound to generate new demand for energy sources.

Therefore, the danger apparently lies first in Vietnam being tempted to take advantage of its new membership in ASEAN and its new friendship with the United States, if only to create an adequate counterweight to China. By the same token, Hanoi may well also be tempted to challenge China again on the territorial issue, and even to enlist the United States in a possible confrontation with China. And in view of the security or strategic considerations of all these countries, it takes only a little persuading and pushing by any one party for such a new anti-China united front to be formed, though perhaps discreetly. In fact, Vietnam did decide to test China's intentions and resolve by seizing two more sand shoals in the Spratly islands in early September 1998.[18] Although Beijing has so far made only verbal protests, such military adventures undertaken by Hanoi are bound to generate new suspicions and anxieties on the part of China, and could even trigger a chain reaction that would not be conducive to the continuing stability of the entire region.

The danger of new conflict also lies in China taking advantage of the power vacuum in Southeast Asia to gain more footholds in the Spratly islands, if not also along the Sino-Vietnamese land border and in the Gulf of Tonkin, the three territorial areas still under dispute. And precisely because China has the smallest share in the Spratly islands compared with all the other disputant parties, and is therefore in the weakest bargaining position, Beijing has no way of substantiating its vast claims without first gaining more control of the island group. Nevertheless, any single, small step taken in that direction, as in the case of Mischief Reef in January 1995, would immediately generate an uproar in Southeast Asia and confirm the latter's long-standing fears and suspicions of China, thereby also pushing the Southeast Asian nations into an alliance against Beijing, if not also inviting the willing United States on to the scene. In this connection, whether and how Beijing will respond to Hanoi's new inroads into the Spratly islands deserves to be watched closely.

Even on the economic side, there may also be increasingly fierce competition between China and Vietnam in the twenty-first century. Although Vietnam's economic reform and open-door policy was implemented nearly ten years later than China's, the much smaller size of the country, the even cheaper labour force, and the fact that the entire southern portion of Vietnam has long practised capitalism, all militate in Vietnam's favour. In fact, spectacular progress in economic development has been achieved since 1988 and on a nationwide scale, a phenomenon that is not paralleled in China. Although in terms of per capita GDP Vietnam is still among the poorest of all nations and lags far behind China, with an average annual growth rate of nine per cent for the past decade, the likelihood of Vietnam catching up with China in the foreseeable future cannot be readily ruled out. After all, Vietnam and China are on the whole still in a similar stage of economic development and are therefore bound to become increasingly keen rivals in the international market.

It is perhaps noteworthy that Vietnam's economic growth has been almost totally unrelated to any Chinese input. Whether by chance or by design, Hanoi has not sought, nor has Beijing provided, any capital aid or expertise to any developmental projects in Vietnam during the past ten years. Rather, new boosters in Vietnam's economy have originated from European, American, Japanese, and Southeast Asian sources. Particularly remarkable is the rapidly growing trade and investment linkages between Vietnam and its ASEAN neighbours. As of the end of 1996, forty per cent of all Vietnam's foreign investment and 48 per cent of its foreign trade were with the other ASEAN countries.[19] The increasingly strong economic links between Vietnam and Western and Southeast Asian countries clearly have the effect of pushing China further apart from Vietnam, with all the political implications that may go along with it.

What may be even worse to Beijing has been the strong economic ties established between Vietnam and Taiwan during the past decade or so, which is in sharp contrast to the stagnation of Sino-Vietnamese economic links. By 1996, Taiwan was already ranked as the number one foreign investor, accounting for 20 per cent of all Vietnam's foreign investment.[20] The new economic links have already generated air links and even discreet political contacts between Hanoi and Taipei, which could also have significant implications for the Spratly dispute. For years the original ASEAN member countries had been reluctant to antagonize China on the issue of Taiwan. Hanoi's ready acceptance of Taiwanese economic initiatives apparently served the political interests of both sides well. Mutual support between Vietnam and Taiwan on the China question certainly would represent a great boost to the strength of any Southeast Asian united front directed against China. Indeed, with its widening economic links with Taipei, Hanoi would be under increasing pressure to make use of Taiwan as a bargaining chip in dealing with China. With Taiwan moving more and more openly towards formal independence since 1996, it would also be interesting to see what new position Taiwan would take on the South China Sea dispute if and when tension flares up again. Here also lies a real danger of new conflict between China and Vietnam with unpredictable consequences. Should Taipei abandon its long-standing position of defending its claims to the South China Sea islands in the same terms of China, and even decide to echo Hanoi's position or co-operate with Vietnam on such matters, Beijing may well view it as a grand conspiracy in the making, involving even the United States, and therefore feel compelled to take a radical stand on all Sino-Vietnamese territorial disputes in general, and the Taiwan-occupied island in particular.[21]

Conclusions

The new era therefore contains opportunities and pitfalls for both China and Vietnam. If China needs to continuously reassure all its Southeast Asian neighbours of its benign nature, as it has in fact been doing energetically with some success during recent years, ASEAN as a whole and Vietnam in particular needs also to accept the continuing growth of China as an economic and political power in the region as a fact to live with, not as a danger to suppress. To be sure, for a Southeast Asia that has been traditionally suspicious of China's imperialist ambitions, and particularly for a Vietnam that has only recently fought bitter battles with China, this reorientation of attitude is a difficult task, particularly at a time when major Western powers, including the United States, has been pursuing a new policy of neo-containment directed against China.[22] Nevertheless Vietnam could in fact play a positive role in this respect and if successful, it would serve the interest of all. If, on the contrary, the new U.S. policy finds ready echoes in the Asia-Pacific region in general and in Southeast Asia in particular, forces increasingly hostile to China would quickly grow, thereby rendering China subject to feelings of being threatened by the surrounding countries again. And out of a sense of insecurity, China might, as it did in the past, resume a militant posture towards its southern neighbours and might even take drastic measures on certain issues still under dispute.

Specifically, if Vietnam refrains from capitalizing on its ASEAN membership or its new friendship with the United States and Taiwan as a counterweight to China and also refrains from pushing for an early solution of the territorial dispute in its favour, peace and stability could be expected for the coming decade in Southeast Asia. If, on the contrary, Hanoi should decide to settle the Spratly dispute in its favour in the near future, and to enlist the support of ASEAN and even the United States, Beijing might be forced to react drastically. In other words, Vietnam should not make the same mistake, as it did in the 1970s and 1980s, of enlisting an outside power, much less a superpower, to confront China. A Vietnam aligned with ASEAN constitutes no threat from the Chinese perspective, but a Vietnam lined up with ASEAN not only hostile to China but also receiving support from the United States is bound to be seen by Beijing as an enormous threat to its security. Similarly, Vietnam must refrain from lining up with Taiwan on any issue against China, otherwise it would also be seen in Beijing as a serious trespassing on Chinese sovereignty that could not be forgiven. The challenge for Vietnam in the coming years, therefore, consists mainly in balancing its ties with China on the one hand, and with Southeast Asia, Taiwan, and the United States on the other, without at the same time attempting to alter the status quo in its disputes with China.

For China, the task of persuading all Southeast Asian neighbours of its peaceful intention is at least an equally difficult one. Here clearly actions speak louder than words. To accomplish this objective, Beijing must refrain from any more show of military force in both the Spratly archipelago and the Taiwan Strait as it has done in recent years. Indeed, it must make at least some concessions in its vast, untenable claim to the South China Sea, a claim that in itself cannot but have only imperialistic implications but no practical value. After all, all of the thirty-six major islands in the Spratly group have been occupied by Southeast Asian countries, and there is little prospect that China could reverse the *fait d'accompli* without a massive use of military force.[23] So far Beijing has repeatedly pledged its intention to settle the territorial dispute in a peaceful manner and according to the Law of the Sea, but more concrete proposals based on the status quo are yet to be forthcoming.

What is even more difficult, Beijing needs also to reassure its neighbours that it would not resort to the use of force against Taiwan unless the latter declares formal independence. In fact, China should exhaust all means to strive for a peaceful resolution of the Taiwan issue. Moreover, it should accept the fact that Taiwan has been an independent political entity for half a century as a basis of any political negotiation between the two sides of the Taiwan Strait. Indeed, to reassure Taiwan of Beijing's good intentions is also to reassure all the Southeast Asian nations of China's non-imperialistic character. And yet this may well be a real challenge to Beijing in view of recent developments. For nearly four decades until the 1990s, the Taiwanese Government had upheld a one-China policy and for nearly ten years after 1987 Taipei had promoted cross-Strait contacts in an effort to normalize relations with China. All these appear to have changed since 1995 with President Lee Teng-hui's visit to the United States, and particularly after Lee's re-election as Taiwan's president in the first-ever direct presidential election in 1996. Hence China's missile test in March 1996 in order to suppress the independence mood,[24] but this show of force immediately rekindled new fears in Southeast Asia. What is worse, Taiwan has not been, and will most likely not be, intimidated into supporting reunification. In fact, it has begun to distance itself from China since the latest Taiwan Strait crisis. How Beijing decides to settle the Taiwan issue in the post-Deng era, therefore, becomes a crucial indicator of its regional policy with immediate implications for Southeast Asia.

To sum up at the risk of oversimplification, the fundamental problem lies in the fact that Vietnam has not been in the habit of co-operating closely with China in its better times. On the other hand, China has not completely abandoned its mentality as a big brother in dealing with Southeast Asian countries in general, and Vietnam and Taiwan in particular. Perhaps what is even more important is that both Hanoi and Beijing could act from a position of unprecedented strength today. Therefore, although the opportunities are here and conspicuous for both countries to work for a lasting peace in Southeast Asia, the temptation of either or both countries to assert its rights or claims at the expense of the other party remains great in spite of the many pressing domestic concerns confronting both countries. Moreover, there are changing variables involving the United States and Taiwan that are beyond the control of both Vietnam and China. For both Hanoi and Beijing, therefore, political foresightedness, military restraint, and diplomatic skills are all required to seize the new opportunities presented to them and to face the new challenges wisely in the years ahead. Let us all hope that a Pax Asiana will indeed reign as we enter the twenty-first century.

Notes

1. For a general historical account of Vietnam's relations with China, see Joseph Buttinger, *A Political History of Vietnam* (London: Andre Deutch, 1969); Nguyen Khac Huyen, *Vision Accomplished?* (New York: Collier Books, 1971).
2. Exchanges of official greetings prior to 1991 and particularly during the Second Indochina War were replete with such terms.
3. See King C. Chen, *China and Vietnam, 1938–1954* (Princeton: Princeton University Press, 1969).
4. For a general account, see Huynh Kim Khanh, *Vietnamese Communism, 1925–1945* (Ithaca: Cornell University Press, 1982).
5. See Chang Pao-min, *Kampuchea Between China and Vietnam* (Singapore: Singapore University Press, 1985).
6. One needs only to read any official policy statement China addressed to Vietnam during the period from November 1978 to May 1979 to get a strong impression of this.
7. Chang Pao-min, *Kampuchea Between China and Vietnam*, op. cit.
8. *Ibid.*
9. See Economist Intelligence Unit, *Country Report: Vietnam* (London: The Economic Intelligence Unit, 1st quarter, 1998), p. 29.
10. This is clearly demonstrated by the fact that the United States deliberately avoided direct confrontation with China during the Taiwan Straits crisis of March 1996, and that U.S.-China relations have not soured since.
11. Between July 1997 and June 1998, property values in Hong Kong were slashed by 40 per cent and the unemployment rate rose from 2.2 per cent to 4.5 per cent; *Hong Kong Monthly Digest of Statistics*, August 1998, p. 8. See also the special issue of *Asian Survey* on Hong Kong published in August 1988.
12. The most recent incident occurred in early October when the shootout took place right in front of the court house where a gang leader was standing trial; *Lianhe Pao* [The United Daily] (Taipei), October 3, 1998, 4.
13. For an elaboration of this argument, see Chang Pao-min, "Jiedu meiguo zai yatai diqu di zhongda liyi" (The Strategic Interests of the

United States: A Critical Analysis), *Ming Pao Monthly* (Hong Kong), February 1997, pp. 28–44.

14. See Chang Pao-min, "Meiguo di xianggang zhengce" (U.S. Policy Towards Hong Kong), *Journal of East Asian Affairs* [Taipei] (July 1998), pp. 71–88.

15. See Chang Pao-min, "China and Southeast Asia: The Problem of a Perception Gap", *Contemporary Southeast Asia* (December 1997): 181–93.

16. William Turley, "Vietnamese Security in Domestic and Regional Focus: The Political-Economic Nexus", in Richard Ellings and Sheldon Simon, eds., *Southeast Asian Security in the New Millenium* (Armonk, New York: M.E. Sharpe, 1996), pp. 175–220.

17. In April 1996, Japan publicized its Exclusive Economic Zone enclosing a total of 2.5 million square kilometres of sea area. A dispute with the Republic of Korea soon followed over a couple of small islands located in the Sea of Japan. See *Lian He Pao*, 21 February 1996 and *Asashi Shimbun* (Tokyo), 29 April 1996. From July to September of the same year, the dispute over Diaoyutai or Senkaku Islands flared up again between Japan, Taiwan, and China.

18. *Ta Kung Pao* (Hong Kong), 10 September 1998, A2.

19. Economist Intelligence Unit, *Country Report: Vietnam* (London: The Economic Intelligence Unit, 1st quarter, 1998).

20. Ibid., Singapore surpassed Taiwan in 1997 to become Vietnam's top foreign investor.

21. The fact that Taipei has not made any protest following the most recent dispute in the Spratly islands may well signal the end of a long-standing policy on the South China Sea.

22. Chang Pao-min, "Meiguo di xianggang zhengce", op. cit.

23. In sharp contrast to Vietnam and the Philippines, China controls only eight tiny rocks or sandbanks which cannot sustain human activity without a massive artificial build-up. For a recent analysis of the Spratly situation, see Cheng-yi Lin, "Taiwan's South China Sea Policy", *Asian Survey* (April 1997): 323–39.

24. For an analysis of the missile crisis, see Chang Pao-min, "The dynamics of Democratization and Crisis in the Taiwan Straits", *Contemporary Southeast Asia* (June 1996): 136–51.

6

BETWEEN CHINA AND ASEAN: THE DIALECTICS OF RECENT VIETNAMESE FOREIGN POLICY

David Wurfel

Introduction

Despite the ideological rhetoric so common in the 1970s, Vietnamese foreign policy practised the age-old strategy of allying with a distant friend against a nearby enemy—both of whom were ideological comrades. China had become that nearby enemy when it supported the aggressively anti-Vietnamese Khmer Rouge regime. When Vietnam moved to liberate Cambodia from that bloody band in December 1978, China undertook to punish Vietnam with a massive border crossing, effectively resisted at great cost.

This sequence of events, far from solving problems, resulted in a multiplication of enemies—for the first time in history Vietnam faced enemies on both the north and the south, as well as to the west. This was a low point for Vietnamese foreign policy. Nevertheless, in 1979 that policy was aimed simply at getting diplomatic recognition for the status quo, i.e. Vietnamese domination in Cambodia. In fact, the brief incursion into Thai territory by the Vietnamese army in 1980 further hardened ASEAN opposition to Vietnam, and made it easier for the Thai to move closer to China with ASEAN approval.

By the mid-1980s there began to be tectonic changes in world politics. Gorbachev was re-evaluating the Soviet role in Asia, which also required rethinking in Hanoi. This rethinking was initiated in large part by the very bright, cosmopolitan foreign minister, Nguyen Co Thach. He saw the need to make accommodations in Cambodia especially to end the embargo and speed normalization of relations with the United States. By 1988 the whole Politburo was moving in this direction, as embodied in Resolution no. 13, which "held that the SRV should establish a new balance in relations with major powers".[1] A decision was also made to try to normalize relations with China. Vietnam was forced into accommodation with neighbours when the "distant friend" showed a desire to withdraw from Southeast Asia. However, these new policy principles were not easy to translate into action, and in any case, there was considerable disagreement within the policy-making élite about what action should be taken.

The purpose of this chapter is to show how the method of, and justification for, rapprochement with China developed and how it was related to the slightly later initiatives towards ASEAN. A brief comparison of Vietnam's China policy with those of its Southeast Asian neighbours notes the interaction of regime maintenance and national security goals. Finally, an evaluation is offered as to whether this combination of policies towards neighbours large and smaller might be characterized as "enmeshment" or "containment", or some mix of the two, and what its prospects of long-term success may be. So far, Vietnam's utilization of ASEAN may have helped to some extent to discourage Chinese expansionism, but whether an "ASEAN Ten" will be of further assistance in this regard is doubtful.

How to approach China

The period 1988–June 1991

After Resolution no. 13, a series of events occurred around the world which were surely cataclysmic in the view of Hanoi leaders: the Tiananmen Square massacre, the collapse of the Berlin Wall, and the dissolution of the Soviet Union and its ruling party. The international conditions for a multidirectional foreign policy had changed. Some had adopted a kind of bunker mentality and wanted to return to the eternal verities of Marxism-Leninism, which, it was thought, would help protect the regime. Others continued to put emphasis on accommodation with the West that would permit the lifting of the American embargo on trade and investment, thus facilitating economic growth under the new policy of renovation. At the ninth plenum of the Central Committee of the Vietnam Communist Party in August 1990 Foreign Minister Thach was attacked as a rightist, partly because the military withdrawal from Cambodia had not achieved the early lifting of the embargo, which he had foreseen. (He was also involved in a larger power cum ideological struggle within the leadership, and was known as a friend of Tran Xuan Bach, who was removed from the Politburo after being accused of advocating pluralism.)[2]

This attack on Thach was in part the fallout from his very tough stance in informal talks with the Chinese, which began to take place in 1989. The fourth round of talks in Hanoi with the Chinese vice foreign minister was particularly stormy. Nevertheless a switch in U.S. policy in July 1990 caused the Chinese to become more accommodating, as they saw new possibilities for an Indochina settlement. They agreed to a summit meeting in September 1990 in Chengdu, attended by premiers and party heads. Thach, at the request of the Chinese, was excluded. The Chengdu summit marked the start of Sino-Vietnamese normalization; there was substantial agreement on the outlines of a Cambodian settlement.[3]

Vietnamese Party leaders were also very much interested in a Chinese suggestion that they would be willing to resume economic aid to Vietnam after a settlement in Cambodia was implemented and normalization with Vietnam was finalized. There was a strong hint, however, that aid would be linked to co-ordination of Chinese and Vietnamese foreign policies. After the Chengdu summit this approach was opposed by other Politburo members, especially Thach.[4] Nevertheless at the January 1991 eleventh plenum of the Central Committee there was again support for drawing closer to China, in the wake of the shocking events in the Soviet Union; the same group reiterated attacks on Thach. The imperative of regime maintenance temporarily strengthened some key elements of the old Vietnamese world-view.[5] In the seventh party congress in June, Foreign Minister Thach counter-attacked with a strong speech criticizing China. This proved his undoing. He was then removed from both the Politburo and the Central Committee, and later from the foreign ministry. Too much co-operation with capitalist countries— which Thach symbolized—would lead to increased pressure on Vietnam's one-party system, it was feared. The goal of regime maintenance dominated foreign policy strategizing.

Between 1991–93, control over policy relating to Cambodia and China was handed to the defence minister, General Le Duc Anh, the second-ranking member of the Politburo, thus marking the end of the transition to a different foreign policy orientation. In July General Anh travelled to Beijing for more discussions, defining further agreement on all outstanding issues, but finding Chinese willingness to offer aid waning.[6] Perhaps they were getting sufficient Vietnamese co-operation without it. In any case, contacts between party officials of the two countries multiplied at all levels. Finally in November 1991, Vietnamese leaders went to Beijing for a summit, which completed the normalization process. A communiqué rejected hegemonism; reiterated Vietnamese commitment to one China, including Taiwan; and affirmed support for the Paris agreement of 23 October on Cambodia. A Vietnamese request for security guarantees from China within the framework of a military alliance indicated that a closer relationship with China was clearly still the desire of the dominant group in the VCP Politburo—but China rebuffed it. Ideological comraderie with a powerful, but very similar regime was needed by those in Hanoi fearful of international trends. Subsequent events, however, made such a partnership more and more difficult to achieve. Those with a more pragmatic, less ideological approach to international affairs would thus be given another chance to play an important role in foreign policy making.

On the one hand, the fruits of a Cambodian settlement—which Thach had promised, somewhat prematurely—began to emerge. Prospects of membership in ASEAN and normalization with the United States improved. At the same time, economic progress under *doi moi* increased regime legitimacy and reduced the chances of a repeat of Eastern European events. But Chinese actions at variance with words were crucial.

In February 1992 China promulgated a law claiming as Chinese territory almost the entire South China Sea. When the matter was referred to the National Assembly in Hanoi, there was a stormy, unpublicized debate. Some delegates advocated economic, even military retaliation, but finally—with advice from the External Affairs Commission of the Party Central Committee—the Assembly adopted an appropriate response: a mild, but firm, declaration. In May Nguyen Van Linh, by then Senior Adviser to the Central Committee, again visited Beijing to hold discussions with Chinese leaders. Only hours before he was ushered into the Great Hall of the People, the Chinese, at the same spot, signed an agreement with Crestone Energy Corporation to engage in exploratory drilling on the Vietnamese continental shelf. Thus, not surprisingly, at the June 1992 third plenum of the party Central Committee, the debate on whether China constituted a long-term threat to Vietnam security was reopened. Those who continued to advocate an alliance with China advised the party to ignore small conflicts.[7] Others were less patient; even Do Muoi was reported to have called China expansionist—a good indication of how the debate was going.[8]

However, the issue was not settled; one source from inside the Party reported that as late as the latter part of 1992 the Central Committee adopted a secret resolution ranking Vietnam's foreign relations in five different priorities, with China and other Marxist-Leninist states first, and the United States last. ASEAN neighbours who have to be won over to co-operate were in the middle.[9] Efforts to deal with China at the highest level continued. In December 1992 Premier Li Peng visited Hanoi, assuring his listeners that China would never become a hegemonistic and expansionist power. The final joint communiqué agreed to speed up negotiations on territorial disputes, on land and in the Gulf of Tonkin, and to refrain from developmental activities in the disputed area pending a final accord. (At this point the South China Sea was excluded from the understanding.) In November 1993 President Le Duc Anh went to Beijing, the first Vietnamese president to do so in thirty-eight years. While finding consensus on the importance of expanding economic relations, he could not secure agreement on conflicting claims in the South China Sea.[10]

In the meantime, the Chinese had been active. For instance, in May 1993, less than six months after Li Peng agreed to the contrary, a Chinese drilling rig entered Vietnamese territorial waters, only to be withdrawn on the eve of a visit to Vietnam by China's defence minister—following a pattern to be repeated. And while Chinese behaviour undermined the position of those favouring an alliance, new options opened up, particularly that of ASEAN. ASEAN foreign ministers, meeting in Manila in July 1992, issued a declaration on the South China Sea calling for restraint by all parties. China, while not mentioned by name, was clearly the target.[11] Vietnam, which had just signed the 1976 Treaty of Amity and Cooperation, quickly endorsed the declaration. In Manila during the same year, Vo Van Kiet and President Cory Aquino had jointly expressed their commitment to the peaceful settlement of the Spratlys dispute.[12] Thus the Vietnamese leadership, which in 1991 had wanted an alliance with China, became more aware of the opportunity to find allies to the south who had a common interest in opposing Chinese incursions. Said one foreign ministry official in 1993 in an interview with Carlyle Thayer, "we tried for a full year to forge new relations with China, but we failed ... They will always pressure us and try to dominate Southeast Asia".[13]

Thus two or three years before Vietnam became a member of ASEAN, most Hanoi policy makers had abandoned the quest for a China alliance; this successful regional organization was beginning to play a major role in Vietnamese élite thinking. Those in Hanoi who favoured membership must have felt that the decision to join ASEAN was vindicated by the results of the China-ASEAN Dialogue in Hangzhou, China, in April 1995. There, for the first time in a multilateral setting, ASEAN officials raised the Spratly issue with the Chinese. ASEAN concerns were expressed in terms that were unusually forceful, according to Philippine Foreign Affairs

Under-secretary Rodolfo Severino.[14] Studies were also undertaken which validated the decision to join. Fear of exploitation by other more advanced ASEAN members was countered with the conclusion that experiences from other economic co-operation organizations have shown that new members with a lower level of economic development often get more benefits than the more developed ones.[15] In the security area it was argued that "any attempt at military and security cooperation would require a certain commonality in strategic outlook and threat perception ... The possibility is there".[16] As early as 1992 a Vietnamese foreign ministry official spelled out the new rationale in a Singapore publication: "Sino-Vietnamese relations will be meshed within the much larger regional network of interlocking economic and political interests. It is an arrangement whereby anybody wanting to violate Vietnam's sovereignty would be violating the interest of other countries as well. This is the ideal strategic option for Vietnam. It is also the most practical".[17] This is a more straightforward formulation than one has heard recently.

Vietnamese China policy in comparative perspective

Fear and distrust of China must surely be the most important emotional foundation of Vietnamese foreign policy, a feeling much older than the ideological camaraderie of the 1950s and 1960s—the revival of which in 1991 was so short-lived. Yet that feeling, quite realistic in view of recent experience, is veiled when officials speak. The manifestation of growing Chinese power and self-confidence has taught them that verbal barbs are quite counterproductive.

China is probably perceived as a greater problem for Vietnam than it is for other Southeast Asian countries, but their policies towards the colossus of the north can be analysed in a common set of categories. First is regime affinity, an influence so powerful at one point in Vietnam as to change the direction of policy. This has also been a strong factor for Laos, Cambodia, and especially Burma. Second is an historical/cultural factor, the size and political/social role of ethnic Chinese minorities and their perceived link with external threats. Indonesia has a large, unassimilated Chinese minority that in 1965 was thought to be linked to foreign intervention, and is still suspect. Despite normalization, Indonesia's relations with China are not warm. In the Philippines, past suspicion of local Chinese complicity in Beijing's aid to insurgents has waned as the reality of such linkages has faded and as local Chinese have better assimilated into Philippine society. Thus closer relations with China in the 1980s became possible, despite memories that linger. In Thailand high levels of Chinese assimilation into both the economic and political élites facilitate good China relations. Vietnam is the only Southeast Asian country to experience repeated Chinese invasions, the most recent in 1979. Suspicion of local Chinese because of links with China are still strong.[18] This was a cause as well as consequence of the 1979 confrontation with China. Third, the geopolitical/strategic factors, which seem to be most important, are the nature of historical and contemporary relations with neighbours, and with other great powers. When immediate neighbours are seen as threats, then this creates the opportunity for China to play the role of protector, as with Cambodia. This was most obvious in the Khmer Rouge era, but may be re-emerging with Hun Sen, reinforced by regime affinity. Thailand moved closest to China when Vietnamese troops were on its border. For Vietnam, on the other hand, China itself is the threatening neighbour.

Friendship with a great power which itself has an antagonistic relationship with China should allow a Southeast Asian state to stand up to China, though the USSR was not of much assistance to Vietnam in 1979, and the United States insists that the mutual defence agreement with the Philippines does not cover the disputed Spratlys. The United States, whatever its intentions may be, is now the only power in Asia with the military capacity to contain China, and is thus quietly courted by both the Philippines and Vietnam. Nevertheless, the realistic limitations on its likely actions cause those two states to seek a degree of accommodation with China as well. Both welcome closer economic ties with Japan, even though, besides economic, Japanese support can be, at most, diplomatic. Fourth, economic factors may influence policy towards China in more than one direction. Investment from Southeast Asia in China, very substantial in the case of Thailand and Malaysia, is appreciated; it is the kind of engagement that fosters closer relations. For those sharing land borders with China, trade—often in the form of smuggling—may as well be a cause of friction as of friendship. This is the Vietnamese case. When relations with China involve major territorial disputes, economic factors are likely to be of secondary importance in determining the tone and direction of foreign relations.

Regardless of the role of local Chinese, the historical memory of frequent Chinese invasion among both élite and populace makes the Vietnamese image of China unique. Thus it is understandable for Vietnam to look to other great powers as a source of some kind of protection against a renewed China threat. Yet Vietnam's approach to China is still moderated by the recognition of regime affinity and the potentially positive consequence this could have for regime maintenance in Hanoi. Thus there may still be debate between ideologues and disciples of *realpolitik*. Though Vietnamese officials will, understandably, deny the existence of factions in foreign policy making, as Brantley Womack has said, immobilism—which he describes as the character of present day élite politics in Hanoi—"is a measure of the severity of factional differences".[19] What is very new about the current era of Vietnamese foreign policy is the recognition that not only great powers, but also small and medium powers within the region, if banded together in a vigorous regional organization, may also have a role to play in dealing with China.

The China policy of Vietnam in ASEAN

There was, of course, some opposition to Vietnam's membership in ASEAN, especially by Thailand, because of a fear that Hanoi was all too eager to use ASEAN as a club against China. One Vietnamese scholar/official recognized in 1994 that "in the short period after joining, it would be difficult for Vietnam to take the lead or put forward its own initiative on security issues as Hanoi needs to learn the mechanism of ASEAN co-operation, and for their part, some ASEAN members might not want to see Vietnam do so".[20] Thus for the first year Vietnam did indeed maintain a low profile. Staff was being trained in English, and in the structures and processes of ASEAN. At the same time, as we shall see, Vietnamese participants in ASEAN seemed to be learning a great deal as well about its political dynamics.

Meanwhile, Vietnam needed to deal with its mammoth neighbour one on one, which was the way China preferred. On the surface it appeared that relations were improving. Rail links were re-established in early 1996, while in June Premier Li Peng attended the Eighth Vietnam Communist Party Congress in Hanoi, the highest-ranked Chinese leader to do so in more than thirty years. Ten rounds of negotiations on border disputes were held, but without any agreements. As Foreign Minister Nguyen Manh Cam said in an interview, "We strive to accelerate all existing ties with China. These ties have created benefits for both countries... Some issues, however, still remain unsolved ...".[21] In any case, trade in 1996 reached US$1 billion. Military exchanges continued with a group of Chinese officers, including the commander of the PLA Navy Air Force, visiting Vietnam—as well as Malaysia and Singapore—in late February 1997.[22] In April a Vietnamese military delegation was received in Beijing by the Chinese Defence Minister, who in his welcome speech said, "The two countries share a common belief and common goals, and both are faced with the challenge of securing peace and development".[23] There seemed to be some attempt to sustain ideological ties.

Other aspects of the relationship were entirely devoid of ideological overtones. To counter a similar tactic used earlier by China, in April 1996 Vietnam awarded a contract for oil exploration in the South China Sea to Conoco—in an area also claimed by China— which China protested. But no drilling has been undertaken. Less than a year later China undertook bolder steps, commencing exploratory drilling on the Vietnamese continental shelf less than sixty-five nautical miles from Vietnam's coast, in an area not covered by claims of any other ASEAN members (and thus designed to antagonize them less). This was despite an October 1993 agreement between the two powers, which said that "while negotiating to settle the [territorial] issues, the two sides shall not conduct activities that may further complicate the disputes".[24] The oil rig began drilling, according to Vietnamese authorities, on 7 March. Vietnam unsuccessfully tried quiet diplomacy before going public with its protest nearly two weeks later. An unnamed official in Hanoi used uncharacteristically strong words: "This action has added another example that the Chinese expansionist policy has remained unchanged".[25] The diplomatic note handed to the Chinese ambassador merely said: "This act of violation runs counter to the good trend in which bilateral relations of friendship and cooperation are developing".[26] Vietnam insisted that China withdraw the rig and discuss the disputed maritime claims. On 7 April it was announced that the rig had been withdrawn; discussions on the claims began in Beijing two days later. The Vietnamese press, however, barely mentioned this apparent diplomatic victory. There was a reason for their reticence; they had boldly played the ASEAN card and wanted to avoid antagonizing China further by gloating over their success. This marked a new stage in Sino-Vietnamese, and in ASEAN-Vietnamese relations.

Vietnam and ASEAN

Vietnam's remarkable diplomatic coup in March 1997 was built on the cultivation of relations with key ASEAN members for some time before that. To review those relationships is a necessary prelude to understanding the events of March.

Indonesia

Indonesia had long been Vietnam's best friend among the noncommunist states in Southeast Asia. Indonesia had recognized the

Provisional Revolutionary Government of South Vietnam before 1975 and became the crucial liaison between Vietnam and ASEAN in preparation for a settlement of the Cambodian crisis. Indonesia shared Vietnam's fear of China, even though it had no claims in the South China Sea that were threatened by China—until a careful reading of Beijing's 1992 legislation. Despite some degree of regime affinity with China, Indonesia was sympathetic with Vietnam's position.

Singapore

Singapore was a major trading partner and source of investment for Vietnam. Lee Kuan Yew had even been invited several times to Hanoi as a senior adviser. Despite somewhat different views of China, Singapore still could appreciate Vietnam's situation.

Malaysia

Malaysia's foreign policy has been determined in the last decade largely by Prime Minister Mahathir Mohamad's personal views, which have shifted. While in the early 1990s he was still talking about his concern for the long term threat of China, recently he has been saying there was nothing to fear from either Japan or China. The Chinese have been supportive of the prime minister's proposal for an East Asian Economic Group. Relations with Vietnam had been particularly rocky in the period of the boat people.

Thailand

Thailand had traditionally been an enemy of Vietnam, particularly on matters concerning Cambodia. Until Premier Chatichai took office, Thailand led the hard-line faction in ASEAN on negotiations for a Cambodian settlement, even joining an alliance with China, receiving Chinese military assistance and allowing transport of supplies from China across Thai territory to the Khmer Rouge. After Vietnam's withdrawal from Cambodia, the Thai began to look at economic opportunities (without abandoning military links with China, which were profitable for the Thai high command). More than US$1 billion was invested in Vietnam (much less than in China), and trade expanded greatly—some illegally transiting Cambodia.

   Thai-Vietnamese relations improved further after Vietnam joined ASEAN. Prime Minister Chavalit Yongchaiyudh's March 1997 state visit to Hanoi—one of several high-level exchanges—was described by the Bangkok press "as a part of Thailand's quest to be treated seriously by Hanoi as an economic partner".[27] That visit also had to deal with serious conflict, derived from overlapping claims to 14,000 square kilometres of the Gulf of Thailand. The Vietnamese had arrested hundreds of Thai fishermen whom they claimed were illegally in Vietnamese waters. Prospects of oil intensified the conflict. In January the Thai Cabinet, on Chavalit's initiative, had unilaterally declared an extension of the Thai continental shelf, over the protest of neighbouring countries. (Perhaps the Thai had learned some techniques from the Chinese.) In fact, the King was so concerned about the impact of this move on relations with Thailand's neighbours that he summoned the Premier to an audience to discuss the matter.[28] The March trip by Chavalit to Hanoi could not resolve this problem, but the two sides agreed that "if agreement cannot be reached, then a joint committee will be established".[29] By April they were talking about joint naval patrols in the disputed area.[30] The constructive approach to bilateral issues was especially impressive for two countries which were traditional enemies and had such different feelings about China.

When Prime Minister Chavalit visited China in early April, he was greeted by the Chinese defence minister with the plea: "China is hopeful that Thailand will help create understanding with neighbouring countries", which probably meant help against the buildup of antipathy towards China within ASEAN. Chavalit responded with effusive praise for China's support of the Thai military, which had just been offered additional Chinese aid. Professor Kusuma Snitwongse of Chulalongkorn University, an experienced observer of Thai foreign policy, commented: "Thailand wants a lead role in ASEAN, and Thailand can act as a bridge to China"—which was denied by foreign ministry officials wary of upsetting ASEAN partners.[31]

Philippines

The Philippines, which had been one of only two Southeast Asian members of the South-East Asian Treaty Organization (SEATO) that had sent troops to help South Vietnam during the Vietnam War and which had had a virulent streak of anti-communism in domestic politics but warmed to China during the Aquino presidency, seemed an unlikely ally for Vietnam. The close relations that have, in fact, developed are a tribute to the potency of a common perception of threat.

Even before the completion of the United Nations Transitional Authority in Cambodia (UNTAC) mission in Cambodia, Vo Van Kiet visited the Philippines in 1992. He and President Aquino "expressed their commitment to the peaceful settlement of the

Spratlys dispute".[32] In 1993 the Vietnamese foreign ministry showed special favours to the Philippines as it was expanding its embassy. There was already an awareness of common problems with China. The Philippines strongly supported Vietnam's admission to ASEAN even before Vietnam officially applied for membership. In March 1994 President Ramos went to Hanoi, where he "sought to strengthen the strategic partnership between the Philippines and Vietnam".[33] A Joint Commission for Bilateral Cooperation was created.

Co-operation intensified after discovery of the Chinese occupation of Mischief Reef in 1995. The Philippines was quite explicit in stating its disappointment with the level of ASEAN support at the time of this incident, and obviously an ASEAN that included Vietnam would have a somewhat different outlook. Vietnam President Le Duc Anh visited Manila later in 1995. In April 1996 Vietnam and the Philippines signed a Memorandum of Understanding on Joint Oceanographic and Marine Scientific Research in the South China Sea. Said Ambassador Rosalinda Tirona, "The example set by the Philippines and Vietnam through this initiative is concrete evidence that despite conflicting territorial claims, states can still cooperate".[34] Was China listening? The first research project undertaken was in the vicinity of Mischief Reef. In January 1997 the commander of the Vietnam People's Navy visited the Philippines to meet the Secretary of National Defense and the Chief of Staff of the Armed Forces, among others. The stage had been well set for the way in which the Philippines would react to incidents involving China in 1997.

Multilateral approaches

On 20 March at the same time that Vietnam went public in its protest against the Chinese oil rig, the deputy foreign minister, Vu Khoan, quietly called together the ASEAN ambassadors to explain Hanoi's position, an event unprecedented in the history of ASEAN.[35] Basically Vietnam was trying to convince other ASEAN members that "if China behaves this way to Vietnam, it could behave the same way towards [them]".[36] The restraint practised by Vietnam within ASEAN up to this point had apparently been helpful. ASEAN diplomats were swayed. A senior ASEAN official noted: "We don't recognize any Chinese rights to Vietnam's continental shelf, nor do we recognize the right of the Chinese to do what they did. Now we're all in this together".[37]

While the Vietnamese tactic may have been helpful in regard to the oil rig, at the same time, China was playing host to a conference on regional security under the auspices of ARF, where it mounted a strident attack on U.S. military presence in the region. And at that conference China refused a request to sign the 1992 Manila Declaration on the South China Sea, which pledged the signatories to use only peaceful means to settle their disputes. There, Beijing had not yet gotten the message from ASEAN.

If ASEAN protests in confidential diplomatic notes did indeed cause the Chinese to withdraw their oil rig shortly after this conference closed, as Vietnamese officials now suggest,[38] then some notes must have been quite forceful, for it appears that only the Philippines released a critical public statement. Foreign Affairs Undersecretary Rodolfo Severino said that his government "is very much concerned over China's reported oil exploration on the Vietnamese continental shelf".[39] On the other hand, when asked to comment on a Chinese oil rig in waters claimed by Vietnam, Thai Premier Chavalit carefully said that "both China and Vietnam are friends of Thailand".[40]

A more important indicator of the accomplishments of Vietnam's strategy was the outcome of the annual China-ASEAN dialogue in mid-April held at the Chinese mountain resort of Huangshan. There issues in the South China Sea were raised forcefully, and for the first time China agreed to talk about the ASEAN member's claims in a multilateral setting. Beijing also offered to negotiate a code of conduct governing ties with ASEAN.[41] At the same time, to mollify China, and in their own interests, Vietnam and Indonesia praised China for fending off a vote on human rights pushed by the West in the United Nations. All agreed that "certain Western powers" were trying to drive a wedge between China and ASEAN—just as China was trying to do to U.S.-ASEAN relations.

Then soon after this somewhat conciliatory conference behaviour, the Chinese again moved assertively in the South China Sea. At the end of April, Chinese vessels appeared near an islet claimed by the Philippines, which quickly deployed air force jets in the area.[42] In addition to making a diplomatic protest to China the presidential palace informed other ASEAN members of the events.[43] Within a few days the vessels did withdraw. The Chinese had first said that navy ships involved were doing "marine survey measurements", but later contended that they were fishing boats approaching the shoal as part of "youth non-government organization" activities![44] Later research revealed that the ships, belonging to the State Oceanic Administration, carried an international group of short wave radio hams, including both Americans and Japanese, who wanted to broadcast from a new and exotic call sign—which just happened to be designated as "Chinese territory".[45] To re-emphasize their position, the Philippine Navy arrested Chinese fishermen in the vicinity, part of the Philippine Economic Zone, a few weeks later—even though international experts now say that the Chinese territorial claim to the islet, far north of the Spratlys, was probably valid.

Nevertheless, this followed a pattern of inconsistency between diplomatic words and seaborne action. Filipino statements regarding what ASEAN should do have been the most open, and blunt, of any from ASEAN members. Said General Arnulfo Acedero, Armed Forces Chief of Staff, in Bangkok, "China is asserting itself too much ... It is about time we put China in its proper place" through diplomatic means.[46] Defense Secretary Renato de Villa put it more cautiously: ASEAN members should allot more time "to take stock of the real situation in the area, with the end in view of enhancing the strength of its defenses, if necessary". Foreign Secretary Domingo Siazon also raised the question of ASEAN involvement with Japan, and the foreign ministry in Tokyo agreed to raise the question of armed Chinese vessels in disputed water of the South China Sea at the ARF meeting in Kuala Lumpur on 27 July 1997.[47]

There is no prospect that ARF would discuss enhancing the strength of ASEAN defences. ASEAN is not a military alliance. Nevertheless, de Villa's comment is interesting because it brings to the fore the question of bilateral military co-operation between ASEAN members, which is already taking place. To a degree one could hardly have expected two years ago, Vietnam itself is involved in this process. Said a leading foreign ministry official, "Integration in South East Asia is the wave of the future ... [It] has both economic and political, i.e. security, aspects. Vietnam has exchanged military delegations with ASEAN countries and joined in military exercises. This helps to maintain Vietnam's security, since Vietnam cannot fight alone".[48]

Vietnam, however, has a problem with confidence building measures (CBMs), the rubric under which so much military dialogue takes place. For it requires transparency, the release of information on military budgets and weapons acquisitions. Said a leading Vietnamese diplomat, "Vietnam is not accustomed to such procedures. If it means revealing secret information, it is very difficult. But it must be done. Even Russia will report to the UN the weapons it has sold to Vietnam".[49] In fact, a Russian scholar/general has already reported that Vietnam was one of the top six purchasers of Russian arms in 1995.[50] Still, among older Party leaders, and, of course, the military, greater transparency is seen as having limited feasibility.[51] Thus Vietnam's military co-ordination with ASEAN will also be limited. This would seem to imply a fairly low priority for such activity.

China and ASEAN: balance or enmeshment?

How then is the role of ASEAN, ARF, and individual ASEAN members, in Vietnamese foreign policy to be evaluated? What is the underlying strategy? Let us first look at Vietnamese views and then at those of observers and analysts from other countries. One senior Party foreign affairs analyst,[52] who revealed himself as being rather conservative on other issues, said that too much cannot be expected of ASEAN. Each country has its own interests and would not join with Vietnam if real action is required. Yet this view was expressed at the same time that he was confident that the Chinese oil rig was withdrawn as a result of protests by most ASEAN members. A younger, U.S. trained foreign ministry official was both more cautious and more positive about ASEAN's role. Said he: "ASEAN protest probably helped in removal of the Chinese oil rig. Some other ASEAN members had a common interest with Vietnam to challenge Chinese territorial claims. ASEAN membership has given Vietnam some comfort in dealing with China, even though ASEAN can never balance China."[53]

In a lecture at the Institute of International Relations in Hanoi, the head of the policy planning staff of the Ministry of Foreign Affairs was even more straightforward in rejecting the concept of ASEAN as balance: "ASEAN does not have the purpose of balancing China. In fact, it cannot, since China is becoming a superpower. But tighter ASEAN integration can strengthen the region's bargaining position with all great powers." He went on to say, "after more than one year it is clear that Vietnam's decision to join ASEAN was correct. Now big powers must deal with Vietnam as a member of ASEAN".

A Japanese scholar has a similar view of Vietnam's stance:

> Convinced that the China threat is real, but anxious to avoid hostilities, Vietnam is ... trying to draw closer to ASEAN, which shares Vietnam's concerns about ambitions in the Spratly Islands. China, it is argued, would hesitate to attack the islands of an ASEAN-related Vietnam, since such an attack would antagonize the other countries of ASEAN, which China looks on ... as potential allies in its struggle with the big countries in the Asia-Pacific region.[54]

Donald Zagoria sees this approach as typical of Southeast Asia generally: "The South East Asian states are aware that their own power resources are limited and that they will not be able to deal to their satisfaction with an aggressive China at any time soon. The best strategy is to engage China as a participant in regional affairs and to increase the incentives for China to play a peaceful and constructive role".[55] An Australian-based scholar advocates such an approach to China for all states in the Asia-Pacific: "A mild form of enmeshment [or engagement], with emphasis on rewards rather than punishments, would seem the most, and really the only satisfactory option. The objective would be to convince Beijing that conciliation pays and heavy-handed unilateralism does not".[56] Vietnam, and Southeast Asia, are thus taking the liberal view that by involving a potential opponent in an international regime, that power may be persuaded to respect the values of the regime and thus modify its behavior accordingly. David Shambaugh is also supportive of this approach: "Engagement ... is a ... vehicle to the ultimate goal of integrating China into the existing rule-based, institutionalized, and normative international system".[57] While entering a realistic caveat, which he explains at some length: "For numerous reasons, China will be reluctant to respond positively to the policy of engagement", he concludes, "yet this remains the best option available to the international community at present". (ASEAN, while following the same rationale, avoids the term "engagement", which the Chinese sometimes characterize as an American plot.)

While ASEAN diplomats and most Western scholars share a consensus that an old-fashioned balance of power approach for dealing with China today would be a great mistake—at best, ineffective—power-based, realistic strategies have not disappeared from the policy horizon. As Allen Whiting puts it, "ASEAN members vary widely in their degrees of apprehension over China's intention, but they concur on the absence of imminent threat. This provides time for a balance of politics [or enmeshment] to reduce Chinese assertiveness so that exercising the balance of power may be unnecessary".[58] This suggests that the relationship between enmeshment and power balancing may be sequential—if the first fails, the second comes into play.

Some Chinese scholars, however, see the two as co-existing today. In an article that is generally balanced, and takes ASEAN quite seriously, Shi Yongming recognizes that ASEAN defence capability "cannot be considered strong",[59] and notes that it is precisely the weak and decentralized defence forces that have motivated ASEAN to use political means to pursue security through strengthened regional multilateral co-operation and negotiation. He adds that "on the other hand, the weak defense forces have also forced ASEAN countries to adopt the military policy of balancing superpowers, namely allowing the U.S. to exercise military functions ... in South East Asia". Even while pointing out that both United States and Japan are attempting to persuade ASEAN to become allies, Shi concludes that "maintaining a balanced relationship with various larger nations is conducive to ASEAN's own security and regional stability" and that of the whole Asia-Pacific. If this were indeed Chinese policy then Vietnam would feel no reluctance to strengthen strategic, as well as economic, links with Japan and the United States—which is, in fact, being done.

When Prime Minister Ryutaro Hashimoto toured Southeast Asia in January 1997, he put more emphasis on security matters than had any previous Japanese premier. While he was in Hanoi, it was reported that throughout the meeting with Premier Vo Van Kiet there were indications of both countries' concern that China may become a common threat for Japan and ASEAN.[60] In the final communiqué Kiet and Hashimoto agreed to promote security dialogue between their countries, at first through vice-ministerial consultations, which have, in fact, proceeded.[61] During a courtesy call on Do Muoi, the Party leader told Hashimoto that it is important that Japan, the United States and China co-operate to maintain stability in the Asia-Pacific. The desire persists for a concert of powers—which plays well in Beijing, but discussions are ongoing to plan for other contingencies.

One concrete result of Hashimoto's tour was the positive, though qualified, ASEAN response to his proposal for a regular summit meeting between ASEAN leaders and Japan.[62] Some members of ASEAN were wary of agreeing to an exclusive ASEAN-JAPAN summit. An earlier proposal to include China and South Korea along with Japan in a high-level meeting was revived and later approved. In December 1998, the first meeting of "ASEAN + 3" (China, Japan and South Korea) was held in Hanoi following the conclusion of the informal ASEAN summit. This meeting represented the *de facto* achievement of Mahathir's dream of an East Asian Economic Group (EAEG) which Japan had initially opposed.

Vietnam's attentions to security relations with the United States were highlighted by the fortuitous presence in Hanoi of Admiral Joseph Prueher, U.S. Pacific Fleet Commander, at the time of the Vietnamese protest about the presence of a Chinese oil rig on their continental shelf. On the occasion of this visit, Deputy Prime Minister Tran Duc Luong praised the contribution of improved Vietnam-U.S. relations to "stability and development in the region".[63] The contribution of the relationship to "security and peace of the Asia Pacific" was reiterated in Hanoi at the time of the Senate confirmation of the new U.S. ambassador to Vietnam. Vietnamese military officers have also had a chance to visit the United States.

All states are aware, therefore, that Vietnam's aspiration is for a concert of powers, consultation, trade, the sharing of goals and the avoidance of overt conflict among the members of ARF. Vietnam will use ASEAN and ARF to raise concerns and seek consensus. When consensus within or beyond ASEAN is not possible, Vietnam will nevertheless use this channel to make protests about violations of its security. At the same time bilateral security dialogue will help prepare for eventualities that Vietnam—along with all ASEAN members—hope to avoid. Constructive dialogues with China and close consultation with ASEAN are the preferred tools by which Vietnam hopes to insure its security. Nevertheless, other courses of action are not ignored.

Prospects

In July 1997 the "ASEAN Seven" became "ASEAN Nine", with the inclusion of Laos and Myanmar. Cambodia was admitted as ASEAN's tenth member on 30 April 1990. How will that affect the utility of Vietnam's policy? Will ASEAN still be as likely to react towards China in a manner basically sympathetic to Vietnam's position? Bilson Kurus, writing in 1995, took an optimistic view: "The inclusion of Vietnam and the other Indochinese states as well as Myanmar would further bolster the ability of ASEAN to deal with extra-regional actors over troublesome issues such as the conflicting claims over the Spratly Islands."[64] A Vietnamese scholar was more cautious: "even though from the prevailing ASEAN viewpoint [China] can pose a direct threat to regional security, ... dealing with China in bilateral and multilateral terms will be a challenge to ASEAN solidarity in the years ahead".[65] In a more recent comment, Lee Poh Ping of the University of Malaya had similar concerns: "It will be more difficult to maintain the cohesion of ten disparate countries".[66] Vietnam itself has been quite enthusiastic about the expansion of ASEAN membership. Though unstated, it seems rather clear that this is because of regime affinity; Vietnam will be more comfortable in ASEAN with a greater preponderance of authoritarian regimes.

The special enthusiasm for Myanmar's entry is also a reaction to U.S. opposition to that move. Vietnam wants to reinforce the principle that human rights are a matter of domestic jurisdiction. Said Foreign Minister Cam of the announcement of U.S. sanctions against Myanmar, "Vietnam shares the view of many countries that economic sanctions are imposed with the aim of interfering in the internal affairs of a nation".[67] In late May, a few weeks after the sanctions were announced, Do Muoi, with a large delegation, made a visit to Yangon.[68] The Burmese were very appreciative of Vietnamese support.

Even Philippine Foreign Minister Domingo Siazon, who was under a lot of pressure at home to oppose Burma's entry into ASEAN, supported the move, arguing that Burma's relations with ASEAN had strategic implications, and could not exist only on one dimension, human rights.[69] This furthered the argument, which had been used elsewhere, that bringing Burma into ASEAN would end its dependency on China—which is, at least, a possibility. Yet why was China itself supporting the expansion of ASEAN so vigorously? Partly, of course, to drive a wedge between ASEAN and the United States. But perhaps it was a more long term strategy. Chinese scholars recognize the fragility of ASEAN unity: "When larger nations have sharp confrontations, it is still unknown whether ASEAN as a whole can insist on neutrality". They noted the economic dimension as well: "If Laos, Burma and Kampuchea are accepted in the ASEAN, problems caused by differences in the economic development of different nations within ASEAN will further worsen".[70]

In fact, it seems unlikely that China would have supported Burma's entry into ASEAN if it had thought that in the process it would be losing a close ally. China has also been wooing Hun Sen, Cambodia's most powerful leader, in recent years. Even Laos is trying to end its dependence on Vietnam by building closer ties to both China and Thailand. Thailand under Chavalit has been open both about its close links to China and its desire for leadership in ASEAN.[71] Therefore, in the future a smaller percentage of ASEAN members are likely to come to the support of Vietnam if it has a problem with China in the South China Sea. Cambodia has no territorial conflict with China and regards Vietnam as its traditional enemy. The two members which joined in 1997 do not have coastlines to the disputed Sea. It may be that Vietnam's eagerness to oppose the United States on human rights and intervention in internal affairs will backfire. It may have helped create a new power structure, a new set of orientations toward China within ASEAN that will be fundamentally inimical to Vietnam's interests.

Vietnam's success in utilizing ASEAN engagement, or enmeshment, with China as a political defence against Chinese incursions may not be a policy with long-term viability. The reluctance of the Vietnamese military to allow greater transparency may also frustrate Vietnam's efforts to establish closer military relations with

ASEAN states. As many have said, the shifting shoals of multilateral diplomacy in a multi-polar world pose considerable risk. Putting high priority on protecting a relatively closed political system complicates an already complex diplomatic task.

The less prominent, but emerging, theme in Vietnam's foreign policy strategy, that of seeking a more traditional form of balancing by increasing military links with Japan and the United States, is also fraught with danger. Quite aside from the question of whether either Japan or the United States has the political will to act in the defence of Vietnam, there is the problem of psychological impact on China. Any hint that neighbours may be involved in a scheme to "contain" China seems to make its government even more militant. So far the level of military contact with those two major powers is lower than that of their interaction with China itself. It is far from the overt strategic alliance with the USSR that caused so many problems for Vietnam in the 1970s. It will be a delicate maneuver indeed to maintain significant military exchanges with two great powers that have their own conflicts with China, at the same time preserving a constructive dialogue with Beijing. In any case, Vietnamese policy-makers seem to be well aware of the dangers of the past, and thus may also be sensitive to the pitfalls of the future.

Notes

1. Gareth Porter, *The Politics of Bureaucratic Socialism* (Ithaca: Cornell University Press, 1993), p. 208.
2. Bui Tin, *Following Ho Chi Minh* (London: Hurst and Co., 1995), p. 160.
3. Carlyle A. Thayer, "Sino-Vietnamese Relations: The Interplay of Ideology and National Interest", *Asian Survey* 34, no. 6 (June 1994): 516–17.
4. Ibid., p. 518.
5. Porter, *The Politics of Bureaucratic Socialism*, op. cit., p. 193.
6. Bui Tin, *Following Ho Chi Minh*, p. 188.
7. Murray Hiebert, *Far Eastern Economic Review*, 16 July 1992, p. 21.
8. Thayer, "Sino-Vietnamese Relations", op. cit., p. 525.
9. Bui Tin, *Following Ho Chi Minh*, op. cit., p. 191.
10. Thayer, "Sino-Vietnamese Relations", op. cit., p. 527.
11. Mark Valencia, "The Spratly Embroglio in the Post-Cold War Era", in David Wurfel and Bruce Burton, eds., *Southeast Asia in the New World Order* (London: Macmillan, 1996), pp. 248–49.
12. Donald Zagoria, "Joining ASEAN", in James W. Morley and Masashi Nishihara, eds., *Vietnam Joins the World* (New York: M.E. Sharpe, 1997), p. 167.
13. Thayer, "Sino-Vietnamese Relations", p. 528.
14. Quoted in Zagoria, "Joining ASEAN", op. cit., p. 158.
15. Hoang Anh Tuan, "Vietnam's Membership in ASEAN: Economic,

Political and Security Implications", *Contemporary Southeast Asia* 16, no. 3 (December 1994): 263.

16. Ibid., p. 266.
17. Nguyen Hong Thach, quoted in Thayer, "Sino-Vietnamese Relations", op. cit., p. 528.
18. Interview by the author with a party official in Hanoi, 28 March 1997.
19. Brantley Womack, "Vietnam 1996: Reform Immobilism", *Asian Survey* 37, no. 1 (January 1997): 86.
20. Hoang Anh Tuan, "Vietnam's Membership in ASEAN", op. cit., p. 267.
21. Saigon Giai Phong, 5 April 1997 in FBIS-EAS-97-105.
22. Xinhua, Beijing, 27 February 1997 in FBIS-CHI-97-039.
23. Xinhua, Beijing, 9 April 1997.
24. Agence France-Presse (AFP), 31 March 1997, in FBIS-EAS-97-090.
25. *Vietnam Investment Review*, 31 March 1997, in FBIS-EAS-97-093.
26. Michael Vatikiotis, *Far Eastern Economic Review*, 3 April 1997, p. 15.
27. *The Nation* (Bangkok), 26 March 1997, in FBIS-EAS-97-058.
28. *Naeo Na*, 31 January 1997, in FBIS-EAS-97-026.
29. *Bangkok Business Day*, 1 April 1997.
30. *Bangkok Post*, 26 April 1997, in FBIS-EAS-97-116.
31. Michael Vatikiotis, *Far Eastern Economic Review*, 17 April 1997, p. 20.
32. Quoted in Zagoria, "Joining ASEAN", op. cit., p. 167.
33. Statement by the Philippines Embassy, Hanoi, 12 July 1996.
34. *Vietnam-Southeast Asia Today* (Hanoi), July 1996, p. 10.
35. *Bangkok Post*, 21 March 1997, in FBIS-EAS-97-079.
36. Michael Vatikiotis, *Far Eastern Economic Review*, 3 April 1997, p. 14.
37. Ibid.
38. Interviews with the author, Hanoi, April 1997.
39. *Business World*, 31 March 1997, in FBIS-EAS-97-090.
40. Quoted in *Far Eastern Economic Review*, 17 April 1997, p. 20.
41. Michael Vatikiotis, *Far Eastern Economic Review*, 8 May 1997, p. 15.
42. AFP, 30 April, 3 May 1997 in FBIS-EAS-97-120, FBIS-CHI-97-123.
43. *International Herald Tribune*, 30 April 1997.
44. AFP, 10 May 1997, in FBIS-EAS-97-130.
45. Andrew Sherry and Rogoberto Tiglao, *Far Eastern Economic Review*, 12 June 1997, pp. 17–21
46. *Business World*, 21 May 1997, in FBIS-EAS-97-141.
47. Kyodo, 16 May 1997, in FBIS-EAS-97-136.
48. Interview with the author, Hanoi, 9 April 1997.
49. Ibid.
50. A. Kotelkin, "Russia and the World Arms Market", *International Affairs* (1996): 34.
51. Interview with the author, Hanoi, 10 April 1997.
52. Interview with the author, Hanoi, 10 April 1997.
53. Interview with the author, Hanoi, 11 April 1997.
54. Tatsumi Okabe, "Coping with China" in Morley and Nishihara, eds., *Vietnam Joins the World*, op. cit., p. 129.
55. Zagoria, "Joining ASEAN", op. cit., p. 157.
56. Denny Roy, "The China Threat Issue: Major Arguments", *Asian Survey* 36, no. 8 (August 1966): 770.

57. David Shambaugh, "Containment or Engagement of China?", *International Security* 21, no. 2 (Fall 1996): 181.
58. Quoted in *Far Eastern Economic Review*, 24 April 1997, p. 28.
59. Shi Yongming, "The Elevated Status and Influence of the ASEAN after the Cold War", *Guoji Wenti Yanjiu* [International Studies], 13 January 1997, 29–33, in FBIS-CHI-97-077.
60. *Mainichi Shimbun*, 13 January 1997, in FBIS-EAS-97-008.
61. Kyodo, 11 January 1997, in FBIS-EAS-97-008.
62. Kyodo, 26 March 1997, in FBIS-EAS-97-085.
63. *Quan Doi Nhan Dan*, 28 March 1997, in FBIS-EAS-97-087.
64. Bilson Kurus, "ASEAN-izing Southeast Asia", in Derek da Cunha, ed., *The Evolving Pacific Power Structure* (Singapore: Institute of Southeast Asian Studies, 1996), p. 75.
65. Hoang Anh Tuan, "ASEAN Dispute Management: Implications for Vietnam and an Expanded ASEAN", *Asian Survey* 18, no. 1 (June 1996): 77.
66. Quoted in *Far Eastern Economic Review*, 12 June 1997, p. 15.
67. *New Light of Myanmar*, 17 May 1997, in FBIS-EAS-97-140.
68. Rangoon Radio, 22 May 1997, in FBIS-EAS-97-143.
69. *The Nation* (Bangkok), 30 April 1997, in FBIS-EAS-97-120.
70. Shi Yongming, "The Elevated Status and Influence of the ASEAN after the Cold War", in FBIS-CHI-97-077.
71. See *Thailand Times*, 16 March 1997, in FBIS-EAS-97-075.

7

DOMESTIC SOURCES OF VIETNAM'S FOREIGN POLICY

Kent Bolton

Introduction

Any number of studies exist in which the *domestic* influences on a multi-party state's foreign policies are examined: who makes said policies; how the media and election cycles affect those policies; how bureaucratic organizations co-opt and constrain policies; and how special influence groups affect those foreign policies.[1] In contrast, relatively few analyses exist in which the domestic influences of a single party state's (e.g. a communist party state's) foreign policies are studied. Those that do exist tend to focus on either the former Soviet Union or China.[2] Three extant single party communist states can be found in East Asia: the People's Republic of China, the Democratic People's Republic of Korea, and the Socialist Republic of Vietnam. This analysis focuses on the domestic sources of Vietnam's foreign policy.

More specifically this chapter examines domestic inputs that have shaped Vietnam's foreign policy reforms and openness during the 1990s, including normalization of relations with the United States, one example of Vietnam's foreign policy "openness". In the summer of 1995, some thirty years after America "officially" sent combat troops into Vietnam, and some twenty years following America's hasty retreat from Indochina, the United States and Vietnam normalized political relations.[3] While various pro-normalization arguments were proffered from both America and Vietnam, some pro-normalization advocates predicted that if Vietnam and the United States normalized, the former would *perforce* become more pluralistic in its political processes.[4] With more than four years of "normalized" relations now as a basis for evaluation, it seems an appropriate time to consider the merit of that prediction, to date.

This chapter discusses Vietnam's foreign policy renovations in the 1990s. The principal focus is on the domestic influences in Vietnam that have affected—either hastened or constrained—its foreign policy renovations. In examining Vietnam's foreign policy reforms, the issue of whether a more pluralistic Vietnam has resulted is also considered.

Normalization as a foreign policy instrument and indicator of renovation

Before turning to Vietnam's foreign policy renovations in the 1990s, a word about normalization is in order. Clearly, normalization with the United States constitutes a narrow area of Vietnam's overall reforms and renovations. Here particular focus is devoted to normalization in the broader context of reform for two reasons. First, Vietnam normalizing relations with the United States is an understandably controversial aspect of Vietnam's foreign policy renovations. Since this study is interested in the domestic influences on Vietnam's foreign policy, normalization serves as a particularly sensitive indicator of the saliency of those domestic forces. Second, normalization is appropriately conceptualized as an instrument (a tool) of foreign policy rather than foreign policy *per se*. As will be seen, defining foreign policy as a function of its conceptually distinctive parts provides a useful way to observe foreign policy (the dependent variable).

Normalization may properly be considered a derivative of Vietnam's foreign policy. Consider a definition of foreign policy. Foreign policy may be defined conceptually as: the goals and objectives a particular country wishes to accomplish abroad, that country's values (*ethos*) which inform said goals, as well as the instruments or tools used by that country to achieve and sustain its goals. Consider "normalization" as an example. Vietnam has an array of goals it wishes to accomplish with respect to the United States. Vietnam's goals conceivably include securing investment capital from foreign partners to sustain its ongoing domestic renovation (*doi moi*), its desire to see political stability in Southeast Asia, and its desire to protect its disputed frontier and sea borders from being settled against its interests by powerful neighbours. The values informing its goals might include Vietnamese nationalism, demonstrated in its historical propensity to protect its sovereignty and territory from historical enemies to the north and to the west, and its near single minded attention to keeping Vietnam unified.[5] Normalization of relations with the United States can therefore be seen as a means (i.e. as an instrument) to achieve Vietnam's foreign policy goals—goals that are animated by Vietnamese values and *ethos*. As will be seen shortly, normalization can be regarded as one of the tools that Vietnam's leaders have used to achieve its broader objectives of renovation and reform.

Vietnam's foreign policy goals

The discussion above on normalization as an instrument of foreign policy, speculated on Vietnam's foreign policy. Obviously, the objective here is to go beyond speculation to Vietnam's actual foreign policy goals. Recurring goals and priorities have emerged from discussions and interviews with a number of Vietnamese, including government officials and academics, as well as from a variety of public statements.[6]

An objective that Vietnamese leaders frequently mention is first and foremost a domestic policy goal (known as *doi moi*): the renovation of Vietnam's economic system, and to some extent its political system. This goal emerged publicly in 1986. Since the mid-1980s, *doi moi* has become a policy rubric for any number of more specific goals and objectives. Inasmuch as Vietnam exists in an international system largely characterized by world trade, Vietnam's renovation has necessarily included a number of foreign policy choices as well. *Doi moi's* foreign policy implications began to emerge in the late 1980s. By the Seventh Party Congress in 1991, "openness" and a "multi-directional approach" were increasingly emblematic of Vietnam's foreign policy renovations.[7] From the 1991 period, through the Eighth Party Congress in June 1996, and now beyond, the "priorities" of foreign policy renovation have included "independence and openness" and have been marked by "continuity" over that period.[8]

Clearly, Vietnam wishes to maintain a stable and peaceful environment in which its domestic renovation can take place.[9] The peaceful environment Vietnam's leaders seek to create is predicated on "multilateralism". Operationally, multilateralism's objectives have been enumerated as: positive "regional relations" with China, Cambodia, Laos, and ASEAN members; positive "relations with major powers"; positive relations with historically "friendly countries" world-wide; and to "integrate Vietnam into regional and world communities", a goal that is primarily described in terms of multilateral economic regimes such as APEC and WTO.[10]

Vietnam's fundamental foreign policy objectives are thus relatively straightforward. Vietnam's leadership is well attuned to international events that affect Vietnam's future. The genesis of today's reforms in Vietnam can be traced to the 1980s when events first compelled Vietnam's leadership to initiate said reforms. Despite recent economic turmoil, Vietnam's neighbours continue to be quite prosperous by comparison. Vietnam's own economic prosperity, which languished prior to renovation, is again causing significant concern among the leadership.[11]

Though views among the leadership may vary on many things, they collectively understand that limits exist to the Vietnamese peoples' forbearance. Fear of reaching those limits, therefore, creates an impetus to continue if not hasten reforms, aimed at improving the well being of Vietnam's people. As noted, the policy rubric under which renovation and reform takes place, both political and economic, is *doi moi. Doi moi* has necessarily involved substantive foreign policy choices. Foreign policy choices in Vietnam, as elsewhere, are guided by normative values. Some of these choices have caused strains within the leadership as historical values (viz., Vietnamese nationalism) have periodically come into conflict with values derived from Marxist Leninist ideology and the thoughts of Ho Chi Minh. The nexus in which the impetus for reform sometimes collides with contradictory values (Party preeminence, democratic centralism, etc.) is therefore conceptualized in this chapter as an important domestic source of Vietnam's foreign policy. The resulting process often appears, to outside observers, to move haltingly; this appearance (characterized as reform inertia below) is an accurate reflection of the competing demands in Vietnam exerting force on Vietnam's foreign policy process.

Sources of Vietnam's foreign policy goals

Systemic-external variables

Vietnam's foreign policy inputs can be divided into two basic types: systemic external and domestic.[12] Dramatic events, external to Vietnam began to occur in the 1980s. Around the time the seventh party congress was formally integrating Vietnam's foreign policy and domestic policy goals under the rubric of *doi moi*, multiple external events exerted influence on Vietnam's foreign policy. Momentous changes transpired in several Eastern European states whereby multi-party regimes replaced single party ones. Similarly, though Gorbachev's reforms had been around since 1986, the forces of change unleashed by those reforms and the implications for Vietnam's own leaders were unmistakable by 1991. In August 1991 a coup that failed to topple Gorbachev nevertheless spelled the demise of Soviet era communism in Russia. By year's end, the Soviet Union had ceased to exist. Although Vietnam withdrew its military forces from Cambodia in September 1989, international negotiations on a peace settlement did not reach their conclusion until October 1991. By 1991, oft strained relations between Vietnam and China moved decisively towards political normalization. Still, with the former USSR no longer a counterbalance to China's actions in Southeast Asia, a number of border issues—particularly, disputed islands— continued to rankle the Vietnamese, causing them to be "attentive" in their monitoring of China.[13] Nor did the occurrence of the Gulf War, during this same period, pass unnoticed in Vietnam. The technologically sophisticated weaponry exhibited in the Gulf War by the allies likely affected Vietnam's foreign policy outlook, especially coming on the heals of their former Soviet ally's demise and China's increasing confidence in Asia.[14]

Another external influence on Vietnam's foreign policy is its regional setting. Vietnam exists in a region whose predominant characteristic, over the past decade or more, has been economic dynamism.[15] Vietnam's leaders are well aware of the influence the regional and larger global economies exert on Vietnam's well being.[16] The relative level of prosperity and well being associated with these economies, as noted above, provides an impetus for continued reform in Vietnam. This is observable, for instance, in the fall 1997 commentary—a surprisingly outspoken one—by former Prime Minister Pham Van Dong, when the elder statesman called for "further and wide ranging reforms" lest Vietnam's economy tailspin into recession and its political leadership be rendered obsolete. High profile and increasingly open criticism has continued in 1998, notably with veteran party member General Tran Do warning, in February, of "disintegration" of the party. As unrest among Vietnamese appeared in 1997 and 1998, Tran Do went further still, suggesting that Vietnam must undertake requisite reforms which met the basic needs of the people, with or without socialism.[17] As the country opened up and as more Westerners travelled and lived in Vietnam, as television (e.g., CNN) and radio permeated Vietnam's borders, Vietnamese have become increasingly aware of the comparative well being of its regional neighbours and people elsewhere. Vietnam's leaders are painfully aware of Vietnam's comparative lack of prosperity as Pham Van Dong's *crise de couer* and Tran Do's various rebukes illustrate.

Domestic variables

The domestic sources of Vietnam's foreign policy—at least those that influence the highest level of foreign policy making—are manifold. The apex of foreign policy decision making in Vietnam is the

Vietnam Communist Party (VCP). The 1992 Constitution is unambiguous in this respect: "The Communist Party of Vietnam, the vanguard of the Vietnamese working class, ... is the force leading the State and society". Additionally, however, the National Assembly's influence is increasing in terms of foreign policy and domestic matters.[18] Given that Vietnam is a single party system, the crucial issue, therefore, is whether intra party groups compete and man- oeuvre to set the policy agenda, more than the relationship between the VCP and the legislature. If so, this would constitute a potent domestic source of Vietnam's foreign policy.

The state bureaucracy including the Ministries of National Defence, Foreign Affairs, Interior, and Planning and Investment also affect foreign policy. Each ministry and persons associated with it can be seen as a potential domestic influence on Vietnam's foreign policy. In between the National Assembly and the state bureaucracy is the "government" (*chinh phu*) as the Vietnamese officially refer to it. The "government", or Cabinet, replaced the Council of Ministers in 1992. The Cabinet exerts some influence on Vietnam's foreign policy as a collective body. Vietnam's Prime Minister who, in the 1990s, has been associated with the apex of state and party power in Vietnam (discussed below) heads the government.

In Western literature on pluralism, interest group influence is often cited as a source of both domestic and foreign policy. Indeed such influence is one of the identifying characteristics of "demo- cratic" or "pluralistic" societies. Though somewhat less potent in Vietnam, there are interest groups that presumably affect policy. The military clearly has affected foreign policy in Vietnam for many years by virtue of its reputation and its representation at both the state (via the Ministry of National Defence and the military's repre- sentation in the National Assembly) and Party levels. Additionally, informal groups like the senior statesmen who are now retired (or semi retired) who struggled and worked with Ho Chi Minh against the French and Americans during respective wars, still exert influ- ence from time to time.[19] One interest group apparently gaining more influence in Vietnam's policy making is the Women's Union. This is a group of some eleven million Vietnamese, roughly five times the roster of party members in Vietnam. It has its own news- paper and exerts influence by its sheer size as well as through its media and campaigns; it may influence Vietnam's foreign policy by virtue of its transnational activities, interacting with various interna- tional organizations.

Perhaps the most potent domestic source of Vietnam's foreign policy, however, is what might be called factionalism,[20] that is ideologically distinct factions or groups within the Vietnam Communist Party pursuing somewhat different agendas. In the case of Vietnam, factionalism may be too severe a word. Nevertheless, ideologically distinct camps exist within the Party and the State/Government whose view of party-state relations, how the Party relates to the citizenry and, importantly, the pace and scope of reform as well as normalization with the West often differ considerably. One long time observer describes their influence on policy this way: "Probably the main source of political change will not come from outside the ranks of the power holders; *it is a split within the political élite* that is of much greater concern".[21] In recent years, these groups (camps) have become identified with the apex of leadership in Vietnam: the so-called troika.[22]

The troika has been instrumental in policy formation in Vietnam throughout much of the 1990s. The troika reflects contrasting and competing ideological views in Vietnam's leadership ranks. President Le Duc Anh, a former military commander, is considered the most ideologically conservative member of the troika. Though the president of Vietnam is largely a symbolic position, during Le Duc Anh's tenure the role of the presidency was greatly magnified. Anh's relationship with the military has been important in the political dynamics of the troika. Prime Minister Vo Van Kiet is clearly the most reform minded of the troika. He has been associated with promoting market mechanisms in Vietnam dating back to the 1980s. As head of the government, Kiet is in a position to shape Vietnam's foreign (and domestic) policy. The third member of the troika is the Secretary-General of the Vietnam Communist Party, Do Muoi. That Vietnam is a single party system clearly puts Muoi in a position of tremendous influence. Many analyses characterize him as a moderator between President Anh's ideological conservative position and Prime Minister Kiet's rapid reform position. Indeed, he has been described as the Confucian Referee.[23] Though Muoi has publicly taken more temperate positions than Anh on occasion, it seems clear that philosophically Muoi leans more towards the more conservative Anh position. For one thing, there is historically a natural alliance between the military, from which former General Anh comes, and the Party, which Muoi heads. Moreover, there is a history of Anh-Muoi co-operation in Politburo manoeuvring to their mutual advantage and, perhaps more importantly, to Kiet's disadvantage. The troika's pre-eminent role is secured by its relationship to the VCP Politburo. One's ranking within the 18-member Politburo[24] is indicative of policy influence. These troika members—Muoi, Anh, and Kiet—occupy the top three slots respectively.[25] In the 1990s, the political dynamic represented in the troika has constituted a strong domestic source of Vietnam's foreign policy, particularly with respect to reform, openness, and normalization with the United States.

Recent leadership changes, long rumoured but repeatedly fore-stalled, produced a new troika. Whether the new troika will continue to represent and reflect intra-party factions, and as such act as a source of Vietnam's foreign policy, remains to be seen. However, two of the new members can be seen as protégés—if not as hand picked successors—of the former troika member whom each replaced. Phan Van Khai and Le Kha Phieu were groomed by Vo Van Kiet and Do Muoi respectively. Early indications are that the new troika has thus far continued to represent ideologically different camps in Vietnam.[26]

Of the several domestic variables enumerated, which ones have affected Vietnam's foreign policy reforms ("openness" generally but also normalization with the United States) and how? These questions are addressed next. First, however, it is worth re-emphasizing several points. The focus here is on domestic influences; this should not be construed as suggesting that systemic external variables are un-important. Further, though it may be useful to separate domestic and systemic external variables for analytic purposes, it is clear that in reality they are not always so simply differentiated. The foreign policy making process is the interaction of domestic and external variables.

Intra-party factions as a domestic source of Vietnam's foreign policy renovations in the 1990s

Around the time that the United States and Vietnam finally normal-ized political relations in 1995, Adam Schwarz penned an article suggesting a relationship between economic openness and political openness—or more precisely, an increasing lack of political open-ness. Schwarz suggested a link between domestic and foreign policy as well as specifying a cause for the lack of political liberalization accompanying economic liberalization. He noted that since political normalization (summer 1995), a pattern had developed: "Analysts note the important openings in foreign affairs and economic policy have regularly been matched by tightening of domestic security, *apparently reflecting the concern of conservative party members* about the possible destabilizing effects of such steps".[27] The highlighted sec-tion is of particular interest. It suggests intra-party factions, their role in foreign policy, and the connection between *doi moi* in terms of domestic and foreign politics. Indeed it is common to read of "party

conservatives" and "ideological conservatives", or simply "conservatives" as opposed to "progressives", or of a "split within the political
élite", even of an "administrator/technocrat" versus a "party/control"
element in Vietnamese policy circles.[28]

If these characterizations accurately reflect philosophical division
in the party and/or state, they serve to explain policy making in Vietnam given Vietnam's single-party regime. Assuming this to be the
case, one ought to be able to establish a timeline relevant to a given
foreign policy, highlighting important junctures at which attendant
decisions of that foreign policy were debated. Furthermore, one
ought to be able to find evidence of the posturing of these camps or
factions at these important decision junctures aimed at affecting
Vietnam's foreign policy.

Beginning with the seventh party congress in 1991 and continuing
through the 1996–97 period, a timeline may be constructed along
which one might reasonably expect to observe important decision
making. Recall that *doi moi* was begun in 1986 which set Vietnam
along a path of economic and political reform. In order for renovation to be successful, Vietnam undertook a series of foreign policy
initiatives including a general openness in its relations with other
countries (e.g. China, ASEAN members, and the United States).
Since Vietnam's 1992 state constitution charges the party with the
responsibility of "leading the State and society", one would obviously
assume that Party Congresses (every five years) as well as yearly
party plenums could constitute important decision points along this
timeline. Given also that the National Assembly is increasingly influential in policy making in Vietnam, National Assembly elections and
its annual deliberations in the 1990s therefore ought to be included
along the timeline as decision making referents.

The sixth national party congress of the VCP (1986) marked the
Party's adoption of *doi moi,* dismantling, to some degree, Vietnam's
"central planning apparatus in favour of a market oriented economy"
and "foreign investment". The foreign policy implications of *doi moi*
had begun to emerge as a "multi-directional foreign policy orientation" in 1987 and 1988; this "multi-directional foreign policy" was
formally adopted by the Party in 1991 at the seventh party congress.
The most recent party congress was the eighth national party congress of the VCP in June–July 1996. The most recent National
Assembly election was held on 20 July 1997: the Tenth National
Assembly.[29] The election for the previous National Assembly, the
Ninth National Assembly, was held on 19 July 1992.

Clearly the adoption of *doi moi* in the mid-1980s constituted
a fairly radical shift in Vietnam's domestic and foreign policy

priorities. To wit, thereafter Vietnam's domestic policies began to move away from its orientation based on a command economy, where the means of production were largely state owned, towards a more market oriented economy, where increasingly the means of production were also owned by private interests. Correspondingly, Vietnam's foreign policy began to reflect a "multi-directional" approach including normalization of relations with the United States. Vietnam's multi-directional approach began to supplant the more ideological oriented approach associated with Vietnam's previous decade. The shift in policy marked a conservative faction mobilization to resist the diminution of ideology.[30]

President Le Duc Anh—member of the ruling troika and from the ranks of the largely conservative military—published an article in the army newspaper in late 1990 seemingly reasserting the military's role in politics generally. (Thayer 1997, p. 24.) The significance of Le Duc Anh's article may well be more in its timing than its substance. That a former general would be reminding the country of the Army's relatively reverential position is hardly noteworthy on its own. Anh's article was published, however, as the conservative camp was mounting a response to the changes in Vietnam's policies, including the then emerging "multi-directional" approach in foreign policy. As such, it serves as the proverbial shot across the bow of Party members whose reforms and openness are seen by Anh and others as going too far too fast. Similarly, it can be seen as timed to marshal conservative forces in anticipation of two important, upcoming events: the seventh party congress; and the critical debates then looming over the soon-to-emerge revised constitution.

Anh's rallying call, notwithstanding, the seventh party congress (June 1991) endorsed the multi-directional approach and Vietnam began to implement that approach soon thereafter.[31] After the Congress, Vietnam's new foreign policy direction of extending friendship to all countries began to bear fruit. Since the rapid reform camp had strongly endorsed foreign policy openness, any benefits associated with said policy would presumably bolster their cause. The fruits included Vietnam and China normalizing relations after several uneasy years; Vietnam actively mending strained relations with ASEAN members; Vietnam agreeing with the international settlement in Cambodia; and a process that would eventually result (1995) in normalization with the United States. Very shortly after the Congress, Phan Van Khai attended a symposium where he extolled the virtues of Vietnam's multi-directional co-operation with all countries. At the time, Khai was both prominently rumoured as the likely successor of his mentor and reform lodestar, Vo Van Kiet, as Prime Minister as well as frequently identified with the rapid reform camp. (Proving the rumour mill accurate, Khai was announced as Kiet's replacement in September 1997.[32])

The conclusion of the seventh party congress and the policies it endorsed marked an apparent victory for the reformers. However, it in no way presaged resignation on the part of conservatives. In fact, what followed was a period particularly notable for its intense intra-party skirmishes. That so intense a struggle ensued was not surprising. From the perspective of either camp, a good deal was at stake at the time. Both the final disposition of the amended constitution and the results of the upcoming election (the ninth National Assembly) were uncertain. Both were critical for conservatives as well as rapid reformers. Both events would be significant in establishing momentum in terms of reform overall and, importantly, the final disposition of the evolving relationship between the Party and the increasingly influential State.

Both conservatives and rapid reformers emerged from the 1991–92 period having succeeded in forestalling complete victory by its opposing faction. The amended constitution "firmly entrenched one-party rule", rejecting the separation-of-power scheme the pro-reform camp had pushed. On the other hand, the Party's (or more accurately, the Politburo's) concentrated control of the policy process was diluted inasmuch as a Cabinet government emerged, headed by what would become an increasingly influential Prime Minister. The state (and by extension the bureaucracy) as well as the state's legislative organ, the National Assembly, therefore explicitly formalized their policy influence. The price of the state's ascendance, however, may have been the creation of a state president to offset the potential for the prime minister to accrue excessive power. What's more, conservative Le Kha Phieu was elevated to the Politburo during this period and the military improved its position in the National Assembly, potentially checking the latter's increasing influence.[33] Nevertheless, reform momentum had been established: Vietnam thereafter continued to pursue foreign policy openness with its neighbours and the West; and the controversial normalization process just under way thereafter continued. Establishing reform momentum gave the rapid reformers a slight advantage by putting conservatives in a reactive and defensive posture.

It should be noted that external variables clearly contributed to Vietnam's foreign policy renovation and openness. At times, such events seemed to play into the hand of the rapid reformers. Vietnam's close ally, the former Soviet Union, collapsed in late 1991 ending what had already become a period of dwindling aid for

Vietnam. Vietnam's need for investment capital to continue its domestic renovations was made even more crucial. At the same time, Vietnam's more proximate neighbour China, continued to establish itself as a military superpower. China sold missiles and other armaments to several countries in the Middle East; and despite its better relations with Vietnam, China's manoeuvrings around disputed offshore islands caused Vietnam no small amount of discomfort.[34] Nor can the impact of the Gulf War be ignored. Notable conservatives in the Army who had previously characterized capitalism as only temporarily ascendant, minimally were inconvenienced by the Gulf War.[35] The military may have been especially shocked by the allies' technological prowess. Thereafter, Vietnam's military actively began to press for an increase in the military budget.[36] It seems clear that many of the external events strengthened the hand of the rapid reformers generally, and hastened the normalization process. In any event, normalization with the United States continued moving forward, establishing its own momentum.[37]

In sum, the 1991–92 period was particularly reflective of intra-party factions mobilizing over reforms and foreign policy openness. Multiple, important decision junctures occurred during the period at which one would expect to find signs of intra-party competition. An important party congress, a National Assembly election, and a revision of Vietnam's constitution all fell during the period. As expected, signs of factional posturing were observable.[38]

On the face of it, the 1993–95 period might appear comparatively bereft of important decision opportunities and therefore less likely indicative of intense factional posturing. One of the curious residues of the previous period's manoeuvrings, however, was the establishment of new venues in which intra-party politics would take place. Establishing the office of Prime Minister, giving real power to the formerly symbolic office of the President, and strengthening the state apparatus resulted in a balance of power between the three offices or troika. The troika's emergence represented a new modality for competition of intra-party camps, divided over reform, openness, and normalization. Henceforth, the troika would become an important feature of factional politics. Beyond establishing the basis for the troika, the seventh congress made provisions for mid-term Party conferences thereafter. The mid-term Party conference constituted a new venue for factional manoeuvring hitherto unknown. That the seventh party congress made such provisions may itself be indicative of factionalism. First, the period for "policy development and leadership change" was effectively shortened by half. (Thayer 1998, Chapter 10.) It likely reflected the unease both rapid reformers and conservatives were feeling in terms of reform momentum. From either camp's perspective, a future undesirable shift in momentum could at least be checked much more rapidly. Minimally the provision is indicative of lack of consensus in the Party leadership regarding reform, both politically and economically. It suggests a bargained outcome indicative of factional competition.

Instead of a quieter 1993–95 period, a period of intensified strife between camps followed. Each camp remobilized its supporters, thus upping the ante. Each redoubled its efforts to affect the direction of reform (both domestically and internationally) in Vietnam. The 1993–95 period is one that can be described in terms of *reform inertia*. Reform momentum had been established in the previous period. Thereafter, reforms continued, but continued in an incremental way. Accordingly, the overt party position was to pursue continued openness and market reforms aimed at attracting foreign investment in Vietnam while preserving the party's dominance over said reforms and mitigating undesirable social consequences. The rapid reform camp repeatedly attempted to increase the pace and scope of reform, apparently hoping to build additional momentum that would ultimately be more difficult to reverse. The rapid reformers were regularly countered by conservatives who continually attempted to put the brakes on, ultimately slowing the momentum. An incremental process resulted: positive moves towards reform being disrupted by conservatives—a campaign, for example, that draws attention to negative social costs. For instance, foreign policy openness—begun in 1991—begat increased Western influence producing a conservative backlash, pointing to the "social evils" such as prostitution, drug use, and corruption.

Troika leaders associated with one camp or the other increasingly found themselves identified with the factional skirmishes over renovation and reform. Ironically, Prime Minister Kiet's association with the rapid reform camp, and President Anh's similar association with conservatives and the military, resulted in party leader Do Muoi being seen as the effective representative of the amorphous middle ground. This may well be why Muoi, despite his probable philosophical comfort with the conservative camp, came to be seen by some as a temperate moderator, or the "Confucian referee". On the one hand, he frequently defended the open door policies under way and the foreign capital those policies were attracting. On the other hand, he lashed out at the West on several occasions, blaming it (as did other notable conservatives) for Vietnam's increasing societal problems, and for various putative schemes to topple the Party peacefully (so-called peaceful evolution). Indicative of Muoi's seeming ideological flexibility is his lauding of foreign policy open-ness (associating himself with the positive windfall of reforms) even while cautioning that too much foreign investment represented a threat to Vietnam's national sovereignty (associating himself with conservatives).

> While concentrating our efforts on national construction, we must not neglect even for a moment the task of defending the fatherland; safe-guarding national independence, sovereignty, territorial integrity, and security; firmly maintaining sociopolitical stability and the socialist orientation of development. ...
>
> We must continue to promote the implementation of an independent, sovereign, *open, diversified, and multilateralized foreign policy,* maximize similarities, and limit differences, thereby creating favorable con-ditions for national construction and defense.[39]

To the observer, Vietnam's foreign policy appeared to have jetti-soned its past ideological constraints. Just below the surface, however, intense posturing over ideology was ongoing. Thus even while Do Muoi publicly evinced a temperate open approach and Vietnam continued the normalization process, conservatives fought a rearguard action with the military asserting a more cautionary view of Vietnam's openness generally and the potential for normalization with the United States specifically. In 1994, for example, Colonel Tran Duy Huong warned of the "peaceful evolution" ploys used by "hostile forces" aimed "at struggling against the party and state" under the guises of "freedom of faith", "democracy," and "human rights".[40] Interestingly, such campaigns neither directly attack the opposing faction nor associated troika members. Rather the skir-mishes are mostly indirect, sometimes subtle attacks.

Intra-party factions typically refrained from directly attacking their opponent publicly. Vietnam's foreign policy reforms had, after all, paid dividends.[41] Conservatives could not ignore the improving economic situation. Approaching normalization with the United States was thought likely to further Vietnam's economic gains. Con-servatives therefore had to be appropriately circumspect in their linking Vietnam's social ills to Western influence. Rapid reformers, in contrast, had momentum in their favour. Why attack their oppo-nent? What was to be gained from it? Intra-party skirmishes therefore remained subrosa in nature.

There were occasional exceptions, however. Towards the end of the 1993–95 period, a particularly intense skirmish erupted that threatened to derail reforms altogether. As the United States and Vietnam consummated the normalization process in 1995, again bolstering Kiet's rapid reformers, preparations were beginning for the important Eighth Party Congress scheduled the following year. Conservatives launched a bold gambit aimed at discrediting Kiet and, by implication, his rapid reform associates. The so-called Dao Duy Tung-Nguyen Ha Phan affair was an effort by conservatives that ultimately failed in causing Kiet's political demise but may have been partially successful in forestalling rumoured leadership changes and in slowing the momentum of the reformers.[42]

Reform momentum seemed to be building in 1995 as Vietnam formally joined ASEAN and normalized diplomatic relations with the United States. Many reforms had of course already been implemented by 1995, but the results of reform were uneven. Though Vietnam's economy had been doing well, a renewed round of public debate regarding the social costs of normalization with the U.S. and Western influences in Vietnam appeared indicative of conservatives attempting to break the momentum. Party leader Do Muoi (who on previous occasions had demonstrated more forbearance) now publicly lamented both the bureaucracy's capriciousness in implementing reform and the results from reform on Vietnamese society.[43] The bureaucracy of course was in Premier Kiet's bailiwick; thus Muoi's criticism was indirectly aimed at Kiet. Muoi's lament appears to have been timed to coincide with other public criticisms. Adam Schwarz noted the angst of the conservative camp associated with the pace of reforms in fall 1995 characterizing it as "concern of conservative party members about the possible destabilising effects of such steps".[44] More important than "concern" by conservatives, "internal party debate" was surfacing in Hanoi, signalling a new and dramatic round of posturing by the respective camps.

Prime Minister Vo Van Kiet prepared and circulated a report to the Politburo to consider foreign policy issues raised by Vietnam's recent normalization of relations. In the draft Kiet warned that the Party must *step up* its renovation efforts or, in effect, risk its own obsolescence. Kiet cited China's assertiveness to support his position of increased interactions with the West—notably with the United States and ASEAN.[45] China had, perhaps unwittingly, provided the rapid reformers new ammunition. "News of the Chinese presence on the aptly named Mischief Reef" had just surfaced "setting off" alarm bells in many Southeast Asian capitals.[46] Among other things, Kiet's report asserted that the struggle between imperialism and socialism had given way to a new era of multipolar international politics having important implications for Vietnam's foreign and domestic policies. He also raised the issue anew of what socialism meant in Vietnam's context. Kiet's report was leaked by conservatives and accompanied by a campaign to characterize Kiet as an ideological "deviant". Dao Duy Tung, then considered a likely contender to replace Do Muoi as Secretary General of the Party, and his protégé Nguyen Ha Phan were instrumental in the campaign against Kiet. Initially, their gambit resulted in renewed, even more shrill denunciations of the "social evils" foisted on Vietnam from abroad. Ultimately both Tung and Phan were ousted and Kiet survived. The gambit did, however, lead to emboldened factional posturing on the eve of the Congress.

As the opening of the congress approached, intra-party groups in Hanoi continued hotly contesting the draft Political Report being circulated. Additionally, rumours abounded regarding succession and sundry associated domestic political problems[47] helping to heighten the tension between the party camps. A "xenophobic tinge ... crept into official commentary" that was a function of the "backroom politicking within the Communist Party" as the Eighth Party Congress loomed large. It was becoming clear "that older party members feel change is occurring too quickly and that a period of political consolidation is in order".[48] Yet Kiet's report had called for nearly the opposite: without more rapid reform, the Party risked its very existence.

The uncertainties over succession and what the party congress would do *vis-à-vis* reforms were combining to produce fierce skirmishes between camps. Party leader Do Muoi warned in a "tough speech" in early May of forces specifically in Ho Chi Minh City, "a fertile ground for hostile forces" who "were politically destabilising, economically sabotaging, and culturally polluting". Various Party members of both "camps" were speaking out prior to the Congress apparently engaging in what Westerners call "spin".[49] The military took advantage of the discord to rejoin the fray with "a screed on perfidious foreign investors" that warned: " 'We are building our country while hostile forces' work to eliminate socialism and to 'completely sabotage the country' ".[50] Le Kha Phieu, a conservative closely associated with both President Anh and Party leader Muoi, publicly staked out a position, in contrast to Kiet's, in the daily *Nhan Dan*.[51] Campaigns to derail Kiet's full speed ahead reform position converged. "Ideological conservatives, located in the Vietnamese Communist Party, the Vietnam People's Army, the ministries of interior and national defence ... formed a loose coalition to put a break on" the rapid reform process.[52] Amid all this action one of Kiet's strongest allies and one "of the principal architects of normalization", Le Mai suddenly died.[53] What impact his death had on the intra-party posturing is unclear but his death, at the very least, left Kiet one fewer high-placed ally. By the end of June *The Economist* reported that "party stalwarts" were seizing on the manifold social consequences of reform (e.g. increase in drug use and prostitution) to successfully defeat the Kiet camp.[54] The final draft of the Political Report to congress appeared to be a compromise position; the changes made to the original draft "reflect the tug of war between the two camps".[55]

Among the compromise positions taken by the Party congress was the decision to keep the ruling troika—Anh, Muoi, and Kiet—in power despite months of open speculation that the Congress would settle on new leadership to take Vietnam into the next five years. Additionally, a new Standing Board of the Politburo, comprised of President Le Duc Anh, Party leader Do Muoi, Prime Minister Vo Van Kiet, as well as Le Kha Phieu, and Nguyen Tan Dung was created and announced. The Standing Board's creation was reportedly intended to act as a bridge between the 170-member Central Committee and 18-member Politburo. There was reportedly "intense jockeying"[56] for placement on the Board. The ruling troika—a balance of ideological camps and geographic regions—formed the critical mass of policy making on the Board. One of the other two members, General Phieu, as noted above, was known to be associated with Do Muoi (and even earlier with President Anh). Though typically characterized as being in the conservative party camp, one report described him as somebody who has been careful not to burn bridges with the Kiet camp,[57] perhaps an indication that he had learned some ideological flexibility from Muoi. The fifth member of the Board was Nguyen Tan Dung, chairman of the Economic Subcommittee of the Party Central Committee. Dung was a young (47 years old) member who ranked last in Politburo seniority. Dung was thought to be a Kiet protégé[58] but lacked enough prestige to help Kiet's position significantly.[59] (In any event, Dung was subsequently "dropped" from the Board after Le Kha Phieu replaced Do Muoi as General Secretary. One report notes that once Phieu became increasingly acclimatized to his new power, he replaced Dung with his own "conservative chum Pham The Duyet".[60])

While Kiet's attempt to set the Party's agenda by drafting and circulating the report was apparently countered, Kiet and his promoters survived and prepared for another day. In July an English language business weekly—a publication of the Ministry of Planning and Investment and supportive of Kiet's rapid reform positions—put a positive spin on the congress by applauding what it characterized as the Party's decision to continue reforms.[61] While *Vietnam Investment*

Review might be excused its exuberance, other more sober assessments saw the outcome of the congress in less sanguine terms.
Carlyle Thayer was quoted as saying: "The party looked at change
and recoiled from it for the sake of unity". Sue Boyd, the Australian
Ambassador to Vietnam, described the politics surrounding the
congress as a "fierce struggle between progressives who want to
accelerate economic change and the conservatives who see this
change as threatening to the fabric of Vietnamese society and the
longer term capacity of the Communist Party to hold on to power".
Far Eastern Economic Review concluded that "[t]he party intends to
reassert its authority over every facet of Vietnamese life: economic,
political and social".[62]

Whichever assessment one cares to believe, the matter was not settled. Just when it looked as if the rapid reform camp was in decline,
an unexpected event occurred that ironically reinvigorated that
camp. President Le Duc Anh fell seriously ill in mid-November
1996.[63] Within weeks, Prime Minister Kiet was quoted as saying that
if Anh's poor health did not improve soon, "then we will have a new
president because the country cannot exist without a president at the
head of that country".[64] If Kiet's words seemed devoid of get-well-
soon sentiment, one must remember that this is the same Le Duc
Anh who reportedly joined with Muoi to ensure that Muoi, not Kiet,
would become the Secretary-General of the Party in 1991.[65]

President Anh's illness notwithstanding, a renewal and intensification of previous differences soon emerged. Among other things, the
Kiet camp (if not Kiet himself) reportedly spread rumours about Le
Duc Anh's activities in Cambodia where then General Anh was said
to have engaged in various wrongdoings. There was speculation that
Kiet's camp had risen like the proverbial phoenix from the ashes of
the eighth party congress fiasco.[66] Party leader Muoi helped lead the
counter attack. Taking a page out of the ideological conservative's
book, Muoi immediately warned of "the enemy's heinous schemes
and sabotage in the current market economy,"[67] a refrain used by
opponents of more rapid reform on many previous occasions.

If Do Muoi's intention had been to stall Kiet's rapid reform
faction's ascendancy long enough for Muoi to evaluate how calls to
hasten reform augured, it may have worked. By April President
Anh's health took a surprising turn for the better. Reuters reported
that:

> The surprise return of Vietnam's President Le Duc Anh to the center-
> stage of politics this week has sparked talk of a push by hardliners to
> make their voices heard as leadership changes loom.

Making his first public speech since suffering a stroke last November, the 76-year-old army general ... delivered a rousing address to the National Assembly on dangers facing Communist Party rule.

Reuters went on to report that Anh's rhetoric—characterized as "the stuff of old style revolutionaries"—referred to recent steps to "defeat the schemes and sabotage of all enemies".[68] Recall that Muoi had used substantially those same words a couple of months earlier. The schemes and sabotage to which both Anh and Muoi referred include the usual suspects: a host of social ills associated with the country's rapid reforms and Western influence generally. Reforms were more vulnerable to criticism than usual due to Vietnam experiencing its first economic downturn since implementing *doi moi*. Days later, Do Muoi made a similar speech effectively backing up President Anh's speech. According to reports, Muoi "emphasized the need to strengthen ideological control so that stability and socialist development could be ensured".[69]

This round of intra-party posturing notably took place at yet another important time in Vietnam to affect reform. In June 1997, the third plenary session of the Central Committee was scheduled. Given the failure to deal with the leadership succession issue at the 1996 Party congress, speculation persisted that the June Central Committee meeting might prove conducive for such change. Additionally, National Assembly elections (last held in 1992) were scheduled for July 1997. The Constitution mandates that the "first session of the newly elected National Assembly be convened two months after its election at the latest"; therefore, according to the Constitution, the National Assembly should have its first session by mid-to-late September.[70] Each of these events represented a decision making juncture where leadership and policy change could have potentially taken place.

The rumours in the run up to these events speculated that Prime Minister Kiet, President Anh, and Party Secretary Muoi were all contemplating retirement. Both the President and the Prime Minister positions are required to be filled from the ranks of elected National Assembly members. While the party Secretary General is not required to be a National Assembly member, nor is the National Assembly charged with electing that position, Do Muoi was said to be looking forward to younger leadership taking over. Late spring and early summer reports had Kiet failing to register for re-election to the National Assembly. Unless Kiet changed his mind at the last minute, therefore, his tenure as prime minister would end. While the National Assembly is constitutionally tasked with electing the prime minister,[71] in fact, the June third plenum of the Central Committee apparently decided on Kiet's replacement. It selected Phan Van Khai (a Kiet protégé) as Kiet's successor. Interestingly, the Central Committee (where one might appropriately expect to hear news of the party Secretary-General being replaced) did not announce a replacement for Do Muoi. Le Kha Phieu (then fifth in the Politburo) had been rumoured to be Muoi's heir apparent but was passed over for the time being showing "the strength of opposition to Le Kha Phieu, even within the military" according to Thayer.[72]

While the internal wrangling over the replacements of Do Muoi as party Secretary-General and Le Duc Anh as president continued, so too did various camps continue to posture to control Vietnam's "renovation" and foreign policy reforms.[73] Momentum for reform and openness in Vietnam has emerged and continues to plod along incrementally. The intra-party efforts at influencing the momentum seem largely aimed at the margins. Rapid reformers seek to hasten reform, building ever-more-difficult-to-counter momentum. Conservatives seek to constrain reform's momentum. Renovation and reform of some fashion will very likely continue in Vietnam.

Momentum seemed to be building in the second half of 1997 for faster and wider reform. In late summer 1997, for example, a "leading economist" in Ho Chi Minh City called for a "new wave of reforms".[74] Interestingly, former Prime Minister Pham Van Dong joined in by calling for more and faster reform. In "an unusually outspoken commentary" Dong called for greater democracy. Apparently his comments were timed for two events: the anniversary of the 19 August 1945 uprising; and "at a critical time for Hanoi, ... currently embroiled in the complex ... process of selecting a new collective leadership".[75] His comments were intriguing in several ways. First, on previous occasions, Pham Van Dong had seemingly taken the position being pushed by the more conservative elements in Vietnam. Second, reports of farmers—an important interest group in Vietnam given that some 80 per cent of Vietnam's population lives in rural, agricultural based areas—becoming disenchanted with government policies were then beginning to surface.[76] Third, some journalists had noticed indications of re-emerging conservatism at about the same time.

> The lengthy period of debate ahead of their planned stepping-down has seen the emergence of conservative groups who favor more cautious reforms coupled with greater social and other controls.[77]

Reactions to these events included Deputy Interior Minister, Vo Thai Hoa making a "blistering attack" against the various subversions of "hostile enemies". The Interior Ministry, as previously noted, has been identified with conservatives whose ideology puts social and political stability ahead of economic liberalization. Hoa's reaction came "amid a string of commentaries and editorials, demanding a new wave of reforms and better conditions...".[78] Thus Pham Van Dong's comments had the appearance of helping to stave off the demise of reforms by more conservative elements in the Party. Even more recently, Tran Do's June (1998) criticism has surfaced, at least appearing to be aimed at sustaining the rapid reformers and reform momentum.

As the reports of unrest in provinces near Hanoi circulated and as both the "leading economist" and Pham Van Dong publicly called for more reform, conservatives raked up the warnings regarding Western and American guests in Vietnam. In one example "[a]n official newspaper warned ... [recently] that foreign criminals were taking advantage of Vietnam's open door policy ...". The report continues noting that the warning "was the latest of several recently to warn about the dangers posed to Vietnam by the activities of foreigners", and that it is "linked to internal political jostling among groups vying for influence ahead of a planned leadership change which is due to be announced in September".[79]

Since these events, the Party's Central Committee nominated replacements for both President Anh and Prime Minister Kiet. The National Assembly ratified the nominated replacements. President Anh was replaced by Tran Duc Luong (formerly a Deputy Prime Minister). Luong defeated others thought to be in contention— notably, the conservative camp's General Doan Khue. As Luong is a geologist by vocation and training, his selection meant that the military had lost their grip on the presidency for the time being. Constitutionally, the state president is also commander-in-chief of the armed forces. Luong's selection may also signal the end to the institutional power Anh had amassed as president. Kiet successfully manoeuvred his own handpicked replacement as Prime Minister: Phan Van Khai. These nominations coupled with other deputy minister nominations suggest that "reform is not dead", according to a Western diplomat.[80] In December 1997 Le Kha Phieu replaced Do Muoi as VCP Secretary-General. The net result, however, suggests partial victories for both camps, and a continuation of reform inertia.

Reports from Vietnam, since Le Kha Phieu replaced Do Muoi as Party Secretary, make clear that intra-party factions continue to contest the ultimate direction of Vietnam's foreign policy, as well as Vietnam's reforms generally. Additional unrest in the countryside has occurred. Recently, a former Party member committed suicide via self immolation—a particularly potent symbolic action for historic reasons. Western lending institutions have continued to push Vietnam for more reform (notably, in state owned enterprises, and banking). Compounding these pressures on the Party, restless citizens in neighbouring Indonesia (an ASEAN partner) recently toppled a seemingly well-entrenched autocrat, with Western governments, lending institutions, and media apparently approving. Meanwhile, intra-party skirmishes over the ultimate future of Vietnam's foreign policy reforms continue.[81]

Balance sheet: more pluralism?

Far Eastern Economic Review's Adam Schwarz was quoted earlier in order to frame ideological factions as important domestic sources of Vietnam's foreign policy. Recall the following passage.

> Analysts note the important *openings in foreign affairs and economic policy have regularly been matched by tightening of domestic security,* apparently reflecting the concern of conservative party members about the possible destabilizing effects of such steps.[82]

This same quote, however, raises another question—the issue of democracy or pluralism; specifically, whether or not Vietnam's foreign policy (in this case normalizing relations with the United States) has led to more political openness in Vietnam. The quote suggests no. On the contrary, it posits an inverse relationship: openings in foreign and economic policy are correlated with the state stifling the emergence of pluralism lest social instability arise.

During summer 1997, Faith Keenan published an article called "Partners in Dialogue" in *Far Eastern Economic Review.* Among other things, the article addresses the recent National Assembly elections. It argues that while the Party is still in control of the important levers of the procedures of democracy (vetting candidates and so forth), the Vietnamese legislature has become a more equal partner: "the assembly's independence is growing, and hints of democracy are emerging...".[83] On the Saturday before the election as well as Election Sunday (19, 20 July 1997), a casual walk around the Hoan Kiem district in Hanoi provided anecdotal support of Keenan's observation. Campaigning, of a sort, was occurring in and around Party and Fatherland Front meeting places. Loudspeakers were blaring patriotic music and political messages. Lorries were moving through the streets with the same messages and music. Small groups of people were congregating around polling areas reading the handbills posted. On Election Day, city residents everywhere seemed to be scurrying to vote wearing what appeared to be their best clothes as they hustled along. If nothing else, it seemed certain that Hanoi's residents were taking their electoral role quite seriously.

Still, that many Vietnamese took their responsibility seriously does not necessarily equate to pluralism or democracy. It was Marx, after all, who warned of normative social controls—albeit associating them with capitalist societies—being more efficient in nature than coercion. He was of course referring to the socialization process which a society's youth undergo that cause them to conform to social norms: the influence of one's peers, schools, churches and one's family environment. It is certainly possible that the bustling voters were simply well socialized. Nor does the fact that the newly elected National Assembly is comprised of better educated delegates, more minorities than the last one, as well as having four independent deputies as members necessarily presage democracy in Vietnam. None the less, it was striking how integral the election appeared to be to the city, at least during those few days.

The basic question is an interesting one. And it is more generalizable than Vietnam. It is this: does economic liberalization perforce lead to political liberalization? The question has been debated in the United States since the 1970s with respect to Vietnam's northern neighbour, China. It is the basic premise behind what has been called "constructive engagement" in past administrations and is presently called "enlargement".

Much like the China example, the evidence of said policies in Vietnam is mixed. In a recent *Asian Wall Street Journal* article by Carlyle Thayer, the author cites some "encouraging signs" indicative of increasing trends of democracy in Vietnam. The party has begun a process whereby its own legitimacy will be based—and presumably therefore evaluated—in terms of its economic performance rather than more abstract ideological bases. The party has opened the electoral process and is permitting the National Assembly limited autonomy, or at least limited power independent of the party. The leadership at least recognizes the need, if not yet embracing it, for "what they term a 'law governed state' ".[84]

As Thayer notes, "Vietnam is not about to become Asia's next democracy". Nor of course did those arguing in favour of normalization of relations with the United States ever actually suggest that it would. The argument was much more limited in scope. The more Americans and American companies are active in Vietnam, and the more cultures and values are exchanged, the more likely Vietnam is to "adopt and adapt" some of those values.[85] If one were to array each of America's Asian allies along a political liberalization continuum, one would see a number of America's close Asia allies rather towards the wanting end of the continuum. Vietnam would be no exception.

Notes

1. For examples of analyses concerning who makes foreign policy, see Richard C. Snyder, H.W. Bruck, and Burton Sapin, *Foreign Policy Decision Making: An Approach to the Study of International Politics* (New York: Free Press, 1962); and James N. Rosenau, "Pre-Theories and Theories of Foreign Policy", in James Rosenau, ed., *The Scientific Study of Foreign Policy*, 2nd edition (New York: Nichols, 1980); and Maurice A. East, Stephen A. Salamore, and Charles F. Hermann, eds, *Why Nations Act: Theoretical Perspectives for Comparative Foreign Policy Studies* (Beverly Hills CA: Sage Publications, 1978). For examples of media and elections respectively, see Eric Alterman, *Sound and Fury* (New York: Harper Perennial, 1992), especially chapter 12; and William Quandt, "The Electoral Cycle and the Conduct of American Foreign Policy", in Eugene R. Wittkopf, ed., *The Domestic Sources of American Foreign Policy*, 2nd edition (New York: St. Martin's Press, 1994). For examples of the bureaucratic impact on foreign policy, see Morton Halperin, Priscilla Clapp and Arnold Kanter, *Bureaucratic Politics and Foreign Policy* (Washington, D.C.: Brookings Institution, 1974). For examples of special interest groups affecting policy, see Bernard C. Cohen, *The Influence of Non-Governmental Groups on Foreign Policy* (Boston: World Peace Foundation, 1959); and M. Kent Bolton, "The Vietnam Crucible", in Abbas Grammy and C. Kaye Bragg, eds., *United States-Third World Relations in the New World Order* (New York: Nova Science Publishers, 1996), where special-interest group influence on U.S. foreign policy *vis-à-vis* Vietnam is examined.

2. For examples concerning the former Soviet Union, see Erik Hoffman and Frederic Fleron, eds., *The Conduct of Soviet Foreign Policy* (New York: Aldine Publishing Company, 1980); and Peter Zwick, "New Thinking and New Foreign Policy Under Gorbachev", *Political Science and Politics* (June 1989): 215–36. For examples of the domestic sources of China's foreign policy see: Richard Solomon, *The China Factor* (Englewood, NJ: Prentice-Hall Inc., 1981); several essays therein, especially Harry Harding, "China and the Third World: From Revolution to Containment".

3. For example, see Doyle McManus, "Clinton Recognizes Vietnam to 'Help Extend Reach of Freedom' ", *Los Angeles Times*, 12 July 1995, A-1; and "Vietnam, US Officially Bury Old Animosities", *San Diego Union-Tribune*, 6 August 1995, A-19.

4. Indicative of this thinking is President Clinton's remarks as the United States announced diplomatic recognition of Vietnam. The President said: "We believe this step will help to extend the reach of freedom in Vietnam". See McManus, "Clinton Recognizes Vietnam to 'Help Extend Reach of Freedom' ", op. cit. Similarly, Senator John McCain (R-AZ) noted that normalization: "was a way of 'increasing the power of the reform elements in the Vietnamese government. Vietnam must make notable improvements on the human rights

issue. If Vietnam is influenced by our (American) values, we will make greater progress in our desire to push Vietnam politically and promote economic liberalization' ". This quote was cited by General Bui Phan Ky in "SRV General on Strategy To Protect Socialism in Vietnam", FBIS-EAS-96-037, *Daily Reports*, 23 February 1996. The reader will doubtless recognize this rationale. It has been used since the Nixon administration to support Nixon's "opening" of China. Similar arguments have been used from time to time to justify policy towards the former USSR, the former apartheid-based South Africa, and recently Saddam Hussein's Iraq in the 1980s.

5. It is of course true that Vietnam's ideology plays a crucial part in its foreign policy; see Eero Palmujoki, "Ideology and Foreign Policy: Vietnam's Marxist-Leninist Doctrine and Global Change, 1986–96", in this volume. Vietnam's ideology is of course based on the historical analysis of world trends by Karl Marx with Lenin's and especially Ho Chi Minh's adaptations for particular circumstances and times. The reader may appropriately ask how such ideology is guiding Vietnam's recent "openness" in foreign policy, particularly when it comes to opening Vietnam to potential capitalist exploitation. In brief, the answer seems to turn on Vietnam's relatively recent adoption of Marxist ideology being somewhat eclipsed by much older Vietnamese nationalist impulses and values. Indeed, this basic conflict may be at the heart of the disparate views on Vietnam's future that are so central to an ongoing debate in Vietnam today.

6. The interviews and meetings cited in this chapter all occurred during the author's trips to Vietnam in 1996 and 1997. Travel during both 1996 and 1997 was generously supported by the California State University system and by California State University, San Marcos with research and travel grants.

7. Carlyle A. Thayer, "Vietnamese Foreign Policy: Multilateralism and the Threat of Peaceful Evolution", paper delivered to the Third European Vietnam Studies Conference, hosted by the International Institute for Asian Studies and the Centre for Asian Studies, at University of Amsterdam, The Netherlands, 2–4 July 1997, p. 8. Thayer notes that since the Seventh Party Congress in 1991, Vietnam attained several accomplishments in diversifying its foreign policy: normalization with China (November 1991); restoration of "official assistance" from Japan (November 1992); normalization of relations with United States (July 1995); and membership in ASEAN (July 1995). Thayer also notes that in 1987, the Politburo adopted Resolution 2 which began Vietnam's adjustments in foreign policy and that by 1988, Vietnam's "new foreign policy orientation was codified"; ibid., 3. The focus of this chapter is primarily on the 1990s.

8. Author's interview with Nguyen Van Tho, Deputy Director, General Political Department, Ministry of Foreign Affairs, 30 July 1997. Hereafter Nguyen Van Tho interview.

9. In this regard, Vietnam's foreign-policy objectives have been identified as "First and foremost to ensure a peaceful environment" by Trinh Quang Thanh, Director of the Department of Policy Planning, Ministry of Foreign Affairs; author's interview on 31 July 1996. Hereafter Trinh Quang Thinh interview. Similarly described as "a peaceful

environment around Vietnam" by Nguyen Van Tho, interview, op. cit.

10. The quotes in the text are from author's interviews with Trinh Quang Thanh and Nguyen Van Tho in 1996 and 1997. For more on Vietnam's multilateralism and its China policy respectively, see comments of then Party leader Do Muoi: "Vietnam hopes to establish peaceful, friendly and cooperative relations with all countries in the region and the world, with priority given to its neighbors, Asean [*sic*] and Asia-Pacific nations.... The Vietnamese Party and State regard the consolidation and expansion of a friendly neighborhood and multi-faceted cooperation with China as an important integration of their foreign policy, ..."; quoted in "Sino-Vietnamese Summit Soothes Old Border Tensions", *Vietnam Investment Review*, 21–27 July 1997, p. 3.

11. Evidence of the Vietnamese leaders" sensitivity to their peoples" patience as well as the link between the adoption of *doi moi* in the 1980s and the unrest of Vietnam's people are from Roger Mitton, "Doi Moi Part 2?", *Asiaweek*, April 1998 [Internet edition]. Interestingly, this may even be more true today in light of the recent events in Indonesia. Vietnam's leaders are said to be "concerned" and to feel "insecure" as they witnessed unrest among the people result in the surprisingly quick removal of neighbouring autocrat Soeharto in the Spring of 1998. See Keiko Watanabe, "Vietnam Closely Following Events in Indonesia", *Yomiuri Shimbun*, 17 June 1998. Regarding relative economic prosperity, or lack thereof, growth rates for Vietnam and its neighbours (e.g. Thailand) are somewhat unrevealing unless they control inflation, unemployment, industrial versus agricultural growth, etc. A comparison between effectiveness in ameliorating poverty may be more useful for illustrative purposes here. During a ten-year period (1985–95), when much of Vietnam's initial reforms were implemented, Vietnam's poverty incidence fell from 75 per cent to 50 per cent. In neighbouring Thailand, poverty has been reduced from about 60 per cent (dating back to the late 1960s) to about 13 per cent at the end of 1997 (even after the turmoil of 1996). World Bank, World Bank *Country Briefs*, Thailand and Vietnam, respectively (http: www.worldbank.org/html/extdr/offrrep/eap/thai.htm and http:// www.worldbank.org/html/prdmg/grthweb/absdol.htm). General economic data on Vietnam since renovation, supplied by Professor Vu Dinh Cu, at a Vietnam-U.S. Society seminar in Hanoi, 30 July 1996.

12. The systemic category dates back at least as far as James Rosenau's efforts in what was then called "comparative foreign policy" analysis. Rosenau suggested five categories of variables that shape all nation-states' foreign policies: systemic, societal, governmental, role, and individual. See Rosenau, "Pre-Theories and Theories of Foreign Policy", op. cit. These same categories have been used in a foreign policy text published more recently. The systemic category was renamed external. See Charles Kegley and Eugene Wittkopf, *American Foreign Policy* (New York: St. Martin's Press, 1991). For present purposes, it is sufficient simply to dichotomize these categories into systemic-external and domestic.

13. Nguyen Van Tho interview, op. cit. When asked about Vietnam's view with respect to China, given the latter's seeming provocations

in the region, Nguyen Van Tho repeatedly pointed to the number of rounds of discussions China and Vietnam had completed on land and sea border disputes. He noted that they had agreements to settle such disputes hospitably, but acknowledged that "yes there were issues" between Vietnam and China and that Vietnam accordingly maintains a "healthy" caution when it comes to China.

14. See Carlyle A. Thayer, "Force Modernization: The Case of the Vietnam People's Army", in *Contemporary South East Asia* 19, no. 1 (June 1997): 9.
15. See, for example, The World Bank, *The World Bank Annual Report 1996* (Washington, D.C.: The World Bank Group, 1996).
16. Nguyen Van Tho interview, op. cit.
17. See "Vietnam's Pham Van Dong Urges Democratic Reform", Reuters News-Wire Service, 16 August 1997. Tran Do's February comments can be found in Pascale Trouillaud, "Communist Party Is Threatened with Disintegration", Agence France Presse, 5 February 1998 and Jim Mann, "High-Level Dissenter Urges Move to Democracy in Hanoi", *Los Angeles Times,* 7 February 1998. For Tran Do's most recent comments, see Andy Soloman, "Dissident Vietnam General Fires New Broadside", Reuters News-Wire Service, 29 June 1998.
18. The Socialist Republic of Vietnam, *The Constitution of 1992* (Hanoi: The Gioi Publishers, 1993) chapter 1, article 4, 14. While the proposition that the Party controls policy is commonly understood, there is a trend in Vietnam to elevate the state (the bureaucracy headed by the Prime Minister as well as the National Assembly) to nearly an equal footing. For example, Nguyen Van Tho described the relationship between the Foreign Ministry and the state with no mention of the party. He said that the state is "the preeminent authority" in determining foreign policy. When asked whether he meant "preeminent authority" or "preeminent state authority" he replied: "Yes, the preeminent state authority". Author's interview with Nguyen Van Tho, op. cit. Another Foreign Ministry official confirmed, in an informal discussion, that while the National Assembly's influence has increased in recent years, there is no question as to where policy initiatives originated—namely the party. Author's interview, Hanoi, 28 July 1997. The National Assembly's increasing influence was noted in Foreign Ministry interviews in the summer 1997. Also, see Faith Keenan, "Partners in Dialogue", *Far Eastern Economic Review,* 24 July 1997 [Internet edition, http://www.feer.com/].
19. Adam Schwarz, "Enemy No. 1", *Far Eastern Economic Review,* 11 July 1996 [Internet edition].
20. The reader will doubtless recognize this term as being associated with politics in the Peoples' Republic of China.
21. David W.P. Elliott, "Vietnam Faces the Future", *Current History* (December 1995): 417. Emphasis added.
22. When the author first began preparing this chapter, the Anh-Kiet-Muoi troika still existed. The subsequent changes in leadership that ultimately reconstituted the troika are discussed below. Though the troika referred to here no longer exists, the discussion that follows will treat it as extant in analysing its association with factional politics through 1997. In the fall of 1997, leadership changes were publicly announced in Vietnam. As previously rumoured, Kiet's

protégé, Phan Van Khai, succeeded his mentor as prime minister. Tran Duc Luong succeeded President Le Duc Anh. Subsequently, General Le Kha Phieu, elevated to status within the Politburo during an earlier round of intra-party promotions, replaced Do Muoi as party Secretary-General. Given the power the troika has wielded thus far in the 1990s, as well as the fact that protégés replaced their mentors, it is not unreasonable to expect its continued role in policy formation. Nor would it be surprising to see former troika members exerting influence over their respective protégés in the new troika. See Kristin Huckshorn, "Vietnam's Economy Hits Skids", *San Jose Mercury News*, 12 October 1997 [Internet edition]; also Ly Thai Hung, "Who to Replace Le Duc Anh", *Vietnam Insight*, January 1997 (http://www.vinsight.org).

23. Seth Mydans, "Domino Effect Is Looming at the Top for Vietnam", *New York Times*, 20 December 1996, A–5. It may be that the political dynamics of factional politics, more than unique attributes of Do Muoi's personality, produced this result (discussed below). In any case, the public positions Muoi had taken during various campaigns and counter-campaigns, suggest that he is, at the very least, ideologically fleet of foot.

24. See Ly Thai Hung, "Who to Replace Le Duc Anh", op cit. It should be noted that *Vietnam Insight* is produced by overseas Vietnamese who make no apologies for having an axe to grind with the current Vietnamese Government.

25. At the eighth party congress, nineteen persons were elected to the Politburo. One member died on the day of his election. When the names of the new Politburo members were released, his was included as a mark of respect. No attempt has been made to fill this vacancy; there are at present (November 1998) eighteen Politburo members.

26. Changes in the apex of leadership are discussed below. However, references to the new "triumvirate" appeared in the fall of 1997. See Ly Thai Hung, "The Newly Elected Triumvirate of the Vietnamese Communist Party", op. cit. where the author discusses the "emergence of the Phieu-Luong-Khai triumvirate" as marking a victory for the "state-power camp". Some arguable indication that ideological representation on the troika continues may be respective responses to recent, increasingly open criticism of the party. In response to Tran Do's "broadside", for example, Phieu's comments were unenthusiastic at best. Khai, by comparison, noted that the critics were entitled to their views. Soloman, "Dissident Vietnam General Fires New Broadside", op. cit.

27. Adam Schwarz, "Arrested Development", *Far Eastern Economic Review*, 7 September 1995, 33. Emphasis added.

28. "Party conservatives" as well as "ideological conservatives" are characterizations Thayer uses; see his "Vietnamese Foreign Policy: Multilateralism and the Threat of Peaceful Evolution", op. cit. The "conservatives" and "progressives" continuum comes from Australian Ambassador Sue Boyd quoted by Adam Schwarz, "Safety First", *Far Eastern Economic Review*, 11 July 1996, pp. 14–16. The administrator/technocrats and party/control dichotomy comes from Elliott, "Vietnam Faces the Future", op. cit., p. 418.

29. Thayer, "Vietnamese Foreign Policy: Multilateralism and the Threat of Peaceful Evolution", p. 2. Nguyen Van Tho used "multilateralism" as a catchall phrase to describe a host of multilateral political and economic relations. Author's interview, op. cit. The demographic changes in Vietnam's National Assembly are noted in "New NA Is Most Educated Yet", *Viet Nam News*, 29 July 1997, p. 1.

30. Thayer, "Vietnamese Foreign Policy: Multilateralism and the Threat of Peaceful Evolution", op. cit., pp. 1–2.

31. It should be pointed out that the seventh party congress saw the military increase its representation on the Central Committee. This was the first time the military had achieved that since 1960. See Thayer, "Force Modernization: The Case of the Vietnam People's Army", op. cit., p. 3. That the congress formally endorsed foreign policy reforms but simultaneously strengthened the conservatives' influence, may well be indicative of a compromise or bargained position coming out of the congress which is itself suggestive of party factions.

32. See Faith Keenan, "Generation Shift", *Far Eastern Economic Review*, 25 September 1997 [Internet edition]. Also see Japan Economic Newswire, "Vietnam Politburo Names President, Premier Nominees", 9 September 1997 (Internet edition).

33. Carlyle Thayer, *Renovating Vietnam: Political Change in a One-Party State* (Sydney: Allen and Unwin, forthcoming 1999), Chapter 10.

34. Thayer notes, for instance, that China's assertiveness in the "Spratly Islands in 1992 served as a catalyst for ASEAN membership" by Vietnam; Thayer, "Vietnamese Foreign Policy: Multilateralism and the Threat of Peaceful Evolution", op. cit.

35. For example, see "Doan Khue Addresses Capital Regiment", in FBIS-EAS-97-008, *Daily Report*, 13 December 1996. General Doan was the Defence Minister; he has been mentioned as an ally of Le Duc Anh's on occasion. See John Chalmers, "Vietnam President's Comeback sets Tongues Wagging", Reuters Wire Service, 2 April 1997 (Internet edition).

36. "Thayer, "Force Modernization: The Case of the Vietnam People's Army", op. cit., p. 5.

37. That normalization took as long as it did may be more attributable to special interest group and presidential campaign politics in the United States than to politics in Vietnam. The presidential election of 1992 was followed by a new United States administration—one with a "Vietnam problem". "The problem" was bluntly described by one journalist in this way: "The decision Clinton faces is mostly political and revolves around a single question: Can a president who avoided serving in Vietnam be the one to renew America's ties there?" Mark Mathews, "Families of MIAs Gird for Final Battle of Vietnam", *Baltimore Sun*, 24 January 1994, 1-A, quoted in Bolton, "The Vietnam Crucible", op. cit.

38. For a detailed analysis of factional posturing surrounding the constitutional revisions and the National Assembly elections, see Thayer, *Renovating Vietnam: Political Change in a One-Party State.*, op. cit., chapters 10 and 11.

39. "Excerpts" from Do Muoi's remarks "At the Midterm National Party

Conference, 20 January 1994 were published in FBIS-EAS-94-134, *Daily Reports*, 13 July 1994. Emphasis added.

40. See Colonel Tran Duy Huong, "Satisfactorily Implementing the Party's Policy on Religion—a Fundamental Countermeasure Against "Peaceful Evolution"", FBIS-EAS-94-216, *Daily Report*, 8 November 1994.

41. Professor Vu Dinh Cu, lecture entitled "Economic Change" delivered to Vietnam-US Society, Hanoi, 30 July 1996. He noted that Vietnam's economy had grown an average of 8.2 per cent between 1991–95. Professor Cu is also a member of the National Assembly.

42. The affair is beyond the limited scope of this chapter. A comprehensive account of the affair can be found in Thayer, *Renovating Vietnam: Political Change in a One-Party State*, op. cit., chapter 11.

43. Elliott, "Vietnam Faces the Future", op. cit., p. 413.

44. Schwarz, "Arrested Development", op. cit., p. 33.

45. Thayer, "Vietnamese Foreign Policy: Multilateralism and the Threat of Peaceful Evolution", op. cit., pp. 15–16.

46. Nayan Chanda et al., "Territorial Imperative", *Far Eastern Economic Review*, 23 February 1995, pp. 14–16.

47. Elliott, "Vietnam Faces the Future", op. cit., p. 417.

48. Adam Schwarz, "Bonfires of the Vanities", *Far Eastern Economic Review*, 7 March 1996, pp. 14–15.

49. For the quotes, see Adam Schwarz, "Guessing Game", *Far Eastern Economic Review*, 6 June 1996, p. 16.

50. Schwarz, "Bonfire of the Vanities", op. cit., p. 15.

51. Thayer, "Vietnamese Foreign Policy: Multilateralism and the Threat of Peaceful Evolution", op. cit., p. 17.

52. Ibid., p. 21.

53. Nayan Chanda, "Big Shoes to Fill", *Far Eastern Economic Review*, 27 June 1996 [Internet edition].

54. *The Economist*, June 1996 [Lexis: New; Major Journals, Major Papers]. By early July, that same journal noted that the old guard were "digging in". See "Vietnam: Where the Communist Sap Doesn"t Rise", *The Economist*, 6 July 1996 [Lexis: New; Major Journals, Major Papers.].

55. Schwarz, "Safety First", op. cit., pp. 15–16.

56. Ibid., p. 16. Also, see: Thayer, "Vietnamese Foreign Policy: Multilateralism and the Threat of Peaceful Evolution", op. cit., p. 18.

57. Ly Thai Hung, "Who to Replace Le Duc Anh", op. cit.

58. See "Senior Leaders 'Make Way for Young Blood' ", *South China Morning Post*, 14 June 97 [Internet edition].

59. Ly Thai Hung, "Who to Replace Le Duc Anh", op. cit.

60. Mitton, "Doi Moi Part 2?," op. cit.

61. See *Vietnam Investment Review*, 1–7 July 1996 and 8–14 July 1996.

62. Schwarz, "Safety First", op. cit., pp. 14–16.

63. See Agence France Press, "Le Duc Anh Remains in 'Critical Condition' After Stroke", in FBIS-EAS-96-223, *Daily Reports*, 17 November 1996.

64. Seth Mydans, "Domino Effect at the Top is Looming for Vietnam", *The New York Times*, 20 December 1996, A-5.

65. Ly Thai Hung, "Who to Replace Le Duc Anh", op. cit.

66. Ibid.

67. Vietnam News Agency, 2 January 1997. Muoi has established himself as being rather rhetorically nimble, one day lambasting reforms or their consequences, another day appearing to be reform's biggest champion. For example, during the summer of 1996—the summer during which the eighth party congress took place—he was quoted as a comforting reassurance to Western business that reforms would continue unabated. See *Vietnam Investment Review*, 1–7 July 1996, p. 1; also see Schwarz, "Safety First", op. cit., p. 16. He has also appeared to temper some of President Anh's more strident remarks on occasion. Yet in May, just prior to the congress while there was still uncertainty as to the congress' outcome, he was lamenting "politically destabilizing, economically sabotaging, and culturally polluting" elements. See Schwarz, "Guessing Game", op. cit., p. 16.

68. John Chalmers, "Vietnam President's Comeback Sets Tongues Wagging", Reuters Wire Service, 3 April 1997 [Internet edition].

69. Adrian Edwards, "Do Muoi Hails Tight Controls as Answer to Vietnam Woes", Reuters Wire Service, 5 April 1997 [Internet edition].

70. *The Constitution of 1992*, op. cit., chapter 6, article 86, 46. This particular deadline does not appear to be a hard-and-fast rule. During the course of interviews in July–August 1997, several specific queries about when the new National Assembly could be expected were made. General consensus was that it would not be until October.

71. *The Constitution of 1992*, op. cit., chapter 6, article 84, 44.

72. Faith Keenan, "Wait and See", *Far Eastern Economic Review*, 3 July 1997 (Internet edition).

73. Though the leadership changes at the top have now been concluded, shuffling of lower level positions continues in 1998, reflecting continued faction manoeuvring. Mitton, "Doi Moi Part 2?" op. cit.

74. Adrian Edwards, Reuters Wire Service, 15 August 1997.

75. Reuters Wire Service, "Vietnam's Pham Van Dong Urges Democratic Reform", 16 August 1997 [Internet edition].

76. For example, Adrian Edwards, "Hanoi Seeks to Placate Farmers amid Unrest Worry", Reuters, Wire Service, 8 August 1997 [Internet edition].

77. Reuters Wire Service, "Vietnam's Pham Van Dong Urges Democratic Reform", 16 August 1997 [Internet edition].

78. Greg Torode, "Debate on Reform Comes into Open", *South China Morning Post,* 20 August 1997 [Internet edition].

79. Reuters Wire Service, "Foreign Criminals Threaten Vietnam, Journal Warns", 13 August 1997 [Internet edition].

80. Keenan, "Generation Shift: Younger Crop of Government Leaders Named", op. cit.

81. Continued factional strife, in Kristin Huckshorn, "Vietnam to Go Slow on Economic Reform", *San Jose Mercury News*, 25 March 1998; Todd Crowell and Ken Stier, "Debate over Directions", *Asiaweek*, April 1998 (Internet edition); Greg Torode, "Pressure on Hanoi Rising with Summer Temperatures", *South China Morning Post*, 1 April 1998 [Internet edition]. On continued unrest in the countryside, see "President Sees Wide Potential for Unrest", *South China Morning Post*, 22 April 1998 (Internet edition). Regarding Nguyen Van Kinh's self-immolation in Ba Dinh Square, see Faith Keenan, "Symptoms of

Malaise", *Far Eastern Economic Review*, 30 April 1998. On Western lenders pushing more reform, see Kristin Huckshorn, "Hanoi's Paralyzing Choice", *San Jose Mercury News*, 18 March 1998. On the impact of events in Indonesia, see Watanabe, "Vietnam Closely Following Events in Indonesia", op. cit.

82. Schwarz, "Arrested Development", op. cit., p. 33. Emphasis added.
83. Keenan, "Partners in Dialogue", op. cit.
84. Carlyle Thayer, "Vietnam's Tardy Reform", *The Asian Wall Street Journal*, 20 August 1997 [Internet: SEASIA-L].
85. The adopt-and-adapt quote comes from Hoan Cong Thuy, deputy secretary, Vietnam-U.S. Society. Thuy pointed out that Vietnam has historically incorporated things from other systems when those things were salient to Vietnam and discarded those things not particularly relevant. Author's interview, Hanoi, August 1997.

8

VIETNAM-U.S. RELATIONS AND VIETNAM'S FOREIGN POLICY IN THE 1990S

Bui Thanh Son

In 1986, Vietnam began to undertake a policy of *doi moi* or "comprehensive renewal". Ten years later, the country has not only emerged from socio-economic crises, but fulfilled the task of establishing a new period of industrialization and modernization of its economy. As a result of the comprehensive renewal, Vietnam also readjusted its foreign policy which, in turn, constituted an important factor in creating a favourable environment for the task of national construction and defence. The success of *doi moi* in general and of the new foreign policy in particular did, among other factors, contribute significantly to the process of normalization of relations between Vietnam and the United States. Finally, on 11 July 1995, President Bill Clinton announced his decision to normalize relations with the Socialist Republic of Vietnam.

This chapter examines Vietnam's current foreign policy and Vietnam-U.S. relations since normalization: how and to what extent does Vietnam's foreign policy affect the development of Vietnam-U.S. relations? What are the areas of co-operation and areas of difficulty or potential difficulty in Vietnam-U.S. relations? How will this bilateral relationship evolve?

Vietnam's Foreign Policy in the 1990s

Tremendous upheavals taking place in the world at the end of 1980s and the early 1990s caused the collapse of the old world order which had existed for almost fifty years. Since then, the world has been entering a transitional period of rapid, complex, and highly unpredictable evolution towards a new world order. In this context, each and every nation has to identify correctly the challenges as well as opportunities that may come in the immediate and long-term future, and fully comprehend major characteristics and trends of the world so as to map out a wise and responsive foreign policy aimed at attaining an optimal or least disadvantageous position in tomorrow's world. Vietnam is no exception.

Actually Vietnam's new thinking on foreign policy had gradually developed since the mid-1980s, when the Vietnamese leadership began to recognize the growing interdependence of the world economies, the trend of détente among major powers, especially between the United States and USSR, the decreased possibility of a world war, and the "economic race" replacing the "arms race" among countries. Based on these assessments, the leadership then came to a conclusion that Vietnam would have to concentrate efforts on economic development while expanding international co-operation in the spirit of "making more friends and reducing the enemies". Such new ideas in foreign policy produced concrete results. In 1989, Vietnam withdrew all troops from Cambodia and this paved the way for the conclusion of the Paris Peace Agreement on Cambodia in 1991. The decision also cleared the biggest obstacle for Vietnam to start the process of normalization with China and the United States and improving its relations with ASEAN countries.

The initial but very important achievements in economic reforms and foreign activities reassured the Vietnamese leadership of the correctness of these policies and contributed to the birth of a general guideline for Vietnam's foreign policy in the 1990s, that is "Vietnam wishes to be a friend of all countries in the world community striving for peace, independence, and development".[1] The active implementation of this new foreign policy significantly contributed to bringing Vietnam out of the state of blockade and embargo, improving its international status, and creating a favourable environment for national development.

During 1995, Vietnam succeeded in joining ASEAN, signed the Framework Agreement on Cooperation with the European Union, and normalized its relations with the United States. By then, Vietnam had established diplomatic relations with more than 160 countries and trade relations with more than 100 countries. Never before in its history have Vietnam's relations with other countries around the world been broader, thus increasing the chances for Vietnam to preserve its independence and sovereignty, enhance self-resilience, and be in a new vantage position to integrate into the world community.

Vietnam's current perception of the world situation

To a large extent how Vietnam views the world will affect its foreign policy decisions and, to lesser extent, the evolution of U.S.-Vietnam relations in the coming years. Vietnam comprehensively set out its perceptions on the world situation in the final resolution adopted by the eighth party congress in mid-1996. In this section, only several major characteristics and trends of the post-Cold War period are highlighted.

First, in years on the threshold of the twenty-first century, we are entering a new stage in the development of world history. It is referred to by many as the "post-Cold War" period. The relations among countries during this period have been influenced and affected not only by the end of the Cold War and the collapse of the socialist regimes in Europe, but mainly by greater changes on a global scale. These changes resulted from the greatest ever revolution in science and technology, which rapidly increases productive forces while accelerating the process of shifting the world economic structures and the internationalization of the economy and social life.

One characteristic of the post-Cold War period is that power is being diffused. It is not concentrated in one or two superpowers as it was during the Cold War; rather it is broken down and spread to several major powers in North America, Europe and Asia. All these existing powers, such as the United States, the European Union, Japan, China, and Russia, are exerting efforts to overcome their weak points and gather forces to secure a better share of the power to influence the international life of the twenty-first century.

Small and medium countries, however, face different problems. They have to find ways to survive and develop in a changed world. New conditions have opened the way for them to secure an independent position so that they can interact and co-operate with all sides. As a result, the trend of diversification and multilateralization has become a universal feature of the post-Cold War era.

Second, the scientific and technological revolution continues to develop at an increasingly higher level which—among other things—has reinforced the level of interdependence among states and accelerated the process of regionalism and globalization. Almost all countries now pursue an outward-looking policy in order to benefit from the international flows of capital, goods, technology, and information. The process of mutual economic interaction and penetration already in existence among national economies has been accelerated. Consequently, economic integration—globally and regionally—has become salient since the end of the 1980s.

Along with the trend of economic integration there exists a contrasting trend, that is nations have heightened their sense of independence, sovereignty, and self-resilience, struggling against any imposition and intervention from outside to preserve their national independence, sovereignty and identity. On the one hand, economic integration is seen as a driving force for economic development of each and every nation. On the other hand, national independence, sovereignty and identity are still considered crucial underpinnings of nation and state building goals. The settlement of these two contrasting trends is of vital importance for the establishment of a new world order in both economic and political spheres.

Third, peace, stability and co-operation for development are increasingly pressing needs of the nations and countries of the world. All countries are giving priority to economic development, considering it of decisive significance for increasing national aggregate strength. This trend together with other factors help push back the danger of a new world war. However, local wars, national, ethnic and religious strife, intervention and terrorism still occur in many places.

Fourth, the Asia-Pacific region, like other parts of the world, has undergone fundamental transformation in the past years. Among the most important developments with implications for Vietnam and other regional countries are the following:

- As a result of the ongoing dynamic development, which continues at a high rate in the Asia-Pacific, global balance of power is increasingly shifting away from Europe and North America towards the Asia-Pacific.

- As Russia has been preoccupied with its internal transformation and the external security environment in Europe, it is clear that the emerging Asia-Pacific order will be built around a triangular structure of relations between the United States, Japan and China. Each leg of this new strategic triangle is itself in a state of flux as the United States, China and Japan reorient relationships with each other. Policies must now be formulated in an environment where no single power can dictate outcomes on the basis of superior economic clout or strategic necessity.

- The emergence of ASEAN as an increasingly influential regional actor has been an important positive development in the Asia-Pacific. With its increased strength, ASEAN has become more resilient and self-confident and has shown its growing capacity for multilateral action. For example, ASEAN was crucial to the formation of APEC and ARF. ASEAN's efforts at co-operative security and economic co-operation have been quite instrumental in facilitating regional dialogues and co-operation. Therefore ASEAN will certainly play an important role in shaping the new regional order.

• Although peace and stability have prevailed in the Asia-Pacific, there still exists a number of sources for concern. They include the intensification of territorial disputes, particularly in the South China Sea; the Korean peninsula, the Cambodian domestic situation; and the new wave of arms modernization.

Main direction of Vietnam's foreign policy

As set out in the resolution of the eighth party congress, the main task of Vietnam's foreign policy in the 1990s and beyond is to "consolidate the peaceful environment and create further favourable international conditions to step up socio-economic development and national industrialization in service of national construction and defence, making active contributions to the common struggle of the world's peoples for peace, national independence, democracy and social progress".[2] In order to fulfil this goal under the perceived international situation, Vietnam has expressed its determination to uphold a foreign policy of independence, sovereignty, openness, diversification and multilateralization of foreign relations, in the spirit of friendship to all nations in the world community, striving for peace, independence and development.

Based on Vietnam's actual foreign activities and the main directions of Vietnam's foreign policy mapped out in the eighth party congress, the following new elements in Vietnam's foreign policy direction for the 1990s may be highlighted. First, as Vietnam concentrates its efforts and resources on economic development, it has accorded greater emphasis to foreign economic issues and a harmonious and flexible combination of political and economic aspects in conducting foreign policy and diplomatic activity. Foreign political activities are aimed at securing a peaceful and stable external environment for domestic economic development and the expansion of foreign economic relations. Foreign economic activities would directly contribute to the course of national industrialization and modernization, which helps strengthen and bolster Vietnam's position in the region and the world. In doing so, Vietnam considers active integration at the regional and global levels, an important issue in the foreign policy agenda. In 1995, Vietnam joined ASEAN and immediately committed to fulfil AFTA's obligations by the year 2006. In 1996, Vietnam submitted its applications for entry into

APEC and WTO and in 1998, Vietnam was admitted to APEC. Preparatory work is in progress for Vietnam to join WTO.

Second, in implementing the policy of diversification and multilateralization, Vietnam gives top priority to consolidation and improvement of friendship and co-operation ties with neighbouring and regional countries. This policy priority is consistent with the world trend and also helps create an environment of peace and stability around Vietnam. For historical and geographical reasons, Vietnam has always attached particular importance to building good relations with neighbouring China, Cambodia and Laos. Since normalization in 1991, Sino-Vietnam relations have turned a new page, one that is marked by frequent exchanges of high level visits, including exchanges of visits by top leaders from both countries, and increased economic and commercial relation. However, whether the two countries can build truly friendly and good neighbourly relation also depends on China's policies towards Vietnam, especially regarding territorial disputes on land and at sea between the two countries. Since the signing of the Paris Agreements on Cambodia, Vietnam has followed a determined policy of non-interference, strict respect for Cambodia's independence and sovereignty, and settlement of bilateral disputes through peaceful negotiations.

During the past six years or so, Vietnam has accomplished a spectacular transformation of its foreign policy *vis-à-vis* ASEAN countries: from confrontation to co-operation and association. By 1995, Vietnam had not only remarkably improved its bilateral relations with each of the ASEAN states, but also succeeded in joining the organization. Active integration into ASEAN is now becoming an important objective of Vietnam's foreign policy.

Third, Vietnam has reserved due attention and efforts to promoting relations with all major powers and political-economic centres of the world, namely China, Japan, the United States, Russia, and the European Union. This policy direction would not only help Vietnam secure an independent position in the new regional and global environment but also create favourable conditions for Vietnam to improve relations with important international organizations, including financial ones such as the World Bank and International Monetary Fund.

Vietnam-U.S. Relations: Present And Future

On 11 July 1995, almost twenty years after the U.S. war with Vietnam, President Bill Clinton announced his decision to normalize relations with Vietnam. The President's decision marked an important step towards closure of a long and sad chapter in the history of the two nations and laid the groundwork for better bilateral co-operation in the years to come. Nearly three years after diplomatic normalization, Vietnamese and Americans, working together, have moved their relations several steps forward. However, the development of Vietnam-U.S. relations are far from commensurate with the potential and desire of the two sides. Bilateral economic and trade relations have yet to be normalized. Both countries still have to overcome many challenges to forge a friendly and constructive relationship as we move on to the twenty-first century.

Reckoning American and Vietnamese interests

As mentioned above, the new American approach towards Vietnam resulted from the country's transition to market economy and a more open society as well as Vietnam's economic potential which attracted the growing interest of the American business community to participate in the process. In April 1997, Secretary of Treasury Robert Rubin visited Hanoi and, in a prepared speech delivered at the U.S.-Vietnam Trade Council, he observed:

> Vietnam is a nation with a proud history ... and it is also a nation with tremendous potential. Already, Vietnam has made great strides in transforming a country shattered by war to one brimming with energy and confidence. Vietnam is blessed by bountiful resources, and with half its population under 25 years old, the advantage of a young, energetic and ambitious population.

To be sure, American economic interests in Vietnam are not as large as in many other regional countries, including China and other individual ASEAN countries. However, Vietnam is seen as the last potential market in Southeast Asia. It is the second most populous country in Southeast Asia. Its economy has grown at 8.2 per cent per annum over the last five years. Furthermore, if the United States regards Vietnam as a member of ASEAN, then U.S. interest seems to be substantial. At present, "U.S. exports to the ASEAN countries exceed those to any other region in the world except northeast Asia and western Europe".[3]

Thus, contrary to the Cold War period, the United States now has a stake in seeing Vietnam succeed in its economic reforms and become a prosperous country with rightful place in Southeast Asia. As Secretary Rubin remarked:

> The United States believes Vietnam's growth and prosperity, while certainly in Vietnam's interest, is also in our interest.[4]

Meanwhile, in Vietnamese eyes, the collapse of the former Soviet Union left the United States the only remaining world superpower. Globally, no other country can approach the United States in economic leverage: being number one in the world in terms of gross national product (GNP), domestic market size, volume of trade, leading edge technologies, military strength, etc. Hence "normal" economic relations with the United States would provide Vietnam's access to most-favoured-nation (MFN) status in the U.S. market at US$7 trillion, the largest in the world. Vietnam is aware that access to the American market constitutes a major factor in the success story of many East Asian economies. In addition, normal economic relations with the United States would also help Vietnam attract more investment capital, more technology and more access to trade opportunities not only from/with the United States but also from/with other countries, international financial and trade organizations.

America's strategic interest in developing relations with Vietnam is no less important. Vietnam does not represent a priority in the U.S. post-Cold War global strategy. However, as a member-state of Southeast Asia, Vietnam has increasingly become an important factor in U.S. regional policy. First, Vietnam is located at a strategic vantage position in Southeast Asia. It is also a large country by regional standards. The combination of these two factors has made Vietnam an important actor in regional affairs. Until the recent past, Vietnam had been a field of competing influence among major powers. In the new regional security environment, a stable and prosperous Vietnam which is not overwhelmingly influenced by any big power is certainly in the U.S. interest. Second, American re-engagement with Vietnam supports regional architecture, of which Vietnam is a part, and bolsters Vietnam's participation in regional groups. Vietnam's reintegration into the region will strengthen multilateral institutions and forums, including ASEAN, ARF, APEC, etc., thus contributing to peace, stability and prosperity of the region.

For its part, Vietnam is aware of the fact that after the Cold War, the Asia-Pacific region is undergoing momentous changes with no few uncertainties ahead. In this context, the United States is considered to be a very important actor in the region due to its economic, political and security leverage. Hence, U.S. positive engagement politically and economically in the region is seen as a stabilizing factor as the Asia-Pacific transforms from bi-polar to multi-polar order in the twenty-first century. The U.S. political interests are, however, still different from that of Vietnam, and the two governments are equally conscious of the differences. In keeping with the four elements of the United States' Asia-Pacific strategy—that is to support democracy and human rights which serve American ideals as well as American interests,[5] President Clinton and his advisers made clear that:

> ... normalization and increased contact between Americans and Vietnamese will advance the cause of freedom in Vietnam, just as it did in Eastern Europe and the Former Soviet Union.[6]

For Vietnam, normalization with the United States has brought the relations between the two countries into a new era of equality, mutual benefit, respect for each other's independence, sovereignty and territorial integrity, as well as non-interference in each other's internal affairs. Therefore, any emerging political issues between the two countries, including the different perceptions over human rights, should be handled on this basis; otherwise conflicts of interest will occur.

Accomplishments

Probably no one can deny the fact that since diplomatic normalization in 1995, Vietnamese and Americans have been working hard together to build the kind of friendly, constructive and mutually beneficial relationship that both peoples envisage and desire. The exchange of Ambassadors between the two countries in May 1997 marked an important step in the direction.

Since normalization, trade and investment have assumed high priority in the development of Vietnam-U.S. relations—both in actual life and on the policy agenda of the two governments. Two-way trade reached US$935 million in 1998 (doubling the 1995 figure and 4.5 times over 1994). Vietnamese exports, valued at US$450 million in 1998, are expected to double once a trade agreement has been signed. Vietnam imported machine tools, aircraft parts, fertilizers, telecommunications equipment, and consumer goods from the United States, and exported coffee, rice, crude oil, garments and textile to the United States. It is noteworthy that Vietnam is running a substantial deficit in bilateral trade with the United States.[7] By the end of 1996 with 63 investment projects worth US$1,319 million, the United States ranked eighth in the list of foreign investors in Vietnam. Additionally, many big U.S. groups are awaiting licences to invest in building power plants and oil refineries.[8] In April 1997, the United States and Vietnam took another important step with the signing of a bilateral agreement on the settlement of debts owed by the former Saigon regime. This agreement removes another important obstacle to closer economic ties between the United States and Vietnam.

Further increases in trade and investment are inevitable, but at this stage they are influenced and constrained by the continuing absence of a trade agreement, which includes U.S. provision of MFN status for Vietnam. After initial discussions about the nature of the two countries' respective economic systems, U.S. and Vietnamese officials met in a series of joint sessions to discuss the main elements of a trade agreement. The two sides have had frank and constructive exchanges throughout the process. In early March 1998, an even bigger step was taken when President Clinton waived the Jackson-Vanik amendment which had placed restrictions on the operations of the Exim Bank and OPIC (Overseas Private Investment Corporation) in specified non-market economies which limit freedom of emigration. Later that month the United States and Vietnam signed a follow-on agreement which permitted OPIC to begin immediate operations in Vietnam. These developments now provide U.S. business with risk protection and financial assistance for investment in Vietnam. Both sides now look to more active negotiations on the provisions of the trade agreement.

Bilateral co-operation in the areas of health, education, environment, science and technology, agriculture, humanitarian aid, etc. have also been expanded, albeit gradually. In the field of education, for example, at present, some thirty American universities are working with Vietnamese counterparts to upgrade Vietnam's education system; and annually, the United States provides about thirty Fulbright scholarships and twenty-five international visitor grants for Vietnamese, not to mention other private and non-governmental funding.

In the security realm, the United States and Vietnam are working at common purposes in multilateral fora such as in the ASEAN Regional Forum to build trust and confidence and promote peaceful resolution of disputes in the region. Bilateral military contact has just been established, and is now only at the initial stage which consists of discussions of regional security perceptions and the exchange of visits.

Vietnam-U.S. political relations appear to be in a temporary period of slow and cautious development. Due to the sensitivity of the political issues, at present, neither leadership expects them to come to the fore in the bilateral relationship. Still the two sides have managed to discuss candidly and quietly some of the most sensitive issues of concern to each side, including the human rights issue. The U.S. political attention, however, has focused on the MIA issue. In his announcement of normalization with Vietnam, President Clinton conditioned the evolution of bilateral relations on continuing progress to the fullest possible accounting for American missing individuals. Vietnam's sustained co-operation on this matter—as acknowledged by high-ranking U.S. officials, including Secretary of State Warren Christopher and Secretary of the Treasury Robert Rubin—has increased popular support for the continuing development of relations between the United States and Vietnam.

Challenges

As noted earlier, accomplishments are considerable and significant, considering the base where Vietnam and the United States started off. However, there remains a lot of work from both sides to move the bilateral relationship forward. In the economic field the absence of a trade agreement have placed U.S. companies that wish to do business in Vietnam in a disadvantageous position compared with other foreign companies. They also prevent Vietnamese companies from getting greater access to the American market because without MFN status, Vietnam's potential products for exports at this stage of economic development, such as woven apparel, footwear, sport bags, assembled electronic products, etc., cannot enter American market at competitive prices.

As the United States and Vietnam enter final negotiations on a draft trade agreement prepared by the U.S. Government, new challenge could arise. It is time for both sides to seriously comprehend the differences in each other's socioeconomic conditions and legal systems in order to move negotiations forward. Meanwhile, progress in negotiating bilateral agreements on civil aviation, investment and copyright protection could serve as fast-track confidence-building measures that would increase the level of mutual trust and provide the momentum towards concluding a comprehensive bilateral trade agreement. The immediate challenge for both sides is to conclude a trade agreement and grant each other most favoured nation status.

In the short term, for reasons noted above, divergence in political interests and perceptions may not represent a major problem in Vietnam-U.S. relations. The challenge for the two governments, however, is to gain better understanding of each other's domestic politics, and to keep on exchanging views and perceptions over existing and emerging political issues. Development of U.S.-Vietnam military-to-military relations depends on progress in other fields of bilateral relations as well as the security environment in East Asia. Current exchanges of perceptions on regional matters and visits by the two sides and increased co-operation in ARF and the Council for Security Cooperation the Asia and the Pacific (CSCAP) will help overcome distrust, build confidence, and lay the groundwork for better co-operation in the future.

Prospects

With the establishment of diplomatic relations and embassies, exchanges of Ambassadors and accomplishments over the past three years, a firm foundation for Vietnam-U.S. relations has been laid. Although there are problems and challenges, the long-term outlook for Vietnam-U.S. relations, which are based on the convergence of major respective national interests, remains bright and positive. Vietnam's determination to continue the process of renewal and integration into the regional and world community would create further opportunities and potential for development of Vietnam-U.S. relations in all fields. Current regional developments and trends in relations among regional countries also—in my view—support the improvement of Vietnam-U.S. relations.

The conclusion of the U.S.-Vietnam Trade Agreement, which is expected before the end of 1999, and the granting of MFN status will ensure rapid growth of bilateral trade and investment, benefiting both sides and facilitating Vietnam's entry into WTO. The United States is likely to become one of Vietnam's leading trade partners and foreign investors. Full diplomatic normalization and increased contacts between the two countries will enhance the opportunities for cultural, educational, scientific and technological exchange between the two peoples in the coming years.

As Vietnam integrates into ASEAN, ARF, and APEC, the two countries can anticipate increasing consonance in their strategic views, thus strengthening the basis for co-operative efforts to solve trans-national problems and other existing or emerging problems in the region.

In order to realize the full potential of this relationship, the United States and Vietnam need to take the following steps:
- For several years to come, both sides need to give top priority to the improvement of economic relations and consider it as a base to expand to other areas;
- The new situation has allowed the two countries to eliminate the "bad faith assumption" about each other which was the legacy of the past, be candid about their perceptions and work together in a spirit of equality, mutual respect and tolerance, taking into account the respectively specific conditions of the two countries.

The United States needs to gain a deeper understanding of the comprehensiveness and complexity of Vietnam's renewal (*doi moi*) and its impact on Vietnamese society and politics. The normalization and improvement of relations with the United States was made possible by the *doi moi* policy, but the establishment of diplomatic relations with the United States is not the exclusive objective of *doi moi*. In any case, Vietnam will certainly go ahead with its reforms, but at its own pace and in its own way.

For its part, the Vietnamese need to comprehend the U.S. political system and the values of its foreign policy. There are different private interest groups and government agencies in America which have different opinions about the normalization with Vietnam. They will influence the pace at which the U.S. Government can move its relations with Vietnam forward. In this context, Vietnam's continued renewal, active co-operation with the United States in solving the MIA issue and keeping the channel of dialogue open with the U.S. on emerging bilateral issues will certainly contribute to the normalization process and changes in American perception about Vietnam in the long-term. Thus, with the goodwill and commitment by both peoples to put the past behind and look forward to a better future, a strong partnership between Vietnam and the United States is not just possible; it has become probable.

Notes

1. This guideline was adopted at the seventh national congress of the VCP in June 1991.
2. *Communist Party of Vietnam*, Eighth National Congress Documents (Hanoi: 1996, p. 77).
3. John Bresnan, *From Dominoes to Dynamos: The Transformation of Southeast Asia* (New York: Council on Foreign Relations Press, 1994), p. 4.
4. Robert Robin, Speech at the U.S.-Vietnam Trade Council, Hanoi, 7 April 1997.
5. Secretary of State Warren Christopher, "America's Strategy for a Peaceful and Prosperous Asia-Pacific", National Press Club, 28 July 1995.
6. Bill Clinton, "U.S. Normalizes Relations with Vietnam", speech delivered in Washington, D.C., 11 July 1995.
7. *Vietnam News Agency*, 17 March 1997.
8. Ministry of Planning and Investment, *Vietnam Business Journal* (January/February 1997), p. 16.

9

CONCLUSION

Carlyle A. Thayer and Ramses Amer

Overview

In the 1980s, Vietnam adopted a foreign policy strategy of improving relations with all nations. To fully comprehend this policy one must look back to the years following unification in 1975. After the end of the Vietnam War, the Vietnamese leadership tried to diversify the country's foreign relations with neighbouring states and with Western Europe. In 1977 Vietnam met with a measure of success with individual members of ASEAN, such as Thailand, but was rebuffed in its overtures further afield. It was not until 1978 that Vietnam made a concerted effort to improve its relations not only with regional states but with ASEAN as an organization. Also in 1978 Vietnam's relations with China, which had been strained, began to sharply deteriorate and eventually led to the Chinese attack on Vietnam in February 1979. That same year Vietnam also failed in its efforts to normalize relations with the United States. Vietnam's military intervention in Cambodia, launched in late December 1978, prompted many non-socialist countries, including the ASEAN members, Australia and Japan, to join in a U.S.-led economic embargo against Vietnam. Thus by early 1979 Vietnam had, contrary to its ambitions in 1975, ended up dependent upon the USSR and even tied to Moscow through a twenty-five year Treaty of Friendship and Co-operation signed in November 1978. This state of affairs—alliance with the USSR and deep conflict with China, confrontation with ASEAN and a deadlocked diplomatic situation in Cambodia—prevailed up to the mid-1980s.

From the mid-1980s, Vietnam's foreign policy underwent a profound transformation as a result of domestic and external pressures. Domestically, Vietnam faced an economic crisis due to the failure of its central planning system to operate efficiently. This crisis was compounded by the costs of Vietnam's military intervention in Cambodia, which included the loss of development assistance, trade and investment opportunities as a result of the embargo imposed by the

United States, ASEAN, Australia, Japan and other states. In September 1979 in response to the economic crisis, Vietnam embarked on piecemeal reforms. It was not until December 1986, at the landmark Sixth National Congress of the Vietnam Communist Party, that Vietnam adopted a comprehensive reform package known as *doi moi* or renovation. The implementation of this programme was thwarted initially by bureaucratic inertia and the opposition of party conservatives and it was not until 1989 that Vietnam's reform effort really began to take effect domestically.

While much attention has been given to the economic measures that Vietnam adopted to transform its centrally planned socialist economy to a market oriented one, less attention has been given to the external or foreign policy dimension of *doi moi*. A key component of Vietnam's programme consisted of opening Vietnam to foreign investment and the development of trade relations with non-traditional partners, primarily the market economies of East Asia. In early 1987 Vietnam promulgated a law on foreign investment, for example. Vietnam's economic fortunes, however, were held hostage by its military intervention in Cambodia. It was clear to some leaders in Hanoi that as long as Vietnam remained militarily engaged in that country, regional states would continue to withhold development assistance and maintain their embargo on trade and investment. In September 1989, in response to these pressures, Vietnam withdrew the last of its formed military units from Cambodia and moved on the diplomatic front to negotiate a comprehensive political settlement to the decade-long conflict. In the context of the withdrawal from Cambodia, it should be noted that Vietnam had carried out troop withdrawals on a yearly basis from 1982, and, beginning in 1985, Vietnam pledged total troop withdrawal by the end of 1990, at the latest. Amer notes that the withdrawal process started before Soviet pressure was applied to Vietnam. He concluded that the economic difficulties may have made Vietnam more eager to speed up the withdrawal but the way in which it was carried out indicated that it was primarily linked to the gradual strengthening of the PRK's defence capability.

While Vietnam was formulating and implementing its programme of comprehensive renovation, it came under external pressures from its major ally, the Soviet Union, not only to speed up the domestic reform process but to transform its external relations as well. In March 1985 Mikhail Gorbachev became Secretary-General of the Communist Party of the Soviet Union (CPSU). Early the following year at a congress of the CPSU he enunciated a reform package which later became synonymous with the words *perestroika*, *glasnost* and "new political thinking". Vietnam was pressured to terminate its military involvement in Cambodia and to normalize its political (that is party-to-party) relations with China. This was not all. Gorbachev completely transformed the ideological and conceptual basis of Soviet foreign policy. Instead of military might, Moscow now stressed the importance of economic strength and the revolution in science and technology as among the most significant factors in determining a nation's strength and the evolution of global politics.

Gorbachev's new political thinking in international relations had a profound impact on Vietnam's foreign policy élite. As Thayer's opening chapter notes, in 1987 Vietnam's leaders adopted Politburo resolution no. 2 which set in motion a fundamental strategic readjustment of that country's national security policy. Vietnam set itself a five-year time frame in which to withdraw its military forces from Cambodia and Laos, and to cut the size of its standing army by half. This followed upon the public commitment in 1985 to a full withdrawal from Cambodia by 1990. In 1988, emboldened by progress on the diplomatic front in reaching a settlement over the Cambodian conflict, Vietnam adopted Politburo resolution no. 13, which aimed to diversify and multilateralize its foreign relations, primarily in the economic field.

It is important to note that the initial transformation in Vietnamese foreign policy was made within the context of its membership in the socialist community headed by the Soviet Union. Palmujoki's chapter makes clear that this resulted in a change in the ideological basis on which the Vietnamese élite framed foreign policy. Increasingly the strictures of Marxist-Leninist doctrine were bypassed in favour of a more pragmatic foreign policy orientation.

The collapse of socialism in Eastern Europe in 1989 and the disintegration of the Soviet Union in 1990–91 were important external factors which led to the transformation of Vietnamese foreign policy. In mid-1991, just prior to the August failed coup against Gorbachev which precipitated the final collapse of the Soviet Union, Vietnam's seventh national party congress adopted an important modification in Vietnam's foreign policy orientation. Vietnam would now "make friends with all countries". Whereas the previous opening had stressed primarily economic ties, the new orientation was aimed at improving political—and later security—ties as well.

The global environment in which Vietnam conducted its foreign policy completely changed in 1991. Not only had communism collapsed but the albatross of Cambodia was finally removed from Hanoi's neck when the Paris International Conference on Cambodia adopted a comprehensive peace settlement in October. Vietnam was no longer a pariah state; the embargo on trade, aid and investment imposed by its regional neighbours and Japan was lifted. Quite remarkably, Vietnam weathered the collapse of the socialist states' system by reorientating its external economic relations from dependency on the Soviet Union and Council for Mutual Economic Assistance (CMEA) countries to the market economies of East Asia.

The resolution of the Cambodian conflict in 1991 paved the way for the full normalization of relations and rapprochement between Vietnam and all ASEAN members. In 1991 relations were also fully normalized with China. As Bui Thanh Son notes, confrontation gave way to co-operation and later association. Vietnam moved determinedly to attain the objective of "making friends with all countries". In July 1995 Vietnam normalized its diplomatic relations with the United States (which had earlier removed an economic embargo extending back to 1964) and became ASEAN's seventh member. Japan, which had taken its lead from the United States, resumed developmental assistance. Finally, relations with the European Union were raised to new levels with the signing of a memorandum of understanding.

Thus, Vietnam's attempt to diversify its foreign relations has proven to be much more successful than the attempts in the 1970s for three main reasons. First, Vietnam's economic reforms have created a domestic environment which is attractive to foreign investors. Second, full normalization and improvement of relations have taken place with ASEAN, Australia, China, France, Japan and even the United States. Third, Vietnam has established closer economic ties with Taiwan and Hong Kong, and diplomatic relations with South Korea.

However, the events described above do not mark the end of a process of transformation but the start of a process of transition in Vietnamese foreign policy as Vietnam's leaders confront new policy challenges such as multilateralism and globalization. The chapters in this book draw attention to the transitional nature of Vietnamese foreign policy in two major domains. The first is concerned with the influence of domestic factors—ideological, economic and political—on foreign policy. The second domain is concerned with the factors which influence three important sets of Vietnam's external relations, that is with ASEAN, China and the United States.

Domestic factors: the role of ideology

Despite that fact that Vietnam is a member of ASEAN and is developing a market-oriented economy, ideology still plays an important role in the conceptualization of Vietnamese foreign policy. Vietnam's 1992 state constitution clearly states that the Vietnam Communist Party is "the force" leading state and society. Party statutes make clear that Marxism-Leninism and the Thoughts of Ho Chi Minh provide the ideological basis for all policy, whether domestic or external. Both Thayer and Palmujoki discuss this important question. As noted above the two authors argue that traditional ideological concepts such as "the two camp thesis" and "three revolutionary currents" have given way to new concepts which were initially borrowed from the vocabulary of reform in Gorbachev's Soviet Union. Palmujoki argues the emphasis is now on the impact of the revolution in science and technology in creating greater interdependence and new modes of production, while Thayer argues that Marxism-Leninism has given way to considerations of national interest and *realpolitik*.

Palmujoki makes the important point that ideology was easily grafted on to previously existing concepts employed by the Confucian literati in the nineteenth century. He notes that such traditional ideological formulations as "who will beat whom" and "which path (capitalism or socialism) will win" have been supplanted. Palmujoki argues that the process is a layered one, and not an abrupt shift from one ideological framework to another. Both Palmujoki and Thayer conclude that the role of ideology has been depreciated but none the less continues to exert an influence on how present day foreign policy is conceptualized and presented rhetorically.

Thayer argues that Vietnam has lost its ideological paradigm but not found another. This has led, in his view, to a certain flatness or shallowness in Vietnam's bilateral relations. The influence of ideology still causes Vietnam to hold back from developing what he terms "fully rounded" bilateral relations. Thayer specifically draws attention to fears expressed by party conservatives that opening up will lead to the introduction of political and economic forces which will undermine one-party rule. This fear is usually expressed as the "threat of peaceful evolution".

The process of modifying and adapting Marxist-Leninist ideological conceptions is not a uni-linear process as Li Ma's chapter demonstrates. A socialist market economy should not be confused with a free market economy or a capitalist one. In her view the jury is still out on how socialist market economies will evolve, but it is clear from Li Ma's chapter that China and Vietnam will continue to use ideology to legitimize party-state dominance over the economy. Further, she argues, because they both face the threat of U.S.-instigated peaceful evolution, they have a common interest which influences their foreign policies. It is clear, therefore, that Vietnam's foreign policy is still in transition on the ideological front.

Domestic factors: the economy

It is quite clear that Vietnam's adoption of comprehensive reforms in 1986, and Vietnam's subsequent reaffirmation that it will continue to pursue comprehensive renovation at the seventh and eighth national party congresses in 1991 and 1996, respectively, has directly contributed to an open door foreign policy and an historic shift from dependency on the socialist states' system to full participation in the global economy. As Bui Thanh Son points out, officially Vietnam's most important foreign policy goal is the maintenance of a peaceful regional and international environment so that it can develop its economy and engage in co-operative relations with other states. This has taken many forms. Vietnam has not only sought official development assistance but has avidly pursued foreign direct investment and trade. Also, Vietnam has fully availed itself of participation in the UN system. It has also sought development loans from a number of international financial institutions such as the Asian Development Bank, International Monetary Fund and World Bank. Vietnam is poised to become a member of the Asia-Pacific Economic Cooperation (APEC) forum and is seeking membership in the World Trade Organization (WTO).

Thus domestic economic factors weigh heavily in Vietnam's foreign policy orientation, and have played a direct role in the development of bilateral relations. For example, since 1991 Vietnam has become linked closely with the market economies of Northeast Asia, especially Japan, Taiwan, Hong Kong and South Korea. Economic issues are a major factor influencing Vietnam's relations with the United States, where only the negotiation of a trade agreement (granting MFN status) remains for economic relations to be fully normalized. As a member of ASEAN, Vietnam has subscribed to the ASEAN Free Trade Area (AFTA) including the Common Effective Preferential Tariff (CEPT) arrangements. As argued by Amer, cross-border smuggling from China, which has serious detrimental effects on Vietnam's domestic industries (and contributes to a loss of revenue), was a major issue in the early 1990s when it was an irritant in Sino-Vietnamese relations. It emerged again as an issue in 1997 when Vietnam stepped up its efforts to curb overall smuggling. Both China and Vietnam are making efforts to combat smuggling in the border areas.

During the second half of 1997 it became apparent that Vietnam's economy was beginning to stall. Weaknesses in the banking system, corruption and red tape contributed to a loss of foreign investor confidence. Disbursement rates for official development assistance began to fall. Vietnam's trade deficit began to grow while GDP growth rates began to taper off. Serious peasant disturbances broke out in the northern province of Thai Binh. These events were described by the Vietnamese leadership as "twin typhoons". Foreign investors and international financial institutions urged Vietnam to step up the pace of reform; some even advocated *"doi moi 2"*. However, economic uncertainty provoked caution. In the face of the third typhoon, Asia's financial crisis, Vietnam appears to have adopted a "wait and see" attitude about what steps to take next. In this sense Vietnamese foreign economic policy is in transition as Vietnam's leaders decide whether the benefits of regional integration outweigh the costs of potential further domestic unrest stemming from the downturn in the economy.

Domestic factors: new political actors

According to Kent Bolton, Vietnam's programme of economic and political renovation has led to the emergence of new institutional actors who have the capacity to affect foreign policy decision making. He mentions in passing the new role in external relations of such bodies as the military, informal groups of retired diplomats and the Vietnam Women's Union. The latter publishes its own newspaper and maintains extensive overseas contacts. Bolton pays particular attention to the decision-making cycle of the Vietnam Communist Party—five yearly congresses and biannual plenary sessions of the Central Committee—as well as to the increasingly autonomous role of the National Assembly and "the government" (council of ministers and individual ministers).

Bolton's case study of the normalization of relations with the United States provides evidence that domestic factors increasingly play a role in foreign policy decision making. He argues that Foreign Minister Nguyen Co Thach was farsighted in his appreciation that Vietnam would have to cut its losses in Cambodia in order to normalize relations with the United States and to balance an ascendant China. Thach also supported Gorbachev's reform efforts in the Soviet Union. As the socialist states' system began to disintegrate, Vietnam's ideological conservatives became increasing apprehensive about the likely impact on Vietnam. When Soviet reform efforts created gross domestic instability, and when the United States failed to reward Vietnam for withdrawing from Cambodia with the normalization of relations, Thach was jettisoned from both his seat on the Politburo and from his posts as Deputy Prime Minister and Foreign Minister.

Amer argues that Nguyen Co Thach's importance should not be overestimated since his diplomatic efforts did not result in advancing the normalization process between China and Vietnam. In fact, the normalization process gained momentum following Thach's removal in July 1991. More generally Amer notes that the interaction between individual political leaders in Vietnam and China may have contributed to the failure in maintaining normal relations and in handling the emerging differences on the 1970s. In the normalization process of the late 1980s and early 1990s, the Vietnamese leadership had been completely revamped compared to the late 1970s, and this may have facilitated contacts with the Chinese leaders.

Initially the VCP sought to depreciate the role of the Ministry of Foreign Affairs (MOFA) and its minister by progressively transferring power to senior members of the party Politburo. Responsibility for policy on China and Cambodia, for example, was reportedly transferred to Le Duc Anh. When the party's *nomenklatura* made clear that Thach would be dropped, none of Vietnam's experienced professional deputy ministers would step forward to take the post. It was in these circumstances that in August 1991 Nguyen Manh Cam, a former ambassador to the Soviet Union, was appointed Minister of Foreign Affairs. Cam was a member of the party Central Committee but not its executive. He reported to Politburo member Le Duc Anh and Secretariat member Hong Ha, the party bureaucracy's top foreign affairs specialist. Following elections for the ninth legislature of the National Assembly in July 1992, Cam was appointed to the newly-created National Defence and Security Council by virtue of his state position as Minister for Foreign Affairs (and not his party standing). The National Defence and Security Council included among its members the state president, prime minister, chairman of the National Assembly Standing Committee, Minister for National Defence and Minister of the Interior (all members of the Politburo).

Cam was not appointed to the Politburo until January 1994. He was later appointed to the five-member Politburo Standing Board when it was first created following the 1996 eighth party congress. His position was further bolstered following the 1997 elections for the tenth legislature of the National Assembly when he was appointed one of five deputy prime ministers and given responsibility for foreign political and economic relations. When the Politburo Standing Board was reconstituted in December 1997, following the elevation of Le Kha Phieu to the post of VCP Secretary-General (replacing Do Muoi), Cam was re-appointed along with the Ministers of Interior and National Defence.

Vietnam's programme of comprehensive renovation has led to greater structural differentiation in the state bureaucracy. Formal responsibility for the conduct of foreign policy rests with the Ministry of Foreign Affairs. In recent years MOFA has created departments responsible for ASEAN affairs and policy planning. Foreign policy is not the exclusive preserve of MOFA, however. For example, Vietnam established a National ASEAN Committee headed by a deputy prime minister who has responsibility for co-ordinating all institutions which interact with ASEAN or ASEAN-affiliated bodies.

Increasingly the Ministries of National Defence, Interior, Trade, and Planning and Investment have become involved in the decision-making process. Defence ministry personnel, for example, now participate in the ASEAN Regional Forum (ARF) activities alongside their MOFA counterparts. More significantly, Vietnam's military establishment has opened defence contacts with nearly thirty countries, including twenty which have accredited defence attachés in Hanoi (three are non-resident). Vietnam's Defence Minister has visited all the ASEAN states with the exception of Brunei. Vietnam has begun participating in bilateral security dialogues with Japan and Australia. Vietnam's defence journal, *Tap Chi Quoc Phong Toan Dan*, has begun carrying articles assessing the contribution of the military's external relations to Vietnam's overall foreign policy. In this context the expanding links between the Vietnamese and Chinese armed forces can be noted with regular visits in both directions.

The role of the VCP's External Relations Department has been expanded to include relations with ruling political parties in countries which have exchanged diplomatic relations with Vietnam. Prior to the collapse of the socialist states' system, for example, the External Relations Department had exclusive carriage for relations with other communist, socialist and other fraternal parties and liberation movements, such as the PLO. The eighth national party congress, for example, was attended by delegations from thirty-five political parties, including communist parties in power, communist and socialist parties and national liberation movements not in power, and ruling political parties such as Singapore's People' Action Party and the United Malays National Organization from Malaysia. The relations between the few remaining ruling communist parties, for example China, Cuba and Laos, have been not only maintained but in the case of the CCP expanded.

On both an institutional and individual basis, Vietnamese foreign policy is in transition as both party and state structures are renovated to meet the challenges of diplomacy in the post-Cold War era. Whereas foreign policy was once (and continues to be) held by a tiny élite, a larger number of ministers are now playing a role in this area as the foreign policy agenda expands. Vietnam is still in the process of adapting its one-party system and ideological outlook to relations with states that are market economies and multi-party systems.

Vietnam and multilateralism

Up until the mid- to late-1980's, Vietnam had little experience in multilateral diplomacy. Most of its experience was gained as a member of the CMEA. In 1994–95, Vietnam became a full member of the ARF and ASEAN respectively. What motivated Vietnam to join? Vietnamese officials argue that three factors influenced Vietnam's decision to join ASEAN: the desire to have friendly relations with regional states, to attract foreign investment and trade, and as a catalyst to its domestic reform process. There are also a number of unstated reasons including gaining familiarity with the norms and practices of a regional organization (e.g. on international trade issues), to assist membership in APEC and the WTO, enhancement of national prestige and security, and strategic considerations (contributing to a more peaceful international environment, and improving Vietnam's bargaining position *vis-à-vis* the United States and China).

On the strategic front, Vietnam's membership in ASEAN has proved useful from a general perspective on Vietnam's position *vis-à-vis* China. With regard to the conflicts in the South China Sea, the benefits of ASEAN membership is not as obvious in constraining Chinese assertiveness. Nevertheless some positive impact from a Vietnamese perspective can be noted, e.g. the South China Sea was raised at the China-ASEAN dialogue in Hangzhou in April 1995. This was the first occasion that the issue of the South China Sea was raised in a multilateral setting (outside of the informal Indonesia-sponsored workshops). The South China Sea issue was raised "forcibly" at the China-ASEAN dialogue held in Huangshan in mid-April 1997. According to David Wurfel, this marked the first time that China had agreed to discuss this issue in a multilateral forum. China responded to ASEAN's united front by offering to negotiate a code of conduct governing their relations. Nevertheless, to cite Wurfel again, Vietnam's success in employing ASEAN enmeshment with China as a political defence against Chinese incursions in the South China Sea "may not have long term viability". This is because ASEAN-Vietnam defence co-operation is unlikely, he argues.

Not all of Vietnam's foreign policy élite fully embrace multi-lateralism. There is concern that Vietnam's interests might be negatively affected by ASEAN's decision-making style of "10 – x" to permit progress when there is a lack of consensus. There is a lingering suspicion that Vietnam might be taken advantage of by ASEAN's richer and more developed members. Some Vietnamese officials are cautious about moving too quickly and are concerned that Vietnam might be disadvantaged by joining an organization in which it must compete with fellow members for development assistance and foreign investment. Others fear that domestic industries will be adversely affected if Vietnam is forced to do away with a number of non-tariff protectionist measures. An influx of cheaper ASEAN goods could undermine local industries, worsen the trade deficit, and erode the government's revenue base, they argue. Finally, Party conservatives are fearful that economic integration could lead to a loss of sovereignty, erode Vietnam's commitment to its "socialist orientation" and eventually undermine one-party rule.

Since 1991 Vietnam has pursued the objective of "diversifying and multilateralizing" its foreign economic relations. Vietnam has played an essentially quiet role within ASEAN and has not been proactive on any particular issue. In some respects it appears that Vietnam became a member of ASEAN almost as an end it itself. This has led to the view that Vietnam has "lost its orientation". While Foreign Minister Cam has called for a "deepening of economic relations", there is little evidence that his ministry has thought through the next stage—how to develop an integrated national strategy which combines the traditional concerns of foreign relations with national security policy and international economic relations (such as trade policy). In this respect Vietnam's foreign policy is still in transition from its traditional focus on bilateral relations to a consideration of how multilateralism should fit into an integrated national foreign policy strategy.

Sino-Vietnamese relations

Four chapters in this book deal with the vexed question of Sino-Vietnamese relations (Li Ma, Ramses Amer, Chang Pao-min and David Wurfel) and the factors which historically have led to alternating patterns of conflict and co-operation. Chang Pao-min makes the important point that historically Vietnam has sought Chinese intervention when its leaders faced domestic turmoil or when Vietnam was threatened externally. China has invariably responded by providing assistance when requested. Vietnam and China have much in common. They are linked geographically and share the same cultural roots and experience of colonial domination. As a result they both adopted the same ideology—nationalism and then communism. Historically, and in the present period of market reforms (dating in China from the late 1970s), China has been a source of inspiration and concrete assistance to its neighbour to the south.

What then explains the "love-hate" relationship and hostility and bitterness of the period from 1975–91? According to Chang, Vietnamese nationalism made cultural affinity with China a liability and was detrimental to the formation of a distinct Vietnamese identity. Chinese bitterness was especially aroused in the late 1970s because Vietnam had not treasured its cultural ties and traditional links with China and had shown ingratitude for Chinese material support during the anti-American war. This led to the cancellation and suspension of Chinese economic assistance to Vietnam in 1978. But other factors were at play which undermined a relationship once described "as close as lips and teeth".

In the twentieth century changes in technology, communication and transport made it possible for the first time for Vietnam to seek an ally "over the horizon" to counterbalance China. How can the sharp deterioration in relations during the second half of the 1970s be explained? Amer's analysis shows that three major issues contributed to the deterioration of relations between China and Vietnam; different perceptions of the USSR, relations to and influence in Cambodia and the ethnic Chinese in Vietnam. He also discusses the relative importance of the territorial disputes, ideology and internal change.

Amer observes that during the normalization process of the late 1980s and early 1990s two of the major issues of controversy in the late 1970s and during the 1980s were removed from the agenda: first were the divergent views concerning the role of the USSR in the world and Vietnam's close relations with the USSR; and second, the Sino-Vietnamese differences over Cambodia were removed through the Vietnamese military withdrawal and the conflict resolution process leading up to the Paris Agreements on Cambodia of October 1991. This left the territorial disputes as a major unresolved issue between Beijing and Hanoi.

What factors explain the remarkable rapprochement between Beijing and Hanoi in the period after 1991? Chang stresses that this new phase in Sino-Vietnamese relations must be analysed in the context of historical patterns and by taking into account changes globally and in the Asia-Pacific region. Three important systemic factors must be considered: Sino-Soviet rapprochement in the mid-1980s, the collapse of the socialist states system, and increased economic interdependence regionally and globally.

The end of the Cold War brought with it not only fundamental structural changes to regional order but peace in the Asia-Pacific. According to Chang, China was no longer confronted or contained by a major external power. It could now turn inward and concentrate on economic development. These systemic changes caused Vietnam to seek reconciliation and co-operation with all its neighbours including China. Thus changes in the international system created an unprecedented opportunity for the revival of friendly and co-operative relations between China and Vietnam. According to Li Ma both countries share many common interests. They both want to retain their one-party regimes in power, overcome U.S. efforts to isolate them from the international community (via containment in the case of China, via an embargo in the case of Vietnam), and resist Western pressures to peacefully evolve into pluralist democracies.

Even more, both share a common interest in the maintenance of a peaceful international environment in which to carry out economic reforms. Both China and Vietnam are committed to successfully creating socialist market economies. In other words, they are following parallel development paths. Both have opened up their economies to the outside and have used diplomacy to attract aid, trade and investment to sustain economic development. Both have included the military as an economic player with a stake in the system. Both face roughly similar problems such as corruption, provincial autonomy and regional disparities. Both have made economic performance the basis of regime legitimacy. Finally, according to Li Ma, both are in a defensive position insofar as they cannot backtrack on reforms and are thus committed to developing their socialist market economies in tandem.

Amer notes that the Sino-Vietnamese relationship has been characterized by two conflicting patterns of interactions: good bilateral relations and tensions related to territorial disputes. On the political level, relations appear especially close since normalization in November 1991. China has hosted two summits involving the leaders of their respective communist parties (November 1995 and July 1997) and there is extensive interaction at all levels, including by uniformed military personnel.

The economies of China and Vietnam are complementary. Vietnam's geographical position serves as a maritime gateway to China's southern provinces. Chang Pao-min argues that Vietnam can serve as a bridge to maritime Southeast Asia. Vietnam represents a substantial market for Beijing.

Tension along their frontier has virtually ceased while border crossings and rail links have been opened. Both sides have signed a number of agreements governing a wide array of co-operative activities. A Sino-Vietnamese Commission for Economic and Commercial Co-operation has been established. China has agreed to provide loans to revitalize industrial plants which it had given as aid to Vietnam before unification. China also provides a symbolic amount of development assistance. However, cross-border smuggling remains a major irritant. It should be noted that China is not a major source of inputs for Vietnam's economic growth. Vietnam is much more oriented towards the economies of Northeast Asia. Despite the progress in recent years in terms of expansion of economic co-operation and a clearly stated political will to further deepen economic co-operation and interaction, noted by Amer, the Chinese-Vietnamese economic relations have not reached their full potential. As China and Vietnam develop they will likely become market rivals in the next century.

Whether or not China and Vietnam can successfully co-operate for development will depend in large measure on how they manage the main obstacle confronting them—territorial disputes along their land border and in the South China Sea. The pattern is mixed. On the one hand, as Amer's overview indicates, the two countries have set up a system of talks and discussions relating to the territorial disputes structured in the following way: expert-level talks; government-level talks (deputy/vice-minister; foreign minister-level talks), and, high-level talks (secretary-generals of the CCP and VCP, presidents and prime ministers). It is notable that in October 1993 the two sides reached a basic agreement on principles for settling territorial disputes along the land border and in the Tonkin Gulf, and during the Beijing summit held in mid-1997 both sides agreed to resolve these disputes by the year 2000.

On the other hand, Amer observes that despite the positive evolution with bilateral talks at different levels the border disputes have not been formally resolved and the parties have been unable to prevent the territorial disputes from causing serious tension. Since full normalization of relations in late 1991, sharp differences relating to all the territorial disputes, i.e. overlapping claims to the Paracel and Spratly archipelagos, to water and continental shelf areas in the South China Sea and in the Gulf of Tonkin, and to areas along the land border, were prevalent between May to November 1992. Differences relating to oil exploration in the South China Sea and the signing of contracts with foreign companies for exploration were prevalent during the periods April–June 1994, April–May 1996 and

March–April 1997. Some more specific examples display the negative impact on unilateral decisions and actions. In 1992 China promulgated a law on territorial waters which incorporated the South China Sea. Again, in 1996, China issued a statement setting out baselines defining its territorial sea adjacent to the mainland and including the Paracel Islands. If this claim were extended to the Spratly Islands, it would enclose the entire archipelago as Chinese territory. In 1992 and again in 1995 China unilaterally took possession of unoccupied features in the South China Sea, Da Lac and Mischief reefs respectively. Other unilateral Chinese actions have included awarding Crestone Energy Corporation, a U.S. company, exploration rights in an area which Vietnam claims is on its continental shelf; drilling in contested areas of the Gulf of Tonkin and in the Tu Chinh reef area, both claimed by Vietnam; and seizing ships bound for Vietnam on the pretext that they are engaged in smuggling. Vietnam unilaterally extended its occupation of features in the South China Sea in 1992 and in April 1994, and took a leaf out of China's book by granting Mobil Oil rights to the Blue Dragon concession, an area claimed by China.

There is undoubtedly a need for the two sides to agree on a "code of conduct" to be observed in disputed areas of the South China Sea in order to maintain the status quo and to prevent the reoccurrence of periods of tension. Amer warns that unless such an agreement is reached, there is a potential risk that tension can escalate into confrontation, thus threatening the positive achievements in expanding bilateral co-operation in recent years.

In 1991 when China and Vietnam issued a joint communiqué announcing the normalization of relations, they devoted the longest section to principles which should guide Vietnam's relations with Taiwan. This important set of bilateral relations has received comparatively little coverage by academic specialists. Chang Pao-min draws attention to the possibility that unresolved bilateral issues and competition for scarce energy sources could generate new tension and conflict between Beijing and Hanoi. Chang argues that Southeast Asian regional states are concerned about a rising China and the development of maritime power projection capabilities. ASEAN's founding members saw Vietnam as a natural ally to restrain and harness potential Chinese expansionism. They moved to incorporate Vietnam as ASEAN's seventh member in order to enhance their bargaining power with China. Chang, however, argues that the confluence of strategic interests which has led to this historic realignment of forces also contains seeds of future conflict. Chang warns of the dire consequences for regional security should Vietnam and an independently-minded Taiwan collude against China. Chang also warns of the possibility of a "chain reaction" leading to hostilities should an anti-China united front develop—which included Vietnam, ASEAN, and the United States—and seek to confront China particularly over disputed territory in the South China Sea.

According to Chang, China must be accepted as a regional power and Vietnam should not turn itself into an anti-China outpost allied with an external power. In Beijing's view, Vietnam can be won over eventually. No relationship with an outside power can negate or replace Vietnam's centuries-old and multifaceted linkages with China, he asserts. China and Vietnam could operate from common strength, a position supported by Li Ma. Both countries are internally focused and are concerned to maintain domestic political stability, or what Wurfel terms regime maintenance. Both need a peaceful international environment in which to undertake economic and political reforms.

In sum, Vietnamese foreign policy is in transition as Hanoi's leaders learn how to manage relations with their large northern neighbour in the post Cold War era. While the past may provide some guide to Vietnam's China specialists on how relations might be managed, the forces of globalization and regionalism have created an entirely new environment for the conduct of such diplomacy. Sino-Vietnamese relations provide opportunities and pitfalls. The challenge for Vietnamese foreign policy is how to balance its relations and not alter the territorial status quo or seek a counter-weight to China. Vietnam's leaders will need political foresightedness, military restraint, and diplomatic skills of the highest order to take advantage of this new opportunity.

Vietnam-U.S. relations

When the old order collapsed in the late 1980s and early 1990s, Vietnam adopted "new thinking" in foreign policy and began to stress the importance of economic interdependence, détente, and the declining possibility of war. Vietnam's leaders studied the success of the so-called Asian tigers and concluded that access to the U.S. market was an important requisite. In order for Vietnam to participate in this process it would need to take steps to end the U.S. economic embargo against it. The Gulf War of the early 1990s came as a shock to Vietnamese leaders, for a U.S. victory implied that capitalism was now in the ascendancy. This strengthened the hands of those who favoured normalization, but the pace of this process was determined by U.S. domestic politics.

According to Kent Bolton, the normalization of relations with the United States was a means to an end for Vietnam. It meant the attainment of two key foreign policy goals: external support for *doi moi* and a stable and peaceful international environment in which to carry out domestic reforms. In other words, the success in carrying out *doi moi*, which included revamping the method for conceptualizing Vietnamese foreign policy, contributed positively to the process of normalization.

Vietnamese leaders correctly identified the Asia-Pacific as a dynamic region of growth where the world revolution in science and technology was taking hold and changing productive forces. National economies were being internationalized, and no one state could dominate because of the economic base and dispersed nature of power. This opened up new possibilities for small and medium countries to interact and co-operate in order to guarantee their own security. This led Vietnam down the path of membership in ASEAN. At the same time, Vietnam's leaders concluded that the balance of power in the Asia-Pacific was shifting towards a tripolar system dominated by the United States, China and Japan, and that membership in ASEAN alone was not sufficient to guarantee national security. Thus normalization of relations with the United States had a strategic rationale.

Vietnam and the United States established diplomatic relations at ambassadorial level in July 1995. There are impediments on both sides to the development of completely normalized relations. Hanoi and Washington must first negotiate a trade agreement in order for Vietnam to be granted most-favoured-nation access to the American market. President Bill Clinton's 1997 waiver of the Jackson-Vanik amendment opened up the possibility of such an agreement being reached in late 1999. A trade agreement will not, however, resolve outstanding political issues such as U.S. concerns about human rights in Vietnam (the MIA issue has largely receded from the agenda).

The normalization of Vietnam-U.S. relations has been a highly contentious issue in Vietnam. The fears of Vietnamese conservatives were heightened by remarks made by President Clinton that normalization of relations would advance the cause of freedom in Vietnam just as it did in Eastern Europe. Clinton's remarks have fuelled fears by Vietnam's ideologues that Washington seeks to overturn one-party rule and convert Vietnam into a pluralist democracy. As Bui Thanh Son makes clear, Vietnam will not only resist such pressures, but will pursue reform at its own measured pace.

Bui Thanh Son also argues that progress in other areas cannot be made until the economic foundations are firmly laid. Thus Vietnamese foreign policy towards the United States will enter a new period of transition once a trade agreement has been reached. This is because for nearly four years now Vietnam has fixated on achieving this objective. Once an agreement is reached, Vietnam will have to develop policies to conduct relations on a much broader front, including political relations and defence/security ties. It is likely that Vietnam-U.S. relations will continue to suffer from the intrusion of domestic politics in both nations (ideological conservatives in the former, according to Thayer; human rights proponents in the latter, according to Bolton). This raises the possibility that Vietnam's conservatives might seek common cause with their cousins in China.

Challenges facing Vietnam's foreign policy

Vietnam faces complex choices about the benefits of multilateralism *à la* ASEAN versus power balancing. The current Asian financial crisis and domestic instability in Indonesia serve to challenge liberal assumptions about the benefits of economic interdependence. Signs of a deepening economic crisis in Japan and the threat of economic instability also in China will further reinforce such thinking and could have negative implications for the regional economy as well as the Vietnamese one. The May 1998 nuclear explosions by India and Pakistan serve to remind regional states that realist assumptions about the nature of the new international order have not passed entirely into history. These developments pose severe challenges for Vietnamese foreign policy.

The limitations of ideology and multilateralism, and the pitfalls of attempting a balance of power approach towards China have been discussed above. According to David Wurfel, Vietnam prefers a concert of powers to alignment, but a concert of powers in which small and medium states can play an important role. Vietnamese foreign policy remains in transition on two counts. First, ideology must catch up with reality. Vietnamese party theorists state that Vietnam is in the "initial phase of the transitional period to socialism". This proposition seems hardly tenable in an era of regionalism and globalization. Second, Vietnam's foreign policy is in transition because power relations in the Asia-Pacific are still in flux. Vietnam has yet to work out what national strategy it should pursue as a regional middle power in order to safeguard national independence, maintain political stability (regime maintenance), develop a socialist market economy, and integrate with the global economy.

SELECT BIBLIOGRAPHY

Carlyle A. Thayer and Ramses Amer, compilers

ASEAN

Acharya, Amitav. "The Association of Southeast Asian Nations: 'Security Community' or 'Defence Community'?" *Pacific Affairs* 64, no. 2 (1991): 159–77.

——. *A New Regional Order in South-East Asia: ASEAN in the Post-Cold War Era.* Adelphi Paper 270. London: International Institute of Strategic and International Studies, 1993.

Amer, Ramses. "Territorial Disputes and Conflict Management in ASEAN". In *The ASEAN: Thirty Years and Beyond*, edited by Lourdes Aranal-Sereno and Joseph Sedfrey S. Santiago, pp. 325–50. Quezon City: University of the Philippines Law Center, Institute of International Legal Studies, 1997.

——. "Expanding ASEAN's Conflict Management Framework in Southeast Asia: The Border Dispute Dimension". *Asian Journal of Political Science* 6, no. 2 (1998): 33–56.

—— and David Hughes. "The Asian Crisis and Economic Cooperation: Implications For an Expanded ASEAN". In *Southeast Asian-Centred Economies or Economics?*, edited by Mason Hoadley, pp. 113–36. NIAS Report Series, No. 39. Copenhagen: Nordic Institute of Asian Studies, 1999.

Antolik, Michael. "ASEAN and the Utilities of Diplomatic Informality". In *The ASEAN: Thirty Years and Beyond*, edited by Lourdes Aranal-Sereno and Joseph Sedfrey S. Santiago, pp. 441–51. Quezon City: University of the Philippines Law Center, Institute of International Legal Studies, 1997.

Aranal-Sereno, Lourdes and Joseph Sedfrey S. Santiago, eds. *The ASEAN: Thirty Years and Beyond.* Quezon City: Institute of International Legal Studies, University of the Philippines Law Center, 1997.

ASEAN Secretariat. *ASEAN Economic Co-operation: Transition and Transformation.* Singapore: Institute of Southeast Asian Studies, 1997.

Askandar, Kamarulzaman. "ASEAN and Conflict Management: The Formative Years of 1967–1976". *Pacifica Review* 6, no. 2 (1994): 57–69.

Australia, Commonwealth of. *The New ASEANs: Vietnam, Burma, Cambodia and Laos.* Canberra: East Asia Analytical Unit, Department of Foreign Affairs and Trade, 1997.

Boisseau du Rocher, Sophie. *L'ASEAN et la construction régionale en Asie du Sud-Est.* Paris and Montreal: L'Harmattan, 1998.

Bowles, Paul. "ASEAN, AFTA and the 'New Regionalism' ". *Pacific Affairs* 70, no. 2 (1997): 219–33.

Caballero-Anthony, Mely. "Mechanisms of Dispute Settlement: The ASEAN Experience". *Contemporary Southeast Asia* 20, no. 1 (1998): 38–66.

Chia, Siow Yue and Marcello Pacini, eds. *ASEAN in the New Asia: Issues and Trends*. Singapore: Institute of Southeast Asian Studies, 1997.

Chin, Kin Wah. "ASEAN: Consolidation and institutional change". *The Pacific Review* 8, no. 3 (1995): 424–39.

———. "ASEAN the Long Road to 'One Southeast Asia' ". *Asian Journal of Political Science* (Special Issue on ASEAN) 5, no. 1 (1997): 1–19.

Doan Manh Giao. "Why Vietnam Joins ASEAN". Paper presented to the international seminar on Vietnam and ASEAN: Business Prospects and Policy Directions, Kuala Lumpur, 19 December 1995.

Funston, John. "ASEAN: Out of its Depth?" *Contemporary Southeast Asia* 20, no. 1 (1998): 22–37.

Gill, Ranjit Gill. *ASEAN Coming of Age*. Singapore: Sterling Corporate Services, 1987.

Hernandez, Carolina G. and Jorge V. Tigno. "ASEAN Labour Migration: Implications for Regional Stability". *The Pacific Review* 8, no. 3 (1995): 544–57.

Hoang Anh Tuan. "Why Hasn't Vietnam Gained ASEAN Membership?" *Contemporary Southeast Asia* 15, no. 3 (1993): 280–91.

———. "Vietnam's Membership in ASEAN: Economic, Political and Security Implications". *Contemporary Southeast Asia* 16, no. 3 (1994): 259–73.

———. "ASEAN Dispute Management: Implications for Vietnam and an Expanded ASEAN". *Contemporary Southeast Asia* 18, no. 1 (1996): 61–80.

Mutalib, Hussin. "At Thirty, ASEAN Looks to Challenges in the New Millennium". *Contemporary Southeast Asia* 19, no. 1 (1997): 74–85.

Huxley, Tim. *ASEAN and Indochina: A Study of Political Responses, 1975–81*. Canberra Studies in World Affairs 19. Canberra: Department of International Relations, The Australian National University, 1985.

Joyaux, François. *L'Association des Nations du Sud-Est Asiatique (ANSEA): "Que sais-je?"*, no. 3153. Paris: Presses universitaires de France, 1997.

Kurus, Bilson. "Understanding ASEAN: Benefits and Raison d'Etre". *Asian Survey* XXXIII, no. 8 (1993): 819–31.

———. 1996 "ASEAN-izing Southeast Asia". In *The Evolving Pacific Power Structure*, edited by Derek da Cunha, pp. 75–80. Singapore: Institute of Southeast Asian Studies, 1996.

Lee, Lai To. "ASEAN and the South China Sea conflicts". *The Pacific Review* 8, no. 3 (1995): 531–43.

Nair, K.K. *ASEAN-Indochina Relations Since 1975: The Politics of Accommodation*. Canberra: Strategic and Defence Studies Centre, Research School of Pacific Studies, The Australian National University, 1984.

Narine, Shaun. "ASEAN and the Management of Regional Security". *Pacific Affairs* 71, no. 2 (1998): 195–214.

Naya, Seiji F. and Michael G. Plummer. "Economic Co-operation after 30 Years of ASEAN". *ASEAN Economic Bulletin* 14, no. 2 (1997): 117–26.

Nguyen Ngoc Truong. "Vietnam's New Home". *Far Eastern Economic Review*, 29 June 1995, p. 33.

Nguyen Vu Tung. "Vietnam-ASEAN Cooperation in Southeast Asia". *Security Dialogue* 34, no. 1 (1993): 85–92.

Paribatra, Sukhumbhand. "Irreversible History: ASEAN, Vietnam, and the Polarization of Southeast Asia". In *ASEAN in Regional and Global Conflict*, edited by Karl D. Jackson, Sukhumbhand Paribatra and J. Soedjati Djiwandono. Berkeley: Institute of East Asian Studies, University of California, 1986.

Paribatra, Sukhumbhand. "From ASEAN Six to ASEAN Ten: Issues and Prospects". *Contemporary Southeast Asia* 16, no. 3 (1994): 243–58.

Paul, Erik. "The Future of ASEAN: A Geopolitical Perspective". In *Global Geopolitical Change and the Asia-Pacific: A Regional Perspective*, edited by Dennis Rumley, pp. 230–50. Aldershot: Avebury, 1996.

Pham Cao Phong. "How Asean's newest member is coping". *Trends, The Business Times Weekend Edition* [Singapore], 29–30 June 1996.

Rajendran, M. *ASEAN's Foreign Relations: The Shift to Collective Action*. Kuala Lumpur: Arenabuku Sdn. Bhd, 1985.

Rush, James. "ASEAN's Neighborhood". In *Postwar Indochina: Old Enemies and New Allies*, edited by Joseph J. Zasloff, pp. 193–223. Washington, D.C.: Center for the Study of Foreign Affairs, Foreign Service Institute, U.S. Department of State, 1988.

Ramasamy, Bala. "The Second Enlargement of ASEAN: The Inclusion of Vietnam". *ASEAN Economies* (ASEAN Secretariat) 25, no. 2 (1996): 29–47.

Report of An International Symposium on Interaction for Progress. "Vietnam's New Course and ASEAN Experiences". *Vietnam Commentary* [Singapore] 24 (1991): 1–43.

Report of The ASEAN-Vietnam Study Group. *Shared Destiny: Southeast Asia in the 21st Century*. Singapore: Information and Documentation Centre, 1993.

Report of The Second International Symposium on Interaction for Progress. "Modernisation of Vietnam and ASEAN Cooperation". *Vietnam Commentary* [Singapore] 29 (1992): 1–47.

Sandhu, K.S. et al., comps. *The ASEAN Reader*. Singapore: Institute of Southeast Asian Studies, 1992.

Simon, Sheldon. "Vietnam's Security: Between China and ASEAN". *Asian Affairs: An American Review* 20, no. 4 (1994): 187–204.

Snitwongse, Kusuma. "ASEAN's Security Cooperation and Regional Order". *The Pacific Review* 8, no. 3 (1995): 518–30.

Soesastro, Hadi. "ASEAN and APEC: Do Concentric Circles Work?" *The Pacific Review* 8, no. 3 (1995): 475–93.

Sukrasep, Vinita. *ASEAN in International Relations*. Bangkok: Institute of Security and International Studies, Faculty of Political Science, Chulalongkorn University, 1989.

Setboonsarng, Suthad, ed. *AFTA Reader*. iv: *The Fifth ASEAN Summit*. Jakarta: ASEAN Secretariat, 1996.

Thambipillai, Pushpa and Johan Saravanamuttu. *ASEAN Negotiations: Two Insights*. Singapore: Institute of Southeast Asian Studies, 1985.

Than, Mya. "Six Plus Four: Economic Cooperation in ASEAN". In *ASEAN Today and Tomorrow* (A Reference Book), by Institute of Southeast Asian Studies, National Centre for Social Sciences and Humanities, pp. 126–55. Hanoi: National Political Publishing House, 1998.

Thayer, Carlyle A. "Indochina and ASEAN: The Trend Towards Dialogue". In *Proceedings of the Third Australia-Indonesia Seminar, Griffith University, 16–17 July 1984*, pp. 26–39. Australia-Asia Papers, Research Paper no. 31, Special Issue. Nathan, Queensland: Centre for the Study of Australian-Asian Relations, School of Modern Asian Studies, Griffith University, 1985.

——. "ASEAN and Indochina: The Dialogue". In *ASEAN Into the 1990s*, edited by Alison Broinowski, pp. 138–61. London: Macmillan Publishers, 1990.

——. "Internal Southeast Asian Dynamics: Vietnam's Membership in ASEAN". In *The Role of Security and Economic Cooperation Structures in the Asia Pacific Region: Indonesian and Australian Views*, edited by Hadi Soesastro and Anthony Bergin, pp. 78–88. Jakarta: Centre for Strategic and International Studies, 1996.

——. "Vietnam and ASEAN: A First Anniversary Assessment". *Southeast Asian Affairs 1997*, pp. 364–74. Singapore: Institute of Southeast Asian Studies, 1997.

Turley, William S., ed. *Confrontation or Coexistence: The Future of ASEAN-Vietnam Relations*. Bangkok: The Institute of Security and International Studies, Chulalongkorn University, 1985.

Wanandi, Jusuf. "ASEAN's Domestic Political Developments and their Impact on Foreign Policy". *The Pacific Review* 8, no. 3 (1995): 440–58.

——. "ASEAN's Future". *The Indonesian Quarterly* XXVI, no. 1 (1998): 21–27.

Wattanayagorn, Panitan. "ASEAN's Arms Modernization and Arms Transfers Dependence". *The Pacific Review* 8, no. 3 (1995): 494–507.

Weatherbee, Donald. *Southeast Asia Divided: The ASEAN-Indochina Crisis*. Boulder: Westview Press, 1985.

Zagoria, Donald. "Joining ASEAN". In *Vietnam Joins the World*, edited by James. W. Morley and Masashi Nishihara, pp. 154–72. Armonk, NY: M.E. Sharpe, 1997.

Cambodian conflict

Acharya, Amitav, Pierre Lizée, and Sorpong Peou, comps. and eds. *Cambodia—The 1989 Paris Peace Conference: Background Analysis and Documents*. New York: Kraus, 1992.

Alagappa, Muthiah. "The Cambodian Conflict: Changing Interests". *The Pacific Review* 3, no. 3 (1990): 266–71.

Amer, Ramses. "The United Nations" Peace Plan for Cambodia: From Confrontation to Consensus". *Interdisciplinary Peace Research* 3, no. 2 (1991): 3–27.

——. *The United Nations and Foreign Military Interventions: A Comparative Study of the Application of the Charter*. Second Edition. Report no. 33. Uppsala: Department of Peace and Conflict Research, Uppsala University, 1994.

——. "Indochinese Perspectives of the Cambodian Conflict". In *The Cambodian Conflict 1979–1991: From Intervention to Resolution*, edited by Ramses Amer, Johan Saravanamuttu, and Peter Wallensteen, pp. 63–117. Penang: Research and Education for Peace, School of Social Sciences, Universiti Sains Malaysia and Department of Peace and Conflict Research, Uppsala University, 1996.

——, Johan Saravanamuttu and Peter Wallensteen, eds. *The Cambodian Conflict 1979–1991: From Intervention to Resolution*. Penang: Research and Education for Peace, School of Social Sciences, Universiti Sains Malaysia, and Department of Peace and Conflict Research, Uppsala University, 1996.

Bach, William. "A Chance in Cambodia". *Foreign Policy* 62 (1986): 75–95.

Buszynski, Leszek. "The Soviet Union and Vietnamese Withdrawal from Cambodia". In *Vietnam's Withdrawal from Cambodia: Regional Issues and Realignments*, edited by Gary Klintworth, pp. 32–47. Canberra Papers on Strategy and Defence, 64. Canberra: Strategic and Defence Studies Centre, Research School of Pacific Studies, The Australian National University, 1990.

Chanda, Nayan. *Brother Enemy: The War after the War: A History of Indochina since the Fall of Saigon*. Orlando: Harcourt Brace Jovanovich, 1986.

Evans, Grant and Kelvin Rowley. *Red Brotherhood at War: Indochina Since the Fall of Saigon*. London: Verso Editions, 1984.

Frost, Frank. "The Cambodian Conflict: The Path towards Peace". *Contemporary Southeast Asia* 13, no. 2 (1991): 119–63.

Gordon, Bernard. "The Third Indochina Conflict". *Foreign Affairs* 65 (1986): 66–85.

Heder, Stephen R. "Origins of the Conflict". *Southeast Asia Chronicle* 64 (1978): 3–18.

——. "The Kampuchean-Vietnamese Conflict". In *The Third Indochina Conflict*, edited by David W.P. Elliott, pp. 21–67. Boulder: Westview Press, 1981.

Klintworth, Gary. *Vietnam's Intervention in Cambodia in International Law*. Canberra: Australian Government Publishing Service, 1989.

Kuroyanagi, Yoneji. "The Cambodian International Civil War and ASEAN Nations: Long Prologue to A Political Settlement". In *Indochina in Transition: Confrontation or Co-prosperity*, edited by Mio Tadashi, pp. 166–84. Tokyo: Japan Institute of International Affairs, 1989.

Leifer, Michael. "Cambodia in Regional and Global Politics". In *Vietnam's Withdrawal from Cambodia: Regional Issues and Realignments*, edited by Gary Klintworth, pp. 7–10. Canberra Papers on Strategy and Defence, 64. Canberra: Strategic and Defence Studies Centre, Research School of Pacific Studies, The Australian National University, 1990.

Lizée, Pierre. "The Challenge of Conflict Resolution in Cambodia". *Canadian Defense Quarterly* 23, no. 1 (1993): 35–42.

Mahbubani, Kishore. "The Kampuchean Problem". *Foreign Affairs* 62 (1983–84): 407–25.

McGregor, Charles. "China, Vietnam and the Cambodian Conflict—Beijing End Game Strategy". *Asian Survey* 30, no. 3 (1990): 266–83.

Okabe, Tatsumi. "The Cambodia Problem and China-Vietnam Relations". In *Indochina in Transition: Confrontation or Co-prosperity*, edited by Mio Tadashi, pp. 152–65. Tokyo: Japan Institute of International Affairs, 1989.

Pouvatchy, J.R. "The Vietnamisation of Cambodia". ISIS Seminar Paper. Kuala Lumpur: Institute of Strategic and International Studies Malaysia, 1986.

"The Vietnamization of Kampuchea: A New Model of Colonialism". *Indochina Report*, *Asian Forecast* special supplement, October 1984.

Chinese foreign policy

Amin, S. "Y a-t-il un projet chinois?" *Alternatives Sud* 3, no. 3 (1996): 16.

Andreyev, M.A. *Overseas Chinese Bourgeoisie—A Peking Tool in Southeast Asia*. Moscow: Progress Publishers, 1975.

Austin, Greg. *China's Ocean Frontier: International, Military Force and*

National Development. St Leonards: Allen & Unwin in association with the Department of International Relations and the Northeast Asia Program, Research School of Pacific and Asian Studies, Australian National University, 1998.

de Beauregard, P., J.P. Cabestan, J.L. Domenach, F. Godement, J. de Glodfiem, and F. Joyaux. *La politique Asiatique de la Chine.* Paris: Fondation pour les études de défense nationale, 1986.

Bhattacharya, J.J. "China: Defence Modernisation after Vietnam". *Strategic Analysis* 3, no. 4 (1979): 136–39.

———. "China: Concerns of the PLA". *Strategic Analysis* 3, no. 8 (1979): 289–91.

Chan, G. "China and International Organizations". *China Review* (1995): 115–35.

Chang, C.Y. "Overseas Chinese in China's Policy". *The China Quarterly* 82 (1980): 281–303.

Chang, Pao-min. "The Dynamics of Democratization and Crisis in the Taiwan Straits". *Contemporary Southeast Asia* 18, no. 1 (1996): 136–51.

———. "China and Southeast Asia: The Problem of a Perception Gap". *Contemporary Southeast Asia* 19, no. 4 (1997): 181–93.

Chen, King C. "Peking's Strategy in Indochina". *The Yale Review* 64, no. 4 (1965): 550–66.

———. *China and the Three Worlds: A Foreign Policy Reader.* White Plains: M.E. Sharpe, 1979.

Chevrier, Y. "Un pays en voie de banalisation? Les paradoxes politiques de la réforme chinoise". *Relations Internationales* 81 (1995): 39–58.

Chi Su. "The Strategic Triangle and China's Soviet Policy". In *China, the United States, and the Soviet Union: Tripolarity and Policy Making in the Cold War,* edited by Robert S. Ross, pp. 48–57. Studies on Contemporary China. Armonk and London: An East Gate Book, M.E. Sharpe, Inc, 1993.

Fitzgerald, Stephen. *China and the Overseas Chinese: A Study of Peking's Changing Policy, 1949–1970.* Cambridge: Cambridge University Press, 1972.

Freymond, Jaques. *La politique ètrangères de la Chine 1971–78: Essai d'interpretation.* Genève: Centre Asiatique, Institut unversitaires des hautes ètudes internationales, 1978.

Faust, John R. and Judith F. Kornberg. *China in World Politics.* Boulder: Lynne Rienner Publishers, 1995.

Garver, John W. "The 'New Type' of Sino-Soviet Relations". *Asian Survey* 29, no. 12 (1989): 1138–40.

———. *Foreign Relations of the People's Republic of China.* Englewood, New Jersey: Prentice Hall, 1993.

Guerassimoff, Carine. *L'état chinois et les communautés chinoises d'outre-mer.* Paris: Editions L'Harmattan and Montréal: L'Harmattan Inc., 1997.

Harding, Harry. "China and the Third World: From Revolution to Containment". In *The China Factor,* edited by Richard Solomon. Englewood, NJ: Prentice-Hall Inc., 1981.

Hunt, Michael H. *The Genesis of Chinese Communist Foreign Policy.* New York: Columbia University Press, 1996.

Jianwen, Y. "China's socialist market economy". *Studia Diplomatica* 49, no. 4–5 (1996): 19–46.

Joyaux, François. *La politique extérieure de la Chine, Que sais-je?* Paris: PUF, 1993.

"Keng Piao's Report on the Situation of the Indochinese Peninsula". *Issues and Studies* 17, no. 1 (1981): 78–96.

Klintworth, Gary. "The Outlook for Cambodia: The China Factor". In *Vietnam's Withdrawal from Cambodia: Regional Issues and Realignments*, edited by Gary Klintworth. Canberra Papers on Strategy and Defence, 64. Canberra: Strategic and Defence Studies Centre, Research School of Pacific Studies, The Australian National University, 1990.

Lardy, N. "Is China Different?" In *The Crisis of Leninism and the Decline of the Left*, edited by D. Chirot, pp. 147–62. Seattle: University of Washington Press, 1991.

Legvold, Robert. "Sino-Soviet Relations: The American Factor". In *China, the United States, and the Soviet Union: Tripolarity and Policy Making in the Cold War*, edited by Robert S. Ross, pp. 80–88. Studies on Contemporary China. Armonk and London: An East Gate Book, M.E. Sharpe, Inc., 1993.

Levine, S. "Perception and Ideology in Chinese Foreign Policy". In *Chinese Foreign Policy, Theory and Practice*, edited by Thomas Robinson and David Shambaugh, pp. 3–46. Oxford: Clarendon Press, 1994.

Lo, Chi-kin. *China's Policy Towards Territorial Disputes: The Case of the South China Sea Islands*. London and New York: Routledge, 1989.

Murphy, W. "Power Transition in Northeast Asia: US-China Security Perceptions and the Challenges of Systemic Adjustment and Stability". *Journal of Northeast Asia Studies* 13, no. 4 (1994): 61–84.

Nolan, Peter. "Democratization, Human Rights and Economic Reform: The Case of China and Russia". *Democratization* 1, no. 1 (1994): 73–99.

Porter, Gareth. "The 'China Card' and US Indochina Policy". *Indochina Issues* 11 (1980): 1–8.

Roy, Denny. "The China Threat Issue: Major Arguments". *Asian Survey* 36, no. 8 (1996): 758–71.

Shambaugh, David. "Containment or Engagement of China?". *International Security* 21, no. 2 (1996): 180–209.

Solomon, Richard, ed. *The China Factor*. Englewood, NJ: Prentice-Hall Inc., 1981.

Suryadinata, Leo. " 'Overseas Chinese' in Southeast Asia and China's Foreign Policy: An Interpretative Essay". *Research Notes and Discussions Paper* 11. Singapore: Institute of Southeast Asian Studies, 1978.

Wang, Gungwu. "China and the Region in Relation to the Chinese Minorities". *Contemporary Southeast Asia* 1, no. 1 (1979): 36–50.

——. "South China Perspectives on Overseas Chinese". *The Australian Journal of Chinese Affairs* 13 (1985): 69–84.

——. *China and the Chinese Overseas*. Singapore: Times Academic Press, 1991.

Zhai Qiang. "China and the Geneva Conference of 1954". *China Quarterly* 129 (1992): 103–22.

Zhang, J. "US-China Relations in the Post-Cold War Period: A Chinese Perspective". *Journal of Northeast Asian Studies* 14, no. 2 (1995): 47–61.

Zou Keyuan. *Chinese Traditional Maritime Boundary Line in the South China Sea: Legal Implications for the Spratly Islands Dispute*. EAI Background Brief, no. 14. Singapore: East Asian Institute, National University of Singapore, 1998.

——. *Maritime Jurisdiction Over the Vessel-Source Pollution in the Exclusive Economic Zone: The Chinese Experience.* EAI Working Paper no. 6. Singapore: East Asian Institute, National University of Singapore, 1998.

General politics (Democratization, Political Theory, Semiotics)

Alterman, Eric. *Sound and Fury.* New York: Harper Perennial, 1992.

Berger, Peter. "The Uncertain Triumph of Democratic Capitalism". In *Capitalism, Socialism, and Democracy Revisited*, edited by L. Diamond, and M. Plattner, pp. 1–10. Baltimore: Johns Hopkins University Press, 1993.

Bernstein, Basil. *Class, Codes and Control: Theoretical Studies Towards a Sociology of Language.* London: Routledge and Kegan Paul, 1971.

Bhagwati, J. "Democracy and Development". In *Capitalism, Socialism, and Democracy Revisited*, edited by L. Diamond, and M. Plattner, pp. 31–38. Baltimore: Johns Hopkins University Press, 1993.

Brodin, Katarina. *Studiet av Utrikespolitiska Doktriner: Teori och tva empiriska tillampningar.* Stockholm: Departementens offsetcentral, 1977.

Broms, H. and H. Gahmberg. "Communication to Self in Organizations and Cultures". *Administrative Science Quarterly* 28 (1983): 482–95.

Callinicos, A. "Liberalism, Marxism, and Democracy: A Response to David Held". *Theory and Society* 22, no. 2 (1993): 283–86.

Chan, S. "Regime Transition in the Asia/Pacific Region: Democratization as a Double-Edged Sword". *The Journal of Strategic Studies* 18, no. 3 (1995): 52–67.

Chang, Pao-min. "Jiedu meiguo zai yatai diqu di zhongda liyi" (The Strategic Interests of the United States: A Critical Analysis). *Ming Pao Monthly* [Hong Kong], February 1997, pp. 28–44.

——. "Meiguo di xianggang zhengce" (US Policy Towards Hong Kong). *Journal of East Asian Affairs* [Taipei] (1998): 71–88.

Chomsky, Noam. *World Orders, Old and New.* London: Pluto Press, 1994.

Dahrendorf, Ralph. *Society and Democracy in Germany.* New York: Doubleday, 1969.

Diamond, Larry, and Marc Plattner, eds. *Capitalism, Socialism, and Democracy Revisited.* Baltimore: Johns Hopkins University Press, 1993.

Diamond, L. "Economic Development and Democracy Reconsidered". *American Behavioral Scientist* 35, no. 4 (1992): 45–99.

Eckstein, Harry. "A Culturalist Theory of Political Change". *American Political Science Review* 82, no. 3 (1988): 789–804.

Emmerson, Donald K. "Region and Recalcitrance: Rethinking Democracy Through Southeast Asia". *The Pacific Review* 8, no. 2 (1995): 223–48.

Fukuyama, F. "The End of History". *The National Interest* 16, no. 4 (1989): 3–18.

——. "Capitalism & Democracy: the Missing Link". In *Capitalism, Socialism, and Democracy Revisited*, edited by L. Diamond, and M. Plattner, pp. 94–104. Baltimore: Johns Hopkins University Press, 1993.

Gellner, E. *Conditions of Liberty: Civil Society and Its Rivals.* London: Penguin, 1994.

Halliday, M.A.K. *Language as a Social Semiotic. The Social Interpretation of Language and Meaning*. London: Edward Arnold (Publishers), 1978.
——. "Language as Code and Language as Behaviour: A Systemic-Functional Interpretation of the Nature and Ontogenesis of Dialogue". In *Semiotics of Culture and Language: Language as Social Semiotic*, vol. 1, edited by Robin P. Fawcett et al., pp. 3–36. London: Frances Pinter (Publishers), 1984.

Haas, R. "Paradigm Lost". *Foreign Affairs* 74, no. 1 (1995): 43–58.

Hassan, M.J. "The Nexus Between Democracy and Stability: The Case of Southeast Asia". *Contemporary Southeast Asia* 18, no. 2 (1996): 163–74.

Hayek, F. *Knowledge, Evolution and Society*. London: Butler and Tanner, 1983.

Heradsveit, D. and Narvesen, O. "Psychological Constraints on Decision-Making: A Discussion of Cognitive Approaches: Operational Code and Cognitive Map". *Cooperation and Conflict* 13 (1978): 77–92.

Huntington, Samuel P. *The Third Wave: Democratization in the Late Twentieth Century*. Norman: University of Oklahoma Press, 1991.
——. "The Clash of Civilizations?" *Foreign Affairs* 73, no. 3 (1993): 22–49.
——. *The Clash of Civilizations and the Remaking of World Order*. New York: Simon and Schuster, 1996.

Ikenberry, G.J. "The Myth of Post-Cold War Chaos". *Foreign Affairs* 75, no. 3 (1996): 79–91.
——. "Just like the Rest". *Foreign Affairs* 76, no. 2 (1997): 162–63.

Kim, K. "Marx, Schumpeter, and the East Asian Experience". In *Capitalism, Socialism, and Democracy Revisited*, edited by L. Diamond and M. Plattner, pp. 11–25. Baltimore: Johns Hopkins University Press, 1993.

Lake, D. "Powerful Pacifists: Democratic States and War". *American Political Science Review* 86, no. 1 (1992): 24–37.

Lam, Peng Er. "Japan and the Spratly's Dispute: Aspirations and Limitations". *Asian Survey* 36, no. 10 (1996): 995–1010.

Layne, C. "Kant or Cant: The Myth of Democratic Peace". *International Security* 19, no. 2 (1994): 5–49.

Lipset, Seymour M. "Some Social Requisites of Democracy: Economic Development and Political Legitimacy". *American Political Science Review* 53 (1959): 69–15.

Londregan, J. and K. Poole. "Does High Income Promote Democracy?" *World Politics* 49, no. 1 (1996): 31–56.

Mansfield, E.D. and J. Snyder. "Democratization and War". *Foreign Affairs* 74, no. 3 (1995): 79–97.

Pei, M. "The Puzzle of East Asian Exceptionalism". *Journal of Democracy* 5, no. 4 (1994): 9–13.

Pye, Lucian W. "Introduction: Political Culture and Political Development". In *Political Culture and Political Development*, edited by Lucian W. Pye and Sidney Verba, pp. 3–26. Princeton, New Jersey: Princeton University Press, 1965.

Quandt, William B. "The Electoral Cycle and the Conduct of American Foreign Policy". In *The Domestic Sources of American Foreign Policy*, 2nd edition, edited by Eugene R. Wittkopf, pp. 132–43. New York: St. Martin's Press, 1994.

Raymond, G.A. "Democracies, Disputes, and Third-Party Intermediaries". *Journal of Conflict Resolution* 38, no. 1 (1994): 24–42.

Russet, Bruce. *Grasping the Democratic Peace: Principles for a Post-Cold War World*. Princeton, New Jersey: Princeton University Press, 1993.

Scalapino, Robert. *The Politics of Development: Perspectives on Twentieth-Century Asia*. Cambridge: Harvard University Press, 1989.

——. "Northeast Asia—Prospects for Cooperation". *The Pacific Review* 5, no. 2 (1992): 101–11.

Shi, Yongming. "The Elevated Status and Influence of the ASEAN after the Cold War". *Guoji Wenti Yanjiu [International Studies]*, 13 January 1997, pp. 29–33.

Spiro, D. "The Insignificance of the Liberal Peace". *International Security* 19 (1994): 5–86.

Susiluoto, Ilmari. "Deritualization of Political Language: The Case of the Soviet Union". In *Texts, Contexts, Concepts: Studies on Politics and Power in Language*, edited by Sakari Hanninen and Kari Palonen, pp. 69–75. Jyvaskyla: The Finnish Political Science Association, 1990.

Talbott, Strobe. "Democracy and the National Interest". *Foreign Affairs* 75, no. 6 (1996): 47–63.

World Bank. *The World Bank Annual Report*. Washington, D.C.: The World Bank Group, 1996.

——. *World Development Record*. Washington, D.C.: The World Bank Group, 1996.

International relations

Cohen, Bernard C. *The Influence of Non-Governmental Groups on Foreign Policy*. Boston: World Peace Foundation, 1959.

da Cunha, Derek, ed. *The Evolving Pacific Power Structure*. Singapore: Institute of Southeast Asian Studies, 1996.

East, Maurice A., Stephen A. Salamore and Charles F. Hermann, eds. *Why Nations Act: Theoretical Perspectives for Comparative Foreign Policy Studies*. Beverly Hills, CA: Sage Publications, 1978.

Halperin, Morton, Priscilla Clapp and Arnold Kanter. *Bureaucratic Politics and Foreign Policy*. Washington, D.C.: Brookings Institution, 1974.

Holsti, Kal. *International Politics: A Framework for Analysis*. Englewood Cliffs, New Jersey: Prentice-Hall, 1977.

Kant, E. *Perpetual Peace*. New York: McMillan, 1957.

Kegley, Charles and Eugene Wittkopf. *American Foreign Policy*. New York: St. Martin's Press, 1991.

Lotman, Yuri M. *Universe of the Mind: A Semiotic Theory of Culture*. London: I.B. Tauris and Co. Ltd. Publishers, 1990.

Mouritzen, Hans. "Prediction on the Basis of Official Doctrines". *Cooperation and Conflict* 16 (1981): 25–38.

Rosenau, James N. "Pre-Theories and Theories of Foreign Policy". In *The Scientific Study of Foreign Policy*, 2nd edition, edited by James Rosenau. New York: Nichols, 1980.

Rosenberg, S.W. and G. Wolsfeld. "International Conflict and the Problem of Attribution". *Journal of Conflict Resolution* 21, no. 1 (1997): 75–103.

Schumpeter, J.A. *Capitalism, Socialism, and Democracy*. New York: Harper and Row, 1995.

Snyder, Richard C., H.W. Bruck, and Burton Sapin. *Foreign Policy Decision*

Making: An Approach to the Study of International Politics. New York: Free Press, 1962.

Wurfel, David and Bruce Burton, eds. *Southeast Asia in the New World Order.* London: Macmillan, 1996.

Soviet/Russian foreign policy

Akino, Yutaka. "Indochinese Nations and the Soviet Bloc". In *Indochina in Transition: Confrontation or Co-prosperity,* edited Mio Tadashi, pp. 114–30. Tokyo: Japan Institute of International Affairs, 1989.

Berry, Peter. *Sovjetunionens Officielle Utrikespolitiska Doktrin.* Stockholm: Utrikespolitiska institutet, forskningsrapport, 1972.

Ellison, Herbert J. "Soviet-Chinese Relations: The Experience of Two Decades". In *China, the United States, and the Soviet Union: Tripolarity and Policy Making in the Cold War,* edited by Robert S. Ross, pp. 99–117. Studies on Contemporary China. Armonk and London: An East Gate Book, M.E. Sharpe, Inc., 1993.

Gaiduk, Ilya V. *The Soviet Union and the Vietnam War.* Chicago: Ivan R., 1996.

George, Alexander. "The 'Operational Code': A Neglected Approach to the Study of Political Leaders and Decision-Making". In *The Conduct of Soviet Foreign Policy,* edited by Erik P. Hoffman and Frederic J. Fleron Jr., pp. 165–90. New York: Aldine Publishing Company, 1980.

Hoffman, Erik P. and Frederic J. Fleron, eds. *The Conduct of Soviet Foreign Policy.* New York: Aldine Publishing Company, 1980.

Institute of International Relations. *The Vietnamese People's Struggle in the International Context.* Hanoi: Foreign Languages Publishing House, 1986.

Kotelkin, A. "Russia and the World Arms Market". *International Affairs* [Moscow] 42, no. 4 (1996): 31–38.

Leites, Nathan. *A Study of Bolshevism.* Glencoe, Illinois: The Free Press Publishers, 1953.

Mitchell, R. Judson. *Ideology of a Superpower: Contemporary Soviet Doctrine on International Relations.* Stanford, CA: Hoover Institution Press, 1982.

Nishihara, Masashi. "The Soviet-Vietnam Alliance and Regional Security". In *Indochina in Transition: Confrontation or Co-prosperity,* edited by Mio Tadashi, pp. 100–13. Tokyo: Japan Institute of International Affairs, 1989.

Pike, Douglas. *Vietnam and the Soviet Union.* Boulder: Westview Press, 1987.

Tadashi, Mio. "Soviet-Vietnamese Relations: An Uneasy Alliance". In *Indochina in Transition: Confrontation or Co-prosperity,* edited by Mio Tadashi, pp. 80–99. Tokyo: Japan Institute of International Affairs, 1989.

Triska, J.F. and Finley, D.D. *Soviet Foreign Policy.* Toronto: Macmillan, 1968.

Thakur, Ramesh and Carlyle A. Thayer. *Soviet Relations with India and Vietnam.* London: Macmillan, 1992.

Thakur, Ramesh and Carlyle A. Thayer. *Soviet Relations with India and Vietnam 1945–1992.* Delhi: Oxford University Press, 1993.

Thayer, Carlyle A. "Vietnam and the Soviet Union: Perceptions and Policies". In *The Soviet Union and the Asia-Pacific Region: Views from the Region*, edited by Pushpa Thambipillai and Daniel C. Matuszewski, pp. 134–53. New York: Praeger Publishers, 1989.

——. "Civil Society and the Soviet-Vietnamese Alliance". In *The Transition from Socialism: State and Civil Society in the USSR*, edited by Chandran Kukathas, David Lovell and William Maley, pp. 198–218. Sydney: Longman Cheshire, 1991.

——. "The Soviet Union and Indochina". In *Soviet Foreign Policy in Transition*, edited by Roger E. Kanet, Deborah Nutter Miner and Tamara J. Resler, pp. 236–55. Cambridge: Cambridge University Press, 1992.

——. "Indochina". In *Reshaping Regional Relations: Asia-Pacific and the Former Soviet Union*, edited by Ramesh Thakur and Carlyle A. Thayer, pp. 201–22. Boulder: Westview Press, 1993.

——. "Russian Policy Toward Vietnam". In *Russian Foreign Policy Since 1990*, edited by Peter Shearman, pp. 201–23. Boulder, San Francisco and Oxford: Westview Press, 1995.

USSR–Vietnam: Distant but Close Friends. Hanoi: Foreign Languages Publishing House. Moscow: Novosti Press Agency Publishing House, 1983.

Zagoria, Donald S. "The Soviet-Vietnamese Alliance". In *Postwar Indochina: Old Enemies and New Allies*, edited by Joseph J. Zasloff, pp. 133–46. Washington, D.C.: Center for the Study of Foreign Affairs, Foreign Service Institute, U.S. Department of State, 1988.

Zwick, Peter. "New Thinking and New Foreign Policy Under Gorbachev". *Political Science and Politics* 22, no. 2 (1989): 215–36.

United States-Vietnam relations

Bresnan, John. *From Dominoes to Dynamos: The Transformation of Southeast Asia*. New York: Council on Foreign Relations Press, 1994.

Brown, Frederick Z. "The U.S. Congressional Perspective on an "Emerging" Indochina". In *Postwar Indochina: Old Enemies and New Allies*, edited by Joseph J. Zasloff, pp. 251–70. Washington, D.C.: Center for the Study of Foreign Affairs, Foreign Service Institute, U.S. Department of State, 1988.

——. *Second Change: The United States and Indochina in the 1990s*. New York: Council on Foreign Relations, 1989.

Colbert, Evelyn. "Southeast Asia: Stand Pat". *Foreign Policy* 54 (1984): 139–55.

——. "U.S. Policy toward Vietnam Since the Fall of Saigon". In *Postwar Indochina: Old Enemies and New Allies*, edited by Joseph J. Zasloff, pp. 225–49. Washington, D.C.: Center for the Study of Foreign Affairs, Foreign Service Institute, U.S. Department of State, 1988.

Goodman, Allan E. "The Political Consequences of Normalization of U.S.-Vietnam Relations". *Contemporary Southeast Asia* 17, no. 4 (1996): 42–49.

Hood, Steven J. "American Influence in the China-Vietnam War: Washington's Unintended but Vital Role". *Asian Thought and Society* 17, no. 49 (1992): 31–46.

Hurst, Steven. *The Carter Administration and Vietnam*. Houndmills: Macmillan Press Ltd and New York: St. Martin's Press, Inc., 1996.

Johnston, Robert H. "The Nixon Doctrine and the New Policy Environment". In *Indochina in Conflict: A Political Assessment*, edited by Joseph J. Zasloff and Allan E. Goodman, pp. 175–200. Lexington: D.C. Heath and Company, 1972.

Kattenburg, Paul M. "Living with Hanoi". *Foreign Policy* 52 (1983–84): 131–49.

Ogasawara, Takayuki. "U.S.-Vietnam Relations: The Long Journey to Rapprochement". In *Indochina in Transition: Confrontation or Co-prosperity*, edited by Mio Tadashi, pp. 185–94. Tokyo: Japan Institute of International Affairs, 1989.

Porter, Gareth. "Vietnam's Soviet Alliance: A Challenge to US Policy". *Indochina Issues* 6 (1980): 1–8.

Pregelj, Vladimir N., Robert G. Sutter, Alan K. Yu and Larry Q. Nowels. *Vietnam: Procedural and Jurisdictional Questions Regarding Possible Normalization of U.S. Diplomatic and Economic Relations*. CRS Report for Congress. Washington, D.C.: Congressional Research Service, The Library of Congress, 1994.

Sidel, Mark. "Vietnam's America Watchers in a New Era". *SAIS Review* 16, no. 2 (1996): 43–69.

Thayer, Carlyle A. "United States Policy Towards Revolutionary Regimes: Vietnam (1975–1983)". In *U.S. Foreign Policy: Adjusting to Change in the Third World*, no. 85–W441, edited by Dick Clark, pp. 121–28. Wye Plantation, Queenstown, MD: Aspen Institute for Humanistic Studies, 1985.

Official sources

Anh Tram. "Portraits of Some Hoa in Vietnam". In *The Hoa in Vietnam Dossier*, pp. 70–79. Documents of Vietnam Courier. Hanoi: Foreign Languages Publishing House, 1978.

Beijing's Expansionism and Hegemonism: Dossier Against Maoism. Hanoi: Vietnam Courier, 1980.

"China's Undisputable Sovereignty over the Xisha and Nansha Islands". *Beijing Review*, 18 February 1980, pp. 15–24.

China's War: Escalation and Aggravation of Tension Along the Vietnam China Border. Hanoi: Ministry of Foreign Affairs, 1984.

Chinese Aggression Against Vietnam: Dossier. Hanoi: Foreign Languages Publishing House, 1979.

"Chinese Foreign Ministry on Xisha and Nansha Islands". *New China News* 18, no. 6 (27 February 1980): 14–16.

Chinese War Crimes in Vietnam, Document. Hanoi: np, 1979.

Clinton, William J. *A National Security Strategy of Engagement and Enlargement*. Washington, D.C.: The White House, 1994.

"Communiqué on the crime of war of aggression of the Chinese expansionists and hegemonists". In *War Crimes of the Pol Pot and Chinese Troops in Vietnam*. Hanoi: Commission of Inquiry into the Chinese Expansionists' and Hegemonists' Crime of War of Aggression, 1979.

"Communiqué of the Eleventh Conference of the Foreign Ministers of the Indochinese Countries (held in Phnom Penh, 15–16 August 1985)". In

On Vietnam and Peace, pp. 48–53. Hanoi: Vietnam Peace Committee, Foreign Languages Publishing House, 1986.

"Communiqué of the Extraordinary Meeting of Foreign Ministers of Laos, Kampuchea and Vietnam in Phnom Penh (April 12, 1983)". In *For Peace and Stability in Southeast Asia*. Hanoi: Vietnam Courier (1983): 54–60.

Communiqué on the Fifth Foreign Ministers Conference of Laos, Kampuchea and Vietnam, 1–8. (Supplement to *Sixth Conference of Foreign Ministers of Laos, Kampuchea and Vietnam (7–1982)*. Hanoi: Vietnam News Agency, 1982.

"Communiqué of the Tenth Conference of the Foreign Ministers of the Indochinese Countries (held in Ho Chi Minh City, Jan. 17–18, 1985)". In *On Vietnam and Peace*, pp. 38–47. Hanoi: Vietnam Peace Committee, Foreign Languages Publishing, 1986.

Communist Party of Vietnam. *Eighth National Congress Documents*. Hanoi: The Gioi Publishers, 1996.

Conventions of 1887 and 1895 on the Delineation of the Border between Vietnam and China. Hanoi: Department of Press and Information, Ministry of Foreign Affairs, Socialist Republic of Vietnam, 1979.

"De l'affaire du Kampuchéa à celle des Hoa ou la main de l'ambassade de Chine à Hanoi (aveux d'agents de Pékin)". In *Kampuchéa, Dossier II*, pp. 82–108. Hanoi: Edité par le Courrier du Vietnam, 1978.

"Decision of the SRV Government Council on the Policy Towards Foreigners Residing and Making a Living in Vietnam (April 25, 1977 —Decision No. 122–CP)". In *Documents Related to the Question of Hoa People in Vietnam*, pp. 7–10. Hanoi: Department of Press and Information, Ministry of Foreign Affairs, Socialist Republic of Vietnam, 1978.

Doan Khue. "Understanding the Resolution of the Third Plenum of the VCP Central Committee: Some Basic Issues Regarding the Party's Military Line in the New Stage". *Tap Chi Quoc Phong Toan Dan*, 8, 3–15 and 45. Translated by U.S. Foreign Broadcast Information Service, *Daily Report East Asia*, FBIS-EAS-92-179, 1992, pp. 42–52.

Documents Related to the Question of Hoa People in Vietnam. Hanoi: Ministry of Foreign Affairs, Socialist Republic of Vietnam, 1978.

Duy Phuong. "La vérité sur la prétendue campagne anti-Hoa à Ho Chi Minh-Ville". In *Les Hoa au Vietnam: Dossier*, pp. 83–93. Hanoi: Documents le *Courrier du Vietnam*, Editions en langues étrangères, 1978.

For a Negotiated Settlement of the Hoang Sa and Truong Sa (Paracels-Spratlys) Affair. Hanoi: Vietnamese Studies, 1988.

"Joint Communiqué of the Sixth Conference of Foreign Ministers of Laos, Kampuchea and Vietnam (July 6–7, 1982)". In *Sixth Conference of Foreign Ministers of Laos, Kampuchea and Vietnam (7–1982)*, pp. 1–10. Hanoi: Vietnam News Agency, 1982. Also re-printed in *For Peace and Stability in Southeast Asia*, pp. 9–18. Hanoi: Foreign Languages Publishing House, 1983.

"Joint Communiqué of Vietnamese, Kampuchean and Lao Foreign Ministers' Conference, First Conference held in Phnom Penh on January 5, 1980". In *Conferences of Foreign Ministers of Vietnam, Laos and Kampuchea (1980–1981)*, pp. 5–18. Hanoi: Information and Press Department, Ministry of Foreign Affairs, Socialist Republic of Vietnam, 1981.

Joint Statement of Chairman Liu Shao-Chi and President Ho Chi Minh. Peking: Foreign Language Press, 1963.

Ky Son. "Quelques Données sur les Hoa". In *Les Hoa au Vietnam: Dossier,* pp. 19–29. Hanoi: Documents le *Courrier du Vietnam.* Editions en langues étrangères, 1978.

Ky Son. "The Hoa in Vietnam: Some Data". In *The Hoa in Vietnam: Dossier,* pp. 19–28. Documents of Vietnam Courier. Hanoi: Foreign Languages Publishing House, 1978.

L'expansionnisme et l'hégémonisme de Pekin. Dossier conte le Maoisme. Hanoi: Édité par le Courrier du Vietnam, 1980.

La souveraineté du Viet Nam sur les archipells Hoang Sa et Truong Sa. Hanoi: Département de la presse et de l'information. Ministère des affaires étrangères, République Socialiste du Viet Nam, 1979.

La lutte du peuple vietnamien dans le contexte international de notre époque. Hanoi: Institut des relations internationales, Editions en langues etrangères, 1986.

Le Duc Anh. "Interview with *Tap Chi Quoc Phong Toan Dan*". Hanoi Domestic Service in Vietnamese, 4 December 1989. Translated in U.S. Foreign Broadcast Information Service, *Daily Report East Asia,* FBIS-EAS-89-234, 1989, pp. 70–75.

Les Hoa au Vietnam. Dossier Hanoi: Documents le *Courrier du Vietnam,* Editions en langues étrangères, 1978.

Mai Thi Tu. "The Hoa people in my neighbourhood". In *The Hoa in Vietnam: Dossier,* pp. 62–69. Documents of Vietnam Courier. Hanoi: Foreign Languages Publishing House, 1978.

"Memorandum of the Ministry of Foreign Affairs of the People's Republic of China on the Question of Xisha and Nasha Islands (May 12, 1988)". In Embassy of the People's Republic of China, *Chinese News Bulletin* [Stockholm], 17 May 1988.

Memorandum of the Ministry of Foreign Affairs of the Socialist Republic of Vietnam Concerning the Chinese Authorities' Provocations and Territorial Encroachments in the Border Region of Vietnam. Hanoi: Department of Press and Information, Ministry of Foreign Affairs, Socialist Republic of Vietnam, 1979.

"Memorandum on Vice-Premier Li Xiannian's Talks with Premier Pham Van Dong, 10 June 1977". In *Beijing Review,* 13 March 1979, pp. 17–22.

Nguyen Vinh Long. "Exode forcé dans une province frontalière". In *Les Hoa au Vietnam: Dossier,* pp. 52–64. Hanoi: Documents le *Courrier du Vietnam,* Editions en langues étrangères, 1978.

Nguyen Yem. "Les rouages de la contrainte". in *Les Hoa au Vietnam: Dossier,* pp. 41–51. Hanoi: Documents le *Courrier du Vietnam,* Editions en langues étrangères, 1978.

Ninth Conference of the Foreign Ministers Laos—Kampuchea—Vietnam (Vientiane 2 July 1984). Phnom Penh: Ministry of Foreign Affairs, People's Republic of Kampuchea, 1984.

"Note addressed by the Government of the Socialist Republic of Vietnam to the Government of the People's Republic of Vietnam (June 17, 1978)". In *17th June Communiqué of the SRV Ministry of Foreign Affairs.* Published in *BBC/FE/5842/A3/1–3,* 19 June 1978.

"Note addressed by the Government of the People's Republic of China to the Government of the Socialist Republic of Vietnam (May 30, 1978)".

In the *17th June Communiqué of the SRV Ministry of Foreign Affairs*. In BBC/FE/5842/A3/6–8, 19 June 1978.

"Note of the Chinese Government to the Government of the Socialist Republic of Vietnam (July 3, 1978)". In *Documents Related to the Question of Hoa People in Vietnam*, pp. 78–79. Hanoi: Ministry of Foreign Affairs, Socialist Republic of Vietnam, 1978.

"Note of the Foreign Ministry of the People's Republic of China to the Embassy of the Socialist Republic of Vietnam in China (May 12, 1978)". In *Documents Related to the Question of Hoa People in Vietnam*, pp. 49–53. Hanoi: Ministry of Foreign Affairs, Socialist Republic of Vietnam, 1978.

"Note of the Government of the Socialist Republic of Vietnam to the Government of the People's Republic of China (May 18, 1978)". In *Documents Related to the Question of Hoa People in Vietnam*, pp. 11–16. Hanoi: Ministry of Foreign Affairs, Socialist Republic of Vietnam, 1978.

"Note of the Government of the People's Republic of China to the Government of the Socialist Republic of Vietnam (May 30, 1978)". In *Documents Related to the Question of Hoa People in Vietnam*, pp. 59–64. Hanoi: Ministry of Foreign Affairs, Socialist Republic of Vietnam, 1978.

"Note of the Ministry of Foreign Affairs of the People's Republic of China to the Ministry of Foreign Affairs of the Socialist Republic of Vietnam (June 2, 1978)". In *Documents Related to the Question of Hoa People in Vietnam*, pp. 65–66. Hanoi: Ministry of Foreign Affairs, Socialist Republic of Vietnam, 1978.

"Note of the Government of the Socialist Republic of Vietnam to the Government of the People's Republic of China (July 6, 1978)". In *Documents Related to the Question of Hoa People in Vietnam*, pp. 43–45. Hanoi: Ministry of Foreign Affairs, Socialist Republic of Vietnam, 1978.

"Note of the Government of the Socialist Republic of Vietnam to the Government of the People's Republic of China (June 17, 1978)". In *Documents Related to the Question of Hoa People in Vietnam*, pp. 29–32. Hanoi: Ministry of Foreign Affairs, Socialist Republic of Vietnam, 1978.

"Note of the Ministry of Foreign Affairs of the People's Republic of China to the Ministry of Foreign Affairs of the Socialist Republic of Vietnam (June 16, 1978)". In *Documents Related to the Question of Hoa People in Vietnam*, pp. 76–77. Hanoi: Ministry of Foreign Affairs, Socialist Republic of Vietnam, 1978.

"Note of the Ministry of Foreign Affairs of the Socialist Republic of Vietnam to the Embassy of the People's Republic of China in Vietnam (June 28, 1978)". In *Documents Related to the Question of Hoa People in Vietnam*, pp. 39–42. Hanoi: Ministry of Foreign Affairs, Socialist Republic of Vietnam, 1978.

"Note of the Ministry of Foreign Affairs of the Socialist Republic of Vietnam to the Ministry of Foreign of the People's Republic of China (May 28, 1978)". In *Documents Related to the Question of Hoa People in Vietnam*, pp. 22–23. Hanoi: Ministry of Foreign Affairs, Socialist Republic of Vietnam, 1978.

Office of the Press Secretary, The White House. "Fact Sheet: Background Paper on Economic Relationships". 11 July 1995, p. 2.

Office of the Press Secretary, The White House. "Remarks by the President in Announcement on Normalization of Diplomatic Relations with Vietnam". Washington, D.C., 11 July 1995.

On the Eve of the Sixth Congress of the Communist Party of Vietnam: Vietnam 1976–1986. Hanoi: Foreign Languages Publishing House, 1986.

On the Vietnamese Foreign Ministry's White Book Concerning Viet Nam-China Relations. By People's Daily and Xinhua News Agency Commentators. Beijing: Foreign Languages Press, 1979.

On Viet Nam's Expulsion of Chinese Residents. Peking: Foreign Languages Press, 1978.

Peace and Stability in Southeast Asia. 1981. Hanoi: Vietnam Courier.

People's Republic of Kampuchea. *Policy of the People's Republic of Kampuchea with regard to Vietnamese residents.* Phnom Penh: Press Department, Ministry of Foreign Affairs, 1983.

Pour le réglement negocié de l'affaire < < Hoang Sa Truong Sa > > (Paracels— Spratly). Hanoi: Publié par la revue *Etudes Vietnamiennes*, 1988.

"Principles governing the peaceful co-existence between the two groups of countries—Indochinese and ASEAN—for peace, stability, friendship and co-operation in Southeast Asia". In *Peace and Stability in Southeast Asia*, pp. 81–88. Hanoi: Vietnam Courier, 1981.

Republic of Vietnam. *White Paper on the Hoang Sa (Paracel) and Truong Sa (Spratly) Islands.* Saigon: Ministry of Foreign Affairs, 1975.

République Socialiste du Viet Nam. *La souveraineté du Viet Nam sur les archipels Hoang Sa et Truong Sa.* Hanoi: Département de la presse et de l'information. Ministère des affaires étrangères, 1979.

"Sino-Vietnamese Joint Communiqué. Full text". In BBC/FE/2477/G/1-2, 4 December 1995.

Socialist Republic of Vietnam. *The Truth About Viet Nam-China Relations Over the Last 30 Years.* Hanoi: Ministry of Foreign Affairs, 1979.

——. *The Constitution of 1992.* Hanoi: The Gioi Publishers, 1993.

——. *Vietnam: Consolidating National Defence, Safeguarding the Homeland.* Hanoi: Ministry of [National] Defence, 1998.

" 'Socialist Transformation' or Anti-China, Expel-the-Chinese Campaign? Commentary by Renmin Ribao Correspondent, July 28, 1978". In *On Viet Nam's Expulsion of Chinese Residents*, pp. 176–80. Peking: Foreign Languages Press, 1978.

"Speech by Chung Hsi-tung, Leader of the Chinese delegation; at the first Session of the Sino-Vietnamese Talks on the Question of Chinese Nationals Residing in Vietnam, (August 8, 1978)". In *On Viet Nam's Expulsion of Chinese Residents*, pp. 29–43. Peking: Foreign Languages Press, 1978.

"Statement by Chung Hsi-tung, Leader of the Chinese Government Delegation, at the Second Session of the Sino-Vietnamese Talks (August, 15 1978)". In *On Viet Nam's Expulsion of Chinese Residents*, pp. 44–58. Hanoi: Foreign Languages, 1978.

"Speech by Chung Hsi-tung, Leader of the Chinese Government Delegation, at the Eighth Session of the Sino-Vietnamese Talks (September 26, 1978)". In *On Viet Nam's Expulsion of Chinese Residents*, pp. 107–19. Peking: Foreign Languages Press, 1978.

"Speech by Chung Hsi-tung, Leader of the Chinese Government Delegation, at the Fifth Session of the Sino-Vietnamese Talks (September 7, 1978)". In *On Viet Nam's Expulsion of Chinese Residents*, pp. 77–88. Peking: Foreign Languages Press, 1978.

"Speech by Chung Hsi-tung, Leader of the Chinese Government Delegation, at the Fourth Session of the Sino-Vietnamese Talks (August 26, 1978)". In *On Viet Nam's Expulsion of Chinese Residents*, pp. 71–76. Peking: Foreign Languages, 1978.

"Speech by Chung Hsi-tung, Leader of the Chinese Government Delegation, at the Seventh Session of the Sino-Vietnamese Talks (September 19, 1978)". In *On Viet Nam's Expulsion of Chinese Residents*, pp. 94–106. Peking: Foreign Languages, 1978.

"Speech by Chung Hsi-tung, Leader of the Chinese Government Delegation, at the Sixth Session of the Sino-Vietnamese Talks (September 12, 1978)". In *On Viet Nam's Expulsion of Chinese Residents*, pp. 89–93. Peking: Foreign Languages Press, 1978.

"Speech by Chung Hsi-tung, Leader of the Chinese Government Delegation, at the Third Session of the Sino-Vietnamese Talks (August 19, 1978)". In *On Viet Nam's Expulsion of Chinese Residents*, pp. 59–70. Peking: Foreign Languages, 1978.

"Speech by Foreign Minister Nguyen Co Thach at the Conference of Foreign Ministers of Non-Aligned Countries in New Delhi (March 3, 1983)". In *For Peace and Stability in Southeast Asia*, pp. 42–53. Hanoi: Foreign Languages Publishing House, 1983.

"Statement by Vice-Minister of Foreign Affairs Hoang Bich Son, Head of the Delegation of the Socialist Republic of Vietnam at the Second Session of the Vietnam-China Talks (August 15, 1978)". In *The Hoa in Vietnam: Dossier II*, pp. 69–78. Hanoi: Vietnam Courier, 1978.

"Statement by Chief Delegate Hoang Bich Son at the Fifth Session of the Vietnam-China Talks (September 7, 1978)". In *The Hoa in Vietnam: Dossier II*, pp. 79–87. Hanoi: Vietnam Courier, 1978.

"Statement by Chief Delegate Hoang Bich Son at the Eighth Session of the Vietnam-China Talks (September 26, 1978)". In *The Hoa in Vietnam: Dossier II*, pp. 88–95. Hanoi: Vietnam Courier, 1978.

"Statement by Spokesman of the Overseas Chinese Affairs Office of the State Council of the People's Republic of China on Viet Nam's Expulsion of Chinese Residents (May 24, 1978)". In *On Viet Nam's Expulsion of Chinese Residents*, pp. 1–6. Peking: Foreign Languages Press, 1978.

"Statement of the Conference of Foreign Ministers of Laos, Kampuchea and Vietnam, Second Conference held in Vientiane on July 17 and 18, 1980". In *Conferences of Foreign Ministers of Vietnam, Laos and Kampuchea (1980–1981)*, pp. 37–44. Hanoi: Information and Press — Department, Ministry of Foreign Affairs, Socialist Republic of Vietnam, 1981.

"Statement by the Conference of Foreign Ministers of Vietnam, Laos and Kampuchea on peace, stability, friendship and cooperation in South-East Asia, Third Conference held in Ho Chi Minh City on January 27 and 28, 1981". In *Conferences of Foreign Ministers of Vietnam, Laos and Kampuchea (1980–1981)*, pp. 21–29. Hanoi: Information and Press Department, Ministry of Foreign Affairs, Socialist Republic of Vietnam, 1981.

"Statement by the Conference of Foreign Ministers of Vietnam, Laos and Kampuchea, Fourth Conference held in Phnom Penh on June 13 and 14, 1981". In *Conferences of Foreign Ministers of Vietnam, Laos and Kampuchea (1980–1981)*, pp. 55–60. Hanoi: Information and Press Department, Ministry of Foreign Affairs, Socialist Republic of Vietnam, 1981.

"Statement of H.E. Nguyen Co Thach, Vice-Chairman of the Council of Ministers, Minister for Foreign Affairs of the S. R. Viet Nam at the International Conference on Cambodia, Paris, 31 July 1989". In *Cambodia—The 1989 Paris Peace Conference: Background Analysis and Documents*, compiled and edited by Amitav Acharya, Pierre Lizée and Sorpong Peou, pp. 43–50. New York: Kraus, 1991.

"Statement of the Ministry of Foreign Affairs of the People's Republic of China on the Expulsion of Chinese Residents by Viet Nam (June 9, 1978)". In *On Viet Nam's Expulsion of Chinese Residents*, pp. 7–17. Peking: Foreign Languages, 1978.

"Statement of the Ministry of Foreign Affairs of the Socialist Republic of Vietnam on the Issue of Hoa People in Vietnam (June 5, 1978)". In *Documents Related to the Question of Hoa People in Vietnam*, pp. 24–27. Hanoi: Ministry of Foreign Affairs, Socialist Republic of Vietnam, 1978.

"Statement of the Spokesman of the Foreign Ministry of the Socialist Republic of Vietnam Regarding the Chinese Distortions of the Vietnamese Government's Policy Towards the Hoa People in Vietnam (May 27, 1978)". In *Documents Related to the Question of Hoa People in Vietnam*, pp. 17–21. Hanoi: Ministry of Foreign Affairs, Socialist Republic of Vietnam, 1978.

"Statement of the Summit Conference of Laos, Kampuchea and Vietnam (March 3, 1983)". In *For Peace and Stability in Southeast Asia*, pp. 26–34. Hanoi: Foreign Languages Publishing House, 1983.

"Statement on the Presence in Kampuchea of Volunteers from the Vietnamese Army Vientiane (February 23, 1983)". In *For Peace and Stability in Southeast Asia*, pp. 35–41. Hanoi: Foreign Languages Publishing House, 1983.

The Chinese Aggression: Why and How it Failed. Hanoi: Foreign Languages Publishing House, 1979.

The Hoa in Vietnam: Dossier. Documents of *Vietnam Courier*. Hanoi: Foreign Languages Publishing House, 1978.

The Hoa in Vietnam. Dossier II. Hanoi: Vietnam Courier, 1978.

The Hoang Sa and Truong Sa Archipelagoes and International Law. Hanoi: Ministry of Foreign Affairs, Socialist Republic of Vietnam, 1988.

The Hoang Sa and Truong Sa Archipelagoes (Paracels and Spratly): Dossier I. Hanoi: Vietnam Courier, 1981.

The Hoang Sa and Truong Sa Archipelagoes (Paracels and Spratly): Dossier II. Hanoi: Ministry of Foreign Affairs, Socialist Republic of Vietnam, 1985.

The Hoang Sa and Truong Sa Archipelagoes Vietnamese Territories. Hanoi: Ministry of Foreign Affairs, Socialist Republic of Vietnam, 1981.

"The Law of the People's Republic of China on its Territorial Waters and Their Contiguous Areas" adopted by the Standing Committee of the National People's Congress on 25 February 1992. In BBC/FE/1316/C1/1–2, 28 February 1992.

The Socialist Republic of Vietnam. Hanoi: Foreign Languages Publishing, 1985.
"The Truth about the Sino-Vietnamese Boundary Question". In *Beijing Review*, 25 May 1979, pp. 14–26.
The Truth About Viet Nam-China Relations Over the Last 30 Years. Hanoi: Ministry of Foreign Affairs, Socialist Republic of Vietnam, 1979.
Thirteenth Conference of the Foreign Minister of Kampuchea—Laos—Vietnam, Hanoi 17–18th, August 1986. Phnom Penh: Press Department, Ministry of Foreign Affairs, People's Republic of Kampuchea, 1986.
Those Who Leave ["The problem of Vietnamese refugees"]. Hanoi: Vietnam Courier, 1979.
Tsai, Maw-kuey. *Les chinois au Sud-Vietnam.* Paris: Ministère de l'éducation nationale, Comité des travaux historiques et scientifiques, Mémoires de la section de géographie, 3, Bibliothèque Nationale, 1968.
Twelfth Conference of the Foreign Minister Laos—Kampuchea—Vietnam [Vientiane, 24th January 1986]". Phnom Penh: Press Department, Ministry of Foreign Affairs. Reprinted in *Vietnam and Peace*, pp. 54–60. Hanoi: Foreign Languages Publishing House, 1986.
"Untenable Arguments of Vietnamese Authorities, Commentary by Hsinhua Correspondent, [July 25, 1978]". In *On Viet Nam's Expulsion of Chinese Residents*, pp. 171–75. Peking: Foreign Languages Press, 1978.
Vo, Long Te. *Les archipels de Hoàng-Sa et de Truong-Sa selon las anciens ouvrages vietnamiens d'histoire et de géographie,* no. 2. Saigon: Publications en langues étrangères de la commission de traduction, Ministère de la culture. de l'éducation et de la jeunesse, 1974.
Who Has Destroyed Vietnamese–Chinese Friendship? Hanoi: Foreign Languages Publishing House, 1983.
"Who is the Instigator by Renmin Ribao Commentator, [June 17, 1978]". In *On Viet Nam's Expulsion of Chinese Residents*, pp. 131–38. Peking: Foreign Languages Press, 1978.

Vietnam's Foreign Relations

Indochina

Brown, MacAlister. "The Indochinese Federation Idea: Learning from History". In *Postwar Indochina: Old Enemies and New Allies*, edited by Joseph J. Zasloff, pp. 77–101. Washington, D.C.: Center for the Study of Foreign Affairs, Foreign Service Institute, U.S. Department of State, 1988.
Elliott, David W.P., ed. *The Third Indochina Conflict.* Boulder: Westview Press, 1981.
Gurtov, Melvin. "Indochina in North Vietnamese Strategy". In *Indochina in Conflict: A Political Assessment*, edited by Joseph J. Zasloff and Allan E. Goodman, pp. 137–54. Lexington: D.C. Heath and Company, 1972.
Hebbel, Hollis C. "The Special Relationship in Indochina". In *Postwar Indochina: Old Enemies and New Allies*, edited by Joseph J. Zasloff, pp. 103–14. Washington, D.C.: Center for the Study of Foreign Affairs, Foreign Service Institute, U.S. Department of State, 1988.
Ljunggren, Börje, ed. *The Challenge of Reform in Indochina.* Cambridge: Harvard Institute for International Development, 1993.

Niksch, Larry A. "Alternate Models for Indochina Relationships: A Bleak Prospect". In *Postwar Indochina: Old Enemies and New Allies*, edited by Joseph J. Zasloff, pp. 115–29. Washington, D.C.: Center for the Study of Foreign Affairs, Foreign Service Institute, U.S. Department of State, 1988.

Porter, Gareth. "Vietnamese Policy and the Indochina Crisis". In *The Third Indochina Conflict*, edited by David W.P. Elliot, pp. 69–137. Boulder: Westview Press, 1981.

Race, Jeffrey and William S. Turley. "The Third Indochina War". *Foreign Policy* 38 (1980): 92–116.

Tadashi, Mio . "Relations Among the Three Indochinese Countries: A Decade of Rise and Fall of 'Strategic Alliance' ". In *Indochina in Transition: Confrontation or Co-prosperity*, edited by Mio Tadashi, pp. 57–79. Tokyo: Japan Institute of International Affairs, 1989.

Tadashi, Mio, ed. *Indochina in Transition: Confrontation or Co-prosperity*. Tokyo: Japan Institute of International Affairs, 1989.

Thayer, Carlyle A. "Indochina". In *Security and Defence: Pacific and Global Perspectives*, edited by Desmond Ball and Cathy Downes, pp. 398–411. Sydney: Allen and Unwin, 1990.

——. *Beyond Indochina*. Adelphi Paper 297. London: Oxford University Press for the International Institute for Strategic Studies, 1995.

——. "Indochina". In *Asia-Pacific Security: Less Uncertainty and New Opportunities?* edited by Gary Klintworth, pp. 132–47. Sydney: Longman Cheshire and New York: St. Martin's Press, 1996.

Turley, William S. "Thai-Vietnamese Rivalry in the Indochina Conflict". In *East Asian Conflict Zones: Prospects for Regional Stability and Deescalation*, edited by Lawrence E. Grinter and Young Whan Kihl, pp. 149–276. New York: St. Martin's Press, 1987.

——. "Vietnam's Strategy for Indochina and Security in Southeast Asia". In *Security, Strategy, and Policy Responses in the Pacific Rim*, edited by Young Whan Kihl and Lawrence E. Grinter. Boulder: Lynn Rienner, 1989.

Zasloff, Joseph J., ed. *Postwar Indochina: Old Enemies and New Allies*. Washington, D.C.: Center for the Study of Foreign Affairs, Foreign Service Institute, U.S. Department of State, 1988.

——. and Allan E. Goodman, eds. *Indochina in Conflict: A Political Assessment*. Lexington: D.C. Heath and Company, 1972.

——. and MacAlister Brown, eds. *Communism in Indochina: New Perspectives*. Lexington: D.C. Heath and Company, 1975.

Laos

Thayer, Carlyle A. "Laos and Vietnam: The Anatomy of a 'Special Relationship' ". In *Contemporary Laos: Studies in the Politics and Society of the Lao People's Democratic Republic*, edited by Martin Stuart-Fox, pp. 245–73. New York: St. Martin's Press, 1982.

Zasloff, Joseph J. "Vietnam and Laos: Master and Apprentice". In *Postwar Indochina: Old Enemies and New Allies*, edited by Joseph J. Zasloff, pp. 37–62. Washington, D.C.: Center for the Study of Foreign Affairs, Foreign Service Institute, U.S. Department of State, 1988.

Refugees (Boat People)

Benoit, Charles. "Vietnam's 'Boat People' ". In *The Third Indochina Conflict*, edited by David W.P. Elliot, pp. 139–62. Boulder: Westview Press, 1981.

Condominas, Georges and Pottier Richard. *Les réfugiés originaires de l'Asie du Sud-Est, rapport au Président de la République*. Paris: La Documentation Française, 1982.

Grant, Bruce. *The Boat People: An "Age" Investigation*. Harmondsworth: Penguin Books, 1979.

Mignot, Michel. "Rapport sur les réfugiés du Vietnam". In *Les réfugiés originaires de l'Asie du Sud-Est, monographies*, pp. 11–49. Paris: La Documentation, 1984.

Thayer, Carlyle A. "Vietnamese Refugees: Why the Outflow Continues". In *Refugees in the Modern World*, edited by Amin Saikal, pp. 45–96. Canberra Studies in World Affairs 25. Canberra: Department of International Relations, The Australian National University, 1989.

Wain, Barry. *The Refused: The Agony of the Indochinese Refugees*. New York: Simon and Schuster, 1981.

Vietnam-Cambodia relations

Amer, Ramses. "The Ethnic Vietnamese in Cambodia—A Minority at Risk?" *Contemporary Southeast Asia* 16, no. 2 (1994): 210–38.

Chanda, Nayan. "Vietnam and Cambodia: Domination and Security". In *Postwar Indochina: Old Enemies and New Allies*, edited by Joseph J. Zasloff, pp. 63–76. Washington, D.C.: Center for the Study of Foreign Affairs, Foreign Service Institute, U.S. Department of State, 1988.

Chou, Meng Tarr. "The Vietnamese Minority in Cambodia". *Race and Class* 34, no. 2 (1992): 34–35.

Hiebert, Murray. "Cambodia and Vietnam: Costs of the Alliance". *Indochina Issues* 46 (1984): 1–8.

Martin, Marie Alexandrine. "Le processus de vietnamisation au Cambodge". *Politique Internationale* 24 (1984): 177–91.

Osborne, Milton E. "Kampuchea and Viet Nam: A Historical Perspective". *Pacific Community* 9, no. 3 (1978).

Porter, Gareth. "Vietnamese Communist Policy Towards Kampuchea, 1930–1970". *Revolution and Its Aftermath in Kampuchea: Eight Essays*, edited by In David P. Chandler and Ben Kiernan. Monograph Series 25. New Haven: Yale University Southeast Asia Studies, 1983.

Pouvatchy, Joseph. "L'éxode des vietnamiens du Cambodge en 1970". *Mondes Asiatiques* 7 (1976): 339–49.

Vietnam-China Relations (1945–90)

Alexiou, Jon James. "The Foreign Policy of the People's Republic of China Towards the Socialist Republic of Vietnam". Ph.D. Dissertation, University of Miami, 1982.

Alley, Rewi. *Refugees from Viet Nam in China*. Beijing: New World, 1980.

Bhattacharya, J.J. "Beijing, Hanoi, and Southeast Asia". *Strategic Analysis* 3, no. 10 (1980): 363–66.

Brewer, Scott Cockey. "The Sino-Vietnamese Conflict". Masters Thesis, Faculty of the College of Public and International Affairs, The American University, 1986.

Chen, King C. "The Chinese Occupation of Vietnam 1945–46". *France Asie, Asia* 196 (1969): 3–28.

——. *Vietnam and China, 1938–1954*. Princeton, NJ: Princeton University Press, 1969.

Chiang, Yung-Ching. "Relations Between the Vietnamese and Chinese Communists 1925–45". Paper presented to the First Sino-American Conference on Mainland China, 14–19 December 1970.

Devillers, Philippe. "Chine-Viêt-Nam: le mythe de la riposte". *Afrique-Asie* 333 (1984): 104–5.

Duiker, William J. *China and Vietnam: The Roots of Conflict*. Indochina Research Monograph 1. Berkeley: Institute of East Asian Studies, University of California, 1986.

——. "China and Vietnam and the Struggle for Indochina". In *Postwar Indochina: Old Enemies and New Allies*, edited by Joseph J. Zasloff, pp. 147–91. Washington, D.C.: Center for the Study of Foreign Affairs, Foreign Service Institute, U.S. Department of State, 1988.

Funnell, Victor C. "Vietnam and the Sino-Soviet Conflict 1965–1976". *Studies in Comparative Communism* 11, nos. 1/2 (1978): 42–169.

Gilks, Anne. *The Breakdown of the Sino-Vietnamese Alliance, 1970–1979*. China Research Monograph 39. Berkeley: Institute of East Asian Studies, University of California, 1982.

Goodstadt, Leo. "Vietnam Stakes in the Conflict with China". *Economic and Political Weekly* [Bombay], 13 July 1978.

Hinton, Harold C. *China's Relations with Burma and Vietnam: A Brief Survey*. New York: Institute of Pacific Research, 1958.

Hood, Steven John. "The Causes and Dynamics of the Sino-Vietnamese Conflict". Ph.D. thesis, Department of Political Science, University of California, Santa Barbara, 1987.

Hood, Steven J. *Dragons Entangled: Indochina and the China-Vietnam War*. Armonk and London: An East Gate Book, M.E. Sharpe Inc., 1992.

Jin, Xudong. "The Sino-Vietnamese Relations: Its Implications for China-ASEAN Relationship". In *The Emerging Relations Between China and Southeast Asia: Limitations and Opportunities*, pp. 145–54. Proceedings and Papers of ASEAN-China Hong Kong Forum 1987. Hong Kong: Centre of Asian Studies, 1988.

Joyaux, François. *La Chine et le règlement du premier conflict d'Indochine: Genève 1954*. Paris: Publications de la Sorbonne, 1979.

Kirk, Donald. "North Vietnam and the Sino-Soviet Dispute: January–August 1963". Master of Arts dissertation, The Faculty of the Division of Social Sciences, The University of Chicago, 1965.

Kleinen, John. "Roots of the Sino-Vietnamese Conflict". *Monthly Review* 34 (1982): 16–36.

Klintworth, Gary. "China's Indochina Policy". *Journal of Northeast Asian Studies* 8, no. 3 (1989): 25–43.

Lawson, Eugene K. *The Sino-Vietnamese Conflict*. New York: Praeger Publishers, 1984.

Li, Man Kin. *Sino-Vietnamese War*. Hong Kong: Kingsway International Publications, 1981.

Maceron, G. "Chine Vietnam les racines historiques du conflit". *Les Temps Modernes*, 395 (1979): 1994–2025.

Nguyen, Huu Thy. "Viet Nam-China: The Root of the Problem". *Vietnamese Studies* 58 (1979): 98–147.

Nguyen, Manh Hung. "The Sino-Vietnamese Conflict: Power Play Among Communist Neighbors". *Asian Survey* 19, no. 11 (1979): 1037–52.

Ou, Hsing-Hung. "Communist China's Foreign Policy Toward the War in Vietnam 1965–1973". Ph.D. dissertation, Southern Illinois University.

Pike, Douglas. "Vietnam's Relationship with China". In *Pacific-Asian Issues: American and Chinese Views*, edited by Robert A. Scalapino and Chen Qimao. Research Papers and Policy Studies 17. Berkeley: Institute of East Asian Studies, University of California, 1986.

——. "Vietnam and China". In *ASEAN and China: An Evolving Relationship*, edited by Joyce K. Kallgren, Noordin Sopiee and Soedjati Djiwandono, pp. 326–41. Research Papers and Policy Studies 24. Berkeley: Institute of East Asian Studies, University of California, 1988.

Quinn-Judge, Paul. "Le Vietnam face à la Chine". *Le Monde Diplomatique*, Septembre 1978.

——. "The Vietnam-China Split: Old Ties Remain". *Indochina Issues* 53 (1985): 1–8.

Ross, Robert S. *The Indochina Tangle: China's Vietnam Policy, 1975–1979*. New York: East Asian Institute, Columbia University, Columbia University, 1988.

Shao, Kuo-Kang. "Zhou Enlai's Diplomacy and the Neutralization of Indo-China, 1954–1955". *The China Quarterly* 107 (1986): 483–504.

Silaphong, Sakoldet. "North Vietnam's Foreign Policy and the Sino-Soviet Dispute". Masters thesis, Department of Political Science, California States University, Long Beach, 1976.

Smyser, William R. *The Independent Vietnamese: Vietnamese Communism Between Russia and China 1956–1969*. Papers in International Studies, Southeast Asia 55. Athens: Center for International Studies, Ohio University, 1980.

Sutter, Robert G. "China's Strategy Toward Vietnam and its Implications for the United States". In *The Third Indochina Conflict*, edited by David W.P. Elliot, pp. 163–92. Boulder: Westview Press, 1981.

Tadashi, Mio. "The Transitions and Prospects of Sino-Vietnam Relations". in Mio Tadashi, ed., *Indochina in Transition: Confrontation or Co-prosperity*, edited by Mio Tadashi, pp. 131–51. Tokyo: Japan Institute of International Affairs, 1989.

Thakur, Ramesh. "Coexistence to Conflict: Hanoi-Moscow-Peking Relations and the China-Vietnam War". *Australian Outlook* 34, no. 1 (1980): 64–74.

Thayer, Carlyle A. "Security Issues in Southeast Asia: The Third Indochina War". Paper presented at the Conference on Security and Arms Control in the North Pacific, organized by the Department of International Relations, Peace Research Centre, and Strategic and Defence Studies, Research School of Pacific Studies, The Australian National University, 12–14 August 1987.

——. "China's Domestic Crisis and Vietnamese Responses, April–July 1989". In *China's Crisis: The International Implications*, edited by Gary Klintworth, pp. 83–97. Canberra Papers on Strategy and Defence 57. Canberra: Strategic and Defence Studies Centre, The Australian National University, 1989.

Woodside, Alexander. "Nationalism and Poverty in the Breakdown of Sino-Vietnamese Relations". *Pacific Affairs* 52, no. 3 (1979): 381–409.

Vietnam-China (Ethnic Chinese)

Amer, Ramses. *The Ethnic Chinese and Sino-Vietnamese Relations*. Kuala Lumpur: Forum Publishers, 1991.

——. "The Chinese Minority in Vietnam Since 1975: Impact of Economic and Political Changes". *Ilmu Masyarakat* [Kuala Lumpur] 22 (1992): 1–39.

——. *China, Vietnam and the Chinese Minority in Vietnam*. Copenhagen Discussion Paper 22. Copenhagen: Center for East and Southeast Asia, University of Copenhagen, 1993.

——. "Les politiques du Viet Nam à l'égard des Chinois d'origine depuis 1975—Continuité et changement". *Réalités Vietnamiennes*, no. 6: 16–45. Cahier d'études du Centre d'Observation de l'Actualité Vietnamienne CODAVI Aix-en-Provence: Institut de Recherche sur le Sud-Est Asiatique IRSEA, 1996.

——. "Vietnam's Policies and the Ethnic Chinese since 1975". *SOJOURN: Journal of Social Issues in Southeast Asia* 11, no. 1 (1996): 76–104.

——. "The Sino-Vietnamese Conflict in 1978–79 and the Ethnic Chinese in Vietnam". *Multiethnica*, nos. 21–22 [Uppsala, Centre for Multiethnic Research, Uppsala University] (1997): 10–16.

——. "The Study of the Ethnic Chinese in Vietnam: Trends, Issues and Challenges". *Asian Culture* 22 (1998): 23–42.

Bhattacharya, J.J. "Migration of Ethnic Chinese from Vietnam". *Strategic Analysis* 3, no. 5 (1979): 176–81.

Chang, Pao-min. *Beijing, Hanoi and the Overseas Chinese*. China Research Monograph 24. Berkeley: Institute of East Asian Studies, University of California, 1982.

——. "Peking, Hanoi, and the Ethnic Chinese of Vietnam". *Asian Affairs: An American Review* 9, no. 4 (1982): 195–207

——. "The Sino-Vietnamese Dispute Over the Ethnic Chinese". *The China Quarterly* 90 (1982): 195–230.

——. *Kampuchea Between China and Vietnam*. Singapore: Singapore University Press, 1985.

Chiu, Hungdah. "China's Legal Position on Protecting Chinese Residents in Vietnam". *American Journal of International Law* 74, no. 3 (1980): 685–89.

Engelbert, Thomas. "Perceptions sur les Hoa après 1975 d'après des sources vietnamiennes et allemandes". In *Viêt Nam: Sources et Approaches*, by Philippe Le Failler and Jean Marie Mancini (texte réunis), pp. 139–55. Actes du colloque international EUROVIET, Aix-en-Provence, 3–5 mai 1995. Aix-en-Provence: Publications de l'Université de Provence, 1996.

Etudes sur le probleme de la nationalite des chinois au Sud-Vietnam. Taipei: Overseas Press, 1957.

Fall, Bernard. "Vietnam's Chinese Problem". *Far Eastern Survey* 27 (1958): 65–72.

Godley, Michael. "A Summer Cruise to Nowhere: China and the Vietnamese Chinese in Perspective". *The Australian Journal of Chinese Affairs* 4 (1980): 35–59.

Honey, P.J. "The Chinese Exodus from Vietnam". *Social Survey* (1978): 203–12.

Kotova, T. "Chinese Community in Vietnam as Peking's Political Weapon". *Far Eastern Affairs* 1 (1979): 88–100.

Luong Nhi Ky. "The Chinese in Vietnam: A Study of Vietnamese-Chinese Relations with Special Attention to the Period, 1862–1961". Ph.D. thesis, University of Michigan, 1962.

Ly, Singko. *Hanoi, Peking and the Overseas Chinese.* Singapore: Asian Writers Publishing House, 1978.

Morice, Jean. "Les chinois au Vietnam". *Revue juridiques et politiques indépendance et coopération* 43 (1987): 315–27.

Porter, Gareth. "Vietnam's Ethnic Chinese and the Sino-Vietnamese Conflict". *Asian Thought and Society* 4, no. 11 (1979): 233–36.

——. "Vietnam's Ethnic Chinese and the Sino-Vietnamese Conflict". *Bulletin of Concerned Asian Scholars* 12, no. 4 (1980): 55–60.

Stern, Lewis. 1984. *Vietnamese Communist Policy Toward the Overseas Chinese, 1920–82.* Ph.D. thesis, University of Pittsburgh.

Stern, Lewis M. "The Overseas Chinese in the Socialist Republic of Vietnam, 1979–1982". *Asian Survey* 25, no. 5 (1985): 521–36.

——. "The Overseas Chinese in Vietnam, 1920–75: Demography, Social Structure, and Economic Power". *Humboldt Journal of Social Relations,* 12, no. 2 (1985): 1–30.

——. "The China Connection and Vietnamese Communist Policy Toward the Overseas Chinese, 1920–1975". *Issues and Studies* 22, no. 4 (1986): 86–119.

——. "Vietnamese Communist Policy Towards the Overseas Chinese During Regime Consolidation and Socialist Transformation, 1955–1960". *Asian Profile* 14, no. 6 (1986): 529–40.

——. "Vietnamese Communist Policy Towards the Overseas Chinese, 1960–1975". *Contemporary Southeast Asia* 7, no. 4 (1986): 281–303.

——. "Vietnamese Communist Policies Towards the Overseas Chinese, 1930–1960". *The Journal of Communist Studies* 2, no. 1 (1986): 49–70.

——. "The Hoa Kieu Under the Socialist Republic of Vietnam". *Issues and Studies* 23, no. 3 (1987): 111–43.

——. "The Vietnamese Expulsion of the Overseas Chinese". *Issues and Studies* 23, no. 7 (1987): 102–35.

——. "The Eternal Return: Changes in Vietnam's Policies Toward the Overseas Chinese, 1982–1988". *Issues and Studies* 24, no. 7 (1988): 118–38.

——. "Vietnamese Communist Policy Towards the Overseas Chinese, 1983–1986". *Asian Profile* 16, no. 2 (1988): 141–46.

Unger, Esta. "Changes in the Chinese Community of Haiphong-Hanoi, 1945–48: The Repudiation of the Congregation System". Paper presented at the Symposium on Changing Identities of the Southeast

Asia Chinese Since World War II. Canberra, The Australian National University, 14–16 June 1985.
——. "The Struggle Over the Chinese Community in Vietnam, 1946–1986". *Pacific Affairs* 60, no. 4 (1987–88): 596–614.
Vairon, Lionel. "Les Chinois du Vietnam: 1975–1979". *Cahiers de l'Asie du Sud-Est* 22 (1987): 135–54.

Vietnam-China (Border War 1979)

Becker, Elizabeth. "The Chinese Invasion of Vietnam: Changing Alliances". *Indochina Issues* 1 (1979): 1–8.
Bhattacharya, J.J. "Military Aspects of the Sino-Vietnam Conflict". *Strategic Analysis* 3, no. 1 (1979): 15–18.
——. "Sino-Vietnam Border Clashes". *Strategic Analysis* 4, no. 9 (1980): 412–15.
Burton, Bruce. "Contending Explanations of the 1979 Sino-Vietnamese War". *International Journal* 34 (1979): 699–722.
Chen, King C. "China's War Against Vietnam: A Military Analysis". *Occasional Paper/Reprint Series* 5. Baltimore: University of Maryland, 1983.
——. "China's War Against Vietnam, 1979: A Military Analysis". *The Journal of East Asian Affairs* 3, no. 1 (1983): 233–63.
——. *Politics and Process of Peiping's Decisions to Attack Vietnam.* Taipei: Institute of International Relations, 1983.
——. *China's War with Vietnam, 1979: Issues, Decisions, and Implications.* Stanford: Stanford University, Hoover Institution Press, 1987.
Do Vang Ly. *Aggression by China: A Peep into the History of Vietnam.* Delhi: Siddaharta Publication Ltd., 1959–60.
Duiker, William J. "Understanding the Sino-Vietnamese War". *Problems of Communism* 38, no. 6 (1989): 84–88.
Duncanson, Dennis. "China's Vietnam War: New and Old Strategic Imperatives". *The World Today* 35, no. 6 (1979): 241–48.
Haggerly, J.J. "The Chinese-Vietnamese Border War of 1979". *Army Quarterly and Defence Journal* 109, no. 3 (1979): 265–72.
Jencks, Harlan W. "China's 'Punitive' War on Vietnam: A Military Assessment". *Asian Survey* 14, no. 8 (1979): 801–15.
Loescher, G.D. "The Sino-Vietnamese Conflict in Recent Historical Perspective". *Survey* 24 (1979): 125–41.
Menguy, Marc. *Hanoi Versus Peking.* Cambridge: Centre for International Affairs, Harvard University, 1979.
Mirsky, Jonathan. "China's Invasion of Vietnam: A View from the Infantry". *Journal of the Royal United Services for Defence Studies* (London) 126, no. 2 (1981): 48–52.
Nelson, Charles R. "The Sino-Viet War: Causes, Conduct and Consequences". *Parameters Journal of the US Army College* 9, no. 3 (1979): 22–30.
Pathania, P.S. "The Sino-Vietnam War—Pattern of Operations". *Strategic Digest* 10, no. 10 (1980): 653–60.
Ray, Hemen. *China's Vietnam War.* New Delhi: Radiant, 1983.
Sola, Richard. "Chine-Indochine: de l'intervention à l'antagonisme: première partie—la Chine en guerre: le conflit du Tonkin en 1979". *Défense Nationale* (1986): 109–124.

Tretiak, Daniel. "China's Vietnam War and its Consequences". *The China Quarterly* 80 (1979): 740–67.

Yee, Herbert S. "The Sino-Vietnamese Border War: China's Motives, Calculations and Strategies". *China Report* 16, no. 1 (1980): 15–32.

Vietnam (Territorial Disputes)

Amer, Ramses. "Vietnam and Its Neighbours: The Border Dispute Dimension". *Contemporary Southeast Asia* 17, no. 3 (1995): 298–318.

——. "The Border Conflicts Between Cambodia and Vietnam". *Boundary and Security Bulletin* 5, no. 2 (1997): 80–91.

——. "The Territorial Disputes Between China and Vietnam and Regional Stability". *Contemporary Southeast Asia* 19, no. 1 (1997): 89–113.

——. "Vietnam's Policy on Territorial Conflicts". In *Vietnam Reform and Transformation: Conference Proceedings*, edited by Björn Beckman, Eva Hansson and Lisa Román, pp. 215–36. Stockholm: Centre for Pacific Asia Studies, 1997.

——. *The Challenge of Managing the Border Disputes Between China and Vietnam*. EAI Working Paper, No. 16. Singapore: East Asian Institute, National University of Singapore, 1998.

Bhattacharya, J.J. "Sino-Vietnam Border Negotiations". *Strategic Analysis* 3, no. 3 (1979): 100–03.

——. "Sino-Vietnam Talks: The Second Round". *Strategic Analysis* 3, no. 5 (1979): 172–76.

Chang, Pao-min. *The Sino-Vietnamese Territorial Dispute*. The Washington Papers 118. New York: The Center for Strategic and International Studies, Georgetown University and Praeger Publishers, 1986.

Gay, Bernard. *La nouvelle frontière lao-vietnamienne. Les acords de 1977–1990*. Paris: L'Harmattan, 1995.

Ghosh, S.K. "Rivalry in the South China Sea". *China Report* 13, no. 2 (1977): 3–8.

Huang Dongdong. "Delimitation of Maritime Boundary Between Vietnam and China in the Gulf Of Tonkin". Dissertation for the LL.D. Degree, Faculty of Law, University of Ottawa, 1992.

Jha, Ganganath. "Vietnam-China Dispute over the Spratleys". *Strategic Analysis* 12, no. 10 (1989): 1201–22.

Les frontières du Vietnam: Histoire des frontières de la péninsule indochinoise. Collection rechrerches asiatiques, dirigee par Alain Forest, Travaux du Centre d'histoire et civilisations de la peninsule indochinoise publiés sous la direction de P.B. Lafont, Ouvrage publié avec le concours du Centre national de la recherche scientifique. Paris: Editions l'Harmattan, 1989.

Luu Van Loi. *Le différend vietnamo-chinois sur les archipels Hoang Sa et Truong Sa*. Hanoi: Editions The Gioi, 1996.

——. *The Sino-Vietnamese Difference on the Hoang Sa and Truonng Sa Archipelagoes*. Hanoi: The Gioi Publishers, 1996.

Murray, Dia. "Conflict and Coexistence: The Sino-Vietnamese Maritime Boundaries in Historical Perspectives". *Wisconsin Papers on Southeast Asia* 13. Madison: Center for Southeast Asian Studies, University of Wisconsin, Madison, 1987.

Nguyen Hong Thao. "Vietnam's First Maritime Boundary Agreement". *Boundary and Security Bulletin* 5, no. 3 (1997): 74–79.
——. "Vietnam and Thailand Settle Maritime Disputes in the Gulf of Thailand". *The MIMA Bulletin* 2/98 (1998): 7–10
Sarin, Chhak. *Les frontières du Cambodge*. Tome I. *Les frontières du Cambodge avec les anciens pays de la Fédération Indochinoise: le Laos et le Vietnam (Cochinchine et Annam)*. Paris: Librairie Dalloz and Centre d'Études des Pays d'Extrême-Orient Asie du Sud-Est, 1966.
Tran Van Minh. "Les frontières du Cambodge et du Vietnam". *Revue Juridique et Politique, Indépendance et Coopération* 32, no. 2 (1978): 647–73.
——. "Les frontières du Cambodge et du Vietnam. Deuxième partie: les frontières maritimes". *Revue Juridique et Politique, Indépendance et Coopération* 33, no. 1 (1979): 37–66.
Valencia, Mark. "The Spratly Embroglio in the Post-Cold War Era". In *Southeast Asia in the New World Order*, edited by David Wurfel and Bruce Burton, pp. 244–72. London: Macmillan, 1996.
Zhou Keyuan. *The Gulf of Tonkin: A Potential Maritime Clash Spot in Sino-Vietnamese Relationship?* EAI Background Brief, No. 17. Singapore: East Asian Institute, National University of Singapore, 1998.

Vietnam-China (1991–)

Amer, Ramses. "Sino-Vietnamese Relations and Southeast Asian Security". *Contemporary Southeast Asia* 14, no. 4 (1993): 314–31.
——. "Sino-Vietnamese Normalization in the Light of the Crisis of the Late 1970s". *Pacific Affairs* 67, no. 3 (1994): 357–83.
Gainsborough, Martin. "Vietnam II: A Turbulent Normalization with China". *World Today* 48, no. 11 (1992): 205–07.
Le dialogue Chine-Viêt-Nam dans un contexte de sécurité multilatérale en Asie Orientale. Sous la direction de Gérard Hervouet. Documents du GERAC 12, Groupe d'études et de recehrcehs sur l'Asie contemporaine. Québec: Institut québéquois des huates études internationales, Université Laval, 1997.
Niquet, Valérie. "le Vietnam face au monde chinois". *Défense nationale* 56 (1994): 131–44.
Okabe, Tatsumi. "Coping with China". In *Vietnam Joins the World*, edited by James W. Morley and Masashi Nishihara, pp. 117–33. New York: M.E. Sharpe, 1997.
Shultz II C.J. and W.J. Ardrey, IV. "The Future Prospects of Sino-Vietnamese Relations: Are Trade and Commerce the Critical Factors for Sustainable Peace?" *Contemporary Southeast Asia* 17, no. 2 (1995): 126–46.
Sutter, Keith. "China's Vietnam Policy: The Road to Normalization and Prospects for the Sino-Vietnamese Relationship". *Journal of Northeast Asian Studies* 12, no. 2 (1993): 21–46.
Thayer, Carlyle A. "Comrade Plus Brother: The New Sino-Vietnamese Relations". *Pacific Review* 5, no. 4 (1992): 402–06.
——. "Sino-Vietnamese Relations: The Interplay of Ideology and National Interest". *Asian Survey* 34, no. 6 (1994): 513–28.

——. "Vietnam: Coping with China". *Southeast Asian Affairs, 1994,* pp. 351–67. Singapore: Institute of Southeast Asian Studies, 1994.

Womack, Brantly. "Sino-Vietnamese Border Trade: The Edge of Normalization". *Asian Survey* 34, no. 6 (1994): 495–512.

Vietnam-General

Abuza, Z. "International Relations Theory and Vietnam". *Contemporary Southeast Asia* 17, no. 4 (1996): 406–19.

Amer, Ramses. "Vietnam's Evolving Relations with the East Asian Countries". In *Current Developments in Asia Pacific*, edited by Bert Edström, pp. 76–92. Stockholm: Center for Pacific Asia Studies, Stockholm University, 1994.

——. "Vietnam and Southeast Asia since the Fall of Saigon in 1975". In *Sydostasien*, edited by Farid Abbaszadegan, pp. 58–76. Skrifter utgivna av Sällskapet för asienstudier 7, Uppsala, 1996.

——. "Le Viet Nam et l'Asie du Sud-Est depuis 1975". *Réalités Vietnamiennes* 9, pp. 18–32. Cahier d'études du Centre d'Observation de l'Actualité Vietnamienne (CODAVI), Institut de Recherche sur le Sud-Est Asiatique (IRSEA), Aix-en-Provence, 1997.

Betts, Richard K. "The Strategic Predicament". In *Vietnam Joins the World*, edited by James W. Morley and Masashi Nishihara, pp. 94–114. New York: M.E. Sharpe, 1997.

Bolton, M. Kent. "Vietnam Crucible: The Political Economy of Normalization in the Post-Cold War World". In *United States-Third World Relations in the New World Order*, edited by Abbas P. Grammy and C. Kaye Bragg, pp. 207–29. New York: NOVA Science Publishers, Inc. 1996.

Bresnan, John. "A Society Emerging from Crisis". In *Vietnam Joins the World,* edited by James W. Morley and Masashi Nishihara, pp. 66–93. New York: M.E. Sharpe, 1997.

Brown, Frederick Z. "Vietnam's Tentative Transformation". *Journal of Democracy* 7, no. 4 (1996): 73–87.

Bui Tin. *Following Ho Chi Minh: The Memoirs of a North Vietnamese Colonel*. London: Hurst & Company, 1995.

Buttinger, Joseph. *A Political History of Vietnam*. London: Andre Deutch, 1969.

Elliott, David W.P. "Vietnam Faces the Future". *Current History* 94, no. 596 (1995): 412–19.

Goodman, Allen E. "Fighting While Negotiating: The View from Hanoi". In *Communism in Indochina: New Perspectives*, edited by Joseph J. Zasloff and MacAlister Brown, pp. 81–107. Lexington: D.C. Heath and Company, 1975.

Hervouet, Gérard and Carlyle A. Thayer. "L'armée populaire vietnamienne, un acteur pour la sécurité de l'Asie du Sud-Est?" *Relations internationales et stratégiques* 27 (1997): 120–28.

Hoang Van Hoan. *A Drop in the Ocean: Hoang Van Hoang's Revolutionary Reminiscences*. Beijing: Foreign Languages Press, 1988.

Honey, P.J. *Communism in North Vietnam*. Cambridge: The MIT Press, 1966.

——, ed. *North Vietnam Today: Profile of a Communist Satellite*. New York: Frederick A. Praeger, 1962.

Huynh Kim Khanh. *Vietnamese Communism, 1925–1945*. Ithaca: Cornell University Press, 1982.

Ikuchi, Tsutomu. "Australia's Policy Toward Indochina: Focusing on the Cambodian Problem". In *Indochina in Transition: Confrontation or Co-prosperity*, edited by Mio Tadashi, pp. 215–31. Tokyo: Japan Institute of International Affairs, 1989.

Inada, Juichi. "Japan's Aid Freeze to Vietnam: Historical Process And Its Diplomatic Implications". In *Indochina in Transition: Confrontation or Co-prosperity*, edited by Mio Tadashi, pp. 195–214. Tokyo: Japan Institute of International Affairs, 1989.

Kattenburg, Paul M. "DRV External Relations in the New Revolutionary Phase". In *Communism in Indochina: New Perspectives*, edited by Joseph J. Zasloff and MacAlister Brown, pp. 109–31. Lexington: D.C. Heath and Company, 1975.

Klintworth, Gary, ed. *Vietnam's Withdrawal from Cambodia: Regional Issues and Realignments*. Canberra Papers on Strategy and Defence 64. Canberra: Strategic and Defence Studies Centre, Research School of Pacific Studies, The Australian National University, 1990.

Lockhart, Greg. "Vietnam: Democracy and Democratisation". *Asian Studies Review* 17, no. 1 (1993): 135–42.

Morley, James W. and Masashi Nishihara, eds. *Vietnam Joins the World*. Armonk, NY: M.E. Sharpe, 1997.

Nakano Ari. "Southeast Asian Policy of Vietnam" In *Indochina in Transition: Confrontation or Co-prosperity*, edited by Mio Tadashi, pp. 232–46. Tokyo: Japan Institute of International Affairs, 1989.

Nguyen Khac Huyen. *Vision Accomplished?* New York: Collier Books, 1971.

Nugent, Nicholas. *Vietnam: The Second Revolution*. Brighton: In Print Publishing, 1996.

Palmujoki, Eero. *Vietnam and the World: Marxist-Leninist Doctrine and the Changes in International Relations, 1975–93*. London: Macmillan Press Ltd., 1997.

Pike, Douglas E. "Operational Code of the North Vietnamese Politburo". *Asia Quarterly* 1 (1971): 91–102.

Pike, Douglas. "Vietnam and Its Neighbours: Internal Influences and External Relations". In *ASEAN in Regional and Global Context*, edited by Karl D. Jackson, Sukhumbhand Paribatra, and J. Soedjati Djiwandono. Research Papers and Policy Studies 18. Berkeley: Institute of East Asian Studies, University of California, 1986.

Pomonti, Jean-Claude and Hugues Tertrais. *Vietnam, communistes et dragons*. Paris: Le Monde-Editions, 1994.

Porter, Gareth. "Vietnam and the Socialist Camp: Center or Periphery?" In *Vietnamese Communism in Comparative Perspective*, edited by William S. Turley, pp. 225–64. Boulder: Westview Press, 1980.

——. "The Transformation of Vietnam's World-view: From Two Camps to Interdependence". *Contemporary Southeast Asia* 12, no. 1 (1990): 1–19.

Porter, Gareth. *The Politics of Bureaucratic Socialism*. Ithaca: Cornell University Press, 1993.

Shiraishi, Masaya. *Japanese Relations with Vietnam: 1951–1987*. Ithaca: Cornell University Southeast Asia Program, 1990.

Shultz II, C.J. and K. Lee. "Vietnam's Inconsistencies Between Political Structure and Socio-economic Practice: Implications for the Nation's Future". *Contemporary Southeast Asia* 15, no. 2 (1993): 179–94.

Stubbs, Richard. *Vietnam Facing the 1990s*. Asia Papers 1. Toronto: University of Toronto-York University Joint Centre for Asia Pacific Studies, 1989.

Thayer, Carlyle A. "Foreign Policy Orientations of the Socialist Republic of Vietnam". In *Southeast Asian Affairs 1977*, edited by Kernial S. Sandhu, pp. 306–24. Singapore: Institute of Southeast Asian Studies, 1977.

——. "Vietnam in World Affairs". *Dyason House Papers* [Melbourne] 3, no. 5 (1977): 5–8.

——. "Vietnam's External Policy: An Overview". *Pacific Community* [Tokyo] 9, no. 2 (1978): 212–31.

——. "Vietnam's Foreign Policy". *World Review* [Brisbane] 20, no. 2 (1981): 30–40.

——. "Vietnamese Perspectives on International Security: Three Revolutionary Currents". In *Asian Perspectives on International Security*, edited by Donald H. McMillen, pp. 57–76. London: Macmillan Press, 1984.

——. "Vietnam: Ideology and the Lessons from Experience". In *Confrontation or Coexistence: The Future of ASEAN-Vietnam Relations*, edited by William S. Turley, pp. 49–74. Bangkok: The Institute of Security and International Studies, Chulalongkorn University, 1985.

——. "Vietnam's Foreign Policy: The Background Factors". *Current Affairs Bulletin* [Sydney] 62, no. 9 (1986): 21–30.

——. *Vietnam*. Asia-Australia Briefing Papers, 1, no. 4. Sydney: The Asia-Australia Institute, The University of New South Wales, 1992.

——. *The Vietnam People's Army Under Doi Moi*. Pacific Strategic Paper 7. Singapore: Institute of Southeast Asian Studies, 1994.

——. *Vietnam's Developing Ties with the Region: The Case for Defence Co-operation*. ADSC Working Paper 24. Canberra: Australian Defence Studies Centre, Australian Defence Force Academy, 1994.

——. "Vietnam's Strategic Readjustment". In *China as a Great Power: Myths, Realities and Challenges in the Asia-Pacific Region*, edited by Stuart Harris and Gary Klintworth, pp. 185–201. Melbourne: Longman Australia Pty Ltd., 1995.

——. "Force Modernization: The Case of the Vietnam People's Army". *Contemporary South East Asia* 19, no. 1 (1997): 1–28.

——. "International Relations and Security: A Rapid Overview of a Decade of Doi Moi". In *Doi Moi Ten Years after the 1986 Party Congress*, edited by Adam Fforde, pp. 25–46. Political and Social Change Monograph 24. Canberra: Department of Political and Social Change, Research School of Pacific and Asian Studies, The Australian National University, 1997.

Trinh Van Thao. *Vietnam: Du confucianisme au communisme*. Paris: Edition's L'Harmattan, 1990.

Ton That Thien. *The Foreign Politics of the Communist Party of Vietnam: A Study of Communist Tactics*. New York: Crane Russak, 1989.

Truong Chinh. *Selected Writings*. Hanoi: Foreign Language Publishing, 1977.

Turley, William S. ed. *Vietnamese Communism in Comparative Perspective*. Boulder: Westview Press, 1980.

——. "Vietnam's Challenge to Southeast Asian Regional Order". In *Asian Pacific Security: Emerging Challenges and Responses*, edited by Young Whan Kihl and Lawrence E. Grinter. Boulder: Lynne Reinner Publishers, 1986.

——. "Vietnamese Security in Domestic and Regional Focus: The Political-Economic Nexus". In *Southeast Asian Security in the New Millennium*, edited by Richard J. Ellings and Sheldon W. Simon, pp. 175–220. Armonk: M.E. Sharpe, 1996.

Vo Nguyen Giap. *People's War, People's Army*. Hanoi: Foreign Language Publishing House, 1961.

Williams, Michael. *Vietnam at the Crossroads*. London: Pinter Publishers, 1992.

Womack, Brantley. "Vietnam 1996: Reform Immobilism". *Asian Survey* 37, no. 1 (1997): 79–87.

Wurfel, David. "*Perestroika*, Vietnamese Style: Problems and Prospects". In *Vietnam Facing the 1990s*, edited by Richard Stubbs, Asia Papers 1. Toronto: University of Toronto-York University Joint Centre for Asia Pacific Studies, 1989.

Vietnamese Language Sources

Bo Ngoai giao, Cong hoa Xa hoi chu nghia Viet Nam and Bo Ngoai giao, Lien bang Cong hoa Xa hoi chu nghia Xo-viet. *Viet Nam Lien Xo: 30 Nam Quan He (1950–1980)*. Moscow: Nha Xuat Ban Tien Bo, 1983.

——. Vien Quan He Quoc Te. *Chu Tich Ho Chi Minh Voi Cong Tac Ngoai Giao*. Hanoi: Nha Xuat Ban Su That, 1990.

——. *Hoi nhap quoc te va giu vung ban sac*. Hanoi: Nha Xuat Ban Chinh Tri Quoc Gia, 1995.

——. Hoc Vien Quan He Quoc Te. *Hoi Dap ve Tinh Hinh The Gioi va Chinh Sach Doi Ngoai cua Dang va Nha Nuoc Ta*. Hanoi: Nha Xuan Ban Chinh Tri Quoc Gia, 1997.

Bui Phan Ky. "May suy nghi ve chien luoc quoc phong trong boi canh quoc te moi". *Tap Chi Cong San* 5 (1993) 58–62.

——. "Ve Nhung Giai Phap Chien Luoc Bao Ve To Quoc Xa Hoi Chu Nghia Trong Hoan Canh Moi". *Tap Chi Quoc Phong Toan Dan* 11 (1995): 20–22 and 78.

——. "May van de ve xay dung va bao ve To quoc xa hoi chu nghia trong boi canh the gioi ngay nay". *Tap Chi Cong San* 16 (1996): 18–20.

Bui Thanh Son. "Nhung yeu to chi phoi chinh sach cua My doi voi Trung Quoc o thoi ky sau chien tranh lanh". *Nghien Cuu Quoc Te* 6 (1995): 10–15.

——. "Danh gia chung ve APEC: Nhung thuan loi va kho khan trong qua trinh hoi nhap cua Viet Nam". *Nghien Cuu Quoc Te* 5, no. 20 (1997): 29–36.

Bui Thien Ngo. "Bao ve an ninh quoc gia trong tinh hinh moi". *Tap Chi Cong San* 9 (1992): 3–7.

Dang Cong San Vietnam. *Du Thao Cac Van Kien Trinh Dai Hoi VIII cua Dang Tai Lieu Dung Tai Dai Hoi Dang Cap Co So*, Mat (Secret), Luu Hanh Noi Bo (Internal Circulation), 1995.

——. *Van Kien Dai Hoi Dai Bieu Toan Quoc Lan Thu VIII*. Hanoi: Nha Xuat Ban Chinh Tri Quoc Gia, 1996.

Do Minh. "Co nen lay chu nghia Mac-Le-nin lam nen tang tu tuong hay khong". *Tap Chi Cong San* 5 (1991): 56–57.

Do Nhu Khue and Nguyen Thi Loan Anh. *Quan He Kinh Te Thuong Mai Giua Viet Nam & ASEAN*. Hanoi: Nha Xuat Ban Thong Ke, 1997.

Doang Chuong. "Bai hoc thoi dai". *Tap Chi Cong San* 2 (1992): 5–9.

Dong Thai. "Ve Van De An Ninh Trong Quan He Viet Nam-ASEAN". In *Quan He Viet Nam-ASEAN*, edited by Duong Phu Hiep. Hanoi: Asia and Pacific Institute, 1992.

"Du Thao Bao Cao Chinh Tri cua Ban Chap Hanh Trung Uong Dang Khoa VII Trinh Dai Hoi Lan Thu VIII cua Dang". *Nhan Dan*, 10 April 1996, supplement.

Duong Phu Hiep, ed. *Quan He Viet Nam-ASEAN*. Hanoi: Asia and Pacific Institute, 1992.

Duy Thao. "Tien trinh khu vuc hoa o Dong Nam A". *Nghien Cuu Quoc Te* 15 (1996): 32–36.

Giai Doan Moi Trong Quan He Viet Nam–Lien Xo. Hanoi: Nha Xuat Ban Su That, 1978.

Ha Nam Binh. "AFTA—thach thuc va trien vong". *Nghien Cuu Quoc Te* 6 (1995): 3–9.

Hoang Nguyen. Doi moi tu duy trong cong tac doi ngoai". *Tap Chi Triet Hoc* 2, no. 57 (1987): 66–78.

Hoang Van Hoan. *Giot Nuoc Trong Bien Ca (Hoi Ky Cach Mang)*. Beijing: Nha Xuat Ban Tin Viet Nam, 1986.

Ho Van Thong. "May van de chung trong nhan thuc tu tuong ve thoi ky qua do hien nay o nuoc ta". In *Quan Triet Nghi Quyet Dai Hoi Lan Thu V cua Dang*, by Truong Dang Cao Cap Nguyen Ai Quoc, Khoa Triet Hoc, pp. 101–22. Hanoi: Nha Xuat Ban Sach Giao Khoa Mac-Lenin, 1984.

Hoang Anh Tuan. "ASEAN–nhung dieu chinh chinh sach sau chien tranh lanh". *Nghien Cuu Quoc Te* 5 (1995): 8–15.

——. "Nhung Tac Dong Cua Viec Mo Rong Tu ASEAN-7 Len ASEAN-10". *Nghien Cuu Quoc Te* 1, no. 16 (1997): 40–45.

Hoang Tung. *May Van De ve Cong Tac Chinh Tri va Tu Tuong Trong Chang Duong Hien Nay cua Cach Mang Xa Hoi Chu Nghia*. Hanoi: Nha Xuat Ban Su That, 1983.

Hong Lam. "Hoi nhap voi kinh te khu vuc va the gioi". *Tap Chi Cong San* 11 (1998): 3–11.

Hung Son. "Nhung phat trien moi o Dong Nam A va chau A-Thai Binh Duong". *Nghien Cuu Quoc Te* 4, no. 6 (1994): 7–10.

Le Dinh Tu. "Quan he van hoa Viet Nam—ASEAN: Mot Cach tiep can". *Nghien Cuu Quoc Te* 5, no. 20 (1997): 49–53.

Le Linh Lan. "Kien truc an ninh khu vuc Chau A-Thai Binh Duong: thach thuc va trien vong". *Nghien Cuu Quoc Te* 2, no. 17 (1997): 8–12.

——. "Cuoc khung hoang tai chinh-kinh te va an ninh khu vuc Chau A-Thai Binh Duong". *Nghien Cuu Quoc Te*, 3, no. 24 (1998): 25–31.

——. "Vai tro cua cac nuoc nho va vua trong quan he quoc te o khu vuc chau A-Thai Binh Duong". *Nghien Cuu Quoc Te* 2, no. 23 (1998): 17–24.

Luu Quy Tan. "Nhung con ho trong ASEAN tu sau suy thoai kinh te nam 1996". *Nghien Cuu Quoc Te* 4, no. 19 (1997): 13–17.

Le Thi. "Tu duy moi ve cuoc dau tranh tu tuong, dau tranh bao ve hoa binh, chong chien tranh hat nhan hien nay". *Tap Chi Triet Hoc* 4, no. 59 (1987): 12 and 21.

Le Tinh. "The gioi nam 1992 co gi moi?" *Tap Chi Cong San* 1 (1993): 57–60.
Le Xuan Luu. "Ban chat cach mang va khoa hoc cua chu nghia Mac-Le-nin". *Tap Chi Cong San* 3 (1992): 3–7.
——. "Su pha hoai ve tu tuong cua cac the luc phan dong trong chien luoc 'dien bien hoa binh' ". *Tap Chi Cong San* 4 (1993): 19–22.
——. "Ve moi quan he giua xay dung va bao ve To quoc trong giai doan cach mang moi". *Tap Chi Cong San* 10 (1996): 7–10 and 14.
Luu Van Loi. "ASEAN—con duong ba muoi nam". *Nghien Cuu Quoc Te* 4, no. 19 (1997): 3–7.
——. *Nam Muoi Nam Ngoai Giao Viet Nam 1945–1995: Ngoai Giao Viet Nam 1945–1975*. Vol. 1. Hanoi: Nha Xuat Ban Cong An Nhan Dan, 1998.
——. *Nam Muoi Nam Ngoai Giao Viet Nam 1945–1995:Ngoai Giao Viet Nam 1975–1995*. Vol. 2. Hanoi: Nha Xuat Ban Cong An Nhan Dan, 1998.
Minh Duc. "Hop Tac Quan Su, Quoc Phong cua cac nuoc ASEAN". *Tap Chi Quoc Phong Toan Dan* (1997): 69–71 and 13.
Ngo Duy Ngo. "Viet Nam va van de gia nhap WTO". *Nghien Cuu Quoc Te* 2, no. 17 (1997): 22–25.
Nguyen Anh Tuan. "WTO, APEC, AFTA: Mot so tac dong toi qua trinh cong nghiep hoa o Viet Nam". *Nghien Cuu Quoc Te* 4, no. 19 (1997): 28–35.
——. "Tac dong cua cuoc khung hoang tien te o Dong Nam A doi voi My, Trung Quoc va Viet Nam". *Nghien Cuu Quoc Te* 1, no. 22 (1998): 32–34.
——. "Ve cuoc khung hoang tien te o Dong Nam A". *Nghien Cuu Quoc Te* 5, no. 20 (1998): 54–61.
Nguyen Co Thach. "Tat ca hoa binh, doc lap dan toc va phat trien". *Tap Chi Cong San* 8 (1989): 1–8.
Nguyen Dinh Luan. "Doi net va dia chinh tri o Chau A sau chien tranh lanh". *Nghien Cuu Quoc Te* 2, no. 17 (1997): 18–21.
——. "Huong toi mot trat tu da trung tam quyen luc dau the ky 21". *Nghien Cuu Quoc Te* 4, no. 25 (1998): 10–14.
Nguyen Duy Trinh. "30 nam dau tranh ngoai giao vi doc lap. tu do cua to quoc va xay dung chu nghia xa hoi". *Hoc Tap* 10 (1975): 5–19 and 28.
Nguyen Dy Nien. "Trien vong tot dep cua nhung quan he hop tac truyen thong". *Nghien Cuu Quoc Te* 4, no. 6 (1994): 4–6.
——. "Tiep tuc doi moi va mo cua vi su nghiep cong nghiep hoa, hien dai hoa dat nuoc". *Tap Chi Cong San* 12 (1996): 47.
Nguyen Hai Yen. "Tam giac tang truong va phat trien kinh te quoc gia, khu vuc". *Nghien Cuu Quoc Te* 2, no. 23 (1998): 36–40.
Nguyen Manh Cam. "Tren duong trien khai chinh sach doi ngoai theo dinh huong moi". *Tap Chi Cong San* 4 (1993): 11–15.
——. "Gia tri lau ben va dinh huong nhat quan". In *Hoi nhap quoc te va giu vung ban sac*, edited by Bo Ngoai Giao, pp. 223–30. Hanoi: Nha Xuat Ban Chinh tri Quoc Gia, 1995.
——. "Chau A trong the ky 21". *Nghien Cuu Quoc Te* 3, no. 18 (1997): 3–8.
——. "Viet nam se tiep tuc no luc dong gop cho cac hoat dong cua LHQ vi hoa binh va phat trien". *Nghien Cuu Quoc Te* 4, no. 25 (1998): 3–9.
——. "Viet Nam Tiep Tuc Day Manh Su Nghiep Doi Moi Vi Phat Trien Va Hop Tac". *Nghien Cuu Quoc Te* 1, no. 22 (1998): 3–8.
Nguyen Manh Hung. "Nhin lai mot nam Viet Nam gia nhap ASEAN". *Nghien Cuu Quoc Te* 13 (1996): 3–5.
Nguyen Phuc Luan. "Ho Chi Minh va tu tuong chung song hoa binh trong

chinh sach doi ngoai dau tien cua Nha nuoc Viet nam doc lap".
Nghien Cuu Quoc Te 1 (1993): 40–43.

Nguyen Phuong Binh. Vai tro cua ASEAN trong viec xay dung co che an
ninh khu vuc". *Nghien Cuu Quoc Te* 46 (1994): 30–34.

——. "Ve viec Viet Nam gia nhap ASEAN". *Nghien Cuu Quoc Te* 3, no. 5
(1994): 24–27.

——. "Vai tro cua ASEAN trong viec xay dung co che an ninh khu vuc".
Nghien Cuu Quoc Te 4, no. 6 (1994): 30–34.

——. "Quan he Viet Nam—ASEAN va nhung van de dat ra trong tuong lai".
Nghien Cuu Quoc Te 4, 19 (1997): 24–27.

Nguyen Trong Thu. "Ve trat tu quoc te moi". *Tap Chi Cong San* 5 (1991):
60.

Nguyen Van Duc. "Mot trat tu the gioi moi hay la mot hinh thai dau tranh
moi?" *Tap Chi Quoc Phong Toan Dan* 1 (1992): 57–61.

Nguyen Van Linh. "Phat bieu cua dong chi tong bi thu Nguyen Van Linh,
Be mac hoi nghi 7 cua BCHTUD". *Tap Chi Cong San* 9 (1989): 5–12.

Nguyen Van Tu. "Chu nghia quoc te cua giai cap cong nhan–nguyen tac
xuyen suot trong hoat dong doi ngoai cua Cong doan Viet Nam". *Tap
Chi Cong San* 18 (1998): 9–11.

Nguyen Vu Tung. "Dien dan khu vuc ASEAN (ARF) va an ninh chau A—
Thai Binh Duong". *Nghien Cuu Quoc Te* 3, no. 5 (1994): 28–33.

Pham Cao Phong. "ASEAN huong ve tuong lai". *Nghien Cuu Quoc Te* 4, no.
19 (1997): 18–23.

Pham Nhu Cuong. "Phan dau nang cao chat luong cua cong tac giang day
nghien cuu ly luan Mac-Le-nin theo tinh than cua nghi quyet dai hoi
Dang lan thu V". *Quan Triet Nghi Quyet Dai Hoi Lan Thu V cua Dang*,
edited by In Truong Dang Cao Cap Nguyen Ai Quoc, Khoa Triet Hoc,
pp. 44–75. Hanoi: Nha Xuat Ban Sach Giao Khoa Mac-Le-nin, 1984.

Pham Thi Mien. "Mot so dieu chinh chinh sach cua My doi voi khu vuc
Dong Nam A". *Nghien Cuu Quoc Te* 5 (1995): 23–27.

Pham Van Bon. "Ve quan ly thi truong ngoai hoi o nuoc ta hien nay". *Tap
Chi Cong San* 16 (1998): 36–40.

Pham Van Chuc. "Suc song va trien vong moi cua Phong trao khong lien
ket". *Tap Chi Cong San* 20 (1998): 61–64.

Phan Doan Nam. "Mot vai suy nghi ve doi moi tu duy doi ngoai". *Tap Chi
Cong San* 2 (1988): 50–54 and 59.

——. "Van de phoi hop giua an ninh, quoc phong va ngoai giao trong giai
doan cach mang moi". *Tap Chi Cong San* 3 (1991): 29–31.

——. "Nhin lai the gioi va chau A Thai Binh Duong sau chien tranh lanh".
Nghien Cuu Quoc Te 15 (1996): 3–11.

——. "Mot vai suy nghi ve van de 'toan cau hoa' ". *Tap Chi Cong San* 8
(1996): 52–56.

——. "Ve mot so mau thuan noi len tren the gioi hien nay". *Nghien Cuu
Quoc Te* 13 (1996): 7–18.

——. "ASEAN—hien tai va tuong lai". *Nghien Cuu Quoc Te* 4, no. 19 (1997):
8–12.

——. "Cach mang khoa hoc cong nghe va quan he quoc te hien dai". *Nghien
Cuu Quoc Te,* 3, no. 24 (1998): 3–8.

——. "De co mot ASEAN hoa binh, on dinh va phat trien dong deu". *Tap
Chi Cong San* 21 (1998): 56–59.

Phuc Cuong. "Con duong dan den hoa binh, doc lap, huu nghi va hop tac
cua cac dan toc Dong Nam A". *Tap Chi Cong San* 6 (1981): 20–34.

Quach Quang Hong. "Trung Quoc va cuoc khung hoang tien te, tai chinh o Dong A". *Nghien Cuu Quoc Te* 4, no. 25 (1998): 31–41.

Quan He Huu Nghi Va Hop Tac Toan Dien Viet Nam–Lien Xo. Hanoi: Nha Xuat Ban Su That, 1988.

Quoc Tuy. "Doi moi tu duy doi ngoai va nhung nguyen tac co ban cua Lenin ve chinh sach doi ngoai". *Tap Chi Cong San* 12 (1989): 12–16.

Song Tung. "Vi sao chu nghia xa hoi hien thuc o Dong Au va Lien xo sup do?" *Tap Chi Cong San* 2 (1992): 10–13 and 17.

Thang Loi Cua Tinh Huu Nghi Va Su Hop Tac Toan Dien Viet Nam—Lien Xo. Hanoi: Nha Xuat Ban Su That, 1983.

Thanh Tin. *Hoa Xuyen Tuyet.* Irvine, CA: Saigon Press, 1991.

To Nghien Cuu Lich Su Chien Tranh, Hoc Vien Quan Su. "Tai thao luoc kiet xuat cua ong cha ta". *Hoc Tap* 11 (1972): 20–34.

Ton Sinh Thanh. "Mo hinh ly thuyet giai thich hien tuong ASEM". *Nghien Cuu Quoc Te* 4, no. 25 (1998): 25–30.

Tran Ba Khoa. "Canh giac voi am muu dien bien hoa binh cua cac the luc thu dich". *Tap Chi Cong San* 1 (1983): 18–20.

——. "Doi thoai va hop tac an ninh o chau A—Thai Binh Duong hien nay". *Tap Chi Quoc Phong Toan Dan* 7 (1996): 120–22.

——. "Cuc dien moi trong quan he quoc te". *Tap Chi Cong San* 17 (1998): 55–57.

——. "Hoa binh, on dinh, an ninh ben vung o khu vuc chau A–Thai Binh Duong". *Tap Chi Cong San* 10 (1998): 56–58.

Tran Con. "Nhan thuc ve van de dau tranh giai cap, dau tranh giua hai con duong o nuoc ta hien nay". *Tap Chi Triet Hoc* 1, no. 40 (1983): 3, 43–65.

——. "Suy nghi ve cuoc dau tranh giai cap, dau tranh giua hai con duong hien nay". In *Quan Triet Nghi Quyet Dai Hoi Lan Thu V cua Dang*, edited by Truong Dang Cao Cap Nguyen Ai Quoc, Khoa Triet Hoc, pp. 123–34. Hanoi: Nha Xuat Ban Sach Giao Khoa Mac—Le-nin, 1984.

Tran Hanh. "Nang cao hieu quu doi ngoai trong su nghiep CNH, HDH dat nuoc". *Tap Chi Quoc Phong Toan Dan* 8 (1997): 3–6.

Tran Mo. "Cuoc Chien Hoa Binh". *Tap Chi Quoc Phong Toan Dan* 11 (1995): 62–63.

Tran Quang Co. "Chang duong phia truoc". *Nghien Cuu Quoc Te* 1 (1993): 3–5.

——. "The gioi huong ve the ky 21". *Nghien Cuu Quoc Te* 5 (1995): 3–7.

——. "Tuong lai cua cac quan he giua Viet Nam va cac nuoc chau A—Thai binh Duong: tac dong den phat trien kinh te cua Viet Nam". In *Hoi Nhap Quoc Te va Giu Vung Ban Sac* (1995): 103–14.

Tran Trong Thin. "Can can quan su dang thay doi chien luoc gi cho ngay mai?" *Tap Chi Cong San* 4 (1991): 56 and 58–59.

Trung Duc. "Tong quan tinh hinh chinh tri-quan su the gioi nam 1997". *Tap Chi Quoc Phong Toan Dan* 2 (1998): 75–79.

Truong Dang Cao Cap Nguyen Ai Quoc, Khoa Lich Su Dang. *Lich Su Dang Cong San Viet Nam, 1920–1954.* Vol. 1. Hanoi: Nha Xuat Ban Sach Giao Khoa Mac-Lenin, 1983.

Truong Giang Long. "Mot So Van De Trong Qua Trinh Hoi Nhap Viet Nam-ASEAN". *Tap Chi Cong San* 3 (1997): 57–59.

Van Tao. "Van de hoa binh trong su chuyen hoa cua cac mau thuan co ban cua thoi dai". *Tap Chi Cong San* 1 (1988): 69–74.

Vo Thu Phuong. "In-do-ne-xi-a, con bao chua qua". *Tap Chi Cong San* 12 (1998): 61–62.

Vo Van Kiet. "Thu Vo Van Kiet goi Bo Chinh Tri". *Viet Luan* [Paris], 1053, 5 January 1996, pp. 30–31 and 58–60.

Vu Khoan. "Tu tuong Ho Chi Minh ve hoat dong quoc te va cong tac ngoai giao". *Nguyen Cuu Quoc Te* 3, no. 5 (1994): 3–14.

——. Mot so van de quoc te cua dai hoi VII". In Bo Ngoai Giao, *Hoi Nhap Quoc Te va Giu Vung Ban Sac*, pp. 71–76. Hanoi: Nha Xuat Ban Chinh Tri Quoc Gia, 1995.

——. "Dai hoi VIII va cong tac doi ngoai". *Tuan Bao Quoc Te* 26 (1996): 1 and 10.

Vu Oanh and Van Thanh. "Tu tuong Ho Chi Minh ve hoa binh, huu nghi co so cua chinh sach hop tac voi My trong giai doan hien nay". *Nghien Cuu Quoc Te* 6 (1995): 20–23.

Journals, Periodicals and News Agencies

Agence France Presse
Asian Wall Street Journal
Baltimore Sun
Beijing Information
Beijing Review
British Broadcasting Corporation, *Summary of World Broadcasts,* Part Three, Asia Pacific.
British Broadcasting Corporation, *Summary of World Broadcasts,* Part Three, Far East
British Broadcasting Corporation, *Summary of World Broadcasts Weekly Economic Report.* Part Three, Asia-Pacific
Bulletin de sinologie
Business Times (Singapore)
Country Report: Vietnam (London: The Economic Intelligence Unit).
The Economist
Far Eastern Economic Review
Hoc Tap
Le Courrier du Vietnam
Le Monde
Libération
Los Angeles Times
Nghien Cuu Quoc Te
Nhan Dan
Quan Doi Nhan Dan
Reuters wire service
San Diego Union Tribune
South China Morning Post
Straits Times
Tap Chi Cong San
Tap Chi Triet Hoc
Tap Chi Quoc Phong Toan Dan
Tuan Bao Quoc Te
U.S. Foreign Broadcast Information Service, *Daily Report Asia Pacific.*
U.S. Foreign Broadcast Information Service, *Daily Report China.*

U.S. Foreign Broadcast Information Service, *Daily Report East Asia.*
Viet Nam News
Vietnam Business Journal
Vietnam Commentary
Vietnam Courier
Vietnam Insight (Internet)
Vietnam Investment Review
Vietnam News Agency

ABBREVIATIONS

AFTA	ASEAN Free Trade Agreement/Area
AMM	ASEAN Ministerial Meeting
APEC	Asia Pacific Economic Cooperation
ARF	ASEAN Regional Forum
ASC	Asian Socialist Community
ASEAN	Association of Southeast Asian Nations
ASEM	Asia Europe Meeting
BBC	British Broadcasting Corporation
CBM	Confidence Building Measure
CCP	Chinese Communist Party
CEPT	Common Effective Preferential Tariff
CGDK	Coalition Government of Democratic Kampuchea
CMEA	Council for Mutual Economic Assistance
CNN	Cable News Network
CPPCC	Chinese People's Political Consultative Conference
CPSU	Communist Party of the Soviet Union
CSCAP	Council for Security Cooperation in Asia Pacific
DPRK	Democratic People's Republic of Korea
DRV	Democratic Republic of Vietnam
EAEG	East Asia Economic Group
EAS	East Asia
EEZ	Exclusive Economic Zone
FBIS	Foreign Broadcast Information Service
FUNCINPEC	Front uni national pour un Cambodge indépendant, neutre, pacifique et coopératif
GATT	General Agreement on Tariffs and Trade
GDP	Gross Domestic Product
GNP	Gross National Product
GSP	Generalized System of Preferences
KPNLF	Khmer People's National Liberation Front

MFN	Most Favoured Nation
MIA	Missing in Action
MOFA	Ministry of Foreign Affairs
MOI	Ministry of the Interior
NIC	Newly Industrializing Country
OECD	Organization for Economic Cooperation and Development
OPIC	Overseas Private Investment Corporation
PDK	Party of Democratic Kampuchea
PLA	People's Liberation Army
PLO	Palestine Liberation Organization
PRC	People's Republic of China
PRK	People's Republic of Kampuchea
RVN	Republic of Vietnam
SEATO	South East Asia Treaty Organisation
SNC	Supreme National Council
SAR	Special Administrative Region
SOC	State of Cambodia
SRV	Socialist Republic of Vietnam
UMNO	United Malays National Organization
UN	United Nations
UNTAC	United Nations Transition Authority Cambodia
UNCLOS	United Nation Convention on Law of the Sea
US	United States
USSR	Union of Soviet Socialist Republics
VCP	Vietnam Communist Party
VFF	Vietnam Fatherland Front
WTO	World Trade Organization

INDEX

CONTRIBUTORS

Ramses Amer, Ph.D. and Associate Professor, is the Coordinator of the Southeast Asia Programme (SEAP) at the Department of Peace and Conflict Research, Uppsala University, Sweden. His major areas of research include: security issues and conflict resolution in Southeast Asia and the wider Pacific Asia, and the role of the United Nations in the international system. His recent publications include *The United Nations and Foreign Military Interventions: A Comparative Study of the Application of the Charter*, second edition (1994), *Peacekeeping in a Peace Process: The Case of Cambodia* (1995) and *The Cambodian Conflict 1979–1991: From Intervention to Resolution* (1996), which he co-authored with Johan Saravanamuttu and Peter Wallensteen. Dr. Amer has also contributed numerous international journal articles, and book chapters, and written commissioned reports on Southeast Asian affairs and the United Nations.

Kent Bolton is an Associate Professor of Political Science at California State University, San Marcos. His research and teaching interests include comparative foreign policy studies generally and U.S.–Vietnam relations specifically. His current chapter is part of on-going research on the U.S.–Vietnam normalization process. He is the author of "Vietnam Crucible: The Political Economy of Normalization in the Post-Cold War World", in Abbas P. Grammy and C. Kaye Bragg, eds., *United States-Third World Relations in the New World Order* (1996).

Bui Thanh Son joined the Institute of International Relations (IIR) in Hanoi in 1985 as Desk Officer in the Information Center. He subsequently served as Researcher in the Department of Asia Pacific Studies and Head of the American Studies Division before his current appointment as Deputy Director General. He holds a B.A. degree from the College of Foreign Affairs in Hanoi and an M.A. degree in International Affairs from the School of International and Public Affairs, Columbia University. He contributes to *Nghien Cuu Quoc Te* (International Studies), the journal of the IIR.

Chang Pao-min is currently Professor and Director of the Graduate Institute of Political Economy, as well as Acting Dean of Social Sciences, at National Cheng Kung University, Tainan, Taiwan. Previously he taught at the Chinese University of Hong Kong, National

University of Singapore, and the University of Macau. He is the author of four English-language books, eight Chinese-language books, and over 100 articles in both languages. Among his major works are *Whither Taiwan: Ideal and Reality* (1996), *China: The Dilemma of Modernization* (1992), *The Sino-Vietnamese Territorial Dispute* (1986), *Kampuchea Between China and Vietnam* (1985), and *Beijing, Hanoi and the Overseas Chinese* (1982).

Li Ma was born in China and now has French nationality. She studied Chinese literature at the University of Jinan (Canton), the Institut National des Langues et Civilisations Orientales (Paris), and at the University of Paris VII. She is presently completing her Ph.D. in international relations at the University of Paris I-Sorbonne on the subject "Communism in Asia (1989–1998): Transition in Continuity". She worked in China as a journalist and editor of a scientific and technical magazine. She has been a resident of Europe since 1989 and returned to China and Hong Kong in 1995 and 1996. Her main field of research concerns international relations and contemporary communist countries. She is also interested in the subject of power and philosophy and the ideological and philosophical basis of political regimes and their legitimacy. She studied the Ming founder in this framework in "Zhu Yuanzhang and the Legalist 'art of ruling' " in *Ming Qing Jianlu* (in press).

Eero Palmujoki is Post-doctoral Fellow and Research Coordinator, Department of Political Science and International Relations, University of Tampere, Finland. He received his Ph.D. at the University of Tampere. He has carried out research at the Institute of Southeast Asian Studies in Singapore, Nordic Institute of Asian Studies in Copenhagen, Institute of International Relations in Hanoi and the Institute of International and Strategic Studies in Kuala Lumpur. He is the author of *Vietnam and the World: Marxist-Leninist Doctrine and the Changes in International Relations, 1975–93* (1997) and several articles on Vietnam's foreign policy, ideology, and the Southeast Asian regional system and ASEAN. Dr. Palmujoki is currently coordinator of the Academy of Finland's project "Regionalism and Globalism in Southeast Asia" and his current research interests focus on the Southeast Asian interstate system.

Carlyle A. Thayer is currently Professor of Southeast Asian security studies at the Asia-Pacific Center for Security Studies in Honolulu, Hawaii. The Center is attached to the U.S. Pacific Command. Previously he was Head of the School of Politics and Coordinator of the

Graduate Program in Defence Studies at the Australian Defence Force Academy, and Director of the Regional Security Studies Program at the Australian Defence Studies Centre in Canberra (1995–97). Prior to that, Professor Thayer taught in the Faculty of Military Studies at The Royal Military College-Duntroon (1979–85). He is the author of *Renovating Vietnam: Political Change in a One-Party State* (1999); "Beyond Indochina", *Adelphi Paper 297* (1995); *The Vietnam People's Army Under Doi Moi* (1994); *War By Other Means: National Liberation and Revolution in Vietnam* (1989); co-author of *Soviet Relations with India and Vietnam* (1992); and co-editor of *Vietnam and the Rule of Law* (1994).

David Wurfel is Professor Emeritus of Political Science at the University of Windsor and Senior Research Associate at the Joint Centre for Asia Pacific Studies, York University/University of Toronto. He received his Ph.D. at Cornell University and has also taught at International Christian University (Tokyo), University of Singapore, University of Missouri (Columbia), and University of Michigan. While at Windsor he served as the founding president of the Canadian Asian Studies Association. He has done research in Vietnam on several visits, dating back to 1956. In 1997 he served as visiting lecturer at the Institute of International Relations, Hanoi. He is the senior editor of *The Political Economy of Foreign Policy in South East Asia* (1990) and *Southeast Asia in the New World Order* (1996), and he has also contributed to *Reinventing Vietnamese Socialism* (1993).